C# – Visual Basic Bilingual Dictionary
Visual Studio 2015 Edition

Tim Patrick

OWANI PRESS

C# – Visual Basic Bilingual Dictionary
Visual Studio 2015 Edition
by Tim Patrick

Published by Owani Press.

For updates to this book and information on other books published by Tim Patrick, contact him online, via email, or through social media.

Website	wellreadman.com
Email	tim@timaki.com
Facebook	facebook.com/wellreadman
Twitter	twitter.com/thewellreadman
Goodreads	goodreads.com/wellreadman

Visit Owani Press online at OwaniPress.com.

Printed by CreateSpace, an Amazon.com company.
Cover art by Kenneth Low.

ISBN: 978-0692433690

To Claudette Moore

a friend to old trees and old technical book authors

Table of Contents

The Two Languages

To paraphrase the renowned playwright George Bernard Shaw, C# and Visual Basic are two languages separated by a common Framework. As for syntax and target audience, Microsoft's two programming systems seem so distant from each other. Despite that separation, they are complete equals when it comes to coding power, computational access, and automation of tasks that users need every day.

VB claims as its grammatical lineage the first edition of BASIC, developed by John Kemeny and Thomas Kurtz in 1964 as a means of bringing ease and clarity to the software development process. Five years later, Dennis Ritchie began work on the C programming language—C#'s own progenitor—crafting a compiler that, according to its author, was "more convenient and effective for many tasks than supposedly more powerful languages."

In .NET, Microsoft brought together these two discrete computing dialects—the simplicity of one software language designed for mere mortals, and the strength of a second language created to solve a large range of coding problems, from device drivers to word processors. The descendants of BASIC and C now sit together on the common foundation of the .NET Framework. From this shared resource, developers in both C# and Visual Basic have access to the same tools, the same platforms, and the same user communities.

Yet they are not the same. Visual Basic code loathes curly braces, and you have to look long and hard to see things spelled out completely in C#. The languages share much in facilitating Rapid Application Development and harnessing powerful technologies such as ADO.NET and XAML. But the way they communicate through source code is quite different. That's where this book comes in.

The *C#-Visual Basic Bilingual Dictionary* helps unify Visual Basic and C# by providing clear, functional equivalents for all syntax and feature differences between the two languages. This linking of the two grammars has never been more essential.

Who Needs this Book?

Decades ago, developers who cut their teeth on C and BASIC could build an entire career by sticking with just one general-purpose language. Today, software houses demand that their programmers be fluent in multiple languages, scripts, data formats, and platforms, both mobile and desktop. If you already speak VB, there's a good chance you will require some proficiency with C# as well, and vice versa.

The *C#-Visual Basic Bilingual Dictionary* is designed for all Visual Basic and C# developers, including those who only use one of those languages. The Internet contains a wealth of support content for .NET developers. However, searching online for an answer to some thorny Framework issue might produce results in that "other" language. Solving your coding problem may require you to act as a foreign-language translator, and having a good dictionary by your side is a must.

This book is also a good resource for Visual Basic developers who target mobile devices with the "VB Core" reduced runtime library. VB Core programs lack access to many features in the `Microsoft.VisualBasic` and `My` namespaces. Often, these missing features can be replaced with language-agnostic .NET Framework library features, and in ways that happen to be identical to the equivalent C# implementation. If you depend on VB Core, locate the missing features in Chapter 2 and Chapter 3 of this text to find useful replacement logic.

This text is a reference work, and not a training manual. While it can teach you a lot about Visual Basic and C#, it is not organized in a way that would be convenient for those new to .NET programming in general. The book assumes that you are at least partially familiar with one of the two languages, or with .NET programming.

What's in the Book?

This reference book exists to make repeated jumps between Visual Basic and C# as painless and informative as possible. Nearly 900 dictionary-like entries cover every keyword and most major grammar concepts found in the two languages. The entries appear in three language-specific chapters.

- *Chapter 1* includes entries for all C# keywords and features, sorted by name. Each entry provides equivalent Visual Basic syntax and usage details for a specific C# construct.
- *Chapter 2* reverses the process, supplying C# substitutes and details for each entry in a sorted list of Visual Basic keywords and features.
- *Chapter 3* is an extension of Chapter 2, listing every member of Visual Basic's "My" Namespace. Each entry documents C# code that allows you to perform the same task as the member in question.

New with Visual Studio 2015

The book includes full coverage of language features introduced with Visual Studio 2015 and the "Roslyn" compiler. For developers who have not yet upgraded to the latest version, all discussions of new features clearly indicate the functionality that existed prior to Visual Studio 2015.

What's Not in the Book?

Although the *C#-Visual Basic Bilingual Dictionary* includes complete coverage of every language keyword and syntactic element in both C# and Visual Basic, it is not an exhaustive reference for .NET development. Except as they appear in specific coding solutions, the book does not discuss the .NET Base Class Libraries. It also excludes other language-neutral .NET technologies, such as ADO.NET and Windows Communication Foundation (WCF).

The name "Visual Basic" refers to the .NET version of the language only, and not to those editions that culminated in Visual Basic 6.0. The book does identify differences between new language updates released with Visual Studio 2015 ("Roslyn") and those that were in effect in Visual Studio 2013. However, it does not document changes introduced in prior releases of the C# and Visual Basic languages. For instance, the text assumes that asynchronous programming keywords (the "async" and "await" operators) already exist in each language, although these keywords were not introduced until Visual Studio 2012.

Although Chapter 1 includes coverage of the `dynamic` C# language keyword, the book does not discuss the `System.Dynamic` namespace, nor any Dynamic Language Runtime features.

Acknowledgements

Reading a reference book from cover to cover is hard work, but several skilled developers across the globe agreed to take the challenge, and the book is much improved as a result. Eric Moreau and Jan Záruba provided extensive comments on the text. Additional input also came from David Fulop, Marcel Meijer, Fanie Reynders, and Alex Sorokoletov. Special thanks goes to Lucian Wischik and all of the Microsoft language MVPs, authors, and insiders who let me eavesdrop and participate in their technical interactions.

About the Author

Tim Patrick is a software architect and developer with more than 30 years of experience in designing and building custom software solutions. He is also an author of books and articles, mostly on technical subjects. You are at this very moment enjoying his eighth book on software development.

In 2007, Microsoft added Tim to its Most Valuable Professional (MVP) program in recognition of his support to the Windows programming community. He is also a Microsoft Certified Solution Developer. Tim earned his degree in computer science from Seattle Pacific University.

You can reach Tim through his web site, wellreadman.com.

Chapter 1

C# to Visual Basic

The C# entries in this chapter appear alphabetically by keyword or feature. Locate a language entry to see its Visual Basic equivalent. Entries identified by symbols appear before those starting with letters, and in the following order.

! # $ % & (* + , - . / : ; < = > ? @ [\ ^ { | ~

! Negation Operator

The Visual Basic equivalent of C#'s ! Boolean-centric operator is the Not operator.

C#
```
bool opposite = !originalValue;
```

VISUAL BASIC
```
Dim opposite As Boolean = Not originalValue
```

The Not operator is also a bitwise complement operator when used with integer operands. The equivalent in C# for that variation is the ~ operator.

See Also

    ~ Bitwise Complement Operator

!= Comparison Operator

When comparing value types, Visual Basic's <> inequality operator is identical to C#'s != operator, and appears in the same binary-operator position.

C#
```
if (teamPlayers != 9)
```

VISUAL BASIC
```
If (teamPlayers <> 9) Then
```

For string comparisons, the <> operator once again replicates C#'s != operator. However, VB's Option Compare statement impacts the way that strings compare to each other. By default, both C# and Visual Basic perform binary-level comparisons of strings. However, if a VB project or source file employs Option Compare Text, the comparison instead uses culture-specific text sorting rules.

For reference types other than strings, C#'s `!=` operator tests whether the two references being compared refer to the same underlying instance. This syntax is invalid in Visual Basic (at least when `Option Strict On` is used). Instead, VB programs should use the `IsNot` operator with a second instance, or with `Nothing`.

C#
```
// ----- Standard instance comparison.
if (firstIntance != secondInstance)

// ----- Comparisons with null.
if (anotherInstance != null)
```

VISUAL BASIC
```
' ----- Standard instance comparison.
If (firstInstance IsNot secondInstance) Then

' ----- Comparisons with null (Nothing in VB).
If (anotherInstance IsNot Nothing) Then
```

#define Directive

In C#, the `#define` directive declares preprocessing constants. These constants are in essence Boolean, in that they either exist (`true`-like) or they don't (`false`-like). The parallel `#undef` directive removes constants previously declared with `#define`.

C#
```
#define TestVersion
```

In Visual Basic, preprocessing constants come into being using the `#Const` directive. Unlike the Boolean nature of C# preprocessing constants, the parallel constants in VB can be Boolean, integer, floating point, string, or date values.

VISUAL BASIC
```
#Const TestVersion = "Beta 0.7"
```

To clear a previously declared VB constant from use, assign it a value of `Nothing`.

VISUAL BASIC
```
#Const TestVersion = Nothing
```

#error Directive

There is no equivalent in Visual Basic for the `#error` directive.

#if Directive

The general syntax of preprocessing conditional statements in Visual Basic parallels closely the usage found in C#, with some minor spelling and casing differences.

C# Term	Visual Basic Term
#if	#If...Then
#elif	#ElseIf...Then
#else	#Else
#endif	#End If

The key difference appears in the conditions themselves. Preprocessor values in C# act like Booleans; they either exist or they don't. In Visual Basic, preprocessor values exist as Booleans, integers, floating-point values, strings, or dates, and you can apply typical VB operators to those values.

C#

```
#if TestVersion
        // ----- Test-specific code here.
#elif (OldVersion == false)
        // ----- Backward-compatible code here.
#else
        // ----- Standard code here.
#endif
```

VISUAL BASIC

```
#If TestVersion Then
        ' ----- Test-specific code here.
#ElseIf (OldVersion = False) Or
        (TargetVersion < 2.5) Then
        ' ----- Backward-compatible code here.
#Else
        ' ----- Standard code here.
#End If
```

C# allows the ==, !=, &&, ||, and ! operators, the true and false constants, and parentheses within the conditional expressions. Visual Basic expressions can include any of the standard VB comparison operators (=, <>, <, >, <=, >=); mathematical, string, and logical operators (+, -, *, /, \, ^, Mod, <<, >>, &, Not, And, Or, Xor, AndAlso, OrElse); intrinsic casting and conversion functions (DirectCast, TryCast, CType, CBool, CByte, CChar, CDate, CDec, CDbl, CInt, CLng, CObj, CSByte, CShort, CSng, CStr, CUInt, CULng, and CUShort); the If function; and parentheses, as long as the final result is Boolean. String values in these expressions use binary-level comparisons instead of culture-specific text comparisons.

#line Directive

There is no equivalent in Visual Basic for the #line directive.

#pragma Directive

In generated Visual Studio source files, C#'s #pragma checksum directive serves the same purpose as Visual Basic's #ExternalChecksum directive. Neither statement should be used directly within code, except as generated by the .NET Framework.

C#

```
// ----- Turn an error off.
#pragma warning disable CS1234

// ----- Turn it back on later.
#pragma warning restore CS1234
```

VISUAL BASIC

```
' ----- Turn an error off.
#Disable Warning BC1234

' ----- Turn it back on later.
#Enable Warning BC1234
```

Both languages accept comma-delimited lists of error codes. For reasons of backward compatibility, C# allows purely numeric error codes. In newer code, these numbers include a *CS* prefix. VB does not permit number-only codes.

#region Directive

Visual Basic's *#Region* directive is equivalent to C#'s *#region* directive. The descriptive tag that follows the directive keyword is enclosed in double-quotes in VB, but such quotes are not used in C#.

C#

```
#region Utility Functions
    // ----- Collapsable code here.
#endregion
```

VISUAL BASIC

```
#Region "Utility Functions"
    ' ----- Collapsable code here.
#End Region
```

Both languages allow nesting of these regions. In C#, additional text (such as the name included with the initial *#region* directive) may appear after the *#endregion* directive. In Visual Basic, such text can only appear as a trailing comment.

C#

```
#endregion Utility Functions
```

VISUAL BASIC

```
#End Region  ' Utility Functions
```

> **New with Visual Studio 2015**
> In C#, regions can appear within method bodies, and a region can even begin in one method and end in a later method. Neither of these options was valid in older editions of Visual Basic, but they were both added to the language starting with its 2015 release.

#undef Directive

To clear a previously declared preprocessor constant in Visual Basic, assign it a value of *Nothing*.

C#
```
#undef TestVersion
```

VISUAL BASIC
```
#Const TestVersion = Nothing
```

#warning Directive

There is no equivalent in Visual Basic for the C# *#warning* directive.

$ Interpolated String Indicator

> **New with Visual Studio 2015**
> In 2015, both C# and Visual Basic added string interpolation, a method of generating formatted strings using string literals. Both languages share an identical syntax for such strings, prefixing them with a *$* symbol, and using curly braces to contain the interpolated sections.

C#
```
message = $"Meet {name} on {meetDate:dddd}";
```

VISUAL BASIC
```
message = $"Meet {name} on {meetDate:dddd}"
```

% Modulo Operator

Visual Basic includes a *Mod* operator that is identical to C#'s *%* modulo operator.

C#
```
int penniesNeeded = totalInCents % 5;
```

VISUAL BASIC
```
Dim penniesNeeded As Integer = totalInCents Mod 5
```

%= Assignment Operator

Visual Basic does not include an equivalent for C#'s *%=* operator. You must perform the modulo (*Mod*) and assignment operations separately in VB.

C#
```
leftOver %= 10;
```

VISUAL BASIC
```
leftOver = leftOver Mod 10
```

See Also

Assignment Operators

& Address Operator

Visual Basic does not include direct support for pointer operations, and therefore does not include an operator that establishes a fixed address for an object.

See Also

Pointers

& Conjunction Operator

In general, Visual Basic's *And* operator is identical to C#'s *&* operator, both for integer (bitwise) and Boolean (logical) operations.

C#
```
bool clapHands = (happy & knowIt);
```

VISUAL BASIC
```
Dim clapHands As Boolean = (happy And knowIt)
```

When applying *Option Strict Off* to a Visual Basic project or source file, using the *And* operator with one integer operand and one Boolean operand forces the Boolean value to an integer (*0* or *-1*), and then performs a bitwise operation. C# does not allow this mixture of operand types.

Visual Basic does include its own *&* operator. However, it is used for string concatenation; it does not process logical or bitwise operations.

&& Conjunction Operator

Visual Basic's *AndAlso* operator is identical to C#'s *&&* short-circuiting conjunction operator.

C#
```
if ((result != null) && (result.Length > 10))
```

VISUAL BASIC
```
If ((result IsNot Nothing) AndAlso
    (result.Length > 10)) Then
```

&= Assignment Operator

Visual Basic does not include an equivalent for C#'s &= operator. You must perform the conjunction (And) and assignment operations separately in VB.

C#
```
finalSet &= testFlag;
```

VISUAL BASIC
```
finalSet = finalSet And testFlag
```

Visual Basic does include its own &= operator. However, it combines string concatenation and assignment, and does not process logical or bitwise operations.

See Also

Assignment Operators

( ) Cast Expression

See

Conversion and Casting

( ) Expression Grouping

When used to group expressions, parentheses in Visual Basic are identical in syntax to grouping parentheses in C#. However, there are times when a set of parentheses is required around an expression in C#, but is optional when creating the equivalent statement in VB. For instance, the condition for an *if* statement in C# must be enclosed in parentheses, but Visual Basic does not have this requirement.

C#
```
// ----- Parentheses required in C#.
if (totalCount >= 100)
```

VISUAL BASIC
```
' ----- Parentheses optional in Visual Basic.
If totalCount >= 100 Then
```

* Dereference Operator

Visual Basic does not include direct support for pointer operations, and therefore does not include a dereferencing operator.

See Also

-> Member Access Operator, Pointers

* Multiplication Operator

The * multiplication operator in Visual Basic uses the same symbol and syntax as in C#.

C#
```
result = originalValue * 5;
```

VISUAL BASIC
```
result = originalValue * 5
```

*= Assignment Operator

Visual Basic's *= assignment operator is identical to the one found in C#, both in syntax and in purpose.

C#
```
originalValue *= 5;
```

VISUAL BASIC
```
originalValue *= 5
```

See Also

Assignment Operators

+ Addition Operator

C#'s + operator serves as both a numeric addition operator and a string concatenation operator.

C#
```
int result = number1 + number2;      // Addition
string greeting = "Hello, " + name;  // Concatenation
```

The + operator in Visual Basic also works for both addition and concatenation.

VISUAL BASIC
```
Dim result As Integer = number1 + number2  ' Addition
Dim greeting As String =
    "Hello, " + name   ' Concatenation
```

However, the rules surrounding concatenation in VB differ depending on the data types of the operands and the state of the *Option Strict* statement in effect. For example, when one operand is numeric and one is string, VB will try to coerce the string to a number (even non-numeric strings) when *Option Strict Off* is used, and will generate a compile-time error when using *Option Strict On*. When confronted with a similar situation, C# converts the number to string before concatenating the operands, a variation not used by VB's + operator. Because of the possibility for ambiguity in such statements, Visual Basic's & operator is the preferred tool for concatenating strings, leaving the + operator for addition only.

VISUAL BASIC
```
Dim result As Integer = number1 + number2   ' Addition
Dim greeting As String =
    "Hello, " & name   ' Concatenation
```

+ Unary-Plus Operator

Both C# and Visual Basic permit a prefix unary-plus operator before numeric literals and expressions. The syntax is identical between the two languages.

++ Increment Operator

Visual Basic does not include an equivalent to C#'s ++ increment operator, in either its prefix or postfix notation. Use the + addition operator or the += assignment operator instead.

C#
```
// ----- result will be 5, originalValue will be 6.
originalValue = 5;
result = originalValue++;
```

VISUAL BASIC
```
' ----- The postfix operation becomes two
'        VB statements.
originalValue = 5
result = originalValue
originalValue += 1
```

See Also

+ Addition Operator, += Assignment Operator, -- Decrement Operator

+= Assignment Operator

Visual Basic's += assignment operator is identical to the one found in C#, both in syntax and in purpose.

C#
```
originalValue += 5;
```

VISUAL BASIC
```
originalValue += 5
```

Although the += operator also performs string concatenation in Visual Basic, the &= assignment operator is a better choice for joining strings in VB.

See Also

Assignment Operators

+= Event Subscription Operator

C# uses the += event subscription operator to attach to an object's events those event handlers that conform to a specific delegate, or to associate a method with a delegate instance in general.

C#
```
// ----- button1_Click method defined elsewhere,
//          and conforms to same delegate used by
//          the Click event.
button1.Click += button1_Click;
```

In Visual Basic, the *AddHandler* statement performs this same type of event handler attachment. The *AddressOf* operator appears before the event handler name.

VISUAL BASIC
```
' ----- Button1_Click method defined elsewhere,
'          and conforms to same delegate used by
'          the Click event.
AddHandler Button1.Click, AddressOf Button1_Click
```

Visual Basic also has an alternate syntax that uses *WithEvents* on the object declaration, and replaces *AddHandler* with the *Handles* clause on the event handler.

VISUAL BASIC
```
' ----- Define the instance.
Public WithEvents Button1 As New Button()

' ----- Define the handler.
Sub Button1_Click(ByVal sender As Object,
        ByVal e As EventArgs) Handles Button1.Click
End Sub
```

Both C# and Visual Basic can attach inline event handlers to an event. See the "delegate Statement" entry in this chapter for an example.

See Also

delegate Statement

, Punctuator

In general, Visual Basic's use of the comma parallels those uses found in C#, with two notable exceptions. The first exception concerns C#'s use of a comma to separate assignments and conditions in *for* Statements.

C#
```
for (counter = 1, mask = "*"; counter <= 10;
        counter++, mask += "*")
```

Visual Basic's *For* Statement is much simpler, restricting control of the loop to a single numeric value, removing the need to support a comma in this context.

VISUAL BASIC
```
Mask = "*"
For counter = 1 To 10
    mask &= "*"
    ' ----- More code.
Next counter
```

The second exception deals with optional arguments. In C#, when calling a method with multiple optional arguments, if you only want to supply one of the later optional arguments, you must employ named arguments.

C#
```
// ----- Assume function Task has three arguments,
//        (a, b, c), where only 'a' is required:
//          void Task(int a, int b = 1, int c = 2)
Task(aValue, c: cValue);
```

This same syntax works in Visual Basic (using the := symbol for the named argument indicator instead of C#'s : symbol). However, Visual Basic also allows you to pass arguments by position, leaving any optional arguments blank as desired.

VISUAL BASIC
```
' ----- b will use its default value.
Task(aValue, , cValue)
```

See Also

Initializers

- Subtraction Operator

The – subtraction operator in Visual Basic uses the same symbol and syntax as in C#.

C#
```
result = originalValue - 5;
```

VISUAL BASIC
```
result = originalValue - 5
```

- Unary-Minus Operator

The – unary-minus operator in Visual Basic uses the same symbol and syntax as in C#.

C#
```
negativeVersion = -originalValue;
```

VISUAL BASIC
```
negativeVersion = -originalValue
```

-- Decrement Operator

Visual Basic does not include an equivalent to C#'s -- decrement operator, in either its prefix or postfix notation. Use the – subtraction operator or the -= assignment operator instead.

C#
```
// ---- result will be 5, originalValue will be 4.
originalValue = 5;
result = originalValue--;
```

```
' ----- The postfix operation becomes two VB statements.
originalValue = 5
result = originalValue
originalValue -= 1
```

-= Assignment Operator

In its typical use, C#'s -= assignment operator is identical to the one found in Visual Basic, both in syntax and in purpose.

C#
```
originalValue -= 5;
```

VISUAL BASIC
```
originalValue -= 5
```

See Also

-= Event Unsubscription Operator, Assignment Operators

-= Event Unsubscription Operator

Visual Basic uses the *RemoveHandler* statement, in conjunction with the *AddressOf* operator, to detach event handlers from object instances, or to disassociate a method from a delegate instance in general.

C#
```
Form1.Click -= ClickEventHandler;
```

VISUAL BASIC
```
RemoveHandler Form1.Click, AddressOf ClickEventHandler
```

See Also

-= Assignment Operator

-> Member Access Operator

Visual Basic does not include direct support for pointer operations, and therefore does not provide access to type members through pointer dereferencing.

VISUAL BASIC
```
value = element.OneMember    ' Standard member access
value = element!OneName      ' Dictionary member access
value = element("OneName")   ' Dictionary member access
```

See Also

. Member Access Operator, [ ] Member Access Operator, Pointers

. Member Access Operator

Both C# and Visual Basic employ a dotted member-access syntax using the period (.) between namespace, class, instance, and member names.

C#
```
value = element.OneMember;
```

VISUAL BASIC
```
value = element.OneMember
```

/ Division Operator

C# defines a single operator that handles numeric division for both integer and floating-point values (and for other types when used with operator overloading).

C#
```
int wholeResult1 = 5 / 3;    // 1
int wholeResult2 = 6 / 3;    // 2
float realResult = 5f / 3f;  // 1.666666...
```

The return type in C# generally follows the type of the operands. The operands are coerced into the same type when needed before the division takes place. This is true for integer and floating-point values. For integer division, rounding always leans toward zero.

Visual Basic also includes a division operator. Unlike C#'s operand-directed return type, the / operator in VB always returns a floating-point quotient.

VISUAL BASIC
```
Dim wholeResult1 As Double = 5 / 3    ' 1.666666...
Dim wholeResult2 As Double = 6 / 3    ' 2.0
Dim realResult As Single = 5! / 3!    ' 1.666666...
```

In most cases, VB's division operation returns a result of type *Double*, even with integer operands. If one operand is *Single* and the other is non-*Double*, the result is *Single*. If one operand is *Decimal* and the other is anything other than *Single* or *Double*, the result is *Decimal*.

Visual Basic also has a \ integer division operator. When used in place of /, the result is always an integer value, with rounding toward zero.

VISUAL BASIC
```
Dim wholeResult1 As Integer = 5 \ 3    ' 1
Dim wholeResult2 As Integer = 6 \ 3    ' 2
Dim realResult As Long = 5! \ 3!       ' 1
```

Floating-point values are coerced to the *Long* data type before processing, and rounded using banker's rounding (0.5 values are rounded toward the nearest even integer). If *Option Strict On* is used, you must manually coerce floating-point values to an appropriate integer type (*Byte*, *Short*, *Integer*, or *Long*).

Both languages follow the same divide-by-zero rules for the / operator, with an exception thrown for *Decimal* operands, and *System.Double.NaN* returned for other data types. For VB's \ operator, divide-by-zero always throws an exception.

/* */ Comment Delimiters

Visual Basic does not include a delimited comment style. Comments always begin with a single quote (') or the *REM* statement and continue to the end of the current physical line. To continue a comment on the next line, start the subsequent line with another comment symbol.

C#
```
/* ----- This is a
 *        multiline comment.
 */
```

VISUAL BASIC
```
' ----- This is an attempt at a
'        multiline comment.
```

C#'s delimited comments also allow you to insert a comment in the middle of a statement.

C#
```
if (/* Annual */ salary >= 100000)
```

This syntax has no equivalent in Visual Basic.

// Comment Symbol

The Visual Basic equivalent of C#'s // comment symbol is the single quote ('). Both symbols start a comment that continues to the end of the current physical line.

C#
```
// ----- This is a full-line comment.
result = DoWork();   // A trailing comment.
```

VISUAL BASIC
```
' ----- This is a full-line comment.
result = DoWork()   ' A trailing comment.
```

> **New with Visual Studio 2015**
> Trailing comments in C# can appear in the middle of a logical line. Such uses are permitted in Visual Basic starting with its 2015 release, but not before.

C#
```
result = DoWork(firstArgument,   // Always allowed in C#
    secondArgument);
```

VISUAL BASIC
```
result = DoWork(firstArgument,   ' VB 2015 and later only
    secondArgument)
```

Visual Basic also includes a *REM* statement that is similar in purpose to the single-quote symbol. Its use in modern VB code is rare.

VISUAL BASIC
```
REM ----- This is an old-style comment. Avoid it.
```

See Also

XML Documentation Comments

/// XML Documentation Comment Symbol

See

XML Documentation Comments

/= Assignment Operator

Visual Basic's /= assignment operator is similar to the same operator in C#, although the data types returned differ between the two languages. In general, C# retains the most relevant operand type, while in VB, the result is always *Double* or *Decimal*.

C#
```
originalValue /= 5.2;
```

VISUAL BASIC
```
originalValue /= 5.2#   ' # suffix indicates Double
```

Visual Basic also includes a \= assignment operator that performs integer division instead of a floating-point operation.

VISUAL BASIC
```
originalInteger \= 5
```

See the "/ Division Operator" entry in this chapter for full information on the differences between the C# and Visual Basic division operators.

See Also

/ Division Operator, Assignment Operators

: Base Declaration Indicator

In C#, classes and interfaces from which a type inherits appear in the declaration, separated from the type name by a colon.

C#
```
public class Dog : Animal, IDomesticate { }
```

In Visual Basic, a type identifies these underlying sources through the *Inherits* and *Implements* statements. For base types, the *Inherits* statement appears on the line immediately after the type definition. You can also use VB's : statement separation symbol to attach the *Inherits* statement to the end of the class declaration's physical line. This results in a more C#-like appearance, although it is not a common practice.

VISUAL BASIC

```
' ----- Standard syntax.
Public Class Dog
    Inherits Animal
End Class


' ----- Syntax using : symbol.
Public Class Dog : Inherits Animal
End Class
```

Interfaces implemented by the new type appear in the *Implements* statement as a comma-delimited list. As with the *Inherits* statement, the *Implements* statement appears immediately after the opening of the type declaration. When a class needs both a base type and one or more interfaces, the *Inherits* statement comes before the *Implements* statement.

VISUAL BASIC

```
Public Class Dog
    Inherits Animal
    Implements IDomesticate
    ' ----- The rest of the class appears here.
End Class
```

Interface inheritance in VB uses the *Inherits* statement within the new interface declaration. For structures that implement an interface, use the *Implements* statement.

VISUAL BASIC

```
Interface IHuman
    Inherits ILifeform
End Interface

Structure Person
    Implements IHuman
End Structure
```

When a C# class or structure implements an interface member, it does so implicitly via the name and argument signature, or explicitly by including the interface name in the method definition.

C#

```
interface IDomesticate
{
    void Train(int daysRequired);
}

class Dog : IDomesticate
{
    // ----- Implicit implementation.
    public void Train(int daysRequired) { }

    // ----- Explicit implementation.
    public void IDomesticate.Train(
        int daysRequired) { }
}
```

In Visual Basic, all interface member implementations must be declared explicitly, and require the *Implements* clause as part of the method declaration.

VISUAL BASIC
```
Interface IDomesticate
    Sub Train(ByVal daysRequired As Integer)
End Interface

Class Dog
    Implements IDomesticate

    Public Sub Train(ByVal daysRequired As Integer) _
            Implements IDomesticate.Train
        ' ----- Implementation code here.
    End Sub
End Class
```

One advantage (or disadvantage, depending on your perspective) of this syntax is that, in Visual Basic, the name of the implementing member need not be the same as the interface member being implemented.

VISUAL BASIC
```
Public Sub TeachTheDog(ByVal daysRequired _
        As Integer) Implements IDomesticate.Train
```

This ability to change the implementation name is not supported in C#.

: Named Argument Indicator

When using named arguments in method calls, Visual Basic uses the := named argument indicator in the same way that C# employs the equivalent : indicator.

C#
```
DefineAbbreviation(fullName:"Montana", shortName:"MT");
```

VISUAL BASIC
```
DefineAbbreviation(fullName:="Montana", shortName:="MT")
```

As in C#, named arguments in VB can follow earlier positional arguments, but a positional argument cannot follow a named argument.

VISUAL BASIC
```
' ----- This syntax is valid...
ProcessData(Date.Today, batchID:="12345")

' ----- ...but this is not.
ProcessData(batchID:="12345", Date.Today)
```

See Also

, Punctuator, Arguments and Parameters

:: Namespace Alias Qualifier

In C#, the `global::` prefix indicates that some fully qualified namespace, type, or member name starts at the root of the namespace hierarchy, removing ambiguity between similarly named library members.

C#

```
// ----- Perhaps you defined a MyApp.System.Exception
//       class in your application's code. This makes
//       it clear you want .NET's Exception class.
global::System.Exception theProblem;
```

In Visual Basic, use `Global` as the first component of the fully qualified type or member path to make it clear that the path begins at the namespace root.

VISUAL BASIC

```
Dim theProblem As Global.System.Exception
```

In C#, you can define other namespace aliases that can appear in place of "global." This allows your code to reference methods from external assemblies, when used in conjunction with the `extern alias` statement. This use of the namespace alias qualifier has no equivalent in Visual Basic.

; Statement Termination Character

Complete C# statements end with the `;` statement termination character, allowing a single statement to flow across as many lines as desired. In Visual Basic, statements terminate at the end of a physical line, unless there is some indication that the statement must continue onto the next physical line.

VISUAL BASIC

```
result = DoSomeWork(withThisData) ' <-- Ends here
```

The traditional VB way to continue a statement onto a subsequent line is to end the physical line with the `_` line continuation character (with at least one space character before it).

VISUAL BASIC

```
result = DoSomeWork(withThisData) _
    + SomeExtraWork(withMoreData)
```

Visual Basic 2010 introduced implicit line continuation, where the syntax of the statement provides hints as to whether a line will continue onto the next physical line. For instance, ending a line with a comma from an argument list indicates that the remaining arguments are on the next line.

VISUAL BASIC

```
result = DoAdvancedWork(withThisData,
    evenMoreData)
```

Implicit line continuation only works when it is clear to the Visual Basic compiler that a physical line ends in the middle of the statement. Typically, this involves ending a line with an operator, or leaving a set of incomplete parentheses open, among other actions.

```
' ----- These split lines require explicit
'       line continuation.
result = 3 _
    + 5
value = someObject _
    .Member

' ----- These split lines are continued implicitly.
result = 3 +
    5
value = someObject.
    Member
```

In some cases, Visual Basic permits multiple statements to appear on a single physical line. Separate the statements with the : statement separation symbol. Typically, such statements are added to the end of a single-line *If* statement, allowing two statements to be processed based on a single Boolean condition.

VISUAL BASIC
```
If (problemMessage) Then _
    RecordError(problemMessage) : Return
```

< > Generic Type Placeholder

In Visual Basic, the type of a generic declaration appears in parentheses with an *Of* clause.

C#
```
Dictionary<long, string> lookupSet;
```

VISUAL BASIC
```
Dim lookupSet As Dictionary(Of Long, String)
```

This syntax extends to class definitions, and anywhere else C# would normally place the type placeholder in angle brackets.

See Also

Generics

< Comparison Operator

When comparing value types, Visual Basic's < operator is identical to C#'s < operator, and appears in the same binary-operator position.

C#
```
if (teamPlayers < 9)
```

VISUAL BASIC
```
If (teamPlayers < 9) Then
```

For string comparisons, C# and VB default to the same method of comparison, checking the binary value of each character in the string. However, VB's *Option*

Compare Text statement, when used within a project or source file, causes the comparison to use culture-specific text sorting rules.

<< Left Shift Operator

Visual Basic's << operator is identical in syntax and usage to C#'s << operator.

<<= Assignment Operator

Visual Basic's <<= operator is identical in syntax and usage to C#'s <<= operator.

See Also

Assignment Operators

<= Comparison Operator

Visual Basic's <= operator is generally the same as C#'s <= operator. The entry for the < operator has additional information about string comparisons.

See Also

< Comparison Operator

= Assignment Operator

When used in a stand-alone assignment statement, Visual Basic's = operator is identical in syntax and purpose to the = operator in C#.

C#
```
taxAmount = subtotal * taxRate;
```

VISUAL BASIC
```
taxAmount = subtotal * taxRate
```

C# allows an assignment to occur within an expression, or multiple assignments to occur within a single statement.

C#
```
// ----- latestValue will be updated before
//       the method call.
ProcessValue(latestValue = incomingValue);

// ----- All three variables will have c's value.
a = b = c;
```

Neither of these forms exists in Visual Basic; you must perform each assignment in a separate statement in VB.

See Also

Assignment Operators

== Comparison Operator

When comparing value types, Visual Basic's = equality operator is identical to C#'s == operator, and appears in the same binary-operator position.

C#
```
if (teamPlayers == 9)
```

VISUAL BASIC
```
If (teamPlayers = 9) Then
```

For string comparisons, the = operator also replicates C#'s == operator. However, VB's *Option Compare* statement impacts the way that strings compare to each other. By default, both C# and Visual Basic perform binary-level comparisons of strings. However, if a VB project or source file employs *Option Compare Text*, the comparison instead uses culture-specific text sorting rules.

For reference types other than strings, C#'s == operator tests whether the two references being compared refer to the same underlying instance. This syntax is invalid in Visual Basic (at least when *Option Strict On* is used). Instead, VB programs use the *Is* operator with a second instance, or with *Nothing*.

C#
```
// ----- Standard instance comparison.
if (firstIntance == secondInstance)

// ----- Comparisons with null.
if (anotherInstance == null)
```

VISUAL BASIC
```
' ----- Standard instance comparison.
If (firstInstance Is secondInstance) Then

' ----- Comparisons with null (Nothing in VB).
If (anotherInstance Is Nothing) Then
```

=> Lambda Operator

Visual Basic includes lambda expressions and anonymous functions that parallel the same features in C#. Single-line lambda expressions in both languages are quite similar, although the VB version does not require any specific replacement for the => lambda operator.

C#
```
// ----- NOTE: These expressions are not meant to
//        be used alone, but are shown here out of
//        context for demonstration purposes only.

// ----- With typed arguments.
(int limit, string code) => code.Length > limit

// ----- With inferred arguments.
(first, second) => first != second
```

```
// ----- With no arguments.
() => LogAction()
```

VISUAL BASIC
```
' ----- With typed arguments.
Function(ByVal limit As Integer,
    ByVal code As String) code.Length > limit

' ----- With inferred arguments.
Function(first, second) first <> second

' ----- With no arguments, and no return value.
Sub() LogAction()
```

Multiline anonymous functions in C# use a set of curly braces after the => operator. In Visual Basic, the same thing is accomplished by starting the function logic on the line following the argument list, and ending the block with *End Sub* or *End Function*.

C#
```
(int someArgument) =>
{
    // ----- Code appears here.
};
```

VISUAL BASIC
```
Sub(ByVal someArgument As Integer)
    ' ----- Or Function...End Function.
End Sub
```

Anonymous functions in both languages can be asynchronous by preceding the entire expression with *async* (C#) or *Async* (Visual Basic).

New with Visual Studio 2015
In 2015, C# added the ability to define method, property, and indexer members in a type using lambda expressions.

C#
```
// ----- Method.
public Position Move(int xOffset, int yOffset) =>
    new Position(CurrentX + xOffset, CurrentY + yOffset);

// ----- Read-only property.
public string FileAs => LastName + ", " + FirstName;

// ----- Indexer.
public Order this[long orderID] =>
    LookupOrderByID(orderID);
```

This use of lambda expressions does not yet exist in Visual Basic.

In C#, older-style anonymous functions use the *delegate* keyword to begin an anonymous function block. In Visual Basic, there is no differentiation between anonymous functions and lambda expressions in terms of syntax. The *Sub* lambda

---

expression in VB is the closest equivalent for `delegate` when creating inline event handlers. See the "delegate Statement" entry in this chapter for an example.

> Comparison Operator

When comparing value types, Visual Basic's > operator is identical to C#'s > operator, and appears in the same binary-operator position.

C#
```
if (teamPlayers > 9)
```

VISUAL BASIC
```
If (teamPlayers > 9) Then
```

The entry for the < operator has additional information about string comparisons.

>= Comparison Operator

Visual Basic's >= operator is generally the same as C#'s >= operator. The entry for the < operator has additional information about string comparisons.

See Also

> Comparison Operator

>> Right Shift Operator

Visual Basic's >> operator is identical in syntax and usage to C#'s >> operator.

>>= Assignment Operator

Visual Basic's >>= operator is identical in syntax and usage to C#'s >>= operator.

See Also

Assignment Operators

? Nullable Type Indicator

See

Nullable Types

?. Null Conditional Operator

New with Visual Studio 2015
In 2015, both C# and Visual Basic added a set of null conditional operators. In general, they are used in exactly the same way between the languages, but with slight differences in syntax.

Usage	C# Syntax	Visual Basic Syntax
Instance Member	A?.B	A?.B
Dictionary Member	Not supported	A?!B
Array or Indexed Member	A?[B]	A?(B)
XML Attribute Axis	Not supported	A?.@B
XML Child Axis	Not supported	A?.<B>
XML Descendant Axis	Not supported	A?...<B>

?: Conditional Operator

In Visual Basic, the conditional operator—traditionally called the ternary operator—has a method-call syntax using the `If` operator. Its syntax varies from C#'s `?:` operator, but it produces the same results.

C#
```
string result = amount > 100 ? "Overflow" :
    amount.ToString();
```

VISUAL BASIC
```
Dim result As String = If(amount > 100, "Overflow",
    amount.ToString())
```

The `If` operator accepts three arguments: (1) a Boolean test condition, (2) the value to return if the condition is true, and (3) the value to return if the condition is false. As in C#, the `If` operator short-circuits; either the true or false part is evaluated, but not both.

Visual Basic also includes an older `IIf` function that is somewhat similar to the newer `If` operator, and has the same syntax. However, `IIf` is not short-circuiting, and its return value is always of type `System.Object`.

C#'s conditional operator is right-associative. Consider the following expressions, which are all equivalent.

C#
```
result1 = a ? b : c ? d : e;
result2 = a ? b : (c ? d : e);
```

VISUAL BASIC
```
result1 = If(a, b, If(c, d, e))
```

?? Coalescence Operator

The `??` operator returns a value if that value is non-`null`, or an alternate second value if that first value is in fact `null`.

C#
```
// ----- Using a domain-specific default.
//       Assumes: string suppliedName;
string customerName = suppliedName ?? "Customer";
```

```
//  ----- Using default for a nullable type.
//        Assumes: int? countFromUser;
int startingValue = countFromUser ?? default(int);
```

In Visual Basic, use the *If* operator with two arguments to defer to a second value when the first is *Nothing*.

VISUAL BASIC

```
'  ----- Using a domain-specific default.
'        Assumes: Dim suppliedName As String
Dim customerName As String = If(suppliedName, "Customer")

'  ----- For nullable value types, you must apply
'        a full conditional statement. Assumes:
'          Dim countFromUser As Integer?
Dim startingValue As Integer
If (countFromUser Is Nothing) Then
    startingValue = Nothing   ' Will become zero
Else
    startingValue = countFromUser
End If
```

@ Verbatim Indicator

C# uses the @ verbatim indicator to give guidance to the compiler when dealing with identifiers and strings. For identifiers, the symbol allows the term that follows it to be treated as an identifier, even if that term conflicts with a C# language keyword.

C#

```
int @double = originalValue * 2;
```

To qualify such names in Visual Basic, enclose them in a set of square brackets.

VISUAL BASIC

```
Dim [Double] As Integer = originalValue * 2
```

The set of keywords differs between the two languages, and a term that may require verbatim qualification in one language can work without it in the other. When doing cross-language development, take care to avoid keywords in both languages.

Because of C#'s case-sensitivity for identifiers, a term that may conflict with a lowercase language keyword will not conflict when entered using uppercase characters. A term that requires verbatim qualification in Visual Basic does so whether it is upper or lower case.

When placed before a C# string, the @ verbatim indicator tells the C# compiler to treat the string more literally. Such strings treat backslashes (\) as ordinary characters; there are no escape sequences in verbatim strings. Within such strings, use a pair of double-quote symbols to embed a lone double-quote within the text.

C#

```
string standard = "C:\\folder\\file.txt";
string verbatim = @"C:\folder\file.txt";
string notice = @"This string contains a ""quote.""";
```

Visual Basic only includes one type of string, one that is identical with C#'s verbatim strings. Strings in VB do not support escape sequences.

VISUAL BASIC
```
Dim standard As String = "C:\folder\file.txt"
Dim notice As String = "This string contains a ""quote."""
```

See Also

Identifiers, Literals

[ ] Array Declaration

Arrays are similar in their use between C# and Visual Basic, but there are differences in how they are declared.

C#
```
// ----- Uninitialized array.
int[] numberSet;
string[] textSet;

// ----- Initialized by size.
int[] setOfFive = new int[5];

// ----- Initialized by members.
string[] setOfThree = {"zero", "one", "two"};
```

VISUAL BASIC
```
' ----- Uninitialized array.
Dim numberSet() As Integer
Dim textSet() As String

' ----- Initialized by size.
Dim setOfFive(4) As Integer

' ----- Initialized by members.
Dim setOfThree() As String = {"zero", "one", "two"}
```

C# uses square brackets to indicate array elements. In Visual Basic, parentheses are used instead. Array declarations in C# always place the brackets with the type; VB allows the parentheses to be with the type or the identifier, but no size is allowed when the parentheses are attached to the type name.

VISUAL BASIC
```
' ----- Both of these will work.
Dim numberSetA() As Integer
Dim numberSetB As Integer()
```

When specifying an array size during declaration, C#'s syntax indicates the number of elements, while Visual Basic's syntax specifies the upper bound of the array. To make it clear that the bound is used, VB includes the optional 0 To prefix. In both languages, the first array element is always numbered zero (0).

VISUAL BASIC
```
' ----- Both of these declare an array of elements
'       numbered from 0 to 4.
Dim setOfFiveA(4) As Integer
Dim setOfFiveB(0 To 4) As Integer
```

As with C#, Visual Basic supports both multidimensional arrays and jagged arrays.

C#
```
int[,] multiArray;
int[][] jaggedArray;
```

VISUAL BASIC
```
Dim multiArray(,) As Integer
Dim jaggedArray()() As Integer
```

Once an array exists in Visual Basic, whether initialized or not, the *ReDim* statement resizes the array, optionally preserving existing elements via the *Preserve* modifier.

VISUAL BASIC
```
Dim storageArea() As Integer   ' Uninitialized

' ----- Initialize the array to include 5 elements,
'       possibly wiping out any existing data.
ReDim storageArea(0 To 4)

' ----- Resize the array to include 10 elements,
'       preserving the existing 0 to 4 elements.
ReDim Preserve storageArea(0 To 9)
```

Member access is the same in both languages, with the exception of the brackets used.

C#
```
int thirdElement = largerArray[2];
```

VISUAL BASIC
```
Dim thirdElement As Integer = largerArray(2)
```

Size requests are also the same, through the *Length*, *GetUpperBound*, and *GetLowerBound* members. Visual Basic also includes two intrinsic functions, *UBound* and *LBound*, which return the limits.

C#
```
size = someArray.Length;
lower = someArray.GetLowerBound(0);
upper = someArray.GetUpperBound(0);
```

VISUAL BASIC
```
size = someArray.Length
lower = someArray.GetLowerBound(0)
upper = someArray.GetUpperBound(0)

' ----- Using VB's intrinsic functions. The second
'       argument is optional, defaulting to zero.
lower = LBound(someArray)
upper = UBound(someArray)
```

```
'  ----- For a multidimensional array, get
'         second-rank bounds.
lower = LBound(multiArray, 1)
upper = UBound(multiArray, 1)
```

See Also

Arrays, Initialization

[ ] Attribute Usage Delimiter

Visual Basic surrounds attributes with angle brackets instead of C#'s square brackets.

C#
```
[System.Serializable]
public class EmployeeData
```

VISUAL BASIC
```
<System.Serializable>
Public Class EmployeeData
```

See Also

Attributes

[ ] Member Access Operator

Dictionary member access is fairly similar in both languages, with Visual Basic using a set of parentheses in lieu of C#'s square brackets.

C#
```
fullName = customerRecord["FullName"];
```

VISUAL BASIC
```
fullName = customerRecord("FullName")
```

Visual Basic also includes a syntax variation that uses an exclamation point to separate the dictionary instance from the member name.

VISUAL BASIC
```
fullName = customerRecord!FullName
```

See Also

this Indexer Declaration

\ Escape Sequence Indicator

See

Literals

\u Unicode Escape Sequence Indicator

See

Literals

^ Exclusive-Or Operator

Visual Basic's *Xor* operator is an exact replacement for C#'s ^ exclusive-or operator, both for integer and Boolean operands.

C#
```
currentState = currentState ^ newInput;
```

VISUAL BASIC
```
currentState = currentState Xor newInput
```

Visual Basic includes a ^ operator, but it is used for exponentiation, the raising of a numeric value to a power.

^= Assignment Operator

Visual Basic does not include an equivalent for C#'s ^= operator. You must perform the exclusive-or (*Xor*) and assignment operations separately in VB.

C#
```
currentState ^= newInput;
```

VISUAL BASIC
```
currentState = currentState Xor newInput
```

Visual Basic includes a ^= operator, but it is used as that language's Exponentiation assignment operator.

See Also

Assignment Operators

{ } Block Statement

In C#, any block of two or more statements that are subordinate to another statement must appear in a set of curly braces.

C#
```
if (warningMessage.Length > 0)
{
    RecordError(warningMessage);
    return -1;
}
```

Visual Basic uses block statements, such as *If...End If* to accomplish the same thing.

VISUAL BASIC

```
If (warningMessage.Length > 0) Then
    RecordError(warningMessage)
    Return -1
End If
```

Any variables declared within a subordinate block are scoped to that block. In C#, you can start a new scoping block at any time by opening a new set of curly braces.

C#

```
// ----- Nothing much going on here, then suddenly...
{
    // ----- Any variables declared here are scoped
    //       to the set of curly braces.
}
```

Visual Basic does not have an equivalent syntax for this scoping construct.

See Also

Lifetime and Scope

{ } Instance Initialization

See

Initializers

| Disjunction Operator

In general, Visual Basic's *Or* operator is identical to C#'s | operator, both for integer (bitwise) and Boolean (logical) operations.

C#

```
bool complain = (hot | humid);
```

VISUAL BASIC

```
Dim complain As Boolean = (hot Or humid)
```

When applying *Option Strict Off* to a Visual Basic project or source file, using the *Or* operator with one integer operand and one Boolean operand forces the Boolean value to an integer (*0* or *-1*), and then performs a bitwise operation. C# does not allow this mixture of operand types.

|= Assignment Operator

Visual Basic does not include an equivalent for C#'s |= operator. You must perform the disjunction (*Or*) and assignment operations separately in VB.

C#

```
daysOpen |= mondayFlag;
```

VISUAL BASIC

```
daysOpen = daysOpen Or mondayFlag
```

See Also

Assignment Operators

|| Disjunction Operator

Visual Basic's *OrElse* operator is identical to C#'s || short-circuiting disjunction operator.

C#
```
if ((result == null) || (result.Length == 0))
```

VISUAL BASIC
```
If ((result Is Nothing) OrElse
    (result.Length == 0)) Then
```

~ Bitwise Complement Operator

The Visual Basic equivalent for C#'s ~ bitwise operator is the *Not* operator.

C#
```
int complement = ~originalValue;
```

VISUAL BASIC
```
Dim complement As Integer = Not originalValue
```

The *Not* operator is also a logical negation operator when used with Boolean operands. The equivalent in C# for that variation is the *!* operator.

See Also

! Negation Operator

~ Destructor Prefix

See

Destructors

abstract Modifier

When applied to a class, Visual Basic's *MustInherit* modifier is equivalent to C#'s class-bound *abstract* modifier.

C#
```
abstract class Creature
{
    // ----- Include members marked as abstract.
}
```

VISUAL BASIC
```
MustInherit Class Creature
    ' ----- Include members marked as MustOverride.
End Class
```

When applied to class members, C#'s *abstract* modifier is the same as Visual Basic's *MustOverride* modifier. The decorated member will not include an implementation.

C#
```
// ----- Abstract method.
public abstract void ProcessResults();

// ----- Abstract property.
public abstract int MaxLevel { get; set; }

// ----- Abstract read-only indexer.
public abstract string this[int index] { get; }
```

VISUAL BASIC
```
' ----- Abstract method.
Public MustOverride Sub ProcessResults()

' ----- Abstract property.
Public MustOverride Property MaxLevel() As Integer

' ----- Abstract read-only indexer.
Public MustOverride Default ReadOnly Property Item(
    ByVal index As Integer) As String
```

C#'s *abstract* member modifier can be applied to methods, properties, indexers, and events. In Visual Basic, the *MustOverride* modifier can be applied to methods and properties, but not events. Just as C# *abstract* members can only appear in a class marked with *abstract*, Visual Basic *MustOverride* members can only appear in a *MustInherit* class.

Access Modifiers

Visual Basic includes access modifiers that parallel those found in C#.

C# Modifiers	Visual Basic Modifiers
internal	Friend
private	Private
protected	Protected
protected internal	Protected Friend
public	Public

In most cases, the use of these modifiers in Visual Basic is identical to how they are used in C#, appearing as a prefix to the type or member being declared.

C#
```
public class Student
```

VISUAL BASIC
```
Public Class Student
```

When declaring fields within types using Visual Basic's *Dim* statement, the access modifier appears as a prefix to the declaration.

```
Class NameTracking
    Private Dim OriginalName As String
```

However, it is more common to omit the *Dim* keyword in this declaration. In fact, Visual Studio automatically removes the *Dim* keyword in field definitions, retaining it only for local variables.

```
Class NameTracking
    Private OriginalName As String
```

Structure members may not use the *protected* (C#) or *Protected* (VB) modifier. For more information on using access modifiers, see the specific statements that employ access modifiers (such as "class Statement") in this chapter.

Anonymous Methods

Visual Basic does not differentiate between anonymous methods and lambda expressions as C# does. See the "=> Lambda Operator" entry in this chapter for information on creating lambda expressions in Visual Basic.

Anonymous Types

C# uses the *new* operator to define a new anonymous type.

C#
```
var samplePerson = new {Name = "John", Age = 42};
```

Visual Basic uses a similar syntax, with the *New* and *With* operators used together. Each field within the type begins with a period (.).

```
Dim samplePerson = New With {.Name = "John",
    .Age = 42}
```

VB also allows you to specify which anonymous type properties are "key" properties, those that can be used for testing for equivalence between two instances.

```
Dim samplePerson = New With {Key .ID = 123,
    .Name = "John", .Age = 42}
```

See Also

Initializers, new Operator

Arguments and Parameters

Parameters are identifiers that are defined with a method, and through which data can be passed into that method. Arguments are the data elements or variables passed through the parameters when the method is called.

C#
```
// ----- Parameters: hour and minute.
public string FormatTime(int hour, int minute)
{
    return string.Format("{0:0}:{1:00}",
        hour, minute);
}

// ----- Later, arguments are passed to the method.
businessStart = FormatTime(5, 30);
```

Both C# and Visual Basic support similar features for working with parameters and arguments. By default, all comma-delimited arguments are passed by-value into the matching parameters. To change this default in C#, use the *ref* or *out* modifier. In Visual Basic, use the *ByRef* modifier to pass by-reference. In C#, the data type for each parameter appears just before the identifier. VB places the data type in an *As* clause just after the identifier.

C#
```
// ----- Parameters are:
//          content:  in/out by-reference
//          method:   by-value
//          warnings: out-only by-reference
public bool CorrectContent(ref string content,
    int method, out string warnings)
```

VISUAL BASIC
```
' ----- Parameters are:
'          content:  in/out by-reference
'          method:   by-value
'          warnings: in/out by-reference
Public Function CorrectContent(
    ByRef content As String,
    ByVal method As Integer,
    ByRef warnings As String)
```

Visual Basic does not have an equivalent for the *out* modifier; use *ByRef* instead, as you would use when replacing *ref*. When passing values by-reference, the calling code must have already assigned a value to the argument being passed. In C#, the calling code applies the *out* or *ref* modifier to match the one in the parameter list. Visual Basic requires no such modifier.

C#
```
// ----- userContent must have been assigned a value.
success = CorrectContent(ref userContent,
    3, out warningText);
```

VISUAL BASIC
```
' ----- userContent must have been assigned a value.
success = CorrectContent(userContent, 3, warningText)
```

Both languages support optional arguments and parameter arrays. See the "Optional Arguments" and "params Modifier" entries in this chapter. Named arguments are also valid in both languages. See the ": Named Argument Indicator" entry in this chapter.

See Also

, Punctuator, Methods, : Named Argument Indicator, Optional Arguments, out Modifier, params Modifier, ref Modifier

Arrays

See

[ ] Array Declaration

as Conversion Operator

C#'s *as* conversion operator is similar to a standard cast, but it returns *null* instead of throwing an exception if the conversion fails.

C#
```
Manager boss = employeeRecord as Manager;
```

In Visual Basic, when working with reference types, the *TryCast* operator performs a similar action, returning *Nothing* on failure.

VISUAL BASIC
```
Dim boss As Manager = TryCast(employeeRecord, Manager)
```

For value types, you need to use one of the intrinsic conversion expressions (such as *CInt*), the *CType* expression, or use one of the *TryParse* methods exposed by the target type (*Integer.TryParse*). This last option is the closest match for the *as* operator, as it indicates a Boolean success code instead of throwing an exception on a failed conversion.

See Also

Conversion and Casting

assembly Modifier

See

Attributes

Assignment Operators

Both C# and Visual Basic include multiple assignment operators, each applying a specific operation to the right-hand value before assigning it to the left hand result.

Operator	C#	Visual Basic
Addition	+=	+=
Assignment	=	=
Concatenation	+=	&=
Conjunction	&=	Not supported
Disjunction	|=	Not supported

Operator	C#	Visual Basic
Division	/=	/=
Event Subscription	+=	Not supported
Event Unsubscription	-=	Not supported
Exclusive-Or	^=	Not supported
Exponentiation	Not supported	^=
Integer Division	Not supported	\=
Left-Shift	<<=	<<=
Modulo	%=	Not supported
Multiplication	*=	*=
Right-Shift	>>=	>>=
Subtraction	-=	-=

For information about these operators, see their entries in this chapter.

C# allows multiple occurrences of assignment operators in a single statement.

C#
```
// ----- Both b and c receive a's value.
int a = 5, b = 10, c = 15;
c = b = a;

// ----- This more unusual use of assignment
//       is still valid.
int d = 5, e = 10, f = 15;
f -= e -= d;
// Result: d-->5, e-->5, f-->10
```

Visual Basic does not permit more than one assignment operator per statement.

Associativity

See

> Operator Precedence and Associativity

async Modifier

Visual Basic's `Async` modifier is identical in use and purpose to C#'s `async` modifier, for both standard and anonymous methods.

C#
```
public async Task<int> ProcessBuffer()
{
    // ----- At least one await appears in code.
}
```

VISUAL BASIC

```
Public Async Function ProcessBuffer() _
        As Task(Of Integer)
    ' ----- At least one Await appears in code.
End Function
```

See Also

await Operator

Asynchronous Processing

See

async Modifier, await Operator

Attributes

Both C# and Visual Basic allow attributes to be attached to types, members, or an entire assembly. C# attributes appear in square brackets; VB uses angle brackets. In both languages, if the defined attribute name ends in "Attribute," that portion can be left off when using the attribute.

C#

```
[System.Obsolete("Use Creature Class Instead")]
class Animal
{
}
```

VISUAL BASIC

```
<System.Obsolete("Use Creature Class Instead")>
Class Animal
End Class
```

In both languages, multiple attributes can appear in separate sets of brackets, or separated by commas within a single set of brackets. When an attribute accepts arguments, you can specify named arguments or initializers with an = sign in C#, or : = in Visual Basic.

C#

```
[AttributeUsage(AttributeTargets.Class,
    AllowMultiple=true)]
```

VISUAL BASIC

```
<AttributeUsage(AttributeTargets.Class,
    AllowMultiple:=True)>
```

Normally, an attribute appears just before the item it modifies. In some cases, it may be necessary to specify the target of the attribute. In both languages, indicate the target with a prefix immediately after the opening bracket.

C#

```
// ----- This attribute is for the whole assembly.
[assembly: AssemblyVersion("1.0.0.0")]
```

```
' ----- This attribute is for the whole assembly.
<Assembly: AssemblyVersion("1.0.0.0")>
```

C# supports more target prefixes than does Visual Basic. The following table lists the targets available as prefixes in both languages.

C#	Visual Basic	Applies to
assembly	Assembly	Entire assembly
module	Module	Current assembly module (not a VB Module)
field	Not supported	Type-level fields
event	Not supported	Events
method	Not supported	Methods, property getters or setters
param	Not supported	Method or property parameters
property	Not supported	Properties
return	Not supported	Return values for methods, indexers, or properties
type	Not supported	Classes, structures, interfaces, enumerations, or delegates

When a prefix is not available in VB, you can only associate it with the target by placing the attribute immediately before that target. For return values in Visual Basic, place the attribute between the As keyword and the data type that follows it in the method's signature.

In addition to the targets listed in the table above, C# allows attributes to be attached to type placeholder variables in generic type declarations.

C#
```
public class FlexibleType<[CSharpOnly]T>
```

This is not supported in Visual Basic.

Automatic Properties

In C#, automatic properties (also known as "auto-implemented properties") include the property declaration, but no getter or setter implementation.

C#
```
public string CoreName { get; set; }
```

This trimmed down version of a property is also used in Visual Basic to create automatic properties.

VISUAL BASIC
```
Public Property CoreName As String
```

> **New with Visual Studio 2015**
> C# lets you create read-only automatic properties. Before 2015, Visual Basic did not support read-only automatic properties. Instead, it was necessary to create a normal property with the ReadOnly modifier, and leave out the setter code. However, its 2015 release added support for read-only auto-properties.

C#

```
public string CoreName { get; }
```

VISUAL BASIC

```
' ----- Before the 2015 release.
Public ReadOnly Property CoreName() As String
    Get
        ' ----- Property-specific logic here.
    End Get
End Property

' ----- Starting with the 2015 release.
Public ReadOnly Property CoreName As String
```

> **New with Visual Studio 2015**
> Originally, C# did not allow automatic properties to be initialized as part of the declaration itself. In 2015, the language gained this functionality for both read-only and read-write properties. Visual Basic already included such initialization features for read-write auto-properties, but initialization of read-only automatic properties came about in that same 2015 release.

C#

```
// ----- Read-write property.
public string CoreName { get; set; } = "Unknown";

// ----- Read-only property.
public string CoreName { get; } = "Unknown";
```

VISUAL BASIC

```
' ----- Read-write property.
Public Property CoreName As String = "Unknown"

' ----- Read-only property.
Public ReadOnly Property CoreName As String = "Unknown"
```

Both languages now also permit assignment to read-only automatic properties within a constructor.

See Also

Properties

await Operator

Visual Basic's *Await* operator is identical to C#'s *await* operator.

C#

```
// ----- The long version.
Task<string> theTask = SomeMethodAsync();
string result = await theTask;

// ----- The short version.
string result = await SomeMethodAsync();
```

VISUAL BASIC

```
' ----- The long version.
Dim theTask As Task(Of String) = SomeMethodAsync()
Dim result As String = Await theTask

' ----- The short version.
Dim result As String = Await SomeMethodAsync()
```

> **New with Visual Studio 2015**
> Starting in 2015, C#'s `await` operator can be used in the `catch` and `finally`
> blocks of a `try` statement, although this option is not yet supported in Visual Basic.

See Also

async Modifier

base Constructor Declaration

In C#, a base constructor can be called from a derived constructor as part of its declaration syntax.

C#

```
// ----- Assumes BaseClass with a default
//        constructor, plus a constructor that
//        accepts an int.
class DerivedClass : BaseClass
{
    public DerivedClass() : base()
    {
        // ----- Default constructor logic here.
    }
    public DerivedClass(int value) : base(value)
    {
        // ----- Constructor logic here.
    }
}
```

In Visual Basic, the call to the base class constructor occurs within the code of the constructor logic itself, using the *MyBase* access keyword.

VISUAL BASIC

```
' ----- Assumes BaseClass with a default constructor,
'        plus a constructor that accepts an Integer.
Class DerivedClass
    Inherits BaseClass

    Public Sub New()
        ' ----- Explicit call to base is optional.
        MyBase.New()
        ' ----- Default constructor logic here.
    End Sub
```

```
Public Sub New(ByVal value As Integer)
    MyBase.New(value)
    ' ----- Constructor logic here.
End Sub
End Class
```

See Also

Constructors, this Constructor Declaration

base Access Expression

Visual Basic's *MyBase* expression provides the same type of access to base type members as does C#'s *base* expression.

C#
```
base.RefreshStatus();
```

VISUAL BASIC
```
MyBase.RefreshStatus()
```

Bitwise Operators

See

See Operators

bool Data Type

Visual Basic's intrinsic *Boolean* data type is identical to C#'s *bool* data type. Both types are aliases for .NET's *System.Boolean* type. For Boolean literals, C# uses *true* and *false* in all lowercase. Although VB is not case-sensitive, the traditional literals are *True* and *False* with an initial capital.

C#
```
bool finished = false;
```

VISUAL BASIC
```
Dim finished As Boolean = False
```

When converting or casting a Boolean value to an integer in C#, *false* always becomes *0* (zero), and *true* becomes *1* (one). In Visual Basic, *False* always becomes zero, as in C#. However, for historical reasons, *True* becomes *1* or *-1* depending on the method used to convert or cast the value.

VISUAL BASIC
```
Dim byDotNet As Integer =
    Convert.ToInt32(True)               ' --> 1
Dim byIntrinsic As Integer = CInt(True) ' --> -1

' ----- Next two require Option Strict Off
Dim byMath As Integer = Int(True)       ' --> 1
Dim byImplicit As Integer = True        ' --> -1
```

break Statement

C# uses a single *break* statement to exit immediately out of *for*, *foreach*, and *do* loops, and the *switch* statement.

C#
```
for (counter = 0; counter < 10; counter++)
{
    // ----- Some code, then...
    break;
    // ----- More code.
}
```

In place of *break*, Visual Basic uses one of four distinct forms of its *Exit* statement, depending on the containing construct.

- *For* and *For Each* loops use the *Exit For* statement.
- *Do* loops use the *Exit Do* statement.
- *While* loops use the *Exit While* statement.
- *Select Case* statements use the *Exit Select* statement.

VISUAL BASIC
```
For counter = 0 To 9
    ' ----- Some code, then...
    Exit For
    ' ----- More code.
Next counter
```

In C#, each *case* or *default* block within a *switch* statement requires at least one *break* statement (or similar exit construct) to confirm the end of block-specific logic.

C#
```
switch (sides)
{
    case 3:
        name = "Triangle";
        break;
    case 4:
        name = "Rectangle";
        break;
```

Visual Basic does not impose this requirement. The *Exit Select* is optional, and a *Case* block will always exit after the last logic line within its block.

VISUAL BASIC
```
Select Case sides
    Case 3
        name = "Triangle"
    Case 4
        name = "Rectangle"
```

byte Data Type

Visual Basic's intrinsic *Byte* data type is identical to C#'s *byte* data type. Both types are aliases for .NET's *System.Byte* type.

C#
```
byte smallCount = 1;
```

VISUAL BASIC
```
Dim smallCount As Byte = 1
```

case Clause

See

switch Statement

Casting

See

Conversion and Casting

catch Clause

See

try Statement

char Data Type

Visual Basic's intrinsic *Char* data type is identical to C#'s *char* data type. Both types are aliases for .NET's *System.Char* type. For *char* literals, C# surrounds a character with single quotes. In Visual Basic, the character appears in double quotes, and is followed by a *c* suffix.

C#
```
char digit = '1';
```

VISUAL BASIC
```
Dim digit As Char = "1"c  ' Or "1"C
```

checked Expression

C#'s *checked* keyword, whether in its statement-block form or expression form, enables run-time integer overflow checking on the contained statements or expression.

Visual Basic enables integer overflow checking by default on a project-wide basis. To enable or disable overflow checking, access the Advanced Compiler Settings within the Project Properties, and set the Remove Integer Overflow Checks field as needed. VB does not include the ability to control integer overflow checks at the statement or expression level.

class Statement

Visual Basic's *Class* statement is equivalent to C#'s *class* statement. When declaring a derived class, VB's *Inherits* clause follows the opening of the class declaration block. Likewise, when a class implements one or more interfaces, the *Implements* clause lists those interfaces, and appears at the top of the class, just after the *Inherits* clause if present.

C#
```csharp
class ActiveCustomer : Customer, IDisposable
{
    // ----- Members appear here.
}
```

VISUAL BASIC
```vbnet
Class ActiveCustomer
    Inherits Customer
    Implements IDisposable
    ' ----- Members appear here.
End Class
```

Classes in both languages contain the same types of members: constructors, destructors, fields, constants, properties, methods, events, operator overloads and user-defined conversions, indexers (called "default properties" in VB), and nested types (including delegates and enumerations). Many of these members can exist as static or instance members.

Classes support the following modifiers in each language.

C# Modifier	Visual Basic Modifier
abstract	MustInherit
internal	Friend
new	Shadows
partial	Partial
private	Private
protected	Protected
protected internal	Protected Friend
public	Public
sealed	NonInheritable
static	Not supported

Classes in C# are *internal* by default, just as classes in Visual Basic are *Friend* by default. Within C# classes, all members are *private* by default. In Visual Basic, fields and constants are *Private* by default, while all other members are *Public* by default.

Visual Basic does not permit static classes (called "shared classes" in VB). Instead, a class with all static (shared) members must be created using the *Module* statement.

```
static class UsefulFunctions
{
    public static string Reverse(string originalText)
    {
        char[] buffer;
        if (originalText == null)
            return "";
        else
        {
            buffer = originalText.ToCharArray();
            Array.Reverse(buffer);
            return new string(buffer);
        }
    }
}
```

Visual Basic

```
Module UsefulFunctions
    Public Function Reverse(ByVal originalText _
        As String) As String
        Dim buffer() As Char
        If (originalText Is Nothing) Then
            Return ""
        Else
            buffer = originalText.ToCharArray()
            Array.Reverse(buffer)
            Return New String(buffer)
        End If
    End Function
End Module
```

See Also

Access Modifiers, Constructors, Destructors

Collection Initializers

See

Initializers

Comments

C# includes comments that terminate at the end of a physical line (those starting with the // symbol) and those that can cover any contiguous span of content, from a partial line to multiple lines (those delimited by /* and */ symbols). Visual Basic only supports the first type, with the single quote symbol (') or the REM keyword.

Visual Basic

```
REM This is a full-line comment.
' Another full-line comment.
Dim counter As Integer ' A line-ending comment
```

See Also

/* */ Comment Delimiters, // Comment Symbol, XML Documentation Comments

Compiler Constants

Both C# and Visual Basic include project-level support for the *DEBUG* and *TRACE* compiler constants. Code throughout the .NET Framework responds to these constants, and you can use them in your own code. To alter the default settings, set the Define DEBUG Constant and Define TRACE Constant fields as needed. In C#, these fields appear on the Project Properties' Build tab; in VB, they appear in the Advanced Compile Options area of the Compile tab.

Although you can always define your own project-specific compiler constants, C# itself does not define any other constants by default. Visual Basic defines four (or up to nine) additional constants.

Constant	Description
CONFIG	The active build configuration, typically "Debug" or "Release."
TARGET	The compiled application type, one of: "winexe," "exe," "library," or "module." Other custom values are also possible.
VBC_VER	The current version of Visual Basic, in *major.minor* format. One of the following values: 8.0 (VB2005), 9.0 (VB2008 and VB2010), 11.0 (VB2012), 12.0 (VB2013), or 14.0 (VB2015).
_MYTYPE	The version of the My pseudo-namespace in use. Depending on the value of this constant, the compiler may define one or more of the following additional constants: *_MYAPPLICATIONTYPE*, *_MYCOMPUTERTYPE*, *_MYFORMS*, *_MYUSERTYPE*, and *_MYWEBSERVICES*.

See Microsoft's MSDN documentation for full information on these constants and how to use them in your code.

const Statement

Both Visual Basic and C# support the declaration of constants at the local and type levels. The syntax of C#'s *const* statement closely parallels standard variable declaration; VB's syntax naturally follows its own variable declaration, replacing *Dim* with *Const*.

C#
```
const int DefaultPort = 25;
```

VISUAL BASIC
```
Const DefaultPort As Integer = 25
```

In both languages, you can string multiple constant declarations together with commas. The two languages also support similar rules on what can be assigned to a constant: literals, enumeration values, and other constants, all joined with basic operators. VB lets you use its intrinsic conversion functions (like *CInt*) as well.

At the field level, each constant declaration can include an access modifier.

C#
```
public const int DefaultPort = 25;
```

VISUAL BASIC
```
Public Const DefaultPort As Integer = 25
```

If *Option Infer On* is used, Visual Basic will infer the data type of the expression when possible, removing the need for a specific type.

VISUAL BASIC
```
Const DefaultPort = 25
```

Some constant declarations are not permitted in C# due to boxing or other reference issues.

C#
```
// ----- This code will not compile:
const object usesBoxing = 10;
const object implicitReference = "Message";
```

Such declarations are permitted in Visual Basic.

Constructors

In C#, constructors are named for the type in which they appear. In Visual Basic, constructors are always named *New*. Constructors in both languages provide functionality that is generally equivalent.

C#
```
class Employee
{
    public Employee()
    {
        // ----- Default constructor.
    }
    public Employee(string empName)
    {
        // ----- Custom constructor.
    }
}
```

VISUAL BASIC
```
Class Employee
    Public Sub New()
        ' ----- Default constructor.
    End Sub
    Public Sub New(ByVal empName As String)
        ' ----- Custom constructor.
    End Sub
End Class
```

By default, the constructor in a derived class calls the default constructor in the base class, if it exists. To call a custom base constructor, or to use another custom constructor as the starting point for a constructor, use the *base* and *this* constructor declarations, respectively.

C#

```
class Employee : Person
{
    public Employee(string empName) : base(empName)
    {
        // ----- Base class handles person's name.
    }
    public Employee(string empName,
        decimal salary) : this(empName)
    {
        // ----- Salary-specific code here.
    }
}
```

In Visual Basic, these base and local constructor foundations are handled within the code of the constructor. Call the relevant base or local constructor as the first line of the new constructor.

VISUAL BASIC

```
Class Employee
    Inherits Person

    Public Sub New(ByVal empName As String)
        ' ----- Base class handles person's name.
        MyBase.New(empName)
    End Sub
    Public Sub New(ByVal empName As String,
            ByVal salary As Decimal)
        ' ----- Another constructor handles the name.
        Me.New(empName)
        ' ----- Salary-specific code here.
    End Sub
End Class
```

Both languages offer static constructors in addition to instance constructors.

C#

```
class Utility
{
    static Utility()
    {
        // ----- Static class initialization here.
    }
}
```

VISUAL BASIC

```
Class Utility
    Shared Sub New()
        ' ----- Static class initialization here.
    End Sub
End Class
```

Constructors support the following modifiers in each language.

C# Modifier	Visual Basic Modifier
Extern	Not supported
Internal	Friend
Private	Private
protected	Protected
protected internal	Protected Friend
Public	Public
Static	Shared

See Also

base Constructor Declaration, this Constructor Declaration

continue Statement

C# uses a single *continue* statement to begin the next iteration of a loop construct.

C#
```
for (counter = 0; counter < 10; counter++)
{
    // ----- Some code, then...
    continue;
    // ----- More code.
}
```

Visual Basic uses one of three distinct forms of its *Continue* statement, depending on the containing loop type.

- *For* and *For Each* loops use the *Continue For* statement.
- *Do* loops use the *Continue Do* statement.
- *While* loops use the *Continue While* statement.

VISUAL BASIC
```
For counter = 0 To 9
    ' ----- Some code, then...
    Continue For
    ' ----- More code.
Next counter
```

Because Visual Basic lets you identify a specific loop type, it is possible to move to the next iteration of a loop containing the innermost loop.

VISUAL BASIC
```
For counter As Integer = 0 To 9
    Do While (content.Length > 0)
        ' ----- This will exit the Do loop, and move
        '       to the next iteration of the For loop.
        Continue For
    Loop
Next counter
```

Conversion and Casting

C# supports both (1) implicit (widening) casting or conversion of data, such as from *int* to *long*; and (2) explicit casting or conversion of data with the *()* casting operator, the *as* operator, and .NET Framework features, such as those from the *System.Convert* class.

Implicit Conversions

Conversions from "smaller" to "larger" data types, including overloaded conversions defined as *implicit* (C#) or *Widening* (VB), occur automatically in both languages.

C#
```
int smallValue = 25;
long largeValue = smallValue;   // Implicit
```

VISUAL BASIC
```
Dim smallValue As Integer = 25
Dim largeValue As Long = smallValue   ' Widening
```

In Visual Basic, when the *Option Strict Off* statement is used at the file or project level, explicit (narrowing) conversions can also occur in code automatically, although run-time errors may result if the source data does not "fit" in the target.

VISUAL BASIC
```
' ----- At the top of the file.
Option Strict Off


' ----- In a method.
Dim largeValue As Long = 100000
Dim smallValue As Integer = largeValue   ' Narrowing
```

When using this non-strict mode, Visual Basic also performs some string-to-number and number-to-string conversions automatically, in ways not supported by C#.

VISUAL BASIC
```
' ----- Assumes: Option Strict Off
Dim trueNumber As Integer = "123"   ' Auto-conversion
Dim trueString As String = 123      ' Auto-conversion
If (trueNumber = trueString) Then
    ' ----- VB performs the conversion and comparison
    '       of the two variables automatically. The
    '       code will reach this conditional block.
End If
```

Explicit Conversions

Explicit casts in C# occur by using the *()* casting operator before an expression.

C#
```
long largeValue = 100000;
int smallValue = (int)largeValue;
```

For intrinsic value types, Visual Basic offers built-in conversion operators, such as *CInt* to convert an expression to an *Integer*. Internally, some of these operators provide additional type checking not found in standard C# casts. However, they are commonly used in Visual Basic in much the same way that C# programmers use the () cast operator.

VISUAL BASIC
```
Dim largeValue As Long = 100000
Dim smallValue As Integer = CInt(largeValue)
```

The following table lists the Visual Basic conversion operators, and shows how they relate to specific C# casts.

C# Cast	Visual Basic Conversion
(bool)	CBool (expression)
(byte)	CByte (expression)
(char)	CChar (expression)
(DateTime)	CDate (expression)
(double)	CDbl (expression)
(decimal)	CDec (expression)
(int)	CInt (expression)
(long)	CLng (expression)
(object)	CObj (expression)
(sbyte)	CSByte (expression)
(short)	CShort (expression)
(float)	CSng (expression)
(string)	CStr (expression)
(uint)	CUInt (expression)
(ulong)	CULng (expression)
(ushort)	CUShort (expression)
(type)	CType (expression, type)

These Visual Basic operators are not exact replacements for the C# casts shown here. In many cases, each operator performs extra steps to ensure a conversion succeeds where it might fail in the equivalent C# code. For example, many of the numeric conversion operators will strip out currency symbols and grouping symbols silently. These characters would cause a failure in the equivalent C# cast.

C#
```
// ----- This will fail.
int trueNumber = (int)"$1,234";
```

VISUAL BASIC
```
' ----- This will succeed, resulting in 1234.
Dim trueNumber As Integer = CInt("$1,234")
```

Visual Basic's CType operator is the most generic of the conversion operators, facilitating conversions between any two types that have a conversion defined. In fact, when defining overloaded conversions in VB, the declaration uses CType as the name for the conversion method.

For reference types that have a derived relationship, VB's DirectCast operator is more casting-friendly, since it is able to make assumptions about the underlying data types involved in the cast.

```
' ----- Bring an elephant into the zoo.
Dim someElephant As Elephant
Dim someAnimal As Animal = GetNewAnimal()
If (TypeOf someAnimal Is Elephant) Then _
    someElephant = DirectCast(someAnimal, Elephant)
```

C#'s *as* operator is similar to casting, but it returns *null* when the conversion fails instead of throwing an exception. Visual Basic includes the *TryCast* operator, which produces similar *Nothing* results on failure.

C#

```
// ----- Might return null if conversion fails.
someElephant = someAnimal as Elephant;
```

VISUAL BASIC

```
' ----- Might return Nothing if conversion fails.
someElephant = TryCast(someAnimal, Elephant)
```

The .NET Framework includes features that convert data from one type to another. The *System.Convert* type hosts many such static functions. The following table shows *System.Convert* member substitutes for most of the VB conversion operators.

Visual Basic Conversion	System.Convert Method
CBool *(expression)*	ToBoolean *(expression)*
CByte *(expression)*	ToByte *(expression)*
CChar *(expression)*	ToChar *(expression)*
CDate *(expression)*	ToDateTime *(expression)*
CDbl *(expression)*	ToDouble *(expression)*
CDec *(expression)*	ToDecimal *(expression)*
CInt *(expression)*	ToInt32 *(expression)*
CLng *(expression)*	ToInt64 *(expression)*
CSByte *(expression)*	ToSByte *(expression)*
CShort *(expression)*	ToInt16 *(expression)*
CSng *(expression)*	ToSingle *(expression)*
CStr *(expression)*	ToString *(expression)*
CUInt *(expression)*	ToUInt32 *(expression)*
CULng *(expression)*	ToUInt64 *(expression)*
CUShort *(expression)*	ToUInt16 *(expression)*

The *ToString* method that is included with every .NET object is available equally in Visual Basic and C#.

Data Types

Visual Basic and C# share a common set of intrinsic data types, with one exception. The following table shows the matching data types, and the underlying .NET data type for which each intrinsic type is an alias.

C# Type	Visual Basic Type	.NET Type
bool	Boolean	System.Boolean
byte	Byte	System.Byte
char	Char	System.Char
decimal	Decimal	System.Decimal
double	Double	System.Double
float	Single	System.Single
int	Integer	System.Int32
long	Long	System.Int64
object	Object	System.Object
sbyte	SByte	System.SByte
short	Short	System.Int16
string	String	System.String
uint	UInteger	System.UInt32
ulong	ULong	System.UInt64
ushort	UShort	System.UInt16
Not supported	Date	System.DateTime

Visual Basic includes an intrinsic *Date* type, an alias for the framework's *System.DateTime* type. C# does not include a parallel date/time type. Instead, you must use *System.DateTime* directly in C#.

For more information about the intrinsic data types, see their individual entries elsewhere in this chapter.

decimal Data Type

Visual Basic's intrinsic *Decimal* data type is identical to C#'s *decimal* data type. Both types are aliases for .NET's *System.Decimal* type. For decimal literals, C# uses an *M* or *m* suffix after the value; in Visual Basic, use *D*, *d*, or *@* instead.

C#
```
decimal cost = 0m;   // or 0M
```

VISUAL BASIC
```
Dim cost As Decimal = 0@   ' or 0D or 0d
```

default Clause

See

> switch Statement

default Operator

In C#, the *default* operator assigns a default value to a variable instance, most commonly for generic type instances.

C#
```
// ----- Somewhere within "class Flexible<T> { }",
//          in one of its methods.
T oneValue = default(T);
```
In Visual Basic, the *Nothing* literal accomplishes the same thing.

VISUAL BASIC
```
' ----- Somewhere within "Class Flexible(Of T)...
'          End Class", in one of its methods.
Dim oneValue As T = Nothing
```
Because Visual Basic assigns a default value to all variable instances automatically, this assignment isn't strictly needed at declaration. But you can also use *Nothing* to reset the instance back to its default value later within the method's logic.

When checking a generic instance for its default value, use the *EqualityComparer(Of T)* type's *Default.Equals* method.

VISUAL BASIC
```
' ----- Assumes: Imports System.Collections.Generic
If (EqualityComparer(Of T).Default.Equals(
    oneValue, Nothing)) Then
```

delegate Statement

Visual Basic's *Delegate* statement is equivalent to C#'s *delegate* statement.

C#
```
public delegate int PerformCalculation(int x, int y);
```
VISUAL BASIC
```
Public Delegate Function PerformCalculation(
    ByVal x As Integer, ByVal y As Integer) _
    As Integer
```
As with standard Visual Basic methods, delegates destined to return a value use the *Function* modifier; those that do not return a value (a *void* return in C#) use the *Sub* modifier instead.

Delegates support the following modifiers in each language.

C# Modifier	Visual Basic Modifier
internal	Friend
new	Shadows
private	Private
protected	Protected
protected internal	Protected Friend
public	Public
static	Shared

C# uses a variation of the *delegate* statement to establish inline event handlers and other anonymous methods.

```
C#
button1.Click += delegate(object o, EventArgs e) {
    /* Event code here. */ };
```

Visual Basic's lambda statements provide this same functionality.

```
VISUAL BASIC
AddHandler Button1.Click, Sub(ByVal o As Object,
         ByVal e As EventArgs)
    ' ----- Event code here.
    End Sub
```

See Also

Anonymous Methods

Destructors

In C# classes, a destructor appears as a method with the same name as the class, prefixed with a tilde character (~).

```
C#
class Customer
{
    ~Customer()
    {
        // ----- Cleanup logic appears here.
    }
}
```

The C# compiler converts this code to the following more verbose equivalent.

```
C#
class Customer
{
    protected override void Finalize()
    {
        try
        {
            // ----- Cleanup logic appears here.
        }
        finally
        {
            // ----- This is called automatically.
            // base.Finalize();
        }
    }
}
```

This converted format closely parallels the version that should be used in Visual Basic classes to create destructors.

```
Class Customer
    Protected Overrides Sub Finalize()
        Try
            ' ----- Cleanup logic appears here.
        Finally
            MyBase.Finalize()
        End Try
    End Sub
End Class
```

In both languages, the garbage collector determines when to call the destructor.

Directives

See

> Preprocessing Directives

do Statement

C#'s *do* statement loops while a condition is true, and is guaranteed to loop at least once, since the condition is not evaluated until the loop completes one iteration.

C#

```
do
{
    content = ProcessChunkOfContent(content);
} while (content.Length > 0);
```

In Visual Basic, the *Do* statement accomplishes the same thing when the condition appears at the bottom of the loop.

VISUAL BASIC

```
Do
    content = ProcessChunkOfContent(content)
Loop While content.Length > 0
```

A variation of this loop uses the *Until* clause instead of *While*.

VISUAL BASIC

```
Do
    content = ProcessChunkOfContent(content)
Loop Until content.Length = 0
```

In Visual Basic, parentheses surrounding the condition are optional. They are required in C#.

See Also

> while Statement

double Data Type

Visual Basic's intrinsic *Double* data type is identical to C#'s *double* data type. Both types are aliases for .NET's *System.Double* type. For double literals, C# uses a *D* or *d* suffix after the value; in Visual Basic, use *R*, *r*, or *#* instead.

C#
```
double factor = 0d;   // or 0D
```

VISUAL BASIC
```
Dim factor As Double = 0#   ' or 0R or 0r
```

Dynamic Binding

See

> dynamic Type

dynamic Type

C#'s *dynamic* type declaration expression enables dynamic binding, often called "late binding" in Visual Basic.

C#
```
dynamic basicValue = 20;
dynamic complexValue = new ExampleType();

// ----- This method call is not checked
//       at compile-time.
complexValue.ProcessData();
```

In Visual Basic, late-bound instances are created as *Object*, and must be defined in a source file or project that uses *Option Strict Off*.

VISUAL BASIC
```
' ----- At the top of the file.
Option Strict Off

' ----- Later, in method code.
Dim basicValue As Object = 20
Dim complexValue As Object = New ExampleType()

' ----- This method call is not checked
'       at compile-time.
complexValue.ProcessData()
```

In both languages, when assigning a value type to a dynamic variable, boxing and unboxing will occur as the value is used throughout your code.

else Clause

See

> if Statement

Entry Point

See

> main Method

enum Statement

Visual Basic's *Enum* statement is equivalent to C#'s *enum* statement.

C#
```
enum DoorState
{
    Closed = 1,
    Ajar,
    Open
}
```

VISUAL BASIC
```
Enum DoorState
    Closed = 1
    Ajar
    Open
End Enum
```

Both languages default each enumeration member to zero (for the first item) or one more than the item that precedes it, unless overridden with a specific value, as was done with `DoorState.Closed` in the prior sample. C# separates members with commas, while VB uses line breaks.

Both Visual Basic and C# support enumerations based on the eight core integer types (*byte*, *sbyte*, *short*, *ushort*, *int*, *uint*, *long*, *ulong*, and their Visual Basic counterparts), with *int* (C#) and *Integer* (VB) used by default.

C#
```
enum DoorState : long
```

VISUAL BASIC
```
Enum DoorState As Long
```

C# enumerations can appear within namespaces, classes, or structures. In addition to these, Visual Basic also permits the nesting of enumerations within interfaces.

Enumerations support the following modifiers in each language.

C# Modifier	Visual Basic Modifier
internal	*Friend*
new	*Shadows*
private	*Private*
protected	*Protected*
protected internal	*Protected Friend*
public	*Public*

Both languages use a dotted notation when accessing enumeration members in code.

New with Visual Studio 2015
In 2015, C# added a new *using static* statement that, when paired with an enumeration, allows use of the enumeration's members without specifying the enumeration name in code. Visual Basic allows this through its *Imports* statement.

C#
```
// ----- Before 2015.
DoorState frontDoor = DoorState.IsClosed;

// ----- Starting in 2015, at the top of the file.
using static DoorNamespace;
using static DoorNamespace.DoorState;

// ----- Later, within a method.
DoorState backDoor = IsClosed;
```

VISUAL BASIC
```
' ----- At the top of the file.
Imports DoorNamespace
Imports DoorNamespace.DoorState

' ----- Later, within a method.
Dim frontDoor As DoorState = DoorState.IsClosed

' ----- This will also work thanks to the Imports.
Dim backDoor As DoorState = IsClosed
```

Error Handling

See

throw Statement, try Statement

Event Handlers

In C#, the *+=* event subscription operator links an object's event to a compatible event handler. The *-=* event unsubscription operator later breaks the association.

C#
```
// ----- Define the instance.
public Button button1 = new Button();
```

```
// ----- Define the handler.
void button1_Click(object sender, EventArgs e)
{
    // ----- Event-handling code here.
}

// ----- Elsewhere...
button1.Click += button1_Click;
```

In Visual Basic, the *AddHandler* and *RemoveHandler* statements, when used in conjunction with the *AddressOf* operator, perform the same function as C#'s *+=* and *-=* event operators.

VISUAL BASIC
```
' ----- Define the instance.
Public Button1 As New Button()

' ----- Define the handler.
Sub Button1_Click(ByVal sender As Object,
        ByVal e As EventArgs)
    ' ----- Event-handling code here.
End Sub

' ----- To connect the event.
AddHandler Button1.Click, AddressOf Button1_Click

' ----- To disconnect the event.
RemoveHandler Button1.Click, AddressOf Button1_Click
```

Visual Basic also has an alternate syntax that uses *WithEvents* on the object declaration, and exchanges *AddHandler* and *RemoveHandler* for the *Handles* clause on the event handler.

VISUAL BASIC
```
' ----- Define the instance.
Public WithEvents Button1 As New Button()

' ----- Define the handler.
Sub Button1_Click(ByVal sender As Object,
        ByVal e As EventArgs) Handles Button1.Click
End Sub
```

Events can also use lambda expressions as event handlers.

C#
```
Button1.Click += (sender, e) => { /* Code here */ };
```

VISUAL BASIC
```
AddHandler Button1.Click, Sub(sender, e)
        ' ----- Code here.
    End Sub
```

See Also

+= Event Subscription Operator, -= Event Unsubscription Operator, event Statement

event Modifier

See

Attributes

event Statement

As in C#, Visual Basic includes support for delegate-based event declaration. Its *Event* statement, when used in this way, closely parallels the functionality of C#'s *event* statement.

C#
```
public delegate void SampleEventHandler(
    object sender, SampleEventArgs e);
public event SampleEventHandler SampleEvent;
```

VISUAL BASIC
```
Public Delegate Sub SampleEventHandler(
    ByVal sender As Object,
    ByVal e As SampleEventArgs)
Public Event SampleEvent As SampleEventHandler
```

Visual Basic also supports a combined syntax, where the signature of the delegate is included in the event declaration.

VISUAL BASIC
```
Public Event SampleEvent(ByVal sender As Object,
    ByVal e As SampleEventArgs)
```

An enhanced version of C#'s *event* statement adds custom logic that runs whenever an event handler is added to or removed from the event being defined. The *add* and *remove* blocks define the event-adding and event-removing logic, respectively. Each block implies a "value" variable, an event handler instance of the delegate type for the event.

C#
```
// ----- Same delegate as above.
public event SampleEventHandler SampleEvent
{
    add { /* Code using "value" here. */ }
    remove { /* Code using "value" here. */ }
}
```

Visual Basic has a similar extended syntax that adds the *Custom* modifier. In addition to add (*AddHandler*) and remove (*RemoveHandler*) blocks, the VB syntax includes a third block named *RaiseEvent* that hosts logic called every time the event is raised. This block has no direct equivalent in C#.

```
' ----- Same delegate as above.
Public Custom Event SampleEvent As SampleEventHandler
    AddHandler(ByVal value As SampleEventHandler)
        ' ----- Custom "add" code here.
    End AddHandler
    RemoveHandler(ByVal value As SampleEventHandler)
        ' ----- Custom "remove" code here.
    End RemoveHandler
    RaiseEvent(ByVal sender As Object,
            ByVal e As SampleEventArgs)
        ' ----- Custom "raise" code here. The
        '       signature is the same as the
        '       delegate signature.
    End RaiseEvent
End Event
```

Events support the following modifiers in each language.

C# Modifier	Visual Basic Modifier
abstract	Not supported
extern	Not supported
internal	Friend
new	Shadows
override	Not supported
private	Private
protected	Protected
protected internal	Protected Friend
public	Public
sealed	Not supported
static	Shared
virtual	Not supported

Exceptions

See

> throw Statement, try Statement

explicit Modifier

C#'s *explicit* modifier indicates that an overloaded conversion from one type to another must be performed explicitly, as the destination type may be too narrow for all the source type's possible values.

```
class BigType
{
    public static explicit operator SmallType(
        BigType source)
    {
        return new SmallType(source.GetCondensed());
    }
}
```

The equivalent Visual Basic overload uses the *Narrowing* modifier to express this same limiting conversion.

```
Class BigType
    Public Shared Narrowing Operator CType(
            ByVal source As BigType) As SmallType
        Return New SmallType(source.GetCondensed())
    End Operator
End Class
```

See Also

implicit Modifier, operator Statement

Extension Methods

In C#, extension methods appear in static classes, and use the *this* modifier to indicate the target type being extended.

```
internal static class LocalExtensions
{
    public static string DigitsOnly(
        this string originalText)
    {
        // ----- Returns a string result.
    }
}
```

In Visual Basic, extension methods always appear in modules, which are akin to static classes in C#. The method must be decorated with the *Extension* attribute (from *System.Runtime.CompilerServices*). Although not marked with any special modifier, the first argument to the method is the target of the extension.

```
Imports System.Runtime.CompilerServices

Friend Module LocalExtensions
    <Extension> Public Function DigitsOnly(
            ByVal originalText As String) As String
        ' ----- Returns a string result.
    End Function
End Module
```

extern alias Statement

Visual Basic has no equivalent for C#'s *extern alias* statement. The closest alternative involves using Reflection to load and access members of an external assembly indirectly, a task that is beyond the scope of this book.

See Also

:: Namespace Alias Qualifier

extern Modifier

When used with the *DllImport* attribute (from *System.Runtime.InteropServices*), the *extern* modifier indicates a method sourced from an external file.

C#
```
[DllImport("avifil32.dll")]
private static extern void AVIFileInit();
```

Visual Basic includes support for this same functionality, but requires no specific modifier comparable to *extern*.

VISUAL BASIC
```
<DllImport("avifil32.dll")>
Private Shared Sub AVIFileInit()
End Sub
```

Beyond this attribute-centric declaration, Visual Basic's *Declare* statement provides a more formal syntax for identifying methods from an external source.

VISUAL BASIC
```
Private Declare Sub InitAVI Lib "avifil32.dll" _
    Alias "AVIFileInit" ()
```

The *Lib* clause indicates the source file, while the optional *Alias* clause identifies the method name in the library for those times when you want to give it a different name within your code. Replace *Sub* with *Function* to import a method that returns data, and update the signature as needed.

Methods imported with the *Declare* statement are *Public* by default. Also, imported methods are assumed to work with ANSI character sets. To alter this default, follow the *Default* keyword with the *Unicode*, *Auto*, or (to make the default clear) *Ansi* keyword.

See Also

Methods

false Boolean Literal

Visual Basic's *False* literal is identical to C#'s *false* literal.

Fields

Fields are variables declared within a class or structure (plus modules in VB), outside of any method. The syntax closely parallels that of local variable declaration. (See the "Variables" entry in this chapter for more declaration details.)

C#

```
// ----- Field declared with initializer.
private int MonitoredValue = 0;
```

VISUAL BASIC

```
' ----- Field declared with initializer.
Private MonitoredValue As Integer = 0

' ----- The "Dim" keyword is optional, but required
'       when no access modifier is used.
Dim AnotherValue As Integer
```

Access modifiers are optional in field declarations. When missing, the access level defaults to *private* in C# classes and structures. Within a Visual Basic *Class* or *Module*, fields are *Private* by default; they are *Public* by default when used in a *Structure*.

Fields support the following modifiers in each language.

C# Modifier	Visual Basic Modifier
internal	Friend
new	Shadows
private	Private
protected	Protected
protected internal	Protected Friend
public	Public
readonly	ReadOnly
static	Shared
volatile	Not supported
Not supported	WithEvents

See Also

[ ] Array Declaration, Access Modifiers, Identifiers, Initializers, new Operator, static Modifier, Variables

field Modifier

See

Attributes

finally Clause

See

try Statement

fixed Modifier

C#'s *fixed* modifier, used to create fixed-size buffers, is only valid in unsafe contexts. Because Visual Basic does not support unsafe code, there is no equivalent for this modifier in VB.

fixed Statement

C#'s *fixed* statement, used to prevent the .NET garbage collector from moving a block of memory, is valid only in unsafe contexts. Because Visual Basic does not support unsafe code, there is no equivalent for this statement in VB.

float Data Type

Visual Basic's intrinsic *Single* data type is identical to C#'s *float* data type. Both types are aliases for .NET's *System.Single* type. For single literals, C# uses an *F* or *f* suffix after the value; in Visual Basic, use *F*, *f*, or *!* instead.

C#
```
float factor = 0f;  // or 0F
```

VISUAL BASIC
```
Dim factor As Single = 0!   ' or 0F or 0f
```

for Statement

For simple C# *for* loops that iterate from a starting number to an ending value, incrementing by a standard amount each time, Visual Basic's *For* loop is an useful replacement.

C#
```
for (int counter = 0; counter < 10; counter++)
{
    // ----- Loops 10 times, from 0 to 9.
}

// ----- Outside-of-loop declaration of counter
//       is also valid.
int counter;
for (counter = 0; counter < 10; counter++)
{
}
```

VISUAL BASIC
```
For counter As Integer = 0 To 9
    ' ----- Loops 10 times, from 0 to 9, inclusive.
Next counter
```

```
' ----- Outside-of-loop declaration of counter
'        is also valid.
Dim counter As Integer
For counter = 0 To 9
Next counter
```

The loop counter in the VB statement can be integer (*Byte*, *Short*, *Integer*, or *Long*, or their signed and unsigned counterparts), a floating-point variable (*Single*, *Double*, or *Decimal*), or an enumeration. If you have another type that has overloaded the +, -, <=, >=, and *CType* operators, it can also be used. By default, the counter variable increases by one (*1*) each time through the loop. You can change this with the *Step* clause, followed by any positive or negative increment.

VISUAL BASIC

```
For counter As Decimal = 10@ To 1@ Step -2.5@
    ' ----- Values will be 10, 7.5, 5, and 2.5.
```

C#'s *for* statement permits even more complex looping scenarios, with support for multiple comma-delimited initializers (of the same data type) and iterators, and a condition section that supports any type of Boolean expression. None of these features are available in Visual Basic's *For* loop. To support such loops, you will need to convert them to a *Do* statement, or manage these other variables in conjunction with a standard *For* loop. Use an *Exit For* or *Exit Do* statement to exit a loop early.

C#

```
string monthCode = "";
for (int month = 1; counter <= 12 &
        !monthCode.Contains("X"); counter++)
    monthCode += ProcessMonth(month);
```

VISUAL BASIC

```
' ----- Using a For statement.
Dim monthCode As String = ""
For month As Integer = 1 To 12
    monthCode &= ProcessMonth(month)
    If (monthCode.Contains("X")) Then Exit For
Next month

' ----- Using a Do statement.
Dim month As Integer = 1
Dim monthCode As String = ""
Do While (month <= 12) And
        (Not monthCode.Contains("X"))
    monthCode &= ProcessMonth(month)
    month += 1
Loop
```

In C#, you can create an infinite loop by leaving the condition portion (or all portions) blank.

C#

```
for (;;) { }
```

To do this in Visual Basic, use a *Do* statement instead.

VISUAL BASIC
```
Do
Loop
```

In both languages, you can alter the counter variable within the body of the loop. The starting, ending, and increment (step) values in a *For* loop, however, are evaluated only once, before the loop begins, and cannot be changed from within the loop.

foreach Statement

Visual Basic's *For Each* statement is equivalent to C#'s *foreach* statement.

C#
```
foreach (DataRow scanRow in customerTable.Rows)
{
    // ----- Logic using scanRow variable.
}
```

VISUAL BASIC
```
For Each scanRow As DataRow In customerTable.Rows
    ' ----- Logic using scanRow variable.
Next scanRow
```

Visual Basic allows the iteration variable to be declared outside of the loop.

VISUAL BASIC
```
Dim scanRow As DataRow
For Each scanRow In customerTable.Rows
```

This is not permitted in C#; you must declare the loop variable type as part of the statement declaration. (The type can be *var* for implicitly typed iterators.)

from Query Expression Operator (LINQ)

Visual Basic's *From* query expression operator is identical to C#'s *from* operator. Both languages allow the clause to appear multiple times within the query. Visual Basic also allows a single *From* clause to include multiple comma-delimited sources.

C#
```
// ----- Single source.
var result = from item in Employees
            select new {item.FullName, item.HireDate};

// ----- Multiple sources.
var result = from item in Employees
            from site in Divisions
            where item.Division == site.ID
            select new {Division = site.Name,
            item.FullName};
```

VISUAL BASIC
```
' ----- Single source.
Dim result = From item In Employees
            Select item.FullName, item.HireDate
```

```
' ----- Multiple comma-delimited sources.
Dim result = From item In Employees, site In Divisions
              Where item.Division = site.ID
              Select Division = site.Name, item.FullName

' ----- Multiple distinct sources.
Dim result = From item In Employees
             From site In Divisions
             Where item.Division = site.ID
             Select Division = site.Name, item.FullName
```

Visual Basic supports multiple *From* clauses when processing nested results.

VISUAL BASIC
```
Dim result = From customer In GetActiveCustomers()
             From order In customer.Orders
             Select order
```

Normally, the range variable is inferred from the collection type. To explicitly identify the range variable type, include an *As* clause.

VISUAL BASIC
```
Dim result = From item As Employee In AllEmployees
```

In C#, the *from* clause is required in all query expressions. In Visual Basic, the *From* clause is normally required. However, when building aggregate queries, the *From* clause is not required if the query expression begins with the *Aggregate* operator.

VISUAL BASIC
```
Dim averageSalary = Aggregate item In Employees
                    Into Average(item.Salary)
```

See Also

Query Expressions

Functions

See

Methods

Garbage Collection

See

Destructors

Generics

Both C# and Visual Basic support generics, also known as "constructed types." One key difference is the syntax used to specify the type placeholders. In C#, these appear within angle brackets after the generic type name, while in Visual Basic, they appear in parentheses as part of an *Of* clause.

C#
```
// ----- As part of a generic declaration.
class SpecialList<T>
{
    private T InternalList;
}

// ----- As part of a generic instantiation.
SpecialList<int> trackNumbers = new SpecialList<int>();
```

VISUAL BASIC
```
' ----- As part of a generic declaration.
Class SpecialList(Of T)
    Private InternalList As T
End Class

' ----- As part of a generic instantiation.
Dim trackNumbers As New SpecialList(Of Integer)
```

Generic constructs can be applied to classes, structures, interfaces, methods, and delegates in both languages. Generic methods can appear within generic or non-generic types.

C#
```
static void ReverseItems<T>(ref T firstItem,
    ref T secondItem)
{
    T holdingArea = firstItem;
    firstItem = secondItem;
    secondItem = holdingArea;
}
```

VISUAL BASIC
```
Shared Sub ReverseItems(Of T)(ByRef firstItem As T,
        ByRef secondItem As T)
    Dim holdingArea As T = firstItem
    firstItem = secondItem
    secondItem = holdingArea
End Sub
```

In both C# and Visual Basic, the generic type parameter list can include type-specific modifiers that provide limits for each parameter. C#'s *where* clause, like VB's *As* clause, lets you limit the specific types that can be used for a type parameter during instantiation. See the "where Clause" entry in this chapter for more information. When defining generic interfaces, optional modifiers specify the variance associated with each type parameter. By default, type parameters are invariant. The "out" modifier in each language specifies covariance, while "in" specifies contravariance.

C#
```
interface IVariant<TInvariant, out TCovariant,
    in TContravariant>
{
}
```

```
Interface IVariant(Of TInvariant, Out TCovariant,
    In TContravariant)
End Interface
```

See Also

where Clause

get Declaration

See

Properties

global Namespace Alias

When used to indicate the root of the namespace hierarchy, Visual Basic's *Global* namespace alias is equivalent to C#'s *global* alias.

C#
```
// ----- Perhaps you defined a MyApp.System.Exception
//       class in your application's code. This makes
//       it clear that you want .NET's Exception class.
global::System.Exception theProblem;
```

VISUAL BASIC
```
Dim theProblem As Global.System.Exception
```

See Also

:: Namespace Alias Qualifier

goto Statement

For ordinary jumps to line labels, Visual Basic's *GoTo* statement is identical to C#'s *goto* statement.

VISUAL BASIC
```
GoTo SkipProcessing
```

Within *switch* statements, C# allows the use of *goto case* and *goto default* to redirect processing to another block within the *switch* statement. This syntax is not supported in VB. Instead, add a line label to the target block, and use a standard *GoTo* statement to jump to the other code.

C#
```
switch (token)
{
    case ">":
        term += "greater than";
        break;
```

```
       case ">=":
           term += "greater than or ";
           goto case "=";
       case "=":
           term += "equal to";
           break;
}
```

VISUAL BASIC

```
Select Case token
    Case ">"
        term &= "greater than"
    Case ">="
        term &= "greater than or "
        GoTo EqualsTo
    Case "="
EqualsTo:
        term &= "equal to"
End Select
```

See Also

Labels

group Query Expression Operator (LINQ)

Visual Basic's *Group* query expression operator parallels C#'s *group* operator. In C#, a single expression or range variable target is grouped by one or more grouping expressions. In Visual Basic, the target can be an expression, a range variable, a comma-delimited list of expressions, or missing altogether, which implies that all range variables or fields should be the target.

C#

```
// ----- Grouping of range variable.
var result = from item in Employees
             group item by item.Department;

// ----- Grouping of specific field.
var result = from item in Employees
             group item.FullName by item.Department;

// ----- Grouping of multiple fields.
var result = from item in Employees
             group new {item.FullName, item.HireDate}
             by item.Department;
```

VISUAL BASIC

```
' ----- Grouping of range variable.
Dim result = From item In Employees
             Group By item.Department Into Group
```

```
' ----- Grouping of specific field.
Dim result = From item In Employees
              Group item.FullName
              By item.Department Into Group

' ----- Grouping of multiple fields.
Dim result = From item In Employees
              Group item.FullName, item.HireDate
              By item.Department Into Group
```

To perform additional processing on the grouped results, the *into* clause (C#) identifies a temporary identifier used in subsequent clauses. In Visual Basic, the *Into* portion is required in all *Group By* expressions, as shown in the previous sample code block. Clauses that follow *Group By* refer to grouping elements directly, often without the alias prefix.

C#

```
var result = from item in Employees
              group item by item.Department into deptSets
              orderby deptSets.Key
              select deptSets;
```

VISUAL BASIC

```
Dim result = From item In Employees
              Group By item.Department Into deptSets = Group
              Order By Department
              Select deptSets
```

Visual Basic's *Into* clause supports additional aggregate functions. This syntax is not supported directly in C#, but requires an additional *select* clause.

C#

```
var result = from item in Employees
              group item by item.Department into deptSets
              select new { DeptName = deptSets.Key,
                           DeptMembers = deptSets.Count() };
```

VISUAL BASIC

```
' ----- In this variation, the results will also include
'        subordinate "item" records, although C# version
'        will only include department name and count.
Dim result = From item In Employees
              Group By item.Department
              Into Group, Count()
```

See Also

Query Expressions

Identifiers

Both C# and Visual Basic use a common set of identifier naming rules, allowing for a mixture of letters, digits, and underscores, with some limitations, such as not starting an identifier with a digit.

Identifiers in C# are case-sensitive. Two variables named *customerName* and *CustomerName* in the same method would not conflict since the first letter is a different case. In Visual Basic, identifiers are case-insensitive. In VB, two identifiers are identical if they are the same when converted to all lower-case letters. It is possible to create an assembly in C# with two exposed type or member names that differ only by case. Such naming would cause problems when consumed by a Visual Basic project, although VB does have rules that attempt to identify the most accessible element when there is a conflict.

Visual Basic allows you to give the same (case-insensitive) name to a type and one of its members.

VISUAL BASIC

```
' ----- This is valid in Visual Basic.
Public Class ItemData
    Public ItemText As String
    Public ItemData As Long
End Class
```

C# does not allow this combination. You must not name a type member the same as its enclosing type in C#. If you create a Visual Basic assembly that has this shared naming of type and member, a C# project will not be able to access the member directly.

C# allows identifiers to include Unicode escape sequences in the form \ *Uhhhh*, where *hhhh* is a 4- or 8-digit hex value. The hex code must still resolve to a character considered valid for identifiers, typically variations of the core alphanumeric characters.

C#

```
string p\00E8re = "French for 'father'";
MessageBox.Show(string.Format("{0} is {1}",
    nameof(p\00E8re), p\00E8re));
// ----- Displays: père is French for 'father'
```

Visual Basic does not include support for these sequences. You can use a Unicode character within an identifier name in VB, but it must be entered as a standard character within the code, and not as an escape sequence.

VISUAL BASIC

```
Dim père As String = "French for 'father'"
MessageBox.Show(String.Format("{0} is {1}",
    NameOf(père), père));
' ----- Displays: père is French for 'father'
```

Both languages allow you to create identifiers that conflict with reserved language keywords. To use such identifiers, prefix them with the @ symbol in C#, or surround them with square brackets in Visual Basic.

C#

```
long @for = 0L;
```

VISUAL BASIC

```
Dim [For] As Long = 0&
```

Microsoft recommends that identifier names be either Pascal-cased or camel-cased. In Pascal casing, every distinct word within the name has an initial capital, including the start of the identifier. Camel casing is similar, but the initial letter is lowercase.

C#

```
int PascalCaseExample;
int camelCaseExample;
```

As indicated in Visual Studio's documentation, camel casing is recommended for parameter names, local variable names, and protected instance fields within types. All other identifiers, including line labels, should use Pascal casing.

if Statement

Visual Basic's *If* statement closely parallels the *if* statement in C#.

C#

```
if (testDate < DateTime.Now)
    era = "Past";
else if (testDate == DateTime.Now)
    era = "Present";
else
    era = "Future";
```

VISUAL BASIC

```
If (testDate < Now) Then
    era = "Past"
ElseIf (testDate = Now) Then
    era = "Present"
Else
    era = "Future"
End If
```

Each condition in VB begins with *If* or *ElseIf*, and ends with *Then* before moving into the logic for that condition. The entire statement ends with *End If*. Visual Basic includes a condensed version of the statement that puts the *Then* and *Else* parts on a single logical line. (This syntax works in C# as well, but that's due to the way that whitespace is used, and not because of the grammar of the *if* statement, as is the case in VB.)

VISUAL BASIC

```
' ----- Simple If with no Else component.
If problemOccurred Then ErrorField.Visible = True

' ----- Simple If with Else component.
If (IsValidZip(zipCode) = True) Then _
    city = GetZipCity(zipCode) Else city = "Unknown"
```

In this simple version of the statement, the *End If* closing token is not used. As shown in the second example, you may need to include a line continuation character (_) if the logical line breaks across more than one physical line.

As in C#, Visual Basic's conditional statements can include any mix of expressions or logical operators, just as long as the result of each expression is a Boolean value. You must surround the condition in C# with a set of parentheses; these parentheses are optional in VB. Visual Basic supports any number of `ElseIf` clauses, and you can nest `If` statements, just like in C#.

implicit Modifier

C#'s *implicit* modifier indicates that an overloaded conversion from one type to another may be performed implicitly, as the destination type is wide enough for all the source type's possible values.

C#

```
class SmallType
{
    public static implicit operator BigType(
        SmallType source)
    {
        return new BigType(source.GetValue());
    }
}
```

The equivalent Visual Basic overload uses the `Widening` modifier to express this same conversion.

VISUAL BASIC

```
Class SmallType
    Public Shared Widening Operator CType(
            ByVal source As SmallType) As BigType
        Return New BigType(source.GetValue())
    End Operator
End Class
```

See Also

explicit Modifier, operator Statement

in Modifier

See

Generics

Indexers

See

this Indexer Declaration

Inheritance

C# indicates a type's base class using the : symbol.

C#

```
// ----- Dog derives from Animal, and
//       implements IDomesticate.
public class Dog : Animal, IDomesticate
```

In Visual Basic, use the *Inherits* statement on the first line within the class definition.

VISUAL BASIC

```
' ----- Dog derives from Animal, and
'       implements IDomesticate.
Public Class Dog
    Inherits Animal
    Implements IDomesticate
```

C# indicates both derived classes and implemented interfaces after the : symbol. In VB, these two relationships must be separated with the *Inherits* and *Implements* statements, as shown in the preceding sample.

See Also

: Base Declaration Indicator, base Constructor Declaration

Initializers

In C#, while you don't need to provide initialization at the moment of declaration for fields and local variables, you must initialize these variables before they are used in code. Visual Basic automatically initializes all fields and local variables to their default values (typically *Nothing* or some variation of zero) when no other initialization is used. Neither language allows you to provide in-line initialization of instance fields in structures. These must be initialized within a constructor.

Basic initialization of variables and constants in both languages is done with an assignment.

C#

```
const decimal closeToPi = 3.2m;
int notInitialized;
int startingZero = 0;
string startingUnused = null;
string startingEmpty = "";
Customer readyToUse = null;
Customer fromExpression = GetCustomer(123);
```

VISUAL BASIC

```
Const closeToPi As Decimal = 3.2@
Dim notInitialized As Integer
Dim startingZero As Integer = 0
Dim startingUnused As String = Nothing
Dim startingEmpty As String = ""
Dim readyToUse As Customer = Nothing
Dim fromExpression As Customer = GetCustomer(123)
```

In both languages, object initializers let you set member fields and properties as part of instance declaration. The member values appear in a set of curly braces. In Visual Basic, this block appears as part of a *With* clause, and each member is prefixed with a period.

C#

```csharp
// ----- Explicit type
Animal cat = new Animal {Age = 5, Name = "Fluffy"};

// ----- Implicit type
var kitten = new Animal {Age = 0, Name = "Kitty"};

// ----- With custom constructor
Employee boss = new Employee("John Smith")
    {Title = "President"};
```

VISUAL BASIC

```vb
' ----- Explicit type
Dim cat1 As New Animal With {.Age = 5, .Name = "Fluffy"}
Dim cat2 As Animal = New Animal With {.Age = 10,
    .Name = "Fang"}

' ----- Implicit type
Dim kitten = New Animal With {.Age = 0, .Name = "Kitty"}

' ----- With custom constructor
Dim boss As New Employee("John Smith") With _
    {.Title = "President"}
```

Both C# and Visual Basic can initialize arrays and collections as part of instance declaration. Notice the *From* clause used when initializing a collection in Visual Basic.

C#

```csharp
// ----- Array. In the explicitSize declaration, "4"
//       refers to the size, not the upper bound.
int[] implicitSize = new int[] {2, 3, 5, 7, 11};
int[] explicitSize = new int[4] {13, 17, 19, 23};
int[] simpler = {29, 31, 37};

int[,] multiDimension = {{1, 2}, {3, 4}};
int[][] jagged = {new int[] {1, 2, 3},
                  new int[] {4, 5, 6, 7, 8}};

// ----- Collection
List<int> basicList = new List<int> {1, 2, 3, 4, 5};
var dayInfo = new Dictionary<int, string>
    {{0, "Sunday"}, {1, "Monday"}};
```

VISUAL BASIC

```vb
' ----- Array. In the explicitSize declaration, "3"
'       refers to the upper bound, not the size.
Dim implicitSize() As Integer = {2, 3, 5, 7, 11}
Dim explicitSize() As Integer =
    New Integer(3) {13, 17, 19, 23}
Dim simpler() As Integer = {29, 31, 37}

Dim multiDimension(,) As Integer = {{1, 2}, {3, 4}}
```

```
Dim jagged()() As Integer = New Integer(1)() _
    {New Integer() {1, 2, 3},
     New Integer() {4, 5, 6, 7, 8}}

' ----- Collection
Dim basicList As New List(Of Integer) From {1, 2, 3, 4, 5}
Dim dayInfo = New Dictionary(Of Integer, String) _
    From {{0, "Sunday"}, {1, "Monday"}}
```

Here is a more involved example that combines collection and object initializers.

C#
```
List<Cat> moreCats = new List<Cat>
{
    new Cat() {Name = "Furrytail", Age = 5},
    new Cat() {Name = "Peaches", Age = 4}
};
```

VISUAL BASIC
```
Dim moreCats As New List(Of Cat) From
{
    New Cat() With {.Name = "Furrytail", .Age = 5},
    New Cat() With {.Name = "Peaches", .Age = 4}
}
```

Collection initializers can be used as expressions, wherever a collection or array is expected.

C#
```
int result = CondenseArray(new int[] {1, 2, 3});
```

VISUAL BASIC
```
Dim result As Integer =
    CondenseArray(New Integer() {1, 2, 3})
```

Initialization of anonymous types in both languages follows the syntax of standard initialization.

C#
```
var pet = new {Age = 3, Name = "Rover"};
```

VISUAL BASIC
```
Dim pet = New With {.Age = 3, .Name = "Rover"}
```

When working with generics, C#'s *default* operator lets you assign the default value of a type to a variable. In Visual Basic, the *Nothing* literal provides the same functionality.

C#
```
class Special<T>
{
    public T watchValue = default(T);
}
```

VISUAL BASIC
```
Class Special(Of T)
    Public watchValue As T = Nothing
End Class
```

> **New with Visual Studio 2015**
> Originally, C# did not allow automatic properties to be initialized as part of the declaration itself. In 2015, the language gained this functionality for both read-only and read-write properties. Visual Basic already included such initialization features for read-write auto-properties, but initialization of read-only automatic properties came about in that same 2015 release.

C#
```
// ----- Read-write property.
public string CoreName { get; set; } = "Unknown";

// ----- Read-only property.
public string CoreName { get; } = "Unknown";
```

VISUAL BASIC
```
' ----- Read-write property.
Public Property CoreName As String = "Unknown"

' ----- Read-only property.
Public ReadOnly Property CoreName As String = "Unknown"
```

> **New with Visual Studio 2015**
> Starting in 2015, C# has a new syntax for initializing indexed collections.

C#
```
Dictionary<int, string> currencyFaces =
    new Dictionary<int, string> {
        [1] = "Washington",
        [5] = "Lincoln",
        [10] = "Hamilton"
    };
```

This new syntax is not available in Visual Basic. Instead, you must add items through the type's standard item-adding features, such as through an *Add* method.

int Data Type

Visual Basic's intrinsic *Integer* data type is identical to C#'s *int* data type. Both types are aliases for .NET's *System.Int32* type. For integer literals, Visual Basic uses an *I*, *I*, or *%* suffix after the value; C# does not include such a suffix.

C#
```
int counter = 0;
```

VISUAL BASIC
```
Dim counter As Integer = 0%   ' or 0I or 0i
```

interface Statement

Visual Basic's *Interface* statement is equivalent to C#'s *interface* statement. When declaring an interface that derives from one or more interfaces, VB's *Inherits* clause lists those interfaces, appearing as the first line within the *Interface* statement.

C#

```
interface ISomethingNew : ISomethingOld
{
    // ----- Members appear here.
}
```

VISUAL BASIC

```
Interface ISomethingNew
    Implements ISomethingOld
    ' ----- Members appear here.
End Interface
```

Interfaces in C# can include methods, properties, events, and indexers. Visual Basic supports all these members, and can also include subordinate interfaces, classes, and structures, none of which can be included in C# interfaces.

C#

```
interface IOptions
{
    // ----- Methods with and without return
    int MethodWithData(string incoming);
    void WorkOnlyMethod();

    // ----- Property and Indexer
    string Name {get; set;}
    string this[int index] {get;}

    // ----- Event (with delegate defined elsewhere)
    event DelegateSignature EventName;
}
```

VISUAL BASIC

```
Interface IOptions
    ' ----- Methods with and without return
    Function MethodWithData(
        ByVal incoming As String) As Integer
    Sub WorkOnlyMethod()

    ' ----- Property and Indexer
    Property Name() As String
    Default ReadOnly Property Item(
        ByVal index As Integer) As String

    ' ----- Event (with and without defined delegate)
    Event EventFromDelegate As DelegateSignature
    Event EventDefinedInline(ByVal source As Object)
```

```
'  ----- Class
Class SubordinateClass
    '  ----- Members here
End Class

'  ----- Structure
Structure SubordinateStructure
    '  ----- Members here
End Structure

'  ----- Interface
Interface ISubordinate
    '  ----- Members here
End Interface
End Interface
```

Interfaces support the following modifiers in each language.

C# Modifier	Visual Basic Modifier
internal	Friend
new	Shadows
partial	Partial (starting in 2015)
private	Private
protected	Protected
protected internal	Protected Friend
public	Public

Interfaces in C# are *internal* by default, just as interfaces in Visual Basic are *Friend* by default. In both languages, all members are public by definition.

During implementation of an interface, Visual Basic uses the *Implements* modifier, both on the type and explicitly on each implementing member.

C#

```csharp
class Employee : IPerson
{
    public string IPerson.Name
    {
        // ----- Implementation here.
    }
}
```

VISUAL BASIC

```vbnet
Class Employee
    Implements IPerson

    Public Property Name As String Implements IPerson.Name
        ' ----- Implementation here.
    End Property
End Class
```

Because the *Implements* clause on the member includes the name of the interface member, the name of the class member implementing the item does not have to be the same in Visual Basic. In C#, the implementing member name is always the same as the interface member name being implemented.

internal Access Modifier

Visual Basic's *Friend* access modifier is equivalent to C#'s *internal* access modifier.

See Also

Access Modifiers

is Comparison Operator

Both C#'s *is* operator and Visual Basic's *TypeOf...Is* operator return true if the object being tested is of a specified type, or can be implicitly converted to that type.

C#
```
if (personVariable is Customer)
```

VISUAL BASIC
```
If (TypeOf personVariable Is Customer) Then
```

> **New with Visual Studio 2015**
> Beginning with its 2015 release, Visual Basic added a new *TypeOf...IsNot* operator that returns the Boolean opposite of the *TypeOf...Is* operator.

Visual Basic includes an *Is* operator (without *TypeOf*) that compares object instances. It is not the same as either *TypeOf...Is* or C#'s *is* operator.

Iterators

In C#, iterators are functions or properties that include the *yield return* statement. In Visual Basic, iterators are also built from functions or properties, include the *Yield* statement, and are declared using the *Iterator* modifier.

C#
```
public IEnumerable<int> FirstFivePrimes()
{
    yield return 2;
    yield return 3;
    yield return 5;
    yield return 7;
    yield return 11;
}
```

VISUAL BASIC
```
Public Iterator Function FirstFivePrimes() As _
        IEnumerable(Of Integer)
    Yield 2
    Yield 3
    Yield 5
```

```
        Yield 7
        Yield 11
End Function
```

When implemented as a read-only property, Visual Basic employs both the *Iterator* and *ReadOnly* modifiers on the property declaration.

C#

```csharp
public IEnumerable<int> EvensOnly(int maximum)
{
    get
    {
        for (int value = 2; value <= maximum; value++)
            yield return value;
    }
}
```

VISUAL BASIC

```vb
Public ReadOnly Iterator Property EvensOnly(
        ByVal maximum As Integer) As _
        IEnumerable(Of Integer)
    Get
        For value As Integer = 2 To maximum
            Yield value
        Next value
    End Get
End Property
```

Visual Basic allows the *Iterator* modifier to be used with an anonymous method. This variation is not supported in C#.

join Query Expression Operator (LINQ)

Visual Basic's *Join* query expression operator is the same as the *join* operator in C#.

C#

```csharp
var result = from item in Employees
             join dept in Departments
             on item.Department equals dept.ID
             select new {item.FullName, dept.DeptName};
```

VISUAL BASIC

```vb
Dim result = From item In Employees
             Join dept In Departments
             On item.Department Equals dept.ID
             Select item.FullName, dept.DeptName
```

As with C#, Visual Basic also supports group joins using the *Group Join* syntax. C# doesn't include an equivalent "group" keyword, but its *into* clause parallels the *Into* clause used in the VB version.

C#

```
var result = from dept in Departments
             join emp in Employees
             on dept.ID equals emp.Department into empSets
             select new {dept.DeptName,
             RecentHires = empSets};
```

VISUAL BASIC

```
Dim result = From dept In Departments
             Group Join emp In Employees
             On dept.ID Equals emp.Department Into Group
             Select dept.DeptName, RecentHires = Group
```

In both languages, you can use multiple "from" and "where" clauses to perform joins between different range sources. See the "from Query Expression Operator" entry in this chapter for an example that uses this syntax.

See Also

Query Expressions

Labels

Both C# and Visual Basic support line labels within methods. In both languages, a colon (:) follows the label.

C#

```
StartOver:
    // ----- Later...
    goto StartOver;
```

VISUAL BASIC

```
StartOver:
    ' ----- Later...
    GoTo StartOver
```

Line labels are case-sensitive in C#; you can include two identically named labels in the same method as long as they vary by case. In Visual Basic, labels are case-insensitive. Do not use two labels of the same name, even if the case varies.

Visual Basic allows labels to be wholly numeric. This is not supported in C#.

VISUAL BASIC

```
100:
    ' ----- Some code here.
```

See Also

goto Statement

Lambda Expressions

See

=> Lambda Operator

Late Binding

See

dynamic Type

let Query Expression Operator (LINQ)

Visual Basic's `Let` query expression operator is identical to C#'s `let` operator.

C#
```
var result = from oneEmployee in Employees
             let annualSalary =
             oneEmployee.WeeklySalary * 52
             where annualSalary >= 50000
             select new {oneEmployee.FullName,
             annualSalary};
```

VISUAL BASIC
```
Dim result = From oneEmployee in Employees
             Let annualSalary =
             oneEmployee.WeeklySalary * 52
             Where annualSalary >= 50000
             Select oneEmployee.FullName, annualSalary
```

See Also

Query Expressions

Lifetime and Scope

With one significant difference within method code, C# and Visual Basic generally follow the same lifetime and scoping rules for variables.

Lifetime

Lifetime indicates how long the value stored within a variable remains available. Both languages mostly follow the same rules for managing variable lifetime. `static` (C#) and `Shared` (VB) fields declared outside of methods have application lifetime, as do fields that appear within Visual Basic `Module` statements. Non-static and non-shared type-level fields have lifetimes that last as long as the instance does. Local `Static` variables in Visual Basic methods have application- or instance-lifetime, depending on whether the containing method is `Shared` or not, respectively. C# does not support local static variables.

The key difference between the languages appears when using non-static local variables. In Visual Basic, all local non-static variables, whether declared inside or outside of a given block, have procedure-lifetime. If you declare a variable within an `If` statement block, its value will remain throughout the entire procedure, although scoping rules limit access to the variable to just that block. This means that if you reenter the block, the variable may retain the value it had the last time you passed through that block. Because of this, you should always initialize variables defined within a block.

In C#, variables have block-level lifetimes. If you declare a variable within an *if* statement block, its lifetime ends upon exiting that block.

Scope

Scope refers to which parts of your source code have access to a specific identifier. C# and Visual Basic follow the same scoping rules for type-level, procedure-level, and block-level variables.

LINQ

See

> Query Expressions

Literals

C# and Visual Basic both support a wide range of value type literals, although there are some significant feature differences between the languages.

Unicode Sequences

String and character literals in C# support Unicode escape sequences, prefixed with the \U or \u escape code.

C#
```
// ----- \u00a3 is the British Pound symbol.
char currencySymbol = '\u00a3';
```

Visual Basic does not support such sequences. You must either embed the character itself within the literal, or use VB's *ChrW* function to obtain a character representation of the Unicode value.

VISUAL BASIC
```
' ----- Embed the symbol directly.
Dim currencySymbol As Char = "£"c

' ----- Use the ChrW function.
Dim currencySymbol As Char = ChrW(&H00A3)
```

C#'s \x variable-length hex-character escape sequence is also not supported in Visual Basic.

Character and String Literals

C# supports two types of string literals: standard literals with support for embedded escape sequences; and verbatim string literals, prefixed with the @ symbol. Visual Basic strings are identical to C#'s verbatim string literals, including the method of embedding double-quote symbols.

C#
```
string notice = @"This is ""verbatim"" text.";
```

VISUAL BASIC
```
Dim notice As String = "This is ""verbatim"" text."
```

C#'s standard string literals have no direct equivalent in Visual Basic. To simulate C#'s escape sequences, you must concatenate variations of these special characters into your target literal. VB includes some useful intrinsic literals for these symbols (found in `Microsoft.VisualBasic.Constants`), or you can use those provided by the .NET Base Class Libraries (such as `System.Environment.NewLine`). You can also use Visual Basic's `Chr` or `ChrW` functions to return a character based on its ASCII or Unicode numeric value, respectively.

C#
```
string endOfLine = "\r\n";
```

VISUAL BASIC
```
Dim endOfLine As String = vbCrLf
```

The following table lists the VB intrinsic literals that you can use in place of C#'s escape sequences.

Character	Hex	C#	Visual Basic
Alert	0x07	\a	Chr(7)
Backslash	0x5c	\\	\ within text
Backspace	0x08	\b	vbBack
Carriage Return	0x0d	\r	vbCr
Double Quote	0x22	\"	"" within text
Form Feed	0x0c	\f	vbFormFeed
Horizontal Tab	0x09	\t	vbTab
Line Feed	0x0a	\n	vbLf
MS-DOS Line Ending	0x0d,0x0a	\r\n	vbCrLf
Null Character	0x00	\0	vbNullChar
Single Quote	0x27	\'	' within text
Vertical Tab	0x0b	\v	vbVerticalTab

New with Visual Studio 2015
C# verbatim strings can break across physical line boundaries, resulting in an embedded line break in the literal string. Beginning in 2015, Visual Basic supports this as well.

C#
```
string multiLine = @"First Line
Second Line";
```

VISUAL BASIC
```
' ----- 2015 and later only.
Dim multiLine As String = "First Line
Second Line"
```

Visual Basic releases before 2015 do not allow an open string to cross a physical line. Concatenate a line ending into the string as needed.

VISUAL BASIC
```
Dim multiLine As String = "First Line" & vbCrLf & _
    "Second Line"
```

Character literals in C# appear in single quotes. In VB, use double-quotes, followed by the *c* suffix.

C#
```
char oneDigit = '0';
```

VISUAL BASIC
```
Dim oneDigit As Char = "0"c
```

New with Visual Studio 2015
In 2015, both C# and Visual Basic added string interpolation, a method of generating formatted strings using string literals. Both languages share an identical syntax for such strings, prefixing them with a *$* symbol, and using curly braces to contain the interpolated sections.

Integer Literals

In C#, a plain integer literal will be typed as *int* if the value fits in that type. If not, it is coerced into the smallest of *uint*, *long*, or *ulong*. In Visual Basic, integer literals are *Integer* by default, or if too large for that type, then *Long*.

Each language supports a set of suffixes that force an integer literal to become a specific type. The following sample includes a long integer value in each language.

C#
```
PassALongValue(123L);
```

VISUAL BASIC
```
PassALongValue(123&)
```

The following table lists the suffixes for each integer type. Each suffix can be uppercase, lowercase, or for suffixes with more than one character, a mix of casing.

Data Type	C# Suffix	Visual Basic Suffix
Short	No suffix	*S*
Unsigned Short	No suffix	*US*
Integer	No suffix	*%* or *I*
Unsigned Integer	*U*	*UI*
Long	*L*	*&* or *L*
Unsigned Long	*UL* or *LU*	*UL*

Floating-Point Literals

In both languages, floating-point literals are *double/Double* by default. You can also alter this default by appending a type suffix to the literal value. The following table lists the suffixes for each floating-point type. Each suffix can be uppercase or lowercase.

Data Type	C# Suffix	Visual Basic Suffix
Single	*F*	*!* or *F*
Double	*D*	*#* or *R*
Decimal	*M*	*@* or *D*

Both Visual Basic and C# allow numeric literals in exponential format (scientific notation). Either the base or the exponent can include a unary + or − sign, and an optional type character can appear as well.

C#
```
bigValue = 9.24E22D;   // double
```

VISUAL BASIC
```
bigValue = 9.24E+22#    ' Double
```

Boolean Literals

Visual Basic's *True* and *False* Boolean literals are exact replacements for C#'s *true* and *false* literals. See the "bool Data Type" entry in this chapter for information on differences between the languages when converting a true value to an integer.

Hexadecimal and Octal Literals

C# supports hexadecimal literals using the *0x* prefix. Visual Basic offers both hexadecimal and octal literals via the *&H* and *&O* prefixes.

C#
```
decimal25 = 0x19;
```

VISUAL BASIC
```
decimal25 = &H19
decimal25 = &O31
```

The various type suffixes, listed earlier in this entry, can follow the hexadecimal and octal literals to force the expression to a specific type.

Date Literals

> **New with Visual Studio 2015**
> Visual Basic includes intrinsic support for date and time literals. The text of the date or time appears between a set of # symbols. Before the 2015 update of Visual Basic, all date literals used a format common in the United States. With the Roslyn update, these literals also support a standard ISO date format.

VISUAL BASIC
```
Dim justDate As Date = #12/31/1999#
Dim justTime As Date = #12:34:56PM#
Dim bothParts As Date = #12/31/1999 12:34:56PM#

' ----- New international format.
Dim worldwideDate As Date = #1999-12-31#
```

The null Literal

C# includes a *null* literal that indicates an undefined reference type. In Visual Basic, the *Nothing* literal does the same for reference types. For value types, *Nothing* acts like C#'s *default* operator, returning the default value.

Local Variables

See

Variables

lock Statement

Visual Basic's *SyncLock* statement is equivalent to C#'s *lock* statement.

C#
```
class VitalMethods
{
    private object HoldLock = new object();
    public void PerformVitalAction()
    {
        lock (HoldLock)
        {
            // ----- Protected code here.
        }
    }
}
```

VISUAL BASIC
```
Class VitalMethods
    Private HoldLock As New Object
    Public Sub PerformVitalAction()
        SyncLock HoldLock
            ' ----- Protected code here.
        End SyncLock
    End Sub
End Class
```

Logical Operators

See

Operators

long Data Type

Visual Basic's intrinsic *Long* data type is identical to C#'s *long* data type. Both types are aliases for .NET's *System.Int64* type. For long literals, C# uses an *L* or *l* suffix after the value; in Visual Basic, use *L*, *l*, or *&* instead.

C#
```
long distance = 0L;  // or 0l
```

VISUAL BASIC
```
Dim distance As Long = 0&  ' or 0L or 0l
```

Main Method

In both C# and Visual Basic, an application uses a *Main* method as the program's entry point. These routines are always *static* (C#) or *Shared* (VB, although the *Shared* modifier is assumed if the method appears in a *Module*), return either no result (*void* or *Sub*) or an integer, and can be defined with one argument, an array of command line argument strings. While C# allows these methods to be *private*, this is not allowed in Visual Basic.

C#
```
// ----- Plain version with no return or arguments.
static void Main()
{
}

// ----- Version with both a return code and arguments.
static int Main(string[] args)
{
}
```

VISUAL BASIC
```
' ----- Plain version with no return or arguments.
Shared Friend Sub Main()
End Sub

' ----- Version with both a return code and arguments.
Shared Friend Function Main(
    ByVal cmdArgs() As String) As Integer
End Function
```

In Visual Basic Windows Forms applications, a form can be defined as the startup object. Although you can include your own custom *Main* method within the form, the compiler will provide the method behind the scenes if one does not exist. In C# Windows Forms applications, the *Main* method is decorated with the *STAThread* attribute.

C#
```
[STAThread] static void Main()
```

The Visual Basic compiler attaches this attribute automatically in Windows Forms applications, so you don't need to provide it as an attribute in code.

In a Windows Forms application, the *Main* method can be used to run custom code before displaying the initial form. This structure is standard in C# applications, although it is less common in VB, since that language provides other features that simplify the application startup process.

C#
```
static void Main()
{
    Application.Run(new Form1());
}
```

VISUAL BASIC
```
Shared Friend Sub Main()
    Application.Run(New Form1())
End Sub
```

An application normally exits when it reaches the end of the *Main* method. A program can be made to exit early by using one of the following features, sorted from most polite to most abrupt.

- Calling *System.Windows.Forms.Application.Exit()*
- Calling *System.Environment.Exit*(exitCode)
- Using Visual Basic's *End* statement

Visual Basic includes its Visual Basic Application Model, activated using the Enable Application Framework field in the Project Properties. When activated, the model enables features that provide for a more structured startup process, plus support for application-wide unhandled error monitoring. For more information on these features, read the Visual Studio documentation. You can also read the following entries in Chapter 3 of this book:

- MinimumSplashScreenDisplayTime Property
- NetworkAvailabilityChanged Event (My.Application)
- SplashScreen Property
- Startup Event
- StartupNextInstance Event
- UnhandledException Event

method Modifier

See

Attributes

Methods

Visual Basic's *Sub* statement is equivalent to C# methods that have a *void* return value.

C#
```
public void LogError(string errorText)
{
    // ----- May optionally include this statement:
    return;
}
```

VISUAL BASIC
```
Public Sub LogError(ByVal errorText As String)
    ' ----- May optionally include this statement:
    Return
End Sub
```

The *Sub* keyword replaces *void* before the method name. In both languages, any parameter definitions appear in parentheses. The statement ends with VB's *End Sub* clause.

In a similar way, the *Function* statement in Visual Basic parallels methods in C# that return anything other than *void*. The syntax is similar to that of the *Sub* statement, but with the keyword *Function* used instead of *Sub*. An *As* clause with the return type follows the parameter list.

C#

```
public bool ParseTimeText(string timeText,
    ref int hours, ref int minutes)
{
    // ----- Core logic, then...
    return success;
}
```

VISUAL BASIC

```
Public Function ParseTimeText(ByVal timeText As String,
    ByRef hours As Integer, ByRef minutes As Integer) _
    As Boolean
    ' ----- Core logic, then...
    Return success
End Function
```

When performing an explicit implementation of an interface member in C#, the name of the method is prefixed with the name of the interface.

C#

```
public void IVocal.Speak(string textToSpeak)
{
```

Visual Basic uses the *Implements* clause to indicate which interface member is being implemented explicitly by the method.

VISUAL BASIC

```
Public Sub Speak(ByVal textToSpeak As String) _
    Implements IVocal.Speak
```

When used to implement an event handler on an object defined with VB's *WithEvents* modifier, the *Handles* clause identifies the source instance and event.

VISUAL BASIC

```
Public Sub Button1_Click(ByVal sender As Object,
    ByVal e As EventArgs) Handles Button1.Click
```

Methods support the following modifiers in each language.

C# Modifier	Visual Basic Modifier
abstract	MustOverride
async	Async
extern	Not supported
internal	Friend
new	Shadows

C# Modifier	Visual Basic Modifier
override	Overrides
partial	Partial
private	Private
protected	Protected
protected internal	Protected Friend
public	Public
sealed	NotOverridable Overrides, or NotOverridable in base class
static	Shared
virtual	Overridable
Not supported	Iterator
Not supported	Overloads

When defined without an access modifier, methods are *private* by default in C# classes and structures. In Visual Basic, all methods are *Public* by default.

When calling methods that include *ref* or *out* modifiers, C# requires that the associated argument in the calling code include those modifiers as well.

C#
```
success = ParseTimeText(timeText, ref hours, ref minutes);
```

Visual Basic does not require the use of any modifiers in the calling code. When calling methods that include no parameters, Visual Basic also does not require that the calling method follow the method name with an empty set of parentheses, although C# requires this, and VB recommends the practice.

New with Visual Studio 2015
In 2015, C# added the ability to define methods using lambda expressions.

C#
```
public Position Move(int xOffset, int yOffset) =>
    new Position(CurrentX + xOffset, CurrentY + yOffset);
```

Visual Basic does not yet support the creation of methods using lambdas.

See Also

, Punctuator, Arguments and Parameters, Access Modifiers, Event Handlers, Identifiers, Named Arguments

module Modifier

See

Attributes

nameof Operator

New with Visual Studio 2015
Visual Basic's *NameOf* operator is identical to C#'s *nameof* operator.

C#
```
string variableName = nameof(customerName);
```

VISUAL BASIC
```
Dim variableName As String = NameOf(customerName)
```

---

namespace Statement

Visual Basic includes a *Namespace* statement that is functionally equivalent to C#'s *namespace* statement. Both languages support nesting of namespaces, either with individual namespaces at each level, or through a dotted-name syntax.

C#
```
namespace Level1
{
    namespace Level2.Level3
    {
    }
}
```

VISUAL BASIC
```
Namespace Level1
    Namespace Level2.Level3
    End Namespace
End Namespace
```

Within the Project Properties, C# includes support for a project's Default Namespace, which Visual Studio uses for the surrounding *namespace* statement when adding new source code files to a project. Visual Basic includes a Root Namespace option in its Project Properties that indicates the top-most namespace for all source code files in the project, even in the absence of a distinct *Namespace* statement. If you include a *Namespace* statement in a file, that block is subordinate to the Root Namespace. To use a namespace outside of that default, you must make use of Visual Basic's *Global* namespace alias.

VISUAL BASIC
```
' ----- Assume Root Namespace is "WindowsApp".
'       Classes here appear in that namespace.

Namespace UtilityCode
    ' ----- Classes here appear in the
    '       "WindowsApp.UtilityCode" namespace.
End Namespace

Namespace Global.SecondRoot
    ' ----- Classes here appear in "SecondRoot"
    '       instead of "WindowsApp".
End Namespace
```

See Also

    :: Namespace Alias Qualifier, global Namespace Alias

---

new Constructor Declaration

See

Constructors

new Modifier

Visual Basic's *Shadows* modifier hides a base member of the same name from being expressed in the derived class, just like C#'s *new* modifier.

C#

```
class DerivedClass : BaseClass
{
    // ----- Hides whatever BaseClass.BaseElement was.
    new public void BaseElement()
    {
    }
}
```

VISUAL BASIC

```
Class DerivedClass
    Inherits BaseClass

    ' ----- Hides whatever BaseClass.BaseElement was.
    Public Shadows Sub BaseElement()
    End Sub
End Class
```

In C#, the *new* modifier is optional; hiding of base elements occurs automatically as part of the declaration. In Visual Basic, the *Shadows* keyword is required to enable hiding.

new Operator

Visual Basic's *New* operator is functionally equivalent to C#'s *new* operator when used to create new type instances. In both languages, the name of the type being instantiated and any parentheses-enclosed constructor arguments follow the operator.

C#

```
// ----- Examples with default and custom constructor.
Employee oneManager = new Employee();
Employee namedManager = new Employee("Jones");
```

VISUAL BASIC

```
' ----- Examples with default and custom constructor.
Dim oneManager As Employee = New Employee
Dim namedManager As Employee = New Employee("Jones")
```

As shown in the previous example, parentheses are required after the type name being instantiated only when constructor arguments are present. Visual Basic also supports a compressed format that combines the type identification and assignment of a new instance.

VISUAL BASIC
```
Dim oneManager As New Employee
```
As in C#, instance creation using the *New* operator can appear within expressions.

C#
```
authenticated = (new PasswordDialog()).PromptUser();
```

VISUAL BASIC
```
authenticated = (New PasswordDialog).PromptUser()
```
Anonymous types in C# use the *new* operator followed by a list of properties in curly braces.

C#
```
var namedAndNumbered = new { ID = 5, Name = "test" };
```
Visual Basic employs a similar syntax, with the inclusion of the *With* keyword. Notice that each property is prefixed with a period.

VISUAL BASIC
```
Dim namedAndNumbered = New With { .ID = 5, .Name = "test" }
```
VB also allows you to specify which anonymous type properties are "key" properties, those that can be used for equivalence testing between two instances.

VISUAL BASIC
```
Dim numberedByID = New With { Key .ID = 5, .Name = "test" }
```
See Also

Initializers

null Literal

C#'s *null* literal is a null reference for reference types and nullable value types.

C#
```
Employee oneManager = null;   // No instance
int? optionalNumber = null;   // No value
```
(When working with "null" values in database interactions, use *System.DbNull* instead of *null*.) In Visual Basic, the *Nothing* literal serves a similar purpose.

VISUAL BASIC
```
Dim oneManager As Employee = Nothing       ' No instance
Dim optionalNumber As Integer? = Nothing   ' No value
```
However, *Nothing* can also be assigned to a standard (non-nullable) value type, in which case it functions much like C#'s *default* operator, assigning the default value to the variable.

VISUAL BASIC
```
Dim requiredNumber As Integer = Nothing    ' Set to zero
```
Assigning *null* to a non-nullable value type in this manner in C# is invalid.

C#

```
// ----- This will not compile.
int requiredNumber = null;

// ----- Use this valid syntax instead.
int requiredNumber = default(int);
```

When comparing variables or expressions to *null* in C#, use the == and !=
comparison operators.

C#

```
if (customerRecord == null)
```

You cannot use the equivalent comparison operators (= and <>) in Visual Basic to
check for *Nothing*. Instead, use VB's *Is* and *IsNot* operators to compare expressions
with *Nothing*.

VISUAL BASIC

```
' ----- Check for the absence of an instance.
If (customerRecord Is Nothing) Then

' ----- Check for the presence of an instance.
If (customerRecord IsNot Nothing) Then
```

Visual Basic propagates or discards *Nothing* in ways that are somewhat different from
how C# uses *null*. This is both for reasons of backward compatibility in VB, and also
because of *Nothing*'s dual nature as a null reference and a default value type. Compare
the following examples to see just one difference.

C#

```
// ----- result will be set to "".
string result = (5 + null).ToString();
```

VISUAL BASIC

```
' ----- result will be set to "5".
Dim result As String = (5 + Nothing).ToString()
```

Visual Basic treats empty strings and *Nothing* as equivalent; C# distinguishes between
null and empty strings.

C#

```
// ----- result will be set to "Not Empty".
string testValue = null;
if (testValue == "")
    result = "Empty";
else
    result = "Not Empty";
```

VISUAL BASIC

```
' ----- result will be set to "Empty".
Dim testValue As String = Nothing
If (testValue = "") Then
    result = "Empty"
Else
```

```
      result = "Not Empty"
   End If
```

To test a VB string to see if it is unassigned, use *Is Nothing* instead.

VISUAL BASIC
```
If (testValue Is Nothing) Then
```

See Also

default Operator

Nullable Types

Both C# and Visual Basic use the *?* symbol after a value type name to indicate a nullable value type.

C#
```
int? optionalNumber = null;
```

VISUAL BASIC
```
Dim optionalNumber As Integer? = Nothing

' ----- This is also a valid syntax.
Dim optionalNumber? As Integer = Nothing
```

In C#, it is valid to compare a nullable variable to *null*.

C#
```
if (optionalNumber == null)
```

In Visual Basic, you cannot directly compare the instance to *Nothing* in this way. Instead, use the *Is* or *IsNot* operators, or use the variable's *HasValue* method.

VISUAL BASIC
```
' ----- This will work instead of = or <>.
If (optionalNumber Is Nothing) Then

' ----- This will also work in both languages.
If (optionalNumber.HasValue() = False) Then
```

In both languages, the nullable syntax is an alias for *Nullable<T>* (in C#) or *Nullable(Of T)* (in Visual Basic).

object Data Type

Visual Basic's intrinsic *Object* data type is identical to C#'s *object* data type. Both types are aliases for .NET's *System.Object* type.

C#
```
object result = null;
```

VISUAL BASIC
```
Dim result As Object = Nothing
```

Object Initializers

See

Initializers

Operator Overloading

See

operator Statement

operator Statement

Visual Basic's *Operator* statement is equivalent to C#'s *operator* statement. In both languages, the "operator" keyword is followed by the specific operator symbol being overloaded, and the operands appear as parameters in the method-style definition.

C#

```csharp
public static Team operator +(Team op1, Player op2)
{
    // ----- Logic to add player to team, then...
    return updatedTeam;
}
```

VISUAL BASIC

```vb
Public Shared Operator +(ByVal op1 As Team,
        ByVal op2 As Player) As Team
    ' ----- Logic to add player to team, then...
    Return updatedTeam
End Operator
```

The overload must be declared as *public static* in C#, and the equivalent *Public Shared* in Visual Basic. VB also allows the *Overloads* modifier to appear between *Public* and *Shared*, but it has no impact on the logic of the overload. In both languages, for unary operators, the parameter list will include only one parameter.

The following table lists the different operators that can be overloaded in each language.

Type	C#	Visual Basic
Addition	+	+
And-also False Test	*false*	*IsFalse*
Bitwise Complement	~	*Not*
Concatenation	+	&
Conjunction	&	*And*
Conversion	See below	*CType*
Decrement	--	Not supported
Disjunction			*Or*
Division	/	/
Equality	==	=

Type	C#	Visual Basic
Exclusive-Or	^	*Xor*
Exponentiation	Not supported	^
Greater Than	>	>
Greater Than Equal	>=	>=
Increment	++	Not supported
Inequality	!=	<>
Integer Division	Not supported	\
Left Shift	<<	<<
Less Than	<	<
Less Than Equal	<=	<=
Modulo	%	*Mod*
Multiplication	*	*
Negation	!	*Not*
Or-else True Test	*true*	*IsTrue*
Pattern Match	Not supported	*Like*
Right Shift	>>	>>
Subtraction	-	-
Unary Minus	-	-
Unary Plus	+	+

In both languages, a few of these operators must be overloaded in pairs.

Type	C#	Visual Basic
Equality Testing	== and !=	= and <>
Less/Greater	> and <	> and <
Less/Greater Equal	>= and <=	>= and <=
And-also/Or-else	*false* and *true*	*IsFalse* and *IsTrue*

Operator overloads support the following modifiers in each language.

C# Modifier	Visual Basic Modifier
explicit	*Narrowing*
extern	Not supported
implicit	*Widening*
public	*Public*
static	*Shared*
Not supported	*Overloads*
Not supported	*Shadows*

User-defined conversions are implemented as part of the operator overloading syntax in both languages. In C#, the source type appears in the parameter list, and the target type is used as the operator name. In Visual Basic, *CType* is used as the operator name for all such conversions. The source type appears in the parameter list, and the target type appears as the return type for the method. In both languages, the type containing the conversion declaration must match either the source or the target type.

C#

```
class CountMonitor
{
    public static explicit operator int(
        CountMonitor source)
    {
        // ----- Converts CountMonitor to int, then...
        return newInt;
    }
    public static implicit operator CountMonitor(
        int source)
    {
        // ----- Converts int to CountMonitor, then...
        return newCountMonitor;
    }
}
```

VISUAL BASIC

```
Class CountMonitor
    Public Shared Narrowing Operator CType(
            ByVal source As CountMonitor) As Integer
        ' ----- Converts CountMonitor to Integer, then...
        Return newInt
    End Operator
    Public Shared Widening Operator CType(
            ByVal source As Integer) As CountMonitor
        ' ----- Converts Integer to CountMonitor, then...
        Return newCountMonitor
    End Operator
End Class
```

Visual Basic's *Widening* modifier is the same as C#'s *implicit* modifier, while VB's *Narrowing* modifier matches C#'s *explicit* modifier. One of these modifiers must be used in each user-defined conversion declaration.

Operator Precedence and Associativity

When an expression includes more than one operator, both C# and Visual Basic use specific precedence and associativity rules to determine, in the absence of grouping parentheses, which operations to apply first. The following table lists the precedence rules for C#, in order from highest (applied first) to lowest (applied last). Operators at the same precedence level are treated as equal in terms of application order.

Category	Operators
Primary	*x.y*, *f(x)*, *a[x]*, *x++*, *x--*, *new*, *typeof*, *default*, *checked*, *unchecked*, *delegate*, *nameof*
Unary	*+*, *-*, *!*, *~*, *++x*, *--x*, *(T) x*
Multiplicative	***, */*, *%*
Additive	*+*, *-*
Shift	*<<*, *>>*

Category	Operators
Comparison	$<$, $>$, $<=$, $>=$, `is`, `as`
Equality	$==$, $!=$
Conjunction	$\&$
Exclusive disjunction	$\wedge$
Disjunction	$|$
Conditional conjunction	$\&\&$
Conditional disjunction	$||$
Coalescence	$??$
Conditional	$?:$
Assignment and lambda	$=$, $*=$, $/=$, $\%=$, $+=$, $-=$, $<<=$, $>>=$, $\&=$, $\wedge=$, $|=$, $=>$

The following table lists Visual Basic's operators by order of precedence.

Category	Operators
Await	`Await`
Exponentiation	$\wedge$
Unary	$+$, $-$
Multiplicative	$*$, $/$
Integer division	$\backslash$
Modulo	`Mod`
Additive	$+$, $-$
Concatenation	$\&$
Shift	$<<$, $>>$
Comparison	$=$, $<>$, $<$, $<=$, $>$, $>=$, `Is`, `IsNot`, `Like`, `TypeOf...Is`, `TypeOf...IsNot`
Negation	`Not`
Conjunction	`And`, `AndAlso`
Disjunction	`Or`, `OrElse`
Exclusive disjunction	`Xor`

In both languages, assignment operators are right-associative; the right side of the operator is evaluated first. For most other binary operators at the same precedence level, operations are left-associative; the expression on the left-side of the operator is determined first, from left to right. For example, $x + y + z$ is evaluated as $(x + y) + z$. The two exceptions are C#'s $?:$ conditional operator and its $??$ null coalescence operator, both of which are right-associative. For an example of how this impacts conditional operations, see the "?: Conditional Operator" entry in this chapter.

Operators

The following table lists the operators available in both languages. Use the "See Also" column in this table to locate related entries in this chapter.

C# Operator	Visual Basic Operator	See Also
!	Not	! Negation Operator
!=	<>	!= Comparison Operator
%	Mod	% Modulo Operator
%=	Not supported	%= Assignment Operator
&	And (Conjunction only)	& Address Operator & Conjunction Operator
&&	AndAlso	&& Conjunction Operator
&=	Not supported	&= Assignment Operator
*	* (Multiplication only)	* Dereference Operator * Multiplication Operator
*=	*=	*= Assignment Operator
+	+ or &	+ Addition Operator, + Unary-Plus Operator
++	Not supported	++ Increment Operator
+=	+= (Assignment only)	+= Assignment Operator, += Event Subscription Operator
–	–	- Subtraction Operator, - Unary-Minus Operator
--	Not supported	-- Decrement Operator
-=	-= (Assignment only)	-= Assignment Operator -= Event Unsubscription Operator
->	Not supported	-> Member Access Operator
?.	?.	?. Null Conditional Operator
.	.	. Member Access Operator
/	/ or \	/ Division Operator
/=	/= or \=	/= Assignment Operator
:?	If(x,y,z)	?: Conditional Operator
<	<	< Comparison Operator
<<	<<	<< Left Shift Operator
<<=	<<=	<<= Assignment Operator
<=	<=	<= Comparison Operator
=	=	= Assignment Operator
==	=	== Comparison Operator
=>	Function(), Sub()	=> Lambda Operator
>	>	> Comparison Operator
>=	>=	>= Comparison Operator
>>	>>	>> Right Shift Operator
>>=	>>=	>>= Assignment Operator
??	If(x,y)	?? Coalescence Operator
[ ]	( )	[] Member Access Operator
^	Xor	^ Exclusive-Or Operator
^=	Not supported	^= Assignment Operator
|	Or	| Disjunction Operator

C# Operator	Visual Basic Operator	See Also
|=	Not supported	|= Assignment Operator
||	OrElse	|| Disjunction Operator
~	Not	~ Bitwise Complement Operator

See Also

Assignment Operators, Operator Precedence and Associativity

Optional Arguments

In C# method signatures, any parameter that includes an assignment becomes an optional argument to the calling procedure.

C#
```
// ----- The times parameter is optional, defaulting to 2.
public string CopyText(string original, int times = 2)
```

Visual Basic optional arguments also include this assignment of a constant expression, as well as the *Optional* modifier.

VISUAL BASIC
```
' ----- The times parameter is optional, defaulting to 2.
Public Function CopyText(ByVal original As String,
    Optional ByVal times As Integer = 2) As String
```

The rules surrounding the use of optional arguments in both languages are similar: no non-optional arguments may appear after an optional argument; parameter arrays and optional arguments cannot be used together; and so on.

See Also

, Punctuator, Arguments and Parameters, Methods

orderby Query Expression Operator (LINQ)

Visual Basic's *Order By* query expression operator is identical to C#'s *orderby* operator. Both languages support a comma-delimited list of sorting fields. Each field is sorted in ascending order by default, or explicitly with the *ascending* (C#) or *Ascending* (VB) option. To sort in descending order, use the *descending* (C#) or *Descending* (VB) option.

C#
```
var result = from oneEmployee in Employees
             orderby oneEmployee.FullName descending
             select oneEmployee;
```

VISUAL BASIC
```
Dim result = From oneEmployee in Employees
             Order By oneEmployee.FullName Descending
             Select oneEmployee
```

In C#, the *orderby* clause must appear before the *select* clause. Visual Basic offers greater flexibility as to the placement of these clauses within the query expression. In

Visual Basic, if the `Select` clause appears first, any calculated fields it includes become available within the `Order By` clause.

VISUAL BASIC
```
Dim result = From oneEmployee in Employees
             Select oneEmployee,
             UpperName = oneEmployee.FullName.ToUpper()
             Order By UpperName Descending
```

See Also

Query Expressions

out Modifier

C#'s *out* modifier appears before a method parameter to indicate that data will transfer in one direction from the method to the calling code's associated argument variable.

C#
```
public bool PerformUpdate(out string updateDetails)
{
    // ----- In code, assign content to updateDetails.
}
```

Visual Basic does not have a direct syntax equivalent for *out*. Instead, use the *ByRef* modifier, which is more akin to C#'s *ref* modifier.

VISUAL BASIC
```
Public Function PerformUpdate(
        ByRef updateDetails As String) As Boolean
    ' ----- In code, assign content to updateDetails.
End Function
```

The *System.Runtime.InteropServices* namespace does include an *OutAttribute* class that can be applied to a Visual Basic parameter to indicate that data comes out of the method through the parameter. However, it does not provide the same level of data enforcement available in the similar C# code.

VISUAL BASIC
```
' ----- Assumes: Imports System.Runtime.InteropServices
Public Function PerformUpdate(
        <Out> ByRef updateDetails As String) As Boolean
```

See Also

Arguments and Parameters, Generics

Overloading

In C#, the overloading of methods occurs automatically whenever a type includes two methods with the same name, but different signatures.

C#

```
public Customer RetrieveCustomer(long customerID)
{
    // ----- Retrieve customer record by numeric ID.
}

public Customer RetrieveCustomer(string email)
{
    // ----- Retrieve customer record by email address.
}
```

The Visual Basic compiler also handles overloading in this way. However, it also provides the optional *Overloads* keyword that makes the overloading clearer to anyone reading the code. You do not need to include the *Overloads* keyword, but if you include it with one of the overloaded methods, you must include it with all of them.

VISUAL BASIC

```
Public Overloads Function RetrieveCustomer(
        ByVal customerID As Long) As Customer
    ' ----- Retrieve customer record by numeric ID.
End Function

Public Overloads Function RetrieveCustomer(
        ByVal email As String) As Customer
    ' ----- Retrieve customer record by email address.
End Function
```

See Also

operator Statement

---

override Modifier

Visual Basic's *Overrides* modifier is equivalent to C#'s *override* modifier.

C#

```
public override int DetermineSize()
```

VISUAL BASIC

```
Public Overrides Function DetermineSize() As Integer
```

C#'s *override* modifier applies to method, property, indexer, and event declarations. In Visual Basic, the *Overrides* modifier cannot be used with event declarations. Also, to override a property, method, or indexer (default property) in VB, the member from the base class must include the *Overridable* modifier (similar to C#'s *virtual* modifier), or have derived from a further base member that has that modifier.

---

param Modifier

See

Attributes

Parameter Arrays

See

params Modifier

Parameters

See

Arguments and Parameters, Methods

params Modifier

Visual Basic's *ParamArray* modifier is functionally identical to C#'s *params* modifier.

C#
```
public int AverageValue(params int[] values)
```

VISUAL BASIC
```
Public Function AverageValue(
    ByVal ParamArray values() As Integer) As Integer
```

partial Modifier

When applied to classes, structures, and interfaces, C#'s *partial* modifier allows you to split the type across multiple files. Each piece must include the *partial* modifier.

C#
```
// ----- From the first *.cs file.
partial class ComplexContent
{
    // ----- Some members defined here.
}

// ----- From the second *.cs file.
partial class ComplexContent
{
    // ----- Other members defined here.
}
```

Visual Basic's *Partial* modifier does the same thing. You can leave the *Partial* keyword off of at most one of the portions.

VISUAL BASIC
```
' ----- From the first *.vb file.
Partial Class ComplexContent
    ' ----- Some members defined here.
End Class
```

```
' ----- From the second *.vb file.
Class ComplexContent
    ' ----- Other members defined here. The
    '          "Partial" modifier was left off of this part,
    '          although it could have been retained.
End Class
```

New with Visual Studio 2015

Visual Basic initially did not allow the *Partial* modifier to be used with interface declarations. However, this feature has been added starting in 2015. That same update also added support for the *Partial* modifier on VB's own *Module* types.

Partial methods allow you to define a method in one file, and provide its implementation in another file, with both parts belonging to the same partial class.

C#
```csharp
// ----- From the first *.cs file.
partial class ComplexContent
{
    // ----- "private" is implied.
    partial void RecordTraceData(string data);
}

// ----- From the second *.cs file.
partial class ComplexContent
{
    // ----- Same "partial void" and signature.
    partial void RecordTraceData(string data)
    {
        // ----- Implementation here.
    }
}
```

VISUAL BASIC
```vb
' ----- From the first *.vb file.
Partial Class ComplexContent
    ' ----- Declaration includes no method body.
    '          Always begins with "Partial Private Sub."
    Partial Private Sub RecordTraceData(
        ByVal data As String)
    End Sub
End Class


' ----- From the second *.vb file.
Partial Class ComplexContent
    ' ----- Implementation excludes "Partial" modifier.
    '          Signature must still match.
    Private Sub RecordTraceData(ByVal data As String)
        ' ----- Implementation here.
    End Sub
End Class
```

C# permits partial methods in both classes and structures. In VB, only classes support partial methods.

Pointers

Visual Basic does not support pointer operations, nor does it support any C# feature that enables pointer functionality.

See Also

    * Dereference Operator, -> Member Access Operator, & Address Operator, fixed Modifier, fixed Statement, stackalloc Modifier, unsafe Modifier, unsafe Statement

Preprocessing Directives

See

    #define Directive, #error Directive, #if Directive, #line Directive, #pragma Directive, #region Directive, #undef Directive, #warning Directive

private Access Modifier

Visual Basic's *Private* access modifier is equivalent to C#'s *private* access modifier.

See Also

    Access Modifiers

Project Properties

C# and Visual Basic offer nearly identical settings through the Project Properties window. Visual Studio presents a tabbed collection of settings, and most of the tabs that exist in C# are found in VB, and in an identical configuration. The set of available tabs and tab features will vary based on the type of project.

This entry describes a few of the differences you will encounter when moving from C# to Visual Basic. To see a list of differences from the perspective of moving from Visual Basic to C#, see the "Project Properties" entry in Chapter 2.

Application Tab

Standalone C# applications begin through a *Main* method. The Application tab's Startup Object includes a list of all valid *Main* methods in your application that can be used as the program's entry point. You will find a similar field in a Visual Basic project's Application tab. However, in Windows Forms projects, the default presentation allows you to select a form as the startup object. Even if you add a *Main* method, it will not appear in the Startup Form list by default (although if you add a compatible *Main* method to the startup form, it will be used instead of a compiler-generated default *Main* method). To use a non-form *Main* method as the entry point in a Visual Basic program, clear the project's Enable Application Framework field on the Project Properties' Application tab. This will change the Startup Form field to a Startup Object field, and will display all eligible *Main* methods.

C# presents various resource management options on the Application tab, only some of which are available in Visual Basic's Application tab. For the Icon and Manifest option, VB has an Icon field that lets you select the default icon. To access the project's "app.manifest" file, click the View Windows Settings button on VB's Application tab.

For C# applications that manage resources through a Win32 resource file, the equivalent configuration in Visual Basic requires the use of the VB compiler's `/win32Resource` command line option.

Build Tab

Most of the features on the Build tab appear in Visual Basic's equivalent Compile tab, although many of the names are altered. In most cases, you should be able to determine fairly quickly what the equivalent field is. Both tabs include an Advanced button, and some of the fields included on the main Build tab in C# (including settings for *DEBUG*, *TRACE*, and custom constants) appear within the Advanced portion of VB's Compile tab.

C#'s Advanced build options include a Check for Arithmetic Overflow/Underflow option. VB's Advanced compile options include a similar Remove Integer Overflow Checks option. Because integer operations are unchecked by default in C#, but checked by default in VB, selecting these options results in different behavior between the languages. If you check the option in C#, you should leave it unchecked in Visual Basic, and vice versa.

C#'s Allow Unsafe Code, Warning Level, and Advanced / Language Version build options have no equivalent in Visual Basic. The Internal Compiler Error Reporting and File Alignment options, both Advanced build options in C#, can only be performed in Visual Basic via its command line compiler options. Use the `/errorreport` and `/filealign` options, respectively.

Build Events Tab

To access these same features in a Visual Basic project, click the Build Events button on the Compile tab.

Reference Paths Tab

The list of reference paths is available in Visual Basic by clicking on the Reference Paths button on the References tab. C# displays project-specific references in a branch of the Solution Explorer. VB also makes project references available in the Solution Explorer, although some editions require that the Show All Files feature of that panel be activated.

Properties

Visual Basic's *Property* statement closely parallels C#'s inclusion of member properties. As with other block statements in VB, the getter, setter, and the property itself all include a closing *End* clause.

C#

```
// ----- Many properties use backing fields.
private int _maxAmount = 0;
```

```csharp
// ----- Here is the property itself.
public int Maximum
{
    get
    {
        return this._maxAmount;
    }
    set
    {
        // ----- A "value" incoming variable is implied.
        if (value > 100)
            this._maxAmount = 100;
        else if (value < 0)
            this._maxAmount = 0;
        else
            this._maxAmount = value;
    }
}
```

VISUAL BASIC

```vb
' ----- Many properties use backing fields.
Private _maxAmount As Integer = 0

' ----- Here is the property itself.
Public Property Maximum As Integer
    Get
        Return Me._maxAmount
    End Get
    Set(ByVal value As Integer)
        ' ----- Although "value" is the default,
        '       you can rename this variable.
        If (value > 100) Then
            Me._maxAmount = 100
        ElseIf (value < 0) Then
            Me._maxAmount = 0
        Else
            Me._maxAmount = value
        End If
    End Set
End Property
```

Read-only and write-only properties in C# exist by leaving out the unneeded getter or setter. This is also done in Visual Basic, but the ReadOnly or WriteOnly modifier must be part of the property declaration as well.

C#

```csharp
public int Status
{
    get
    {
        // ----- return statement appears here.
    }
    // ----- But no setter appears.
}
```

```
Public ReadOnly Property Status As Integer
    Get
        ' ----- Return statement appears here.
    End Get
    ' ----- But no setter appears.
End Property
```

When crafting a read-write property, both languages allow you to apply an access modifier to either the getter or setter (but not both) that differs from the modifier applied to the property itself. Properties are *private* by default in C# classes and structures, but *Public* by default in Visual Basic types.

C#

```
public int Status
{
    get
    {
        // ----- Publicly accessible getter code.
    }
    private set
    {
        // ----- Privately accessible setter code.
    }
}
```

VISUAL BASIC

```
Public Property Status As Integer
    Get
        ' ----- Publicly accessible getter code.
    End Get
    Private Set
        ' ----- Privately accessible setter code.
    End Set
End Property
```

In C#, when a property explicitly implements an interface member, the name is modified to include the interface name. In Visual Basic, an *Implements* clause appears after the *As* clause.

C#

```
public int IMonitor.Status
```

VISUAL BASIC

```
Public Property Status As Integer _
    Implements IMonitor.Status
```

New with Visual Studio 2015

In 2015, C# added the ability to define properties using lambda expressions.

C#

```
public string FileAs => LastName + ", " + FirstName;
```

Visual Basic does not yet support the creation of properties using lambdas.

New with Visual Studio 2015

C# allows a property defined as read-only in an interface to be managed by a full read-write property member in the implementing type. Visual Basic formerly did not allow this combination, but this feature was added to that language starting in 2015.

Properties support the following modifiers in each language.

C# Modifier	Visual Basic Modifier
abstract	MustOverride
extern	Not supported
internal	Friend
new	Shadows
override	Overrides
private	Private
protected	Protected
protected internal	Protected Friend
public	Public
sealed	NotOverridable Overrides, or NotOverridable in base class
static	Shared
virtual	Overridable
Not supported	Default
Not supported	Overloads
Not supported	Iterator
Not supported	ReadOnly
Not supported	WriteOnly

Properties in Visual Basic can include parameters, as with methods. The parameter list appears after the property name in the initial declaration. This method for creating parameterized properties is not supported in C#.

VISUAL BASIC

```
Public Property Status(ByVal day As DayOfWeek) As Integer
    Get
        ' ----- Return day-specific status.
    End Get
    Set(ByVal value As Integer)
        ' ----- Set day-specific status to value.
    End Set
End Property
```

In Visual Basic, a property can be passed to a method by reference, something not supported in C#.

See Also

Automatic Properties

property Modifier

See

Attributes

protected Access Modifier

Visual Basic's `Protected` access modifier is equivalent to C#'s `protected` access modifier.

See Also

Access Modifiers

protected internal Access Modifier

Visual Basic's `Protected Friend` access modifier is equivalent to C#'s `protected internal` access modifier.

See Also

Access Modifiers

public Access Modifier

Visual Basic's `Public` access modifier is equivalent to C#'s `public` access modifier.

See Also

Access Modifiers

Query Expressions (LINQ)

Both C# and Visual Basic include native support for many features of LINQ. Each language includes a set of query operators, and many of them have counterparts in the other language. The following table lists the methods supported by LINQ's `Queryable` class, and indicates the equivalent query operator available within each language.

Queryable Member	C# Operator	Visual Basic Operator
`Aggregate`	Not supported	Not supported
`All`	Not supported	`Aggregate...Into All`
`Any`	Not supported	`Aggregate...Into Any`
`AsEnumerable`	Not supported	Not supported
`AsQueryable`	`from` with TypeName	`From...As`
`Average`	Not supported	`Aggregate...Into Average`
`Cast`	Not supported	Not supported
`Concat`	Not supported	Not supported

Queryable Member	C# Operator	Visual Basic Operator
Contains	Not supported	Not supported
Count	Not supported	Aggregate...Into Count
DefaultIfEmpty	Not supported	Not supported
Distinct	Not supported	Distinct
ElementAt	Not supported	Not supported
ElementAtOrDefault	Not supported	Not supported
Empty	Not supported	Not supported
Except	Not supported	Not supported
First	Not supported	Not supported
FirstOrDefault	Not supported	Not supported
GroupBy	group	Group By
GroupJoin	join...into	Group Join
Intersect	Not supported	Not supported
Join	join	Join
Last	Not supported	Not supported
LastOrDefault	Not supported	Not supported
LongCount	Not supported	Aggregate...Into LongCount
Max	Not supported	Aggregate...Into Max
Min	Not supported	Aggregate...Into Min
OfType	Not supported	Not supported
OrderBy	orderby	Order By
OrderByDescending	orderby	Order By
Range	Not supported	Not supported
Repeat	Not supported	Not supported
Reverse	Not supported	Not supported
Select	from and select	From and Select
SelectMany	from (multiple)	From (multiple)
SequenceEqual	Not supported	Not supported
Single	Not supported	Not supported
SingleOrDefault	Not supported	Not supported
Skip	Not supported	Skip
SkipWhile	Not supported	Skip While
Sum	Not supported	Aggregate...Into Sum
Take	Not supported	Take
TakeWhile	Not supported	Take While
ThenBy	orderby	Order By
ThenByDescending	orderby	Order By
ToArray	Not supported	Not supported
ToDictionary	Not supported	Not supported
ToList	Not supported	Not supported
ToLookup	Not supported	Not supported
Union	Not supported	Not supported

Queryable Member	C# Operator	Visual Basic Operator
Where	*where*	*Where*
Not applicable	*let*	*Let*

To see specific examples of these native operators, use the "See Also" block later in this entry to locate related query expression entries in this chapter.

When a specific LINQ method is not supported natively, each language allows that method to be included directly as part of the query expression syntax.

C#

```
var allNames = (from set1 in oldCustomers
                select set1.FullName).Union(
                from set2 in newCustomers
                select set2.FullName);
```

VISUAL BASIC

```
Dim allNames = (From set1 In oldCustomers
                Select set1.FullName).Union(
                From set2 In newCustomers
                Select set2.FullName)
```

Both languages support the LINQ providers supplied with Visual Studio: LINQ to Objects, LINQ to DataSet, LINQ to Entities, and LINQ to XML. (LINQ to SQL, formerly supported in both languages, has been deprecated in favor of LINQ to DataSet and LINQ to Entities.) Visual Basic's interaction with LINQ to XML includes the ability to generate new XML content natively as part of its XML Literals support. C# does not include this feature.

LINQ queries in C# support the * transparent identifier as part of its *from* clause. These transparent identifiers are not supported in Visual Basic.

As with other statements in C#, a query expression that completes a statement must be followed by a semicolon. In Visual Basic, the compiler attempts to detect the end of the statement syntactically. However, there may be times when the compiler will not be able to correctly determine whether the statement that follows a query expression is part of the query or not. In some cases, a blank line must appear between the query expression and the subsequent statement to ensure a proper separation. Also, a line continuation character (_) may be needed within some queries to ensure that all lines of those queries remain connected.

See Also

from Query Expression Operator, group Query Expression Operator, join Query Expression Operator, let Query Expression Operator, orderby Query Expression Operator, select Query Expression Operator, where Query Expression Operator

readonly Modifier

As with C#'s *readonly* modifier, Visual Basic's *ReadOnly* modifier can appear as part of a field definition.

C#

```
class TaxInformation
{
    // ----- Must be set in a constructor or declaration.
    private readonly int TaxYear;
}
```

VISUAL BASIC

```
Class TaxInformation
    ' ----- Must be set in a constructor or declaration.
    Private ReadOnly TaxYear As Integer
End Class
```

Visual Basic's *ReadOnly* modifier can also be used to create a read-only property. In C#, this is done by omitting the property's setter.

See Also

Properties

ref Modifier

Visual Basic's *ByRef* modifier is equivalent to C#'s *ref* modifier, both of which indicate that an argument is to be passed by reference instead of by value.

C#

```
public bool ModifyDate(ref DateTime activeDate)
{
    // ----- Use or update activeDate as needed.
}
```

VISUAL BASIC

```
Public Function ModifyDate(
        ByRef activeDate As Date) As Boolean
    ' ----- Use or update activeDate as needed.
End Function
```

In Visual Basic, a property can be passed to a method by reference, something not supported in C#.

See Also

Arguments and Parameters, Generics

return Modifier

See

Attributes

return Statement

Visual Basic's *Return* statement is identical in use and syntax to C#'s *return* statement, both for methods with return values and for those without.

C#

```
// ----- For methods with void return type.
return;

// ----- For methods with non-void return type.
return someValue;
```

VISUAL BASIC

```
' ----- For methods with void return type (Sub).
Return

' ----- For methods with non-void return type (Function).
Return someValue
```

For methods that do not return a value (*Sub* methods), Visual Basic also supports the *Exit Sub* statement, which is functionally equivalent to *Return*. (A related *Exit Property* statement exists for properties.)

VISUAL BASIC

```
' ----- For methods with a void return type.
Exit Sub
```

For methods that return a value in VB (*Function* methods), that value can be assigned to the name of the function, and the *Exit Function* can be used to exit the method early.

VISUAL BASIC

```
Public Function DetermineValue() As Integer
    Dim theValue As Integer

    ' ----- Calculating logic, then...
    DetermineValue = theValue
    Exit Function

    ' ----- More logic can appear here.
End Function
```

This variation exists for backward compatibility. The use of the newer *Return* syntax is recommended.

sbyte Data Type

Visual Basic's intrinsic *SByte* data type is identical to C#'s *sbyte* data type. Both types are aliases for .NET's *System.SByte* type.

C#

```
sbyte offset = 0;
```

VISUAL BASIC

```
Dim offset As SByte = 0
```

Scope

See

Lifetime and Scope

sealed Modifier

When applied to a class, C#'s *sealed* modifier is the same as Visual Basic's *NotInheritable* modifier.

C#
```
sealed class CoreSettings
```

VISUAL BASIC
```
NotInheritable Class CoreSettings
```

When applied to members of a derived class overriding the matching virtual member in the base class, C#'s *sealed* modifier is replaced in Visual Basic with the *NotOverridable* modifier. In both languages, the *override* (C#) or *Overrides* (VB) modifier must also be present.

C#
```
sealed protected override void Refresh()
```

VISUAL BASIC
```
Protected NotOverridable Overrides Sub Refresh()
```

For such members, C#'s *sealed* modifier can apply to methods, properties, indexers, and events. In Visual Basic, events cannot be marked with the *NotOverridable* modifier.

select Query Expression Operator (LINQ)

Visual Basic's *Select* query expression operator is identical to C#'s *select* operator. When crafting query expressions in VB, the *Select* clause is optional, even in situations where its C# counterpart would be required. When *Select* is left out, the member identified in the *From*, *Aggregate*, or *Group* clause is returned. Additionally, Visual Basic allows more flexibility concerning the placement of the *Select* clause within the query expression.

C#
```
var result = from oneEmployee in Employees
             where oneEmployee.IsManager == true
             select oneEmployee;
```

VISUAL BASIC
```
' ----- The Select clause can also appear before Where.
Dim result = From oneEmployee In Employees
             Where oneEmployee.IsManager = True
             Select oneEmployee
```

As in C#, Visual Basic supports the return of anonymous types, either implicitly with a restricted selection list, or explicitly via the *New With* syntax. You can also create new instances of named types using this same syntax.

C#

```
// ----- Anonymous type.
var result = from oneEmployee in Employees
             where oneEmployee.IsManager == true
             select new {Name = oneEmployee.FullName,
             oneEmployee.Salary, oneEmployee.HireDate};

// ----- Named type.
var result = from oneEmployee in Employees
             where oneEmployee.IsManager == true
             select new Person {
             Name = oneEmployee.FullName};
```

VISUAL BASIC

```
' ----- Anonymous type.
Dim result = From oneEmployee In Employees
             Where oneEmployee.IsManager = True
             Select New With {.Name = oneEmployee.FullName,
             oneEmployee.Salary, oneEmployee.HireDate}

' ----- Named type.
Dim result = From oneEmployee In Employees
             Where oneEmployee.IsManager = True
             Select New Person With {
             .Name = oneEmployee.FullName}
```

See Also

Query Expressions

---

set Declaration

See

Properties

Short Circuiting

See

&& Conjunction Operator, || Disjunction Operator, ?: Conditional Operator

---

short Data Type

Visual Basic's intrinsic *Short* data type is identical to C#'s *short* data type. Both types are aliases for .NET's *System.Int16* type. For short literals, Visual Basic uses an *S* or *s* suffix after the value; C# does not include such a suffix.

C#

```
short baseYear = 0;
```

```
Dim baseYear As Short = 0s    ' or 0S
```

sizeof Operator

Visual Basic does not include a direct equivalent for C#'s *sizeof* operator. One option is to use the *System.Runtime.InteropServices.Marshal.SizeOf* method, which provides similar, though not identical, results. Consider the following table, which compares the output (in bytes) of both *sizeof* and *Marshal.SizeOf* using the same data types as arguments. The *bool* and *char* types provide different results. Visual Basic also includes a *Len* method that returns similar, but not identical, results for its intrinsic value types.

C# Type	sizeof	Marshal.SizeOf	Len Method
byte, sbyte	1	1	1
short, ushort	2	2	2
int, uint	4	4	4
long, ulong	8	8	8
bool	1	4	2
char	2	1	2
float	4	4	4
double	8	8	8
decimal	16	16	8

The *sizeof* operator also returns sizes for pointers and certain structures in unsafe contexts. You can use .NET's *System.IntPtr.Size* method in VB to obtain the platform-specific size of a pointer or handle. For structures, the *Marshal.SizeOf* method will return the total size of the structure type passed to it. This may or may not result in the same value provided by C#'s *sizeof* operator.

```
Dim structSize As Integer =
    Marshal.SizeOf(GetType(structName))
```

stackalloc Modifier

Visual Basic has no equivalent for C#'s *stackalloc* modifier.

Statements

In C#, the semicolon determines the end of a statement. For the purposes of statement structure, a block of statements surrounded with a set of curly braces is treated as a single semicolon-terminated statement.

C#
```
// ----- A simple single-line statement.
quotient = numerator / denominator;
```

```
// ----- An if condition, with its subordinate statement.
if (totalPercent > 100)
    totalPercent = 100;

// ----- An if condition with a subordinate block.
if (totalPercent > 100)
{
    ReportOverage(totalPercent);
    totalPercent = 100;
}
```

In Visual Basic, the end of a physical line indicates where the statement ends. For block statements (such as *For* loops), opening, closing, and subordinate portions each terminate at the end of a physical line, although multiple statements may appear within the subordinate block.

VISUAL BASIC
```
' ----- A simple single-line statement.
quotient = numerator / denominator

' ----- An If condition, with its subordinate statement.
If (totalPercent > 100) Then
    totalPercent = 100
End If

' ----- An If condition with a subordinate block.
If (totalPercent > 100) Then
    ReportOverage(totalPercent)
    totalPercent = 100
End If
```

C# allows a single logical line to span physical lines by employing as much or as little whitespace as needed, as long as the entire statement ends with a semicolon.

C#
```
expirationDate = string.Format("{0:00}/{1:0000}",
    monthPortion, yearPortion);
```

Traditionally, Visual Basic accomplishes this by adding a line continuation character (an underscore preceded by at least one space character) to the end of all lines except the last in a logical statement.

VISUAL BASIC
```
expirationDate = String.Format("{0:00}/{1:0000}", _
    monthPortion, yearPortion)
```

Newer editions of Visual Basic do a better job at determining when two physical lines constitute a logical statement, even in the absence of the line continuation character. In general, when a line ends with a clearly incomplete statement—such as a set of parentheses being left open—the VB compiler will assume that the line continues, even when not explicitly indicated.

```
' ----- A line ending in a comma indicates continuation.
expirationDate = String.Format("{0:00}/{1:0000}",
    monthPortion, yearPortion)
```

C# allows multiple statements to sit on a single physical line.

C#
```
// ----- Two simple statements on one line.
firstName = "John"; lastName = "Doe";

// ----- A block statement can be single-line as well.
while (status > 0) status = DoMoreWork();
```

To do this in Visual Basic, you must connect the statements with a colon character.

VISUAL BASIC
```
' ----- Two simple statements on one line.
firstName = "John" : lastName = "Doe"

' ----- A block statement can be single-line as well.
Do While (status > 0) : status = DoMoreWork() : Loop
```

A special case of this statement joining in VB occurs in the single-line form of the *If* statement, where linked statements are processed in response to the condition.

VISUAL BASIC
```
' ----- Both assignments will occur if true.
If (counter > 100) Then overflow = True : counter = 0
```

In C#, these subordinate statements must be enclosed in a set of curly braces. Using a syntax that more closely parallels that of VB will produce the wrong results.

C#
```
// ----- This is equivalent to the earlier VB code.
if (counter > 100) { overflow = true; counter = 0; }

// ----- This code is wrong; counter will be reset
//       whether the condition is true or false.
if (counter > 100) overflow = true; counter = 0;
```

C# permits you to start a distinctly scoped block by using a set of curly braces without an associated block construct.

C#
```
{
    // ----- Code here is locally scoped.
}
```

There is no built-in way to accomplish this in Visual Basic, although you can simulate by using a superfluous *If* statement.

VISUAL BASIC
```
If (True) Then
    ' ----- Code here is locally scoped.
End If
```

As with other Visual Basic statements, LINQ queries can span multiple physical lines, explicitly using line continuation characters, or implicitly when the context leads to implicit line continuation. However, it is possible to design a query for which the end of the statement is not easily recognized by the VB compiler. In such cases, you must leave a blank line after the query before beginning the next logical statement.

See Also

; Statement Termination Character

static Modifier

C#'s *static* modifier, when attached to a class or to individual members of a structure or class, identifies members (or an entire class' members) that are accessible outside of any specific instance of that class. When a class uses *static* as part of its declaration, all of its members must also be marked as *static*.

C#
```
static class CoreFeatures
{
    public static void LogError(string errorText)
    {
        // ----- Callable as CoreFeatures.LogError()
    }
}
```

In Visual Basic, the *Shared* modifier performs the same function. However, it can only be attached to class and structure members, not to the class itself.

VISUAL BASIC
```
Class CoreFeatures
    Public Shared Sub LogError(ByVal errorText As String)
        ' ----- Callable as CoreFeatures.LogError()
    End Sub
End Class
```

If every member of the class will be shared, you can use a Visual Basic *Module* statement. All members of modules are implicitly shared, as with a static class in C#. Therefore, the *Shared* modifier does not appear in this context.

VISUAL BASIC
```
Module CoreFeatures
    Public Sub LogError(ByVal errorText As String)
        ' ----- Implicitly shared. Callable as LogError()
    End Sub
End Module
```

Visual Basic does include a *Static* statement. It is used to declare local variables, just like the *Dim* statement, but the lifetime of static variables is the lifetime of the instance (when found in instance methods of classes and structures) or the application (when found in modules, or in static methods of classes and structures).

```
Public Sub ProcessData()
    ' ----- Track errors over multiple calls.
    Static countErrors As Integer = 0

    Try
        ' ----- Processing logic here.
    Catch ex As System.Exception
        countErrors += 1
        If (countErrors >= 5) Then Throw
    End Try
End Sub
```

C# does not include support for local static variables. Such variables must appear as type-level fields instead.

string Data Type

Visual Basic's intrinsic *String* data type is identical to C#'s *string* data type. Both types are aliases for .NET's *System.String* type.

C#
```
string name = "";
```

VISUAL BASIC
```
Dim name As String = ""
```

Historically, Visual Basic has provided a *$* suffix that could be attached to string identifiers or certain intrinsic functions. Although the .NET versions of Visual Basic still support this for backward compatibility, its use is not recommended.

struct Statement

Visual Basic's *Structure* statement is equivalent to C#'s *struct* statement. When declaring a structure that implements one or more interfaces, VB's *Implements* clause lists those interfaces, appearing as the first line within the *Structure* statement.

C#
```
struct Variable : IDataPart
{
    // ----- Members appear here.
}
```

VISUAL BASIC
```
Structure Variable
    Implements IDataPart
    ' ----- Members appear here.
End Structure
```

Structures in both languages contain the same types of members: constructors, fields, constants, properties, methods, operator overloads and user-defined conversions, indexers, events, and nested types (including delegates and enumerations). Instance fields within a structure cannot include an initialization value with the declaration, but static fields can.

Structures support the following modifiers in each language.

C# Modifier	Visual Basic Modifier
internal	Friend
new	Shadows
partial	Partial
private	Private
protected	Protected
protected internal	Protected Friend
public	Public

Structures in C# are *internal* by default, just as structures in Visual Basic are *Friend* by default. C# structure members are *private* by default; they are *Public* by default in VB. Structure members cannot use the *protected* (C#) or *Protected* (VB) modifier.

See Also

Access Modifiers, Constructors

switch Statement

Visual Basic's *Select Case* statement is generally equivalent to C#'s *switch* statement. Both statements include "case" blocks, plus an optional default/else block.

C#

```csharp
switch (position)
{
    case 1:
        positionName = "ones";
        break;
    case 10:
        positionName = "tens";
        break;
    case 100:
        positionName = "hundreds";
        break;
    default:
        positionName = "too large!";
        break;
}
```

VISUAL BASIC

```vb
Select Case position
    Case 1
        positionName = "ones"
    Case 10
        positionName = "tens"
    Case 100
        positionName = "hundreds"
```

```
    Case Else
        positionName = "too large!"
End Select
```

As with other C# block statements, the condition that appears after the *switch* keyword must be enclosed in parentheses. The parentheses are optional in VB. C#'s *case* clause becomes *Case* with no trailing colon; *default* becomes *Case Else*. In both languages, the first block that matches is used; those that follow, even if they match the test value, will be skipped.

Each *case* block in C# must be explicitly exited using a *break* statement or some other exiting statement. In Visual Basic, a matched block is automatically exited after its last statement; no equivalent for *break* is needed. You can also exit a C# *case* block using a *goto case* or *goto default* statement.

C#
```
case DayOfWeek.Monday:
    // ----- Day-specific processing, then...
    goto default;
default:
    // ----- General processing.
```

To do the same thing in Visual Basic, use a standard *GoTo* statement with a line label placed in the target *Case* block.

VISUAL BASIC
```
Case DayOfWeek.Monday
    ' ----- Day-specific processing, then...
    GoTo DoDefault
Case Else
DoDefault:
    ' ----- General processing.
```

In C#, the *case* clauses each contain a single comparison value: an integer number, a character or string, a Boolean literal, an enumeration member, or *null*. Visual Basic adds floating-point numbers, dates, and general *Object* instances to the list. In C#, two values can trigger the same block of matching code by placing their *case* clauses next to each other.

C#
```
case DayOfWeek.Monday:
case DayOfWeek.Wednesday:
    // ----- Day-specific processing.
```

In Visual Basic, both values can appear in a single *Case* clause, separated by commas. Also, VB supports value ranges, expressions, and relative comparisons.

VISUAL BASIC
```
Case 1, 2
    ' ----- Matches one of the comma-delimited values.
    tableSize = "small"
Case 3 To 6
    ' ----- Matches inclusive range.
    tableSize = "medium"
```

```
Case TableForSeven()
    ' ----- Matches result of expression or method call.
    tableSize = "oddball"
Case Is > 7
    ' ----- Matches using comparison operator.
    tableSize = "large"
```

For the comparison operator method, the *Is* keyword is followed by one of =, <>, <, <=, >, or >=, and then a comparison value. When comparing string values, the current state of the *Option Compare* statement will impact the comparison.

You can mix any number of comparison alternatives by including them in a single comma-delimited list.

VISUAL BASIC
```
Case 1, 3 To 6, 3 * 12, SpecialValue(), Is >= 100
```

The associated block will execute if any of the comma-delimited values match the test value. That is, they are implicitly connected with an *Or* comparison operator. Because of this, take care when using more than one *Is* keyword.

VISUAL BASIC
```
Case Is >= 100, Is <= 500
```

This will match all values, since every value is either more than 100 or less than 500. Instead, you should use a *100 To 500* range specification instead.

See Also

goto Statement

Ternary Operator

See

?: Conditional Operator

---

this Constructor Declaration

C#'s *this* constructor declaration, when attached to an instance constructor, calls another of the type's instance constructors before processing its own logic.

C#
```
class Person
{
    public string FullName;
    public int CurrentAge;

    public Person(string name)
    {
        FullName = name;
    }
```

```
public Person(string name, int age) : this(name)
{
    CurrentAge = age;
}
}
```

Visual Basic does not have a direct equivalent for this syntax. Instead, you must call one constructor from the other.

VISUAL BASIC
```
Class Person
    Public FullName As String
    Public CurrentAge As Integer

    Public Sub New(ByVal name As String)
        Me.FullName = name
    End Sub

    Public Sub New(ByVal name As String,
            ByVal age As Integer)
        Me.New(name)
        Me.CurrentAge = age
    End Sub
End Class
```

See Also

base Constructor Declaration, Constructors

this Extension Method Modifier

See

Extension Methods

this Indexer Declaration

C# uses *this* as part of a property declaration to define an indexer.

C#
```
public string this[int index]
{
    get
    {
        return InternalStorage[index];
    }
    set
    {
        // ----- "value" is implicitly defined
        InternalStorage[index] = value;
    }
}
```

In Visual Basic, indexers are known more commonly as "default properties," due in part to the use of the `Default` modifier on the property definition. Unlike other property modifiers, `Default` appears before the access modifier.

VISUAL BASIC

```
' ----- You may indicate the name, "Item" in this case.
Default Public Property Item(
        ByVal index As Integer) As String
    Get
        Return InternalStorage(index)
    End Get
    Set(ByVal value As String)
        ' ----- If the "value" declaration is omitted,
        '        "value" will be implicitly defined as in
        '        C#. When present, you can alter its name.
        InternalStorage(index) = value
    End Set
End Property
```

Both languages support overloading of the indexer via a different argument signature. The name of the property must be the same across all overloads in VB, and `Default` must appear as a modifier in each overload. Both languages allow indexers to appear in classes, structures, or interfaces.

C#

```
// ----- Interface-based indexer.
interface IIndexed
{
    string this[int index] {get; set;}
}
```

VISUAL BASIC

```
' ----- Interface-based indexer.
Interface IIndexed
    Default Property Item(ByVal index As Integer) As String
End Interface
```

> **New with Visual Studio 2015**
> In 2015, C# added the ability to define indexers using lambda expressions.

C#

```
public Order this[long orderID] =>
    LookupOrderByID(orderID);
```

Visual Basic does not yet support the creation of default properties using lambdas.

In addition to Visual Basic's `Default` modifier, indexers support the following modifiers in each language.

C# Modifier	Visual Basic Modifier
abstract	MustOverride
extern	Not supported
internal	Friend

C# Modifier	Visual Basic Modifier
new	Shadows
override	Overrides
private	Private
protected	Protected
protected internal	Protected Friend
public	Public
sealed	NotOverridable Overrides, or NotOverridable in base class
virtual	Overridable
Not supported	ReadOnly
Not supported	WriteOnly

See Also

[] Member Access Operator, Properties

this Instance Expression

Visual Basic's *Me* expression provides access to members of the local type, just like C#'s *this* expression.

C#
```csharp
class SimpleAdder
{
    public int Value = 0;

    public void Increment()
    {
        this.Value++;
    }
}
```

VISUAL BASIC
```vb
Class SimpleAdder
    Public Value As Integer = 0

    Public Sub Increment()
        Me.Value += 1
    End Sub
End Class
```

Visual Basic also includes a *MyClass* expression that is similar to *Me*, but where *Me* would reference overridden members in derived classes when relevant, *MyClass* always references members as they were originally defined in the current class. There is no C# equivalent for *MyClass*.

throw Statement

Visual Basic's *Throw* statement is identical to C#'s *throw* statement.

C#

```
throw new System.Exception("Something bad happened.");
```

VISUAL BASIC

```
Throw New System.Exception("Something bad happened.")
```

Within the *catch* block of a *try* statement, the *throw* statement can be used by itself (without any operand) to re-throw the *catch* block's exception.

C#

```
catch (System.Exception ex)
{
    // ----- Local logic, then...
    throw;
}
```

Visual Basic supports this same syntax.

VISUAL BASIC

```
Catch ex As System.Exception
    ' ----- Local logic, then...
    Throw
```

true Boolean Literal

When limited to Boolean operations, Visual Basic's *True* literal is identical to C#'s *true* literal. When a Boolean value is converted or cast to an integer, C#'s *true* value will always become *1* (one). In VB, *True* will become *1* or *-1* depending on the type of cast or conversion. See the "bool Data Type" in this chapter for details.

See Also

bool Data Type

try Statement

Visual Basic's *Try* statement is generally equivalent to C#'s *try* statement.

C#

```
try
{
    customerRecord = RetrieveCustomer(customerID);
}
catch (System.Expression ex)
{
    LogError("Problem with customer record.", ex);
    return;
}
finally
{
    InProcessField.Visible = false;
}
```

```
Try
    customerRecord = RetrieveCustomer(customerID)
Catch ex As System.Expression
    LogError("Problem with customer record.", ex)
    Return
Finally
    InProcessField.Visible = False
End Try
```

Both languages share a common set of rules surrounding the use of try/catch statements: at least one catch or finally block must appear; nesting is supported; jumps into any of the blocks from outside are restricted; multiple catch blocks may appear, and are processed in order; and so on.

> **New with Visual Studio 2015**
> Beginning in 2015, *catch* clauses in C# can include conditions that limit access to a given exception handler. Visual Basic already included support for this same functionality through its *When* clause.

C#

```
try
{
    customerRecord = RetrieveCustomer(customerID);
}
catch (System.Exception ex) if (errorCount < 5)
{
    errorCount += 1;
    LogWarning("Problem with customer record.", ex);
}
catch (System.Exception ex) if (errorCount >=5)
{
    LogFatalError("Problem with customer record.", ex);
    return;
}
```

VISUAL BASIC

```
Try
    customerRecord = RetrieveCustomer(customerID)
Catch ex As System.Exception When (errorCount < 5)
    errorCount += 1
    LogWarning("Problem with customer record.", ex)
Catch ex As System.Exception When (errorCount >=5)
    LogFatalError("Problem with customer record.", ex)
    Return
End Try
```

Visual Basic includes an *Exit Try* statement that can be used in a *Try* or *Catch* block (but not a *Finally* block) to exit the innermost *Try* structure. Execution continues with the statement after the entire *Try* statement; the *Finally* block, when present, will be processed. In C#, such a jump out of the *try* statement requires a line label after the statement, and the use of *goto* to perform the jump out of the *try* or *catch* block.

type Modifier

See

Attributes

typeof Operator

Visual Basic's *GetType* operator is identical to C#'s *typeof* operator.

C#
```
System.Type numberType = typeof(int);
```

VISUAL BASIC
```
Dim numberType As System.Type = GetType(Integer)
```

uint Data Type

Visual Basic's intrinsic *UInteger* data type is identical to C#'s *uint* data type. Both types are aliases for .NET's *System.UInt32* type. For unsigned integer literals, C# uses a *U* or *u* suffix after the value; in Visual Basic, use *UI* or *ui* instead.

C#
```
uint counter = 0u;
```

VISUAL BASIC
```
Dim counter As UInteger = 0UI   ' or 0ui
```

ulong Data Type

Visual Basic's intrinsic *ULong* data type is identical to C#'s *ulong* data type. Both types are aliases for .NET's *System.UInt64* type. For unsigned long literals, both C# and Visual Basic use a *UL* suffix after the value, or some uppercase/lowercase variation of *UL*.

C#
```
ulong counter = 0ul;
```

VISUAL BASIC
```
Dim counter As ULong = 0UL
```

unchecked Expression

C#'s *unchecked* keyword, whether in its statement-block form or expression form, disables run-time integer overflow checking on the contained statements or expression.

Visual Basic enables integer overflow checking by default on a project-wide basis. To enable or disable overflow checking, access the Advanced Compiler Settings within the Project Properties, and set the Remove Integer Overflow Checks field as needed. VB does not include the ability to control integer overflow checks at the statement or expression level.

unsafe Expression

C#'s *unsafe* expression, whether in its statement-block or modifier form, indicates a section of unsafe (unmanaged) code. Because Visual Basic does not support unsafe contexts, it has no equivalent for *unsafe*.

ushort Data Type

Visual Basic's intrinsic *UShort* data type is identical to C#'s *ushort* data type. Both types are aliases for .NET's *System.UInt16* type. For unsigned short literals, Visual Basic uses a *US* suffix after the value, or some uppercase/lowercase variation of *US*; C# does not include such a suffix.

C#
```
ushort counter = 0;
```

VISUAL BASIC
```
Dim counter As UShort = 0US
```

using Directive

C#'s *using* directive identifies namespaces that will be used within the current source file without the need to provide the full, absolute namespace path to its members.

C#
```
// ----- At the top of a source code file.
using System.Text;

// ----- Later, in a method in the same file, you don't
//       need the full System.Text.StringBuilder path.
StringBuilder content = new StringBuilder();
```

Visual Basic's *Imports* statement performs this same identification of namespaces.

VISUAL BASIC
```
' ----- At the top of a source code file.
Imports System.Text

' ----- Later, in a method in the same file, you don't
'       need the full System.Text.StringBuilder path.
Dim content As New StringBuilder()
```

Both languages support the assignment of alias names to imported namespaces (and imported types in Visaul Basic).

C#
```
using TextStuff = System.Text;
```

VISUAL BASIC
```
Imports TextStuff = System.Text
```

The alias can be prefixed to member names within that same file.

C#

```
TextStuff.StringBuilder content =
    new TextStuff.StringBuilder();
```

Visual Basic

```
Dim content As New TextStuff.StringBuilder()
```

Visual Basic also provides project-wide importing of namespaces, allowing programmers to reference such namespaces without the need to include an *Imports* statement in every file. Relevant namespaces are imported by default into new projects through this feature. To access the list of project-wide imports, open the Project Properties panel, access the References tab, and use the Imported Namespaces field to select those namespaces that should be imported across your project.

New with Visual Studio 2015

Starting in 2015, C#'s *using static* directive can specify a static type (or an instance type with static members), such as an enumeration or a static class. This allows your code to reference members of those types without a full namespace qualification. Visual Basic's *Imports* statement has always included this same functionality.

C#

```
using static System.Drawing.SystemColors;

// ----- Later, in method code in the same file, members
//       of SystemColors can be used directly.
displayColor = ControlText;
```

Visual Basic

```
Imports System.Drawing.SystemColors

' ----- Later, in method code in the same file, members
'       of SystemColors can be used directly.
displayColor = ControlText
```

---

using Statement

Visual Basic's *Using* statement is generally equivalent to C#'s *using* statement. C# requires parentheses around the block variable declaration, but they are optional in VB.

C#

```
using (SqlConnection myDB = new SqlConnection(dbPath))
{
    // ----- myDB is disposed on exit of using block.
}
```

Visual Basic

```
Using myDB As SqlConnection = New SqlConnection(dbPath)
    ' ----- myDB is disposed on exit of Using block.
End Using
```

```
' ----- This compressed format is also supported.
Using myDB As New SqlConnection(dbPath)
End Using
```

Both languages allow multiple resources to be created at once in the same *using* or *Using* statement. The compiler converts these to nested blocks, which are also permitted in each language. In C#, all variables declared with the same *using* statement must be of the same data type; VB allows these variables to be of different types.

C#

```
using (Type1 firstVal = new Type1(),
    secondVal = new Type1())
```

VISUAL BASIC

```
' ----- Variables of the same type.
Using firstVal As New Type1, secondVal As New Type1

' ----- Variables of different types.
Using firstVal As New Type1, secondVal As New Type2
```

var Implicit Type

C#'s *var* keyword allows your code to create a strongly type variable whose type is determined by context. Such values are commonly used as recipients of LINQ queries, since those statements return anonymous types.

C#

```
// ----- These two statements create an int and an
//       anonymous type with two members.
var basicValue = 10;
var moreComplex = new { ID = 10, Name = "Ten" };
```

In Visual Basic, the standard *Dim* declaration keyword, when used without an *As* clause, accomplishes this same purpose.

VISUAL BASIC

```
Dim basicValue = 10
Dim moreComplex = New With { .ID = 10, .Name = "Ten" }
```

To enable this implicit typing, VB requires that the *Option Infer On* statement be used, either at the top of the relevant source file, or configured for all files through the project's properties.

See Also

Query Expressions

Variables

In C#, local variables appear without any special keyword.

C#

```
int basicValue;              // No initializer
string greeting = "hi";      // With initializer
byte[] storage;              // Array
```

In Visual Basic, the *Dim* statement declares local variables.

VISUAL BASIC

```
Dim basicValue As Integer        ' No initializer
Dim greeting As String = "hi"    ' With initializer
Dim storage() As Byte            ' Array
```

Just like in C#, VB allows multiple variables to be declared in a single statement, using a comma to separate the identifiers.

C#

```
// ----- Both variables typed as DateTime.
DateTime startDate, endDate;

// ----- Different types require different statements.
int i1, i2, i3;
short s4, s5;
```

VISUAL BASIC

```
' ----- Both variables typed as Date.
Dim startDate, endDate As Date

' ----- Three Integer, two Short
Dim i1, i2, i3 As Integer, s4, s5 As Short
```

In C#, all variables must be assigned an initial value before they can be used elsewhere in code. In Visual Basic, all variables are initialized automatically to their default values: *Nothing* for reference types; some variation of zero for intrinsic value types and enumerations; and an instance with initialized members for structures.

Inferred variables in C# use the *var* instance type.

C#

```
// ----- Inferred as string.
var message = "Hello, world.";
```

In Visual Basic, you use the standard *Dim* statement, but leave off the *As* clause to trigger local type inference. *Option Infer On* must be used at the file or project level for this to work.

VISUAL BASIC

```
' ----- Inferred as string.
Dim message = "Hello, world."
```

Locally defined variables in VB can be used as the iteration variable in a *For Each* loop. In C#, the iteration variable must be defined as part of the *foreach* loop declaration itself.

See Also

[ ] Array Declaration, const Statement, Fields, Identifiers, Initializers, Lifetime and Scope, var Implicit Type

virtual Modifier

Visual Basic's *Overridable* modifier is equivalent to C#'s *virtual* modifier.

C#
```
public virtual long DetermineImpact()
```

VISUAL BASIC
```
Public Overridable Function DetermineImpact() As Long
```

C#'s *virtual* modifier can be used with class methods, properties, indexers, and events. In Visual Basic, the *Overridable* modifier cannot be used with events.

void Data Type

When used as the return type for a method, C#'s *void* intrinsic data type indicates that no value will be returned from that method.

C#
```
public void UpdateStatistics()
{
    // ----- May include a return with no value.
    return;
}
```

In Visual Basic, use the *Sub* keyword to indicate a method with no return value.

VISUAL BASIC
```
Public Sub UpdateStatistics()
    ' ----- May include a return with no value.
    Return
End Sub
```

The *void* type can also be used in C# to indicate a pointer for which the true type is unknown. Because Visual Basic does not include support for pointers, this use of *void* has no direct equivalent in VB. Although *void* is an alias for .NET's *System.Void* type, the use of that type is very limited in Visual Basic.

volatile Modifier

Visual Basic does not include a direct substitute for C#'s *volatile* modifier. To protect access to a local variable in your code, consider using VB's *SyncLock* statement, or use other .NET Framework features that allow a thread to safely manage access to a shared resource.

where Clause

In C# generics, conditions can be placed on type parameters with the *where* clause.

C#
```
// ----- Clause applied to one type parameter.
class SingleGeneric<T> where T : IEnumerable
```

```
// ----- Constraints applied to two type parameters
//          requires two where clauses.
class DoubleGeneric<T, U>
    where T : IEnumerable
    where U : IDisposable
```

In Visual Basic, the As clause parallels C#'s where clause, and appears immediately after the type parameter being constrained.

VISUAL BASIC
```
' ----- Clause applied to one type parameter.
Class SingleGeneric(Of T As IEnumerable)

' ----- Constraints applied to two type parameters
'          requires two As clauses.
Class DoubleGeneric(Of T As IEnumerable, U As IDisposable)
```

To apply multiple constraints to a single parameter, enclose the comma-delimited VB constraints within a set of curly braces.

C#
```
class ComplexGeneric<T> where T : class, IDisposable
```

VISUAL BASIC
```
Class ComplexGeneric(Of T As {class, IDisposable})
```

Both languages support the same types of constraints on parameters. The following table lists the equivalent constraints.

Constraint	C#	Visual Basic
Specific type	Customer	Customer
Specific interface	IEnumerable	IEnumerable
Another type parameter	U	U
Any class	class	Class
Any structure	struct	Structure
Class with default constructor	new()	New

See Also

Generics

where Query Expression Operator (LINQ)

Visual Basic's Where query expression operator is identical to C#'s where operator. As in C#, Visual Basic's Where clause supports the full set of language-specific logical operators.

C#
```
var result = from oneEmployee in Employees
             where oneEmployee.IsManager == true
             select oneEmployee;
```

```
' ----- The Select clause can also appear before Where.
Dim result = From oneEmployee in Employees
            Where oneEmployee.IsManager = True
            Select oneEmployee
```

In C#, the *where* clause must appear before the *select* clause. Visual Basic offers greater flexibility as to the placement of these clauses within the query expression.

See Also

Query Expressions

while Statement

C#'s *while* statement loops while a condition is true, and may not loop at all if the condition is initially false.

C#
```
while (content.Length > 0)
{
    content = ProcessChunkOfContent(content);
}
```

In Visual Basic, the *Do* statement accomplishes the same thing when the condition appears at the top of the loop.

VISUAL BASIC
```
Do While content.Length > 0
    content = ProcessChunkOfContent(content)
Loop
```

A variation of this loop uses the *Until* clause instead of *While*.

VISUAL BASIC
```
Do Until content.Length = 0
    content = ProcessChunkOfContent(content)
Loop
```

In both cases, the parentheses surrounding the condition are optional, although they are required in C#.

See Also

do Statement

XML Documentation Comments

Both C# and Visual Basic support XML comments as a means of documenting code and prompting Visual Studio's IntelliSense to display extended information about types and type members. In C#, these comments begin with the /// symbol.

C#
```
/// <summary>
///     Tracks details about living creatures.
/// </summary>
```

```
class Animal
{
}
```

In Visual Basic, use the ' ' ' symbol instead.

```
''' <summary>
'''    Tracks details about living creatures.
''' </summary>
Class Animal
End Class
```

C# also allows XML comments within multi-line comment blocks, by starting the block with the /** symbol. This variation has no equivalent in Visual Basic.

C#
```
/** <summary>
    . . .
  */
```

Both languages use the same set of recommended XML tags for documenting code. See Microsoft's MSDN documentation for information on using these tags in your projects.

yield Statement

When defining a method iterator or get-accessor iterator, C#'s *yield return* statement identifies the next value to emit. The related *yield break* statement aborts an iterator early, before any other logic in the iterator code can run.

C#
```
// ----- Assumes a LimitedEdition value defined elsewhere.
public IEnumerable<int> SmallNumbers()
{
    yield return 1;
    yield return 2;
    yield return 3;
    if (LimitedEdition)
        yield break;
    yield return 4;
    yield return 5;
}
```

In Visual Basic, the *Yield* statement returns the next iterator value, and appears in a function or property that includes the *Iterator* modifier. VB's standard *Return* statement (or the older *Exit Function* and *Exit Property* statements) takes the place of C#'s *yield break* statement.

VISUAL BASIC
```
' ----- Assumes a LimitedEdition value defined elsewhere.
Public Iterator Function SmallNumbers() As _
        IEnumerable(Of Integer)
    Yield 1
    Yield 2
    Yield 3
```

```
        If (LimitedEdition) Then Return
        Yield 4
        Yield 5
    End Function
```

If a *yield* statement appears in a C# *try* statement, that statement cannot have *catch* clauses, only a *finally* clause. Visual Basic allows *Try* statements that contain *Yield* statements to use both *Catch* and *Finally* clauses.

See Also

Iterators

Chapter 2

Visual Basic to C#

The Visual Basic entries in this chapter appear alphabetically by keyword or feature. Locate a language entry to see its C# equivalent. Entries identified by symbols appear before those starting with letters, and in the following order.

! # $ % & ' (* + , - . / : < = > ? @ [\ ^ _ {

! Dictionary Access Operator

Visual Basic's *!* member access operator acts as a shortcut for parentheses-based dictionary lookup.

VISUAL BASIC

```
' ----- Shortcut syntax using ! operator.
customerName = CStr(allRecords!FullName)

' ----- Standard dictionary syntax.
customerName = CStr(allRecords("FullName"))
```

C# uses this full version of the syntax for dictionary lookups, replacing the parentheses with square brackets.

C#

```
customerName = (string)allRecords["FullName"];
```

! Type Character

When attached as a suffix to a numeric literal, Visual Basic's *!* type character coerces the value to the *Single* data type. In C#, use the *F* or *f* suffix instead to coerce the value to the *float* data type.

VISUAL BASIC

```
Dim value As Single = 123!
```

C#

```
float value = 123F;
```

See Also

Single Data Type

Date Literal Marker

C# does not include support for date literals. Instead, you must create an instance of *System.DateTime*, passing the initial values to its constructor.

VISUAL BASIC
```
Dim dateValue = #12/31/1999#
```

C#
```
DateTime dateValue = new DateTime(1999, 12, 31);
```

Type Character

When attached as a suffix to a numeric literal, Visual Basic's # type character coerces the value to the *Double* data type. In C#, use the *D* or *d* suffix instead to coerce the value to the *double* data type.

VISUAL BASIC
```
Dim value As Double = 123#
```

C#
```
double value = 123D;
```

See Also

Double Data Type

#Const Directive

In Visual Basic, preprocessing constants come into being using the *#Const* directive. These constants can be Boolean, integer, floating-point, string, or date values.

VISUAL BASIC
```
' ----- A string preprocessing constant.
#Const TestVersion = "Beta 0.7"
```

In C#, the *#define* directive declares preprocessing constants. These constants are in essence Boolean, in that they either exist (*true*-like) or they don't (*false*-like).

C#
```
#define TestVersion
```

To clear a previously declared constant from use in Visual Basic, assign it a value of *Nothing*. In C#, use the *#undef* directive to remove the constant and give it a *false*-like state.

VISUAL BASIC
```
#Const TestVersion = Nothing
```

C#
```
#undef TestVersion
```

#Disable Directive

New with Visual Studio 2015
In 2015, Visual Basic received a new *#Disable* preprocessing directive that
prevents the compiler from reporting specific error conditions. C# uses the
#pragma warning statement for this same purpose.

VISUAL BASIC
```
' ----- Turn an error off.
#Disable Warning BC1234
```

C#
```
// ----- Turn an error off.
#pragma warning disable CS1234
```

Both languages accept comma-delimited lists of error codes.

#Enable Directive

New with Visual Studio 2015
In 2015, Visual Basic received a new *#Enable* preprocessing directive that prompts
the compiler to once again report specific error conditions. C# uses the *#pragma
warning* statement for this same purpose.

VISUAL BASIC
```
' ----- Turn an error back on.
#Enable Warning BC1234
```

C#
```
// ----- Turn an error back on.
#pragma warning restore CS1234
```

Both languages accept comma-delimited lists of error codes.

#ExternalChecksum Directive

In generated ASP.NET source files, C#'s *#pragma checksum* directive serves the
same purpose as Visual Basic's *#ExternalChecksum* directive. Neither statement
should be used directly within code, except as generated by the .NET Framework.

#ExternalSource Directive

There is no equivalent in C# for the *#ExternalSource* directive. Even in Visual
Basic it is only used within generated code, and not normally added directly by
developers.

#If Directive

The general syntax of preprocessing conditional statements in C# parallels closely the
usage found in Visual Basic, with some minor spelling and casing differences.

Visual Basic Term	C# Term
#If...Then	#if
#ElseIf...Then	#elif
#Else	#else
#End If	#endif

The key difference appears in the conditions themselves. In Visual Basic, preprocessor values exist as Booleans, integers, floating-point values, strings, or dates, and you can apply typical VB operators to those values. Preprocessor values in C# act like Booleans; they either exist or they don't.

VISUAL BASIC

```
#If TestVersion Then
    ' ----- Test-specific code here.
#ElseIf (OldVersion = False) Or (TargetVersion < 2.5) Then
    ' ----- Backward-compatible code here.
#Else
    ' ----- Standard code here.
#End If
```

C#

```
#if TestVersion
    // ----- Test-specific code here.
#elif (OldVersion == false)
    // ----- Backward-compatible code here.
#else
    // ----- Standard code here.
#endif
```

In these preprocessing expressions, Visual Basic supports all of its standard comparison operators; mathematical, string, and logical operators; and intrinsic conversion functions. In C#, expressions are much more limited, allowing just the ==, !=, &&, ||, and ! operators; the true and false constants; and parentheses within the conditional expressions. All expressions assume you are working with Boolean-like defined constants. Expressions using non-Boolean types are not permitted in C#.

#Region Directive

C#'s #region directive is equivalent to Visual Basic's #Region directive. The descriptive tag that follows the directive keyword is enclosed in double-quotes in VB, but quotation marks are not used in C#.

VISUAL BASIC

```
#Region "Utility Functions"
    ' ----- Collapsable code here.
#End Region
```

C#

```
#region Utility Functions
    // ----- Collapsable code here.
#endregion
```

Nesting of these regions is allowed in both languages.

$ Interpolated String Indicator

New with Visual Studio 2015
In 2015, both Visual Basic and C# added string interpolation, a method of generating formatted strings using string literals. Both languages share an identical syntax for such strings, prefixing them with a $ symbol, and using curly braces to contain the interpolated sections.

VISUAL BASIC
```
message = $"Meet {name} on {meetDate:dddd}"
```

C#
```
message = $"Meet {name} on {meetDate:dddd}";
```

$ Type Character

In pre-.NET versions of Visual Basic, the $ suffix was used to differentiate between "string" and "variant" versions of string identifiers and functions. The *Variant* data type no longer exists in modern Visual Basic, making the $ type character irrelevant. Also, there is no need for it in equivalent C# code.

See Also

String Data Type

% Type Character

When attached as a suffix to a numeric literal, Visual Basic's % type character coerces the value to the *Integer* data type. In C#, numeric literals that fit within the *int* data type are *int* by default, although you can also coerce a value to an *int* by using a cast.

C#
```
int someIntValue = (int)someLongValue;
```

See Also

Integer Data Type

& Concatenation Operator

C# uses its + addition operator for concatenation.

VISUAL BASIC
```
Dim greeting As String = "Hello, " & name
```

C#
```
string greeting = "Hello, " + name;
```

Visual Basic also allows concatenation with the + operator. However, the rules surrounding such concatenations vary depending on the data types of the operands and the state of the *Option Strict* statement in effect. For this reason, & is preferred. In C#, no such variations exist; it always concatenates when string operands are involved.

C# does include its own & operator. However, it is the equivalent of VB's *And* conjunction operator; it does not perform string concatenation.

& Type Character

When attached as a suffix to a numeric literal, Visual Basic's & type character coerces the value to the *Long* data type. In C#, use the *L* or *l* suffix instead to coerce the value to the *long* data type.

VISUAL BASIC
```
Dim value As Long = 123&
```

C#
```
long value = 123L;
```

See Also

Long Data Type

&= Assignment Operator

When used for string concatenation, C#'s *+=* assignment operator provides the same results as Visual Basic's *&=* operator.

VISUAL BASIC
```
originalValue &= "The end."
```

C#
```
originalValue += "The end.";
```

Visual Basic also allows concatenation with the *+=* operator. However, the rules surrounding such concatenations vary depending on the data types of the operands and the state of the *Option Strict* statement in effect. For this reason, *&=* is preferred. In C#, no such variations exist; the *+=* operator always concatenates when string operands are involved.

Although C# includes an *&=* operator, that is the assignment operator for the *&* conjunction operator, and should not be confused with the identical-looking VB operator.

See Also

Assignment Operators

' Comment Symbol

The C# equivalent of Visual Basic's *'* comment symbol is *//*. Both symbols start a comment that continues to the end of the current physical line.

VISUAL BASIC
```
' This is a full-line comment.
result = DoWork()   ' A trailing comment.
```

C#
```
// This is a full-line comment.
result = DoWork();   // A trailing comment.
```

See Also

REM Statement, XML Documentation Comments

''' XML Documentation Comment Symbol

See

XML Documentation Comments

( ) Array Declaration

Arrays are similar in their use between Visual Basic and C#, but there are differences in how they are declared.

VISUAL BASIC
```
' ----- Uninitialized array.
Dim numberSet() As Integer
Dim textSet() As String

' ----- Initialized by size.
Dim setOfFive(4) As Integer

' ----- Initialized by members.
Dim setOfThree() As String = {"zero", "one", "two"}
```

C#
```
// ----- Uninitialized array.
int[] numberSet;
string[] textSet;

// ----- Initialized by size.
int[] setOfFive = new int[5];

// ----- Initialized by members.
string[] setOfThree = {"zero", "one", "two"};
```

Visual Basic uses parentheses to indicate array elements. In C#, square brackets are used instead. Array declarations in VB allow the parentheses to follow either the identifier name or the type (although no size is permitted with this second format); C# always places the brackets with the type.

VISUAL BASIC
```
' ----- Both of these will work.
Dim numberSetA() As Integer
Dim numberSetB As Integer()
```

C#
```
// ----- Only this placement of brackets is valid.
int[] numberSet;
```

When specifying an array size during declaration, Visual Basic's syntax indicates the upper bound of the array, while C#'s syntax specifies the number of elements. The lower bound of all C# arrays is zero. There is no equivalent to VB's *0 To* array declaration prefix.

VISUAL BASIC
```
' ----- Both of these declare an array of elements
'        numbered from 0 to 4.
Dim setOfFiveA(4) As Integer
Dim setOfFiveB(0 To 4) As Integer
```

C#
```
// ----- Only this syntax is supported in C#.
int[] setOfFive = new int[5];
```

As with Visual Basic, C# supports both multidimensional arrays and jagged arrays.

VISUAL BASIC
```
Dim multiArray(,) As Integer
Dim jaggedArray()() As Integer
```

C#
```
int[,] multiArray;
int[][] jaggedArray;
```

C# does not include an equivalent for Visual Basic's *ReDim* statement, with or without its *Preserve* option. To resize an array without preservation, assign a new array to the identifier. To preserve the contents, use the *Array.Resize* method.

VISUAL BASIC
```
Dim storageArea() As Integer   ' Uninitialized

' ----- Initialize the array to include 5 elements,
'       possibly wiping out any existing data.
ReDim storageArea(0 to 4)

' ----- Resize the array to include 10 elements,
'       preserving the existing 0 to 4 elements.
ReDim Preserve storageArea(0 to 9)
```

C#
```
int[] storageArea;   // Uninitialized

// ----- Initialize the array to include 5 elements,
//       wiping out any existing data.
storageArea = new int[5];

// ----- Resize the array to include 10 elements,
//       preserving the existing 0 to 4 elements.
Array.Resize(ref storageArea, 10);
```

Member access is the same in both languages, with the exception of the brackets used.

VISUAL BASIC
```
Dim thirdElement As Integer = largerArray(2)
```

C#

```
int thirdElement = largerArray[2];
```

Size requests are also the same, through the *Length*, *GetUpperBound*, and *GetLowerBound* members. Visual Basic also includes two intrinsic functions, *UBound* and *LBound*, that return the limits, but C# has no such intrinsic methods.

VISUAL BASIC

```
size = someArray.Length
lower = someArray.GetLowerBound(0)
upper = someArray.GetUpperBound(0)

' ----- Using VB's intrinsic functions. The second
'       argument is optional, defaulting to zero.
lower = LBound(someArray)
upper = UBound(someArray)

' ----- For a multidimensional array, get
'       second-rank bounds.
lower = LBound(multiArray, 1)
upper = UBound(multiArray, 1)
```

C#

```
size = someArray.Length;
lower = someArray.GetLowerBound(0);
upper = someArray.GetUpperBound(0);
```

See Also

( ) Array Declaration, Initialization

( ) Expression Grouping

When used to group expressions, parentheses in C# are identical in syntax to grouping parentheses in Visual Basic. However, there are times when a set of parentheses is required around an expression in C#, but is optional when creating the equivalent statement in VB. For instance, the condition for an *if* statement in C# must be enclosed in parentheses, but Visual Basic does not have this requirement.

VISUAL BASIC

```
' ----- This If-statement condition is valid.
If totalCount >= 100 Then
```

C#

```
// ----- The parentheses must be added in C#.
if (totalCount >= 100)
```

( ) Member Operator

Dictionary member access is fairly similar in both languages, with C# using a set of square brackets in lieu of Visual Basic's parentheses.

```
fullName = customerRecord("FullName")
```

C#
```
fullName = customerRecord["FullName"];
```

Visual Basic's use of the *!* operator as a dictionary access shortcut does not have a direct equivalent in C#. Instead, you use this same square-bracket syntax to access members of a dictionary.

See Also

Indexers

---

* Multiplication Operator

The * multiplication operator in C# uses the same symbol and syntax as in Visual Basic.

VISUAL BASIC
```
result = originalValue * 5
```

C#
```
result = originalValue * 5;
```

---

*= Assignment Operator

C#'s *= assignment operator is identical to the one found in Visual Basic, both in syntax and in purpose.

VISUAL BASIC
```
originalValue *= 5
```

C#
```
originalValue *= 5;
```

See Also

Assignment Operators

+ Addition Operator

For mathematical operations, C#'s + operator is identical to the one found in Visual Basic, both in syntax and in purpose.

VISUAL BASIC
```
Dim result As Integer = number1 + number2
```

C#
```
int result = number1 + number2;
```

In both languages, the + operator also performs string concatenation. However, while C# performs simple concatenation on string operands, Visual Basic may perform addition or concatenation depending on the operand data types and the current setting

---

of `Option Strict`. Therefore, for string concatenation operations, C#'s + operator is more consistent with VB's & operator.

VISUAL BASIC
```
Dim greeting As String = "Hello, " & name
```

C#
```
string greeting = "Hello, " + name;
```

+ Unary-Plus Operator

Both Visual Basic and C# permit a prefix unary-plus operator before numeric literals and expressions. The syntax is identical between the two languages.

+= Assignment Operator

For mathematical operations, C#'s += assignment operator is identical to the one found in Visual Basic, both in syntax and in purpose.

VISUAL BASIC
```
originalValue += 5
```

C#
```
originalValue += 5;
```

In both languages, the += operator also performs string concatenation. However, while C# performs simple concatenation on string operands, Visual Basic may perform addition or concatenation depending on the operand data types and the current setting of `Option Strict`. Therefore, for string concatenation operations, C#'s += operator is more consistent with VB's &= assignment operator.

C# also uses this operator to attach event handlers to an object's events, or to associate a method with a delegate instance in general.

See Also

Assignment Operators

, Punctuator

In general, C#'s use of the comma parallels those uses found in Visual Basic, with two notable exceptions. The first concerns C#'s use of a comma to separate assignments and conditions in `for` Statements, a variation not supported by Visual Basic's counter-centric `For` statement.

C#
```
for (counter = 1, mask = "*", counter <= 10;
     counter++, mask += "*") { /* ... */ }
```

The second exception deals with optional arguments. In C#, when calling a method with multiple optional arguments, if you want to supply only one of the later optional arguments, you must employ named arguments.

C#
```
// ----- Assume function Task has three arguments,
//       (a, b, c), where only 'a' is required, as in:
//           void Task(int a, int b = 1, int c = 2)
Task(aValue, c: cValue);
```

This parallels the implementation found in Visual Basic (using the := symbol for the named argument indicator instead of C#'s : symbol). However, Visual Basic also allows you to pass arguments by position, leaving any optional arguments blank as desired.

VISUAL BASIC
```
' ----- b will use its default value.
Task(aValue, , cValue)
```

This argument-skipping syntax is not supported in C#.

See Also

Initializers

- Subtraction Operator

The – subtraction operator in C# uses the same symbol and syntax as in Visual Basic.

VISUAL BASIC
```
result = originalValue - 5
```

C#
```
result = originalValue - 5;
```

- Unary-Minus Operator

The – unary-minus operator in C# uses the same symbol and syntax as in Visual Basic.

VISUAL BASIC
```
negativeVersion = -originalValue
```

C#
```
negativeVersion = -originalValue;
```

-= Assignment Operator

For mathematical and overloaded operations, Visual Basic's -= assignment operator is identical to the one found in C#, both in syntax and in purpose.

VISUAL BASIC
```
originalValue -= 5
```

C#
```
originalValue -= 5;
```

C# also uses this operator to detach event handlers from an object's events, or to disassociate a method from a delegate instance in general.

RemoveHandler Statement

. Member Access Operator

Both Visual Basic and C# employ a dotted member access syntax using the period (.)
between namespace, class, instance, and member names.

VISUAL BASIC
```
value = element.OneMember
```

C#
```
value = element.OneMember;
```

/ Division Operator

Visual Basic's / division operator returns a floating-point quotient.

VISUAL BASIC
```
Dim wholeResult1 As Double = 5 / 3    ' 1.666666...
Dim wholeResult2 As Double = 6 / 3    ' 2.0
Dim realResult As Single = 5! / 3!;   ' 1.666666...
```

In most cases, VB's division operation returns a result of type *Double*, even with
integer operands. If one operand is *Single* and the other is non-*Double*, the result is
Single. If one operand is *Decimal* and the other is anything other than *Single* or
Double, the result is *Decimal*.

C# also includes a / operator. It handles numeric division for both integer and floating-
point values (and for other types when used with operator overloading).

C#
```
int wholeResult1 = 5 / 3;     // 1
int wholeResult2 = 6 / 3;     // 2
float realResult = 5f / 3f;   // 1.666666...
```

The return type in C# generally follows the type of the operands. The operands are
coerced into the same type before the division takes place. This is true for integer and
floating-point values. For integer division, rounding always leans toward zero.

Both languages follow the same divide-by-zero rules for the / operator, with an
exception thrown for *Decimal* operands, and *System.Double.NaN* returned for
other data types.

See Also

\ Integer Division Operator

/= Assignment Operator

C#'s /= assignment operator is similar to the same operator in Visual Basic, although
the data types involved and returned differ between the two languages. In general, C#

retains the most relevant operand type, while in VB, the result is always *Double* or *Decimal.*

VISUAL BASIC
```
originalValue /= 5.2#
```

C#
```
originalValue /= 5.2D;
```

See the "/ Division Operator" entry in this chapter for full information on the differences between the Visual Basic and C# division operators.

See Also

/ Division Operator, Assignment Operators

: Statement Separation Symbol

In Visual Basic, a : statement separation symbol can be used to join multiple distinct statements onto a single physical line.

VISUAL BASIC
```
' ----- Ordinary statements.
ProcessData(actDate) : actDate = actDate.AddDays(1)

' ----- Condensed loop.
For count = 1 To 5 : Initialize(count) : Next count

' ----- With multiple triggered statements.
If (ProcessData() = Fail) Then LogError() : Return False
```

Because C# does not use line breaks to identify the end of a statement, C# naturally allows multiple statements to appear on a single line, divided by the *;* statement termination character. When multiple statements need to be processed together in response to some condition, those statements must be enclosed in a set of curly braces.

C#
```
// ----- Ordinary statements.
ProcessData(actDate); actDate = actDate.AddDays(1);

// ----- Condensed loop.
for (count = 1; count <= 5; count++) Initialize(count);

// ----- With multiple triggered statements. In this
//       case, curly braces are required around the
//       subordinate statements.
if (ProcessData() == Fail) { LogError(); return false; }
```

See Also

Statements

:= Named Argument Indicator

When using named arguments in method calls, C# uses the : named argument indicator in the same way that Visual Basic employs the equivalent : = indicator.

VISUAL BASIC
```
DefineAbbreviation(fullName:="Montana", shortName:="MT")
```

C#
```
DefineAbbreviation(fullName:"Montana", shortName:"MT");
```

As in Visual Basic, named arguments in C# can follow earlier positional arguments, but a positional argument cannot follow a named argument.

C#
```
// ----- This syntax is valid...
ProcessData(DateTime.Today, batchID:"12345");

// ----- ...but this is not.
ProcessData(batchID:"12345", DateTime.Today);
```

When using named arguments in attributes, Visual Basic uses the : = indicator as it does with method named arguments. C# uses the = sign, which differs from its own method named argument syntax.

VISUAL BASIC
```
<AttributeUsage(AttributeTargets.Class,
    AllowMultiple:=True)>
```

C#
```
[AttributeUsage(AttributeTargets.Class,
    AllowMultiple=true)]
```

See Also

, Punctuator, Arguments and Parameters

< > Attribute Usage Delimiter

C# surrounds attributes with square brackets instead of Visual Basic's angle brackets.

VISUAL BASIC
```
<System.Serliazable>
Public Class EmployeeData
```

C#
```
[System.Serializable]
public class EmployeeData
```

See Also

Attributes

< Comparison Operator

When comparing value types, C#'s < operator is identical to Visual Basic's < operator, and appears in the same binary-operator position.

```
If (teamPlayers < 9) Then
```

C#

```
if (teamPlayers < 9)
```

For string comparisons, VB and C# default to the same method of comparison, checking the binary value of each character in both strings. However, VB's *Option Compare Text* statement, when used within a project or source file, causes the comparison to use culture-specific text sorting rules. C# does not include native support for this style of comparison. Instead, you can use the *string* type's *Compare* method and its various overloads to indicate culture-specific comparisons.

C#

```
if (string.Compare(title1, title2,
    StringComparison.CurrentCultureIgnoreCase) < 0)
```

<< Left Shift Operator

C#'s << operator is identical in syntax and usage to Visual Basic's << operator.

<<= Assignment Operator

C#'s <<= operator is identical in syntax and usage to Visual Basic's <<= operator.

See Also

Assignment Operators

<= Comparison Operator

C#'s <= operator is generally identical to Visual Basic's <= operator. The entry for the < operator has additional information about string comparisons.

See Also

< Comparison Operator

<> Comparison Operator

When comparing value types, C#'s *!=* inequality operator is identical to Visual Basic's <> operator, and appears in the same binary-operator position.

```
If (teamPlayers <> 9) Then
```

C#

```
if (teamPlayers != 9)
```

For string comparisons, the `!=` operator once again replicates VB's `<>` operator. However, Visual Basic's `Option Compare` statement impacts the way that strings compare to each other. By default, both Visual Basic and C# perform binary-level comparisons of strings. However, if a VB project or source file employs `Option Compare Text`, the comparison instead uses culture-specific text sorting rules. C# has no way to specify this style of comparison using language features. See the "< Comparison Operator" entry in this chapter for a C# example that employs .NET Framework features to accomplish this.

For reference types other than strings, Visual Basic's `IsNot` operator appears in place of `<>`, especially when comparing an instance to `Nothing`. In C#, the `!=` operator is also used for these types of comparisons.

VISUAL BASIC

```
' ----- Standard instance comparison
If (firstInstance IsNot secondInstance) Then

' ----- Comparison with null (Nothing in VB).
If (anotherInstance IsNot Nothing) Then
```

C#

```
// ----- Standard instance comparison.
if (firstIntance != secondInstance)

// ----- Comparison with null.
if (anotherInstance != null)
```

See Also

Nothing Literal

= Assignment Operator

When used in a stand-alone assignment statement, C#'s = operator is identical in syntax and purpose to the = operator in Visual Basic.

VISUAL BASIC

```
taxAmount = subtotal * taxRate
```

C#

```
taxAmount = subtotal * taxRate;
```

C# allows an assignment to occur within an expression, or multiple assignments to occur within a single statement, a syntax not supported in Visual Basic.

C#

```
// ----- latestValue will be updated before method call.
ProcessValue(latestValue = incomingValue);

// ----- Both a and b will receive c's value.
a = b = c;
```

Assignment Operators

= Comparison Operator

When comparing value types, C#'s == equality operator is identical to Visual Basic's = operator, and appears in the same binary-operator position.

VISUAL BASIC
```
If (teamPlayers = 9) Then
```

C#
```
if (teamPlayers == 9)
```

For string comparisons, the == operator once again replicates VB's = operator. However, VB's Option Compare statement impacts the way that strings compare to each other. By default, both Visual Basic and C# perform binary-level comparisons of strings. However, if a VB project or source file employs Option Compare Text, the comparison instead uses culture-specific text sorting rules. C# has no way to specify this style of comparison using language features. See the "< Comparison Operator" entry in this chapter for a C# example that employs .NET Framework features to accomplish this.

For reference types other than strings, Visual Basic's Is operator appears in place of =, especially when comparing an instance to Nothing. In C#, the == operator is also used for these types of comparisons.

VISUAL BASIC
```
' ----- Standard instance comparison.
If (firstInstance Is secondInstance) Then

' ----- Comparison with null (Nothing in VB).
If (anotherInstance Is Nothing) Then
```

C#
```
// ----- Standard instance comparison.
if (firstIntance == secondInstance)

// ----- Comparison with null.
if (anotherInstance == null)
```

See Also

Nothing Literal

> Comparison Operator

When comparing value types, C#'s > operator is identical to Visual Basic's > operator, and appears in the same binary-operator position.

VISUAL BASIC
```
If (teamPlayers > 9) Then
```

C#
```
if (teamPlayers > 9)
```
The entry for the < operator has additional information about string comparisons.

>= Comparison Operator

C#'s >= operator is generally identical to Visual Basic's >= operator. The entry for the < operator has additional information about string comparisons.

See Also

> Comparison Operator

>> Right Shift Operator

C#'s >> operator is identical in syntax and usage to Visual Basic's >> operator.

>>= Assignment Operator

C#'s >>= operator is identical in syntax and usage to Visual Basic's >>= operator.

See Also

Assignment Operators

? Nullable Type Indicator

See

Nullable Types

?. Null Conditional Operator

New with Visual Studio 2015
In 2015, both Visual Basic and C# added a set of null conditional operators. In general, they are used in exactly the same way between the languages, but with slight differences in syntax.

Usage	Visual Basic Syntax	C# Syntax
Instance Member	A?.B	A?.B
Dictionary Member	A?!B	Not supported
Array or Indexed Member	A?(B)	A?[B]
XML Attribute Axis	A?.@B	Not supported
XML Child Axis	A?.<B>	Not supported
XML Descendant Axis	A?...<B>	Not supported

@ Type Character

When attached as a suffix to a numeric literal, Visual Basic's @ type character coerces the value to the *Decimal* data type. In C#, use the *M* or *m* suffix instead to coerce the value to the *decimal* data type.

VISUAL BASIC
```
Dim value As Decimal = 123@
```

C#
```
decimal value = 123M;
```

See Also

Decimal Data Type

[ ] Verbatim Indicator

Enclosing a Visual Basic reserved word within a set of square brackets allows that term to be used as an identifier.

VISUAL BASIC
```
Dim [double] As Integer = originalValue * 2
```

C# uses the @ verbatim indicator for this same purpose.

C#
```
int @double = originalValue * 2;
```

The set of keywords differs between the two languages, and a term that may require verbatim qualification in one language can work without it in the other. When doing cross-language development, take care to avoid keywords in both languages.

A term that requires verbatim qualification in Visual Basic does so whether it is upper or lower case. Because of C#'s case-sensitivity for identifiers, a term that may conflict with a lowercase language keyword will not conflict when entered with uppercase characters.

See Also

Identifiers, Literals

\ Integer Division Operator

Visual Basic's \ integer division operator, when used in place of /, always returns an integer value, with rounding toward zero.

VISUAL BASIC
```
Dim wholeResult1 As Integer = 5 \ 3    ' 1
Dim wholeResult2 As Integer = 6 \ 3    ' 2
Dim realResult As Long = 5! \ 3!       ' 1
```

Floating-point values are coerced to the *Long* data type before processing, rounded using banker's rounding (0.5 values are rounded toward the nearest even integer). If *Option Strict On* is used, you must manually coerce floating-point values to an appropriate integer type (*Byte*, *Short*, *Integer*, or *Long*).

In C#, there is no distinct integer division operator. Instead, there is a single / division operator that handles both floating-point and integer operations (and for other types when used with operator overloading).

C#
```
int wholeResult1 = 5 / 3;    // 1
int wholeResult2 = 6 / 3;    // 2
float realResult = 5f / 3f;  // 1.666666...
```

The return type in C# generally follows the type of the operands. The operands are coerced into the same type when needed before the division takes place. This is true for integer and floating-point values. For integer division, rounding always leans toward zero.

For Visual Basic's \ operator, divide-by-zero always throws an exception. In C#, an exception is only thrown for *decimal* operands. For other data types, the operation returns *System.Double.NaN* when the denominator is zero.

\= Assignment Operator

C# has no direct equivalent to Visual Basic's \= assignment operator. It does include a /= operator that combines aspects of VB's /= and \= operators. See the division operator entries in this chapter for information on language differences over division.

See Also

/ Division Operator, \ Integer Division Operator, Assignment Operators

^ Exponentiation Operator

C# does not include a dedicated operator to raise a value to a power. Use the *System.Math.Pow* method instead.

VISUAL BASIC
```
Dim result As Double = base ^ power
```

C#
```
double result = Math.Pow(base, power);
```

C# includes a ^ operator, but it is used as that language's Exclusive-Or operator.

^= Assignment Operator

C# does not include a dedicated assignment operator to raise a value to a power. Use the *System.Math.Pow* method instead.

VISUAL BASIC
```
base ^= power
```

C#
```
base = Math.Pow(base, power);
```

C# includes a ^= operator, but it is used as that language's Exclusive-Or assignment operator.

See Also

Assignment Operators

_ Line Continuation Character

C# does not require the use of any special character to continue a statement onto the next physical line. A single line may break across multiple lines as long as the statement terminates with a semicolon.

{ } Instance Initialization

See

Initializers

Access Modifiers

C# includes access modifiers that parallel those found in Visual Basic.

Visual Basic Modifiers	C# Modifiers
Friend	internal
Private	private
Protected	protected
Protected Friend	protected internal
Public	public

In most cases, the use of these modifiers in C# is identical to how they are used in Visual Basic, appearing as a prefix to the type or member being declared.

VISUAL BASIC
```
Public Class Student
```

C#
```
public class Student
```

When declaring fields within types using Visual Basic's *Dim* statement, the access modifier appears as a prefix to the declaration.

VISUAL BASIC
```
Class NameTracking
    Private Dim OriginalName As String
```

However, it is more common to omit the *Dim* keyword in this declaration. In fact, Visual Studio automatically removes the *Dim* keyword in field definitions, retaining it only for local variables. Since C# includes no special keyword for these declarations, the access modifier remains as an optional prefix.

```
Class NameTracking
    Private OriginalName As String
```

C#

```
class NameTracking
{
    private string OriginalName;
```

Structure members may not use the *Protected* (VB) or *protected* (C#) modifier in either language. For more information on using access modifiers, see the specific statements that employ access modifiers (such as "Class Statement") in this chapter.

AddHandler Custom Event Declaration

See

Custom Event Statement

AddHandler Statement

In Visual Basic, the `AddHandler` statement attaches an event handler to an object's events. The `AddressOf` operator appears before the event handler name.

VISUAL BASIC

```
' ----- Button1_Click method defined elsewhere, and
'       conforms to the same delegate used by Click event.
AddHandler Button1.Click, AddressOf Button1_Click
```

C# uses the *+=* event subscription operator to attach to an object's events those event handlers that conform to a specific delegate.

C#

```
// ----- button1_Click method defined elsewhere, and
//       conforms to the same delegate used by Click event.
button1.Click += button1_Click;
```

Visual Basic lets you use a lambda statement to establish inline event handlers.

VISUAL BASIC

```
AddHandler Button1.Click, Sub(ByVal o As Object,
            ByVal e As EventArgs)
        ' ----- Event code here.
    End Sub
```

C# uses a variation of its *delegate* statement to provide this same functionality, or a more plain syntax without the *delegate* keyword.

C#

```
' ----- The delegate syntax.
button1.Click += delegate(object o, EventArgs e) {
    /* Event code here. */ };
```

```
' ----- Alternate syntax without delegate keyword.
button1.Click += (object o, EventArgs e) {
    /* Event code here. */ };
```

AddressOf Operator

C# does not include an equivalent for Visual Basic's *AddressOf* operator. However, its functionality is implied when attaching event handlers to instance events.

VISUAL BASIC
```
' ----- Button1_Click method defined elsewhere, and
'         conforms to the same delegate used by Click event.
AddHandler Button1.Click, AddressOf Button1_Click
```

C#
```
// ----- button1_Click method defined elsewhere, and
//         conforms to the same delegate used by Click event.
button1.Click += button1_Click;
```

See Also

AddHandler Statement, RemoveHandler Statement

Aggregate Query Expression Operator (LINQ)

C# does not include a direct equivalent for Visual Basic's *Aggregate* query expression operator. However, you can use LINQ's aggregate extension methods, such as *Sum*, to generate an aggregated result.

VISUAL BASIC
```
Dim taxPaid = Aggregate order In AllOrders
              Into Sum(order.SalesTax)
```

C#
```
var taxPaid = (from order in AllOrders
              select order.SalesTax).Sum();
```

For aggregates by group, use the *group* operator, which parallels Visual Basic's own *Group* operator.

VISUAL BASIC
```
Dim stateCustomers = From customer In AllCustomers
                     Group By customer.State
                     Into Total = Count()
                     Order By State
```

C#
```
var stateCustomers = from customer in AllCustomers
                     group customer by customer.State
                     into aggregate
                     select new
                     {
```

```
                    State = aggregate.Key,
                    Total = aggregate.Count()
              } into results
              orderby results.State
              select results;
```

See Also

Query Expressions

And Conjunction Operator

In general, C#'s & operator is identical to Visual Basic's And operator, both for integer (bitwise) and Boolean (logical) operations.

VISUAL BASIC
```
Dim clapHands As Boolean = (happy And knowIt)
```

C#
```
bool clapHands = (happy & knowIt);
```

When applying *Option Strict Off* to a Visual Basic project or source file, using the And operator with one integer operand and one Boolean operand forces the Boolean value to an integer (*0* or *-1*), and then performs a bitwise operation. C# does not allow this mixture of operand types.

AndAlso Conjunction Operator

C#'s && operator is generally identical to Visual Basic's AndAlso short-circuiting conjunction operator.

VISUAL BASIC
```
If ((result IsNot Nothing) AndAlso
      (result.Length > 10)) Then
```

C#
```
if ((result != null) && (result.Length > 10))
```

Anonymous Methods

See

Lambda Expressions

Anonymous Types

Visual Basic uses the *New* and *With* operators to define a new anonymous type.

VISUAL BASIC
```
Dim samplePerson = New With {.Name = "John", .Age = 42}
```

C# uses a similar syntax with its *new* operator. The period that appears before each VB field is not included in the C# equivalent.

C#

```
var samplePerson = new {Name = "John", Age = 42};
```

VB also allows you to specify which anonymous type properties are "key" properties, those that can be used for testing for equivalence between two instances.

VISUAL BASIC

```
Dim samplePerson = New With {Key .ID = 123,
    .Name = "John", .Age = 42}
```

C# does not include support for these key fields. Instead, you must create a standard named type, and provide your own custom overrides for the *Equals* and *GetHashCode* base methods.

See Also

Initializers, New Operator

AppActivate Method

C# does not include an equivalent for Visual Basic's *AppActivate* method. The following code defines two methods that provide functionality that is comparable to what *AppActivate* provides.

C#

```
[System.RunTime.InteropServices.
    DllImportAttribute("User32.dll")]
private static extern int SetForegroundWindow(int hWnd);

private void AppActivate(string windowTitle)
{
    System.Diagnostics.Process[] allProcesses =
        System.Diagnostics.Process.GetProcesses();
    var targetProcess = from oneProcess in allProcesses
        where oneProcess.MainWindowTitle == windowTitle
        select oneProcess;
    if (targetProcess != null)
        SetForegroundWindow(targetProcess.First().
        MainWindowHandle.ToInt32());
}

private void AppActivate(int processID)
{
    System.Diagnostics.Process targetProcess =
        System.Diagnostics.Process.
        GetProcessById(processID);
    if (targetProcess != null)
        SetForegroundWindow(targetProcess.
        MainWindowHandle.ToInt32());
}
```

Arguments and Parameters

Parameters are those identifiers that are defined with a method, and through which data can be passed into that method. Arguments are the data elements or variables passed through the parameters when the method is called.

VISUAL BASIC

```
' ----- Parameters: hour and minute.
Public Function FormatTime(ByVal hour As Integer,
        ByVal minute As Integer) As String
    Return String.Format("{0:0}:{1:00}", hour, minute)
End Function

' ----- Later, the arguments are passed to the method.
businessStart = FormatTime(5, 30)
```

Both Visual Basic and C# support similar features for working with parameters and arguments. By default, all comma-delimited arguments are passed by-value into the matching parameters. To change this default in Visual Basic, use the *ByRef* modifier. In C#, use the *ref* or *out* pass-by-reference modifiers to provide bidirectional and out-only reference content passing, respectively. In VB, the data type for each parameter appears in an *As* clause after the identifier. C# places the data type by itself just before the identifier.

VISUAL BASIC

```
' ----- Parameters are:
'          content:  in/out by-reference
'          method:   by-value
'          warnings: in/out by-reference
Public Function CorrectContent(ByRef content As String,
    ByVal method As Integer, ByRef warnings As String)
```

C#

```
// ----- Parameters are:
//          content:  in/out by-reference
//          method:   by-value
//          warnings: out-only by-reference
public bool CorrectContent(ref string content,
        int method, out string warnings)
```

Normally, you can simply use C#'s *ref* modifier in place of the Visual Basic *ByRef* modifier. If you know that data will never be passed in through that parameter, and will only have data sent out, you can use the *out* modifier instead. When passing values by reference, the calling code must have already assigned a value to the argument being passed. In C#, the calling code applies the *out* or *ref* modifier to match the one in the parameter list, something not needed in VB.

VISUAL BASIC

```
' ----- userContent must have been assigned a value.
success = CorrectContent(userContent, 3, warningText)
```

C#

```
// ----- userContent must have been assigned a value.
success = CorrectContent(ref userContent, 3,
    out warningText);
```

Both languages support optional arguments and parameter arrays. See the "Optional Modifier" and "ParamArray Modifier" entries in this chapter. Named arguments are also valid in both languages. See the ":= Named Argument Indicator" entry in this chapter.

See Also

, Punctuator, := Named Argument Indicator, ByRef Modifier, Methods, Optional Modifier, ParamArray Modifier

Arrays

See

( ) Array Declaration

As Clause

Note

This entry discusses the *As* clause that appears after the *Of* clause in generic declarations. For information about the *As* clause used in variable and constant declarations and method parameter lists, see the following entries in this chapter: "Arguments and Parameters," "Const Statement," "Dim Statement," "Fields," and "Variables."

In Visual Basic generics, conditions can be placed on type parameters with the *As* clause.

VISUAL BASIC

```
' ----- Clause applied to one type parameter.
Class SingleGeneric(Of T As IEnumerable)

' ----- Constraints applied to two type parameters
'       requires two As clauses.
Class DoubleGeneric(Of T As IEnumerable, U As IDisposable)
```

In C#, the *where* clause replicates VB's *As* clause, and appears immediately after the type parameter being constrained.

C#

```
// ----- Clause applied to one type parameter.
class SingleGeneric<T> where T : IEnumerable

// ----- Constraints applied to two type parameters
//       requires two where clauses.
class DoubleGeneric<T, U>
    where T : IEnumerable
    where U : IDisposable
```

Multiple constraints appear as a comma-delimited list. C# does not require the surrounding curly braces used in Visual Basic.

VISUAL BASIC
```
Class ComplexGeneric(Of T As {class, IDisposable})
```

C#
```
class ComplexGeneric<T> where T : class, IDisposable
```

Both languages support the same types of constraints on parameters. The following table lists the equivalent constraints.

Constraint	Visual Basic	C#
Specific type	Customer	Customer
Specific interface	IEnumerable	IEnumerable
Another type parameter	U	U
Any class	Class	class
Any structure	Structure	struct
Class with default constructor	New	new()

See Also

Generics

Asc Method

Visual Basic's *Asc* method converts a character (or the first character of a longer string) to its integer equivalent, taking into account single-byte and double-byte character set rules for the current platform and language encoding. The following code provides a C# equivalent for the conversion performed by *Asc*.

C#
```
public int Asc(char oneChar)
{
    // ----- Convert char to integer,
    //       taking character set into account.
    int charAsInt;
    System.Text.Encoding charSize;
    char[] asArray;
    byte[] asBytes;
    int length;
    byte holdByte;

    // ----- Seven-bit values are simple.
    charAsInt = Convert.ToInt32(oneChar);
    if (charAsInt < 128)
        return charAsInt;

    // ----- Convert the character to raw bytes.
    charSize = System.Text.Encoding.Default;
    asArray = new char[] {oneChar};
    asBytes = new byte[2];
    length = charSize.GetBytes(asArray, 0, 1, asBytes, 0);
```

```
// ----- SBCS or single-byte character from DBCS.
if ((charSize.IsSingleByte) | (length == 1))
    return asBytes[0];

// ----- Double-byte character set from now on.
if (System.BitConverter.IsLittleEndian)
{
    // ----- Platform bytes are reversed internally.
    holdByte = asBytes[0];
    asBytes[0] = asBytes[1];
    asBytes[1] = holdByte;
}
return System.BitConverter.ToInt16(asBytes, 0);
}
```

The related *AscW* method performs a similar conversion, but in a more platform-neutral way. See the "AscW Method" entry in this chapter for more information.

See Also

AscW Method

AscW Method

Visual Basic's *AscW* returns the character passed to it, or the first character of the string passed to it, converted to an *Integer*. The same thing can be done directly with casts in C#.

VISUAL BASIC
```
' ----- Both of these return the integer value of "A"
Dim charVal As Integer = AscW("A"c)   ' Char version
Dim strVal As Integer = AscW("ABC")   ' String version
```

C#
```
// ----- Both of these return the integer value of "A"
int charVal = (int)'A';            // Char version
int strVal = (int)("ABC"[0]);      // String version
```

The related *Asc* method performs a similar conversion, but takes single-byte and double-byte character set rules into account. See the "Asc Method" entry in this chapter for more information.

See Also

Asc Method

Assembly Modifier

See

Attributes

Assignment Operators

Both Visual Basic and C# include multiple assignment operators, each applying a specific operation on the right-hand value before assigning it to the left hand result.

Operator	Visual Basic	C#
Addition	`+=`	`+=`
Assignment	`=`	`=`
Concatenation	`&=`	`+=`
Conjunction	Not supported	`&=`
Disjunction	Not supported	`|=`
Division	`/=`	`/=`
Event Subscription	Not supported	`+=`
Event Unsubscription	Not supported	`-=`
Exclusive-Or	Not supported	`^=`
Exponentiation	`^=`	Not supported
Integer Division	`\=`	Not supported
Left-Shift	`<<=`	`<<=`
Modulo	Not supported	`%=`
Multiplication	`*=`	`*=`
Right-Shift	`>>=`	`>>=`
Subtraction	`-=`	`-=`

For information about these operators, see their entries in this chapter.

C# allows multiple occurrences of assignment operators in a single statement, a syntax not supported by Visual Basic.

C#
```
// ----- Both b and c receive a's value.
int a = 5, b = 10, c = 15;
c = b = a;

// ----- This more unusual use of assignment
//       is still valid.
int d = 5, e = 10, f = 15;
f -= e -= d;
// Result: d-->5, e-->5, f-->10
```

Associativity

See

   Operator Precedence and Associativity

Async Modifier

C#'s `async` modifier is identical in use and purpose to Visual Basic's `Async` modifier, for both standard and anonymous methods.

```
Public Async Function ProcessBuffer() As Task(Of Integer)
    ' ----- At least one Await appears in code.
End Function
```

C#

```
public async Task<int> ProcessBuffer()
{
    // ----- At least one await appears in code.
}
```

See Also

Await Operator

Asynchronous Processing

See

Async Modifier, Await Operator

Attributes

Both Visual Basic and C# allow attributes to be attached to types, members, or an entire assembly. VB attributes appear in angle brackets; C# uses square brackets. In both languages, if the defined attribute name ends in "Attribute," that portion can be left off when using the attribute.

VISUAL BASIC

```
<System.Obsolete("Use Creature Class Instead")>
Class Animal
End Class
```

C#

```
[System.Obsolete("Use Creature Class Instead")]
class Animal
{
}
```

In both languages, multiple attributes can appear in separate sets of brackets, or separated by commas within a single set of brackets. When an attribute accepts arguments, you can specify named arguments or initializers with an : = sign in Visual Basic, or = in C#.

VISUAL BASIC

```
<AttributeUsage(AttributeTargets.Class,
    AllowMultiple:=True)>
```

C#

```
[AttributeUsage(AttributeTargets.Class,
    AllowMultiple=true)]
```

Normally, an attribute appears just before the item it modifies. In some cases, it may be necessary to specify the target of the attribute. In both languages, indicate the target with a prefix immediately after the opening bracket.

VISUAL BASIC
```
' ----- This attribute is for the whole assembly.
<Assembly: AssemblyVersion("1.0.0.0")>
```

C#
```
// ----- This attribute is for the whole assembly.
[assembly: AssemblyVersion("1.0.0.0")]
```

C# supports more target prefixes than does Visual Basic. The following table lists the targets available as prefixes in both languages.

Visual Basic	C#	Applies to
Assembly	assembly	Entire assembly
Module	module	Current assembly module (not a VB Module)
Not supported	event	Events
Not supported	field	Type-level fields
Not supported	method	Methods, property getters or setters
Not supported	param	Method or property parameters
Not supported	property	Properties
Not supported	return	Return values for methods, indexers, or properties
Not supported	type	Classes, structures, VB modules, interfaces, enumerations, or delegates

When a prefix is not available in VB, you can only associate it with the target by placing the attribute immediately before that target. For return values in Visual Basic, place the attribute between the As keyword and the data type that follows it in the method's signature.

Automatic Properties

In Visual Basic, automatic properties (also known as "auto-implemented properties") include a property name and data type, but no implementation.

VISUAL BASIC
```
Public Property CoreName As String
```

C# uses a similar trimmed down property declaration syntax to create automatic properties.

C#
```
public string CoreName { get; set; }
```

New with Visual Studio 2015
Before 2015, Visual Basic did not support read-only automatic properties. Instead, it was necessary to create a normal property with the ReadOnly modifier, and leave out the setter code. However, its 2015 release added support for read-only auto-properties. C# already supported such read-only automatic properties.

VISUAL BASIC
```
' ----- Before the 2015 release.
Public ReadOnly Property CoreName() As String
    Get
        ' ----- Property-specific logic here.
    End Get
End Property

' ----- Starting with the 2015 release.
Public ReadOnly Property CoreName As String
```
C#
```
public string CoreName { get; }
```

New with Visual Studio 2015
In Visual Basic, you can initialize a read-write automatic property as part of the declaration, without needing to perform that step in a constructor. Beginning in 2015, VB also enabled such initializations for read-only auto-properties. C# also gained the ability to initialize both read-only and read-write automatic properties as part of their declarations with its 2015 release.

VISUAL BASIC
```
' ----- Read-write property.
Public Property CoreName As String = "Unknown"

' ----- Read-only property.
Public ReadOnly Property CoreName As String = "Unknown"
```
C#
```
// ----- Read-write property.
public string CoreName { get; set; } = "Unknown";

// ----- Read-only property.
public string CoreName { get; } = "Unknown";
```
Both languages now also permit assignment to read-only automatic properties within a constructor.

See Also

Properties

Await Operator

C#'s *await* operator is identical to Visual Basic's *Await* operator.

VISUAL BASIC
```
' ----- The long version.
Dim theTask As Task(Of String) = SomeMethodAsync()
Dim result As String = Await theTask

' ----- The short version.
Dim result As String = Await SomeMethodAsync()
```

C#

```
// ----- The long version.
Task<string> theTask = SomeMethodAsync();
string result = await theTask;

// ----- The short version.
string result = await SomeMethodAsync();
```

> **New with Visual Studio 2015**
> Starting in 2015, C#'s *await* operator can be used in the *catch* and *finally*
> blocks of a *try* statement, although this option is not yet supported in Visual Basic.

See Also

Async Modifier

Beep Method

To initiate a system beep in C#, use the *Console.Beep* method.

VISUAL BASIC
```
Beep()
```

C#
```
System.Console.Beep();
```

Bitwise Operators

See

Operators

Boolean Data Type

C#'s intrinsic *bool* data type is identical to Visual Basic's *Boolean* data type. Both
types are aliases for .NET's *System.Boolean* type. For Boolean literals, C# uses
true and *false* in all lowercase. Although VB is not case-sensitive, the traditional
literals are *True* and *False* with an initial capital.

VISUAL BASIC
```
Dim finished As Boolean = False
```

C#
```
bool finished = false;
```

When converting or casting a Boolean value to an integer in Visual Basic, *False* always
becomes zero, as in C#. However, for historical reasons, *True* becomes *1* or *-1*
depending on the method used to convert or cast the value.

VISUAL BASIC
```
Dim byDotNet As Integer = Convert.ToInt32(True)    ' --> 1
Dim byIntrinsic As Integer = CInt(True)            ' --> -1
```

```
' ----- Next two require Option Strict Off
Dim byMath As Integer = Int(True)          ' --> 1
Dim byImplicit As Integer = True           ' --> -1
```

When performing similar conversions in C#, *true* always becomes *1* (one).

ByRef Modifier

C#'s *ref* modifier is equivalent to Visual Basic's *ByRef* modifier, both indicating that an argument is to be passed by reference instead of by value.

VISUAL BASIC
```
Public Function ModifyDate(
        ByRef activeDate As Date) As Boolean
    ' ----- Use or update activeDate as needed.
End Function
```

C#
```
public bool ModifyDate(ref DateTime activeDate)
{
    // ----- Use or update activeDate as needed.
}
```

C# also includes an *out* modifier that is a unidirectional version of *ref*, allowing data to be passed out from the called method, but not sent in. Within the method, the *out* parameter must be assigned a return value. Visual Basic does not include an equivalent feature.

C#
```
public bool ConfirmChanges(out string correctionDetails)
{
    // ----- Set correctionDetails before exiting.
}
```

When calling a method in C# that includes a *ref* or *out* parameter, the calling code must also use the *ref* or *out* modifier on the passed argument.

C#
```
// ----- workingDate must be previously assigned a value.
result = ModifyDate(ref workingDate);
```

In Visual Basic, a property can be passed to a method by reference, something not supported in C#.

See Also

Arguments and Parameters, Generics

Byte Data Type

C#'s intrinsic *byte* data type is identical to Visual Basic's *Byte* data type. Both types are aliases for .NET's *System.Byte* type.

VISUAL BASIC
```
Dim smallCount As Byte = 1
```

C#

```
byte smallCount = 1;
```

ByVal Modifier

C# does not include an equivalent modifier for Visual Basic's *ByVal* modifier. The absence of a modifier when defining the C# parameter is sufficient to indicate that it uses a pass-by-value mechanism.

VISUAL BASIC

```
Public Sub LogError(ByVal errorText As String)
```

C#

```
public void LogError(string errorText)
```

Call Statement

C# does not include an equivalent to Visual Basic's *Call* statement. In general, the equivalent C# code parallels the VB version, but without the *Call* keyword.

VISUAL BASIC

```
Call New ActionClass().ActionMethod()
```

C#

```
(new ActionClass()).ActionMethod();
```

CallByName Method

Visual Basic's *CallByName* method lets you call an instance's method or property accessor by passing the member name as a string, and any arguments as an array. C# does not include a direct equivalent for *CallByName*, but you can use .NET's *MethodInfo* and *PropertyInfo* classes (both in the *System.Reflection* namespace) to provide similar functionality.

VISUAL BASIC

```
' ----- Set a property value (TextBox1.Text).
CallByName(TextBox1, "Text", CallType.Set, "Success")

' ----- Get a property value (TextBox1.Visible).
Dim isShowing As Boolean = CBool(CallByName(TextBox1,
    "Visible", CallType.Get))

' ----- Call a method (TextBox1.Clear).
CallByName(TextBox1, "Clear", CallType.Method)
```

C#

```
// ----- Set a property value (TextBox1.Text).
PropertyInfo textProperty =
    typeof(TextBox).GetProperty("Text");
textProperty.SetValue(TextBox1, "Success", null);
```

```
// ----- Get a property value (TextBox1.Visible).
PropertyInfo visibleProperty =
    typeof(TextBox).GetProperty("Visible");
bool isShowing = (bool)visibleProperty.GetValue(
    TextBox1, null);

// ----- Call a method (TextBox1.Clear).
MethodInfo clearMethod =
    typeof(TextBox).GetMethod("Clear");
clearMethod.Invoke(TextBox1, null);
```

C# also supports traditional late binding through the *dynamic* type.

Case Clause

See

> Select Case Statement

Casting

See

> Conversion and Casting

Catch Clause

See

> Try Statement

CBool Conversion Operator

C# does not have an exact replacement for Visual Basic's *CBool* operator. Instead, it has several similar features that can convert from other data types to *bool*.

VISUAL BASIC
```
result = CBool(originalValue)
```

C#
```
// ----- Casting with exception on failure.
result = (bool)originalValue;

// ----- Casting with null return on failure.
nullableResult = originalValue as bool?;

// ----- System.Convert functions offer the
//       most flexibility.
result = System.Convert.ToBoolean(originalValue);

// ----- Parse works on strings of "true" or "false".
result = System.Boolean.Parse(originalValue);
```

See Also

Conversion and Casting

CByte Conversion Operator

C# does not have an exact replacement for Visual Basic's *CByte* operator. Instead, it has several similar features that can convert from other data types to *byte*.

VISUAL BASIC
```
result = CByte(originalValue)
```

C#
```
// ----- Casting with exception on failure.
result = (byte)originalValue;

// ----- Casting with null return on failure.
nullableResult = originalValue as byte?;

// ----- System.Convert functions offer the
//       most flexibility.
result = System.Convert.ToByte(originalValue);

// ----- Parse works on numeric strings.
result = System.Byte.Parse(originalValue);
```

See Also

Conversion and Casting

CChar Conversion Operator

C# does not have an exact replacement for Visual Basic's *CChar* operator. Instead, it has several similar features that can convert from other data types to *char*.

VISUAL BASIC
```
result = CChar(originalValue)
```

C#
```
// ----- Casting with exception on failure.
result = (char)originalValue;

// ----- Casting with null return on failure.
nullableResult = originalValue as char?;

// ----- System.Convert functions offer the
//       most flexibility.
result = System.Convert.ToChar(originalValue);

// ----- Parse works on numeric strings.
result = System.Char.Parse(originalValue);
```

See Also

Conversion and Casting

CDate Conversion Operator

C# does not have an exact replacement for Visual Basic's `CDate` operator. Instead, it has several similar features that can convert from other data types to `DateTime`.

VISUAL BASIC
```
result = CDate(originalValue)
```

C#
```
// ----- Casting with exception on failure.
result = (DateTime)originalValue;

// ----- Casting with null return on failure.
nullableResult = originalValue as DateTime?;

// ----- System.Convert functions offer the
//       most flexibility.
result = System.Convert.ToDateTime(originalValue);

// ----- Parse works on strings with date content.
result = System.DateTime.Parse(originalValue);
```

See Also

Conversion and Casting

CDbl Conversion Operator

C# does not have an exact replacement for Visual Basic's `CDbl` operator. Instead, it has several similar features that can convert from other data types to `double`.

VISUAL BASIC
```
result = CDbl(originalValue)
```

C#
```
// ----- Casting with exception on failure.
result = (double)originalValue;

// ----- Casting with null return on failure.
nullableResult = originalValue as double?;

// ----- System.Convert functions offer the
//       most flexibility.
result = System.Convert.ToDouble(originalValue);

// ----- Parse works on numeric strings.
result = System.Double.Parse(originalValue);
```

See Also

Conversion and Casting

CDec Conversion Operator

C# does not have an exact replacement for Visual Basic's *CDec* operator. Instead, it has several similar features that can convert from other data types to *decimal*.

VISUAL BASIC
```
result = CDec(originalValue)
```

C#
```
// ----- Casting with exception on failure.
result = (decimal)originalValue;

// ----- Casting with null return on failure.
nullableResult = originalValue as decimal?;

// ----- System.Convert functions offer the
//       most flexibility.
result = System.Convert.ToDecimal(originalValue);

// ----- Parse works on numeric strings.
result = System.Decimal.Parse(originalValue);
```

See Also

Conversion and Casting

Char Data Type

C#'s intrinsic *char* data type is identical to Visual Basic's *Char* data type. Both types are aliases for .NET's *System.Char* type. In Visual Basic, character literals appear in double quotes, followed by a *c* suffix. C# surrounds *char* literals with single quotes.

VISUAL BASIC
```
Dim digit As Char = "1"c   ' Or "1"C
```

C#
```
char digit = '1';
```

ChDir Method

In C#, the .NET Framework's *SetCurrentDirectory* method accomplishes the same result as Visual Basic's *ChDir* method.

VISUAL BASIC
```
ChDir("C:\temp")
```

C#
```
System.IO.Directory.SetCurrentDirectory("C:\\temp");
```

The *ChDir* method silently adjusts some path expressions into a form recognized by Windows. For example, the method accepts the backslash character (\) by itself to indicate the root of the current directory. In C#, you must use a valid full or relative path when changing directories.

C#
```
if (targetPath.Trim() == "\\")
    targetPath = System.IO.Directory.GetDirectoryRoot(
        System.IO.Directory.GetCurrentDirectory());
System.IO.Directory.SetCurrentDirectory(targetPath);
```

ChDrive Method

In C#, the .NET Framework's *SetCurrentDirectory* method accomplishes the same result as Visual Basic's *ChDrive* method when supplied with a drive letter.

VISUAL BASIC
```
' ----- No colon required; only letter is used.
ChDrive("C")
```

C#
```
// ----- Colon required after drive letter.
System.IO.Directory.SetCurrentDirectory("C:");
```

Choose Method

C# does not include a method that is similar to Visual Basic's *Choose* method. The following code implements a method in C# that provides comparable functionality.

C#
```
public static object Choose(double index,
    params object[] choice)
{
    // ----- Don't bother if there is nothing to choose.
    if ((choice == null) || (choice.Length == 0))
        return null;

    try
    {
        int indexAsInt = Convert.ToInt32(index);
        if ((indexAsInt < 0) |
            (indexAsInt >= choice.Length))
            return null;
        return choice[indexAsInt];
    }
    catch
    {
        return null;
    }
}
```

Chr Method

Visual Basic's *Chr* method converts an integer value to its character equivalent, taking into account single-byte and double-byte character set rules for the current platform and language encoding. The following code provides a C# equivalent for the conversion performed by *Chr*.

C#

```csharp
public char Chr(int oneValue)
{
    // ----- Convert char to integer,
    //       taking character set into account.
    System.Text.Encoding charSize;
    System.Text.Decoder converter;
    int numChars;
    char[] asArray = new char[2];
    byte[] asBytes = new byte[2];

    // ----- Ignore out-of-range values.
    if ((oneValue < -32768) | (oneValue > 65535))
        throw new ArgumentException("Invalid argument.");

    // ----- Seven-bit values are simple.
    if ((oneValue >= 0) & (oneValue <= 127))
        return Convert.ToChar(oneValue);

    try
    {
        // ----- Rules may vary by region.
        charSize = Encoding.GetEncoding(
            System.Threading.Thread.CurrentThread.
            CurrentCulture.TextInfo.ANSICodePage);

        // ----- Single-byte encoding.
        if (charSize.IsSingleByte)
        {
            if ((oneValue < 0) | (oneValue > 255))
                throw new ArgumentException(
                    "Invalid argument.");
        }

        // ----- Same code for single-byte or
        //       double-byte encoding.
        converter = charSize.GetDecoder();
        if ((oneValue >= 0) & (oneValue <= 255))
        {
            asBytes[0] = Convert.ToByte(oneValue & 0xff);
            numChars = converter.GetChars(
                asBytes, 0, 1, asArray, 0);
        }
        else
        {
            asBytes[0] = Convert.ToByte(
                (oneValue & 0xff00) >> 8);
            asBytes[1] = Convert.ToByte(oneValue & 0x00ff);
```

```
            numChars = converter.GetChars(
                asBytes, 0, 2, asArray, 0);
        }
        return asArray[0];
    }
    catch (System.Exception ex)
    {
        throw ex;
    }
}
```

The related *ChrW* method performs a similar conversion, but in a more platform-neutral way. See the "ChrW Method" entry in this chapter for more information.

See Also

ChrW Method

ChrW Method

In C#, use the *Convert.ToChar* method with a mask to return results similar to Visual Basic's *ChrW* method.

VISUAL BASIC
```
Dim result As Char = ChrW(intValue)
```

C#
```
char result = Convert.ToChar(intValue & 0xffff);
```

CInt Conversion Operator

C# does not have an exact replacement for Visual Basic's *CInt* operator. Instead, it has several similar features that can convert from other data types to *int*.

VISUAL BASIC
```
result = CInt(originalValue)
```

C#
```
// ----- Casting with exception on failure.
result = (int)originalValue;

// ----- Casting with null return on failure.
nullableResult = originalValue as int?;

// ----- System.Convert functions offer the
//       most flexibility.
result = System.Convert.ToInt32(originalValue);

// ----- Parse works on numeric strings.
result = System.Int32.Parse(originalValue);
```

See Also

Conversion and Casting

Class Statement

C#'s *class* statement is equivalent to Visual Basic's *Class* statement. When declaring a C# class that derives from another class, or implements an interface, those base types appear in a comma-delimited list following the class name, instead of through distinct *Inherits* or *Implements* statements.

VISUAL BASIC
```
Class ActiveCustomer
    Inherits Customer
    Implements IDisposable
    ' ----- Members appear here.
End Class
```

C#
```
class ActiveCustomer : Customer, IDisposable
{
    // ----- Members appear here.
}
```

Classes in both languages contain the same types of members: constructors, destructors, fields, constants, properties, methods, events, operator overloads and user-defined conversions, default properties (called "indexers" in C#), and nested types (including delegates and enumerations). Many of these members can exist as static or instance members.

Classes support the following modifiers in each language.

Visual Basic Modifier	C# Modifier
Friend	internal
MustInherit	abstract
NonInheritable	sealed
Partial	partial
Private	private
Protected	protected
Protected Friend	protected internal
Public	public
Shadows	new
Not supported	static

Classes in Visual Basic are *Friend* by default, just as classes in C# are *internal* by default. In Visual Basic, fields and constants within classes are *Private* by default, while all other members are *Public* by default. Within C# classes, all members are *private* by default.

See Also

Access Modifiers, Constructors, Destructors, Module Statement

CLng Conversion Operator

C# does not have an exact replacement for Visual Basic's *CLng* operator. Instead, it has several similar features that can convert from other data types to *long*.

VISUAL BASIC
```
result = CLng(originalValue)
```

C#
```
// ----- Casting with exception on failure.
result = (long)originalValue;

// ----- Casting with null return on failure.
nullableResult = originalValue as long?;

// ----- System.Convert functions offer the
//       most flexibility.
result = System.Convert.ToInt64(originalValue);

// ----- Parse works on numeric strings.
result = System.Int64.Parse(originalValue);
```

See Also

Conversion and Casting

CObj Conversion Operator

C# does not have an exact replacement for Visual Basic's *CObj* operator. Instead, use a cast to treat any instance as the underlying *System.Object* type.

VISUAL BASIC
```
result = CObj(originalValue)
```

C#
```
result = (object)originalValue;
```

See Also

Conversion and Casting

Collection Initializers

See

Initializers

Collection Class

Visual Basic's *Collection* class exists for backward compatibility with a class of the same name in pre-.NET editions of the language. Its functionality overlaps some of the collections in the *System.Collections* and *System.Collections.Generic* namespaces.

For collections that require a dictionary key, consider the `Hashtable` class from the `System.Collections` namespace. The `ArrayList` collection from that same namespace provides comparable functionality, but without a dictionary-key requirement. For strongly typed collections, consider the classes in the `System.Collections.Generic` namespace instead.

Command Method

Visual Basic's `Command` method returns a single string that includes all command-line arguments used to initiate the application. In C#, use the command-line-related features of the `System.Environment` class to obtain the same content.

VISUAL BASIC
```
Dim result As String = Command()
```

C#
```
string result = string.Join(" ",
    Environment.GetCommandLineArgs());
```

The previous C# example strips out redundant whitespace between arguments. If you need to access the raw command line text, including the program name, use the `CommandLine` property instead.

C#
```
string result = Environment.CommandLine;
```

Comments

In Visual Basic, all comments begin with a comment marker, either the single quote symbol (') or the `REM` keyword. The comment continues through the end of the physical line. C# includes this same type of comment, with a pair of slash characters (//) used as the comment marker.

C#
```
// This is a full-line comment.
int counter; // A line-ending comment
```

C# also supports an alternate comment syntax that can span multiple lines, or can appear in the middle of a line, surrounded by valid C# statements. Such spans of content appear within a set of /* and */ symbols.

C#
```
/* ----- Here is a multi-line comment that ends
 *        when the closing comment symbol appears.
 */
int /* A comment within a statement. */ counter;
```

As with Visual Basic, C# does not support nested comments.

See Also

' Comment Symbol, XML Documentation Comments

Compiler Constants

Both Visual Basic and C# include project-level support for the *DEBUG* and *TRACE* compiler constants. Code throughout the .NET Framework responds to these constants, and you can use them in your own code. To alter the default settings, set the Define DEBUG Constant and Define TRACE Constant fields as needed. In VB, these fields appear in the Advanced Compile Options area of the Project Properties' Compile tab. In C#, they appear on the Build tab.

Visual Basic defines four (or up to nine) additional constants.

Constant	Description
CONFIG	The active build configuration, typically "Debug" or "Release."
TARGET	The compiled application type, one of: "winexe," "exe," "library," or "module." Other custom values are also possible.
VBC_VER	The current version of Visual Basic, in *major.minor* format. One of the following values: 8.0 (VB2005), 9.0 (VB2008 and VB2010), 11.0 (VB2012), 12.0 (VB2013), or 14.0 (VB2015).
_MYTYPE	The version of the My pseudo-namespace in use. Depending on the value of this constant, the compiler may define one or more of the following additional constants: *_MYAPPLICATIONTYPE*, *_MYCOMPUTERTYPE*, *_MYFORMS*, *_MYUSERTYPE*, and *_MYWEBSERVICES*.

C# does not automatically define equivalents for these constants.

Const Statement

Both C# and Visual Basic support the declaration of constants at the local and type levels. The syntax of VB's *Const* statement closely parallels standard variable declaration, replacing *Dim* with *Const*. C#'s syntax similarly follows its own variable declaration, adding *const* before the core declaration.

VISUAL BASIC
```
Const DefaultPort As Integer = 25
```

C#
```
const int DefaultPort = 25;
```

In both languages, you can string multiple constant declarations together with commas. The two languages also support similar rules on what can be assigned to the constant: literals, enumeration values, and other constants, all joined with basic operators.

At the field level, each constant declaration can include an access modifier.

VISUAL BASIC
```
Public Const DefaultPort As Integer = 25
```

C#
```
public const int DefaultPort = 25;
```

If `Option Infer On` is used, Visual Basic will infer the data type of the expression when possible, removing the need for a specific type.

```
Const DefaultPort = 25
```

C# requires that a data type be indicated for every constant. Additionally, some constant declarations are not permitted in C# due to boxing or other reference issues.

```
// ----- This code will not compile:
const object usesBoxing = 10;
const object implicitReference = "Message";
```

Such declarations are permitted in Visual Basic.

Constants Class

The `Microsoft.VisualBasic.Constants` class contains miscellaneous constants useful to Visual Basic developers. Most of these constants are useful only in relation to other VB features that aren't found in C#. There are a few constants, such as `vbCrLf`, that have special string-based equivalents in C#. For information on these constants, see the "ControlChars Class" entry in this chapter.

ControlChars Class

The `Microsoft.VisualBasic.ControlChars` class exposes several fields that represent special characters, such as a carriage return or backspace character. The related `Microsoft.VisualBasic.Constants` class includes these same characters, and they appear in VB code with more frequency than the equivalent `ControlChars` members. Both sets of fields have equivalents in C# string escape sequences.

```
Dim backspace As String = vbBack
```

```
string backspace = "\b";
```

The following table lists the fields in the `ControlChars` class, the matching members of the `Constants` class, and the equivalent escape sequence in C# strings.

ControlChars Field	Constants Field	C# Escape Sequence
Back	vbBack	\b
Cr	vbCr	\r
CrLf	vbCrLf	\r\n
FormFeed	vbFormFeed	\f
Lf	vbLf	\n
NewLine	vbNewLine	\r\n
NullChar	vbNullChar	\x00
Quote	Not available	\"
Tab	vbTab	\t

ControlChars Field	Constants Field	C# Escape Sequence
VerticalTab	*vbVerticalTab*	*\v*
Not available	*vbNullString*	*null*

Constructors

In Visual Basic, constructors are always named *New*. In C#, constructors are named for the type in which they appear. Constructors in both languages provide functionality that is generally equivalent. Unlike other type methods, C#'s *void* return type is implied in a constructor. Do not include that keyword in the declaration.

VISUAL BASIC
```
Class Employee
    Public Sub New()
        ' ----- Default constructor.
    End Sub
    Public Sub New(ByVal empName As String)
        ' ----- Custom constructor.
    End Sub
End Class
```

C#
```
class Employee
{
    public Employee()
    {
        // ----- Default constructor.
    }
    public Employee(string empName)
    {
        // ----- Custom constructor.
    }
}
```

By default, the constructor in a derived class calls the default constructor in the base class, if it exists. To call a custom base constructor in Visual Basic, or to call one of the other constructors in the derived class, call the specific constructor as the first line of the new constructor.

VISUAL BASIC
```
Class Employee
    Inherits Person

    Public Sub New(ByVal empName As String)
        ' ----- Base class handles person's name.
        MyBase.New(empName)
    End Sub
    Public Sub New(ByVal empName As String,
            ByVal salary As Decimal)
        ' ----- Another constructor handles the name.
        Me.New(empName)
```

```
        ' ----- Salary-specific code here.
    End Sub
End Class
```

To call a custom base constructor in C#, or to use another custom constructor as the starting point for a constructor, use the *base* and *this* constructor declarations, respectively. They appear after the constructor signature, separated by a colon.

C#
```
class Employee : Person
{
    public Employee(string empName) : base(empName)
    {
        // ----- Base class handles person's name.
    }
    public Employee(string empName,
        decimal salary) : this(empName)
    {
        // ----- Salary-specific code here.
    }
}
```

Both languages offer static constructors in addition to instance constructors.

VISUAL BASIC
```
Class Utility
    Shared Sub New()
        ' ----- Static class initialization here.
    End Sub
End Class
```

C#
```
class Utility
{
    static Utility()
    {
        // ----- Static class initialization here.
    }
}
```

Constructors support the following modifiers in each language.

Visual Basic Modifier	C# Modifier
Friend	internal
Private	private
Protected	protected
Protected Friend	protected internal
Public	public
Shared	static
Not supported	extern

Continue Statement

Visual Basic uses one of three distinct forms of its *Continue* statement, depending on the containing loop type.

- *For* and *For Each* loops use the *Continue For* statement.
- *Do* loops use the *Continue Do* statement.
- *While* loops use the *Continue While* statement.

VISUAL BASIC

```
For counter = 0 To 9
    ' ----- Some code, then...
    Continue For
    ' ----- More code.
Next counter
```

C# uses a single *continue* statement to begin the next iteration of a loop construct. The type of loop is not important; the statement always initiates the next iteration of the innermost loop.

C#

```
for (counter = 0; counter < 10; counter++)
{
    // ----- Some code, then...
    continue;
    // ----- More code.
}
```

Because Visual Basic lets you identify a specific loop type, it is possible to move to the next iteration of a loop containing the innermost loop.

VISUAL BASIC

```
For counter As Integer = 0 To 9
    Do While (content.Length > 0)
        ' ----- This will exit the Do loop, and move
        '       to the next iteration of the For loop.
        Continue For
    Loop
Next counter
```

C#'s combined *continue* statement doesn't support this level of jumping. Instead, you must use other methods, such as a *goto* statement, to exit the innermost loop.

C#

```
for (int counter = 0; counter < 10; counter++)
{
    while (content.Length > 0)
    {
        // ----- This will exit the while loop, and move
        //       to the next iteration of the for loop.
        goto NextIteration;
    }
```

```
        // ----- Any code here will be skipped by goto.

NextIteration:
    ; // ----- Innermost jump comes here.
}
```

Conversion and Casting

Visual Basic supports (1) implicit (widening) casting or conversion of data, such as from *Integer* to *Long*; (2) enhanced implicit conversions of data when *Option Strict Off* is used; and (3) explicit casting or conversion of data through VB's intrinsic conversion operators (such as *CInt*), the *DirectCast* operator, the *TryCast* operator, and .NET Framework features, such as those from the *System.Convert* class.

Implicit Conversions

Conversions from "smaller" to "larger" data types, including overloaded conversions defined as *Widening* (VB) or *implicit* (C#), occur automatically in both languages.

VISUAL BASIC
```
Dim smallValue As Integer = 25
Dim largeValue As Long = smallValue   ' Widening conversion
```

C#
```
int smallValue = 25;
long largeValue = smallValue;   // Implicit conversion
```

In Visual Basic, when the *Option Strict Off* statement is used at the file or project level, explicit (narrowing) conversions can also occur automatically in code, although run-time errors may result if the source data does not "fit" in the target.

VISUAL BASIC
```
' ----- At the top of the file.
Option Strict Off

' ----- In a method.
Dim largeValue As Long = 100000
Dim smallValue As Integer = largeValue   ' Narrowing
```

When using this non-strict mode, Visual Basic also performs some string-to-number and number-to-string conversions automatically.

VISUAL BASIC
```
' ----- Assumes: Option Strict Off
Dim trueNumber As Integer = "123"   ' Auto-conversion
Dim trueString As String = 123      ' Auto-conversion
If (trueNumber = trueString) Then
    ' ----- VB performs the conversion and comparison
            of the two variables automatically. The
    '       code will reach this conditional block.
End If
```

C# supports none of these "enhanced" implicit conversions. C# has no equivalent for `Option Strict Off`, and all such non-strict conversions must be performed explicitly, as described below.

Explicit Conversions

For intrinsic value types, Visual Basic offers built-in conversion functions, such as `CInt` to convert an expression to an `Integer`.

VISUAL BASIC
```
Dim largeValue As Long = 100000
Dim smallValue As Integer = CInt(largeValue)
```

In C#, the comparable language feature for these explicit conversions is the cast operator, which places the target data type in a set of parentheses before the source expression.

C#
```
long largeValue = 100000;
int smallValue = (int)largeValue;
```

The following table lists the Visual Basic conversion functions, and shows how they relate to specific C# casts.

Visual Basic Conversion	C# Cast
CBool *(expression)*	(bool)
CByte *(expression)*	(byte)
CChar *(expression)*	(char)
CDate *(expression)*	(DateTime)
CDbl *(expression)*	(double)
CDec *(expression)*	(decimal)
CInt *(expression)*	(int)
CLng *(expression)*	(long)
CObj *(expression)*	(object)
CSByte *(expression)*	(sbyte)
CShort *(expression)*	(short)
CSng *(expression)*	(float)
CStr *(expression)*	(string)
CType *(expression, type)*	(type)
CUInt *(expression)*	(uint)
CULng *(expression)*	(ulong)
CUShort *(expression)*	(ushort)

These C# casts are not exact replacements for the Visual Basic operators shown here. In many cases, each VB operator performs extra steps to ensure a conversion succeeds where it might fail in the equivalent C# code. For example, many of the numeric conversion operators will strip out currency symbols and grouping symbols silently. These characters would cause a failure in the equivalent C# cast.

VISUAL BASIC
```
' ----- This will succeed, resulting in a value of 1234.
Dim trueNumber As Integer = CInt("$1,234")
```

C#
```
// ----- This will fail.
int trueNumber = (int)"$1,234";
```

Visual Basic's `DirectCast` operator also equates to a standard cast in C# code. VB's `TryCast` operator is similar to `DirectCast`, but it returns `Nothing` when the conversion fails instead of throwing an exception. C# includes the `as` operator, which produces similar `null` results on failure.

VISUAL BASIC
```
' ----- Might return Nothing if conversion fails.
someElephant = TryCast(someAnimal, Elephant)
```

C#
```
// ----- Might return null if conversion fails.
someElephant = someAnimal as Elephant;
```

The .NET Framework includes features that convert data from one type to another. The `System.Convert` type hosts many such static functions. The following table shows `System.Convert` member substitutes for most of the VB conversion operators. These Framework equivalents can be used in C# code.

Visual Basic Conversion	System.Convert Method
CBool *(expression)*	ToBoolean *(expression)*
CByte *(expression)*	ToByte *(expression)*
CChar *(expression)*	ToChar *(expression)*
CDate *(expression)*	ToDateTime *(expression)*
CDbl *(expression)*	ToDouble *(expression)*
CDec *(expression)*	ToDecimal *(expression)*
CInt *(expression)*	ToInt32 *(expression)*
CLng *(expression)*	ToInt64 *(expression)*
CSByte *(expression)*	ToSByte *(expression)*
CShort *(expression)*	ToInt16 *(expression)*
CSng *(expression)*	ToSingle *(expression)*
CStr *(expression)*	ToString *(expression)*
CUInt *(expression)*	ToUInt32 *(expression)*
CULng *(expression)*	ToUInt64 *(expression)*
CUShort *(expression)*	ToUInt16 *(expression)*

The `ToString` method that is included with every .NET object is available equally in C# and Visual Basic.

CreateObject Method

Visual Basic's `CreateObject` method returns a COM instance from an external source. In C#, once the program ID and optional server name have been converted to a valid type, the `System.Activator.CreateInstance` method will instantiate and return the same COM content.

```
' ----- With just a program ID.
Dim external1 As Object = CreateObject(programID)

' ----- With both a program ID and a server name.
Dim external2 As Object = CreateObject(
    programID, serverName)
```

C#
```
// ----- With just a program ID.
Type external1Type = Type.GetTypeFromProgID(programID);
dynamic external1 =
    Activator.CreateInstance(external1Type);

// ----- With both a program ID and a server name.
Type external2Type = Type.GetTypeFromProgID(
    programID, serverName);
dynamic external2 =
    Activator.CreateInstance(external2Type);
```

CSByte Conversion Operator

C# does not have an exact replacement for Visual Basic's *CSByte* operator. Instead, it has several similar features that can convert from other data types to *sbyte*.

VISUAL BASIC
```
result = CSByte(originalValue)
```

C#
```
// ----- Casting with exception on failure.
result = (sbyte)originalValue;

// ----- Casting with null return on failure.
nullableResult = originalValue as sbyte?;

// ----- System.Convert functions offer the
//       most flexibility.
result = System.Convert.ToSByte(originalValue);

// ----- Parse works on numeric strings.
result = System.SByte.Parse(originalValue);
```
See Also

Conversion and Casting

CShort Conversion Operator

C# does not have an exact replacement for Visual Basic's *CShort* operator. Instead, it has several similar features that can convert from other data types to *short*.

VISUAL BASIC
```
result = CShort(originalValue)
```

C#
```
// ----- Casting with exception on failure.
result = (short)originalValue;

// ----- Casting with null return on failure.
nullableResult = originalValue as short?;

// ----- System.Convert functions offer the
//       most flexibility.
result = System.Convert.ToInt16(originalValue);

// ----- Parse works on numeric strings.
result = System.Int16.Parse(originalValue);
```

See Also

Conversion and Casting

CSng Conversion Operator

C# does not have an exact replacement for Visual Basic's *CSng* operator. Instead, it has several similar features that can convert from other data types to *float*.

VISUAL BASIC
```
result = CSng(originalValue)
```

C#
```
// ----- Casting with exception on failure.
result = (float)originalValue;

// ----- Casting with null return on failure.
nullableResult = originalValue as float?;

// ----- System.Convert functions offer the
//       most flexibility.
result = System.Convert.ToSingle(originalValue);

// ----- Parse works on numeric strings.
result = System.Single.Parse(originalValue);
```

See Also

Conversion and Casting

CStr Conversion Operator

C# does not have an exact replacement for Visual Basic's *CStr* operator. Instead, it has several similar features that can convert from other data types to *string*.

VISUAL BASIC
```
result = CStr(originalValue)
```

C#
```
// ----- Casting with exception on failure.
result = (string)originalValue;

// ----- Casting with null return on failure.
result = originalValue as string;

// ----- System.Convert functions offer the
//       most flexibility.
result = System.Convert.ToString(originalValue);

// ----- ToString method is available on all types.
result = originalValue.ToString();
```

All instances in .NET include a *ToString* method that can generate a string version of the instance content. The format of the resulting string varies by type, and some *ToString* methods include arguments that let you adjust the result.

Casting directly from a *char* value to a *string* value is not permitted. Use the *char* instance's *ToString* method to generate a string version of the character.

See Also

Conversion and Casting

CType Conversion Operator

C# does not have an exact replacement for Visual Basic's *CType* operator. Instead, it includes casting features that let you convert from one data type to another.

VISUAL BASIC
```
result = CType(originalValue, NewType)
```

C#
```
// ----- Casting with exception on failure.
result = (NewType)originalValue;

// ----- Casting with null return on failure.
result = originalValue as NewType;
```

See Also

Conversion and Casting

CUInt Conversion Operator

C# does not have an exact replacement for Visual Basic's *CUInt* operator. Instead, it has several similar features that can convert from other data types to *uint*.

VISUAL BASIC
```
result = CUInt(originalValue)
```

C#
```
// ----- Casting with exception on failure.
result = (uint)originalValue;
```

```
// ----- Casting with null return on failure.
nullableResult = originalValue as uint?;

// ----- System.Convert functions offer the
//       most flexibility.
result = System.Convert.ToUInt32(originalValue);

// ----- Parse works on numeric strings.
result = System.UInt32.Parse(originalValue);
```

See Also

Conversion and Casting

CULng Conversion Operator

C# does not have an exact replacement for Visual Basic's *CULng* operator. Instead, it has several similar features that can convert from other data types to *ulong*.

VISUAL BASIC
```
result = CULng(originalValue)
```

C#
```
// ----- Casting with exception on failure.
result = (ulong)originalValue;

// ----- Casting with null return on failure.
nullableResult = originalValue as ulong?;

// ----- System.Convert functions offer the
//       most flexibility.
result = System.Convert.ToUInt64(originalValue);

// ----- Parse works on numeric strings.
result = System.UInt64.Parse(originalValue);
```

See Also

Conversion and Casting

CurDir Method

Visual Basic's *CurDir* method returns the current directory, either on the default drive or on a specified drive letter. In C#, use features in the *System.IO.Path* class to retrieve these same paths.

VISUAL BASIC
```
' ----- On the default drive.
Dim defaultPath As String = CurDir()

' ----- On "E" drive.
Dim drivePath As String = CurDir("E")
```

C#

```
// ----- On the default drive.
string defaultPath = System.IO.Path.GetCurrentDirectory();

// ----- On "E" drive. Follow the letter with ":."
string drivePath = System.IO.Path.GetFullPath("E:.");
```

CUShort Conversion Operator

C# does not have an exact replacement for Visual Basic's *CUShort* operator. Instead, it has several similar features that can convert from other data types to *ushort*.

VISUAL BASIC

```
result = CUShort(originalValue)
```

C#

```
// ----- Casting with exception on failure.
result = (ushort)originalValue;

// ----- Casting with null return on failure.
nullableResult = originalValue as ushort?;

// ----- System.Convert functions offer the
//       most flexibility.
result = System.Convert.ToUInt16(originalValue);

// ----- Parse works on numeric strings.
result = System.UInt16.Parse(originalValue);
```

See Also

Conversion and Casting

Custom Event Statement

Visual Basic's *Custom Event* statement adds custom logic to event subscription, unsubscription, and invocation for a specific delegate. Its *AddHandler*, *RemoveHandler*, and *RaiseEvent* blocks host the custom logic.

VISUAL BASIC

```
' ----- The delegate for the custom event.
Public Delegate Sub SampleEventHandler(
    ByVal sender As Object, ByVal e As SampleEventArgs)

Public Custom Event SampleEvent As SampleEventHandler
    AddHandler(ByVal value As SampleEventHandler)
        ' ----- Custom "add" code here.
    End AddHandler
    RemoveHandler(ByVal value As SampleEventHandler)
        ' ----- Custom "remove" code here.
    End RemoveHandler
```

```
      RaiseEvent(ByVal sender As Object,
            ByVal e As SampleEventArgs)
         ' ----- Custom "raise" code here. The signature
         '          is the same as the delegate signature.
      End RaiseEvent
   End Event
```

An enhanced version of C#'s *event* statement provides similar functionality, allowing custom logic to be invoked when an event handler is added or removed based on a defined delegate. The *add* and *remove* blocks define the event-adding and event-removing logic, respectively. Each block implies a "value" variable, an event handler instance of the delegate type for the event.

C#
```
// ----- The delegate for the custom event.
public delegate void SampleEventHandler(
    object sender, SampleEventArgs e);

public event SampleEventHandler SampleEvent
{
    add { /* Code using "value" here. */ }
    remove { /* Code using "value" here. */ }
}
```

C# does not include an equivalent block for Visual Basic's *RaiseEvent* declaration block.

Custom events support the following modifiers in each language.

Visual Basic Modifier	C# Modifier
Friend	internal
Private	private
Protected	protected
Protected Friend	protected internal
Public	public
Shadows	new
Shared	static
Not supported	abstract
Not supported	extern
Not supported	override
Not supported	sealed
Not supported	virtual

Data Types

C# and Visual Basic share a common set of intrinsic data types, with one exception. The following table shows the matching data types, and the underlying .NET data type for which each intrinsic type is an alias.

Visual Basic Type	C# Type	.NET Type
Boolean	bool	System.Boolean
Byte	byte	System.Byte
Char	char	System.Char
Date	Not supported	System.DateTime
Decimal	decimal	System.Decimal
Double	double	System.Double
Integer	int	System.Int32
Long	long	System.Int64
Object	object	System.Object
SByte	sbyte	System.SByte
Short	short	System.Int16
Single	float	System.Single
String	string	System.String
UInteger	uint	System.UInt32
ULong	ulong	System.UInt64
UShort	ushort	System.UInt16

Visual Basic includes an intrinsic *Date* type, an alias for the framework's *System.DateTime* type. C# does not include a parallel date/time type. Instead, you must use *System.DateTime* directly in C#.

For more information about the intrinsic data types, see their individual entries in this chapter.

Date Data Type

C# does not include intrinsic support for Visual Basic's *Date* data type. Instead, you must use the underlying .NET Framework type *System.DateTime* directly in C# code.

DateAdd Method

Visual Basic's *DateAdd* method returns a *Date* instance based on adding a date or time component to another date expression. An interval string or *DateInterval* enumeration value indicates the type of component to adjust.

VISUAL BASIC
```
' ----- Add three days.
Dim someTimeLater As Date = DateAdd("d", 3, originalDate)

' ----- Or use an enumeration value.
someTimeLater = DateAdd(DateInterval.Day, 3, originalDate)
```

In C#, various methods of the *DateTime* type provide similar functionality.

C#
```
// ----- Add three days.
DateTime someTimeLater = originalDate.AddDays(3);
```

The following table shows matching *DateTime* type methods that provide the same functionality as the various *DateAdd* method interval values.

DateInterval Member	String Interval	DateTime Member
Day	d	AddDays
DayOfYear	y	AddDays
Hour	h	AddHours
Minute	n	AddMinutes
Month	m	AddMonths
Quarter	q	3 * AddMonths
Second	s	AddSeconds
Weekday	w	AddDays
WeekOfYear	ww	7 * AddDays
Year	yyyy	AddYears

DateDiff Method

C# has no direct equivalent for Visual Basic's *DateDiff* method. Instead, many date components can be obtained by subtracting one date from another. This subtraction creates a *TimeSpan* instance, with members representing the different time components.

VISUAL BASIC

```
' ----- Days, hours, minutes, seconds, weeks, years.
Dim days As Long = DateDiff("d", date1, date2)
Dim hours As Long = DateDiff("h", date1, date2)
Dim minutes As Long = DateDiff("n", date1, date2)
Dim seconds As Long = DateDiff("s", date1, date2)
Dim weeks As Long = DateDiff("w", date1, date2)

Dim years As Long = DateDiff("yyyy", date1, date2)
Dim months As Long = DateDiff("m", date1, date2)
Dim quarters As Long = DateDiff("q", date1, date2)
```

C#

```
// ----- Days, hours, minutes, seconds, weeks.
//       All values are fractional, and should be
//       truncated or rounded for whole components.
long days = (long)(date2 - date1).TotalDays;
long hours = (long)(date2 - date1).TotalHours;
long minutes = (long)(date2 - date1).TotalMinutes;
long seconds = (long)(date2 - date1).TotalSeconds;
long weeks = (long)((date2 - date1).TotalDays / 7);

// ----- Years, months, quarters don't require TimeSpan.
long years = date2.Year - date1.Year;
long months = ((date2.Year - date1.Year) * 12) +
    (date2.Month - date1.Month);
long quarters = ((date2.Year - date1.Year) * 4) +
    ((long)(date2.Month / 3) - (long)(date1.Month / 3));
```

DateDiff also calculates a "week of year" difference. It is similar to the standard week calculation, but focuses on whole instead of partial weeks. In C#, adjust each date to the start of its week before subtracting.

VISUAL BASIC

```
' ----- Uses the specified day-of-week.
Dim weeksOfYear As Long = DateDiff("ww", date1, date2,
    FirstDayOfWeek.Sunday)
```

C#

```
// ----- Assumes Sunday as the start of the week.
DateTime startOfWeek1 = date1.AddDays(
    -(int)date1.DayOfWeek);
DateTime startOfWeek2 = date2.AddDays(
    -(int)date2.DayOfWeek);
long weeksOfYear = (long)((startOfWeek2 -
    startOfWeek1).TotalDays / 7);
```

DatePart Method

Visual Basic's *DatePart* method returns one component of a *Date* instance as an integer. For example, the following code returns the year component, and shows the equivalent code in C# using the members of a *DateTime* instance.

VISUAL BASIC

```
Dim whichYear As Integer = DatePart("yyyy", sourceDate)
```

C#

```
int whichYear = sourceDate.Year;
```

The *DatePart* method accepts, as its first argument, a value that indicates the type of information to return. This value can be a string or a member of VB's *DateInterval* enumeration. The following table shows the available (case-insensitive) string and enumeration options, and the member of the *DateTime* instance that should be used in C# to return the equivalent component.

Interval (String)	Interval (Enum)	DateTime Member
d	DateInterval.Day	Day
h	DateInterval.Hour	Hour
m	DateInterval.Month	Month
n	DateInterval.Minute	Minute
q	DateInterval.Quarter	See below
s	DateInterval.Second	Second
w	DateInterval.Weekday	See below
ww	DateInterval.WeekOfYear	See below
y	DateInterval.DayOfYear	DayOfYear
yyyy	DateInterval.Year	Year

To obtain the quarter in C#, extrapolate it from the month.

C#

```
int quarter = Math.Floor(sourceDate.Month - 1) / 3) + 1;
```

For the day of the week, Visual Basic returns a 1-based position within the week, where the first day of the week is the system default, or specified through an optional argument. In C#, the `DateTime` type's `DayOfWeek` property always returns a `DayOfWeek` enumeration value. When converted to an integer, this enumeration's values run from 0 (Sunday) to 6 (Saturday).

VISUAL BASIC
```
Dim whichDay As Integer = DatePart(
    "w", sourceDate, vbSunday)
```

C#
```csharp
int whichDay = ((int)sourceDate.DayOfWeek) + 1;
```

For week-of-year calculations, use the `Calendar.GetWeekOfYear` method in the `System.Globalization` namespace. It accepts arguments similar to those used in VB's `DatePart` method. For example, to return the current week for a year that starts on January 1, use the following code.

VISUAL BASIC
```
Dim whichWeek As Integer = DatePart("ww", sourceDate,
    vbSunday, vbFirstJan1)
```

C#
```csharp
// ----- Assumes: using System.Globalization;
int whichWeek = Calendar.GetWeekOfYear(sourceDate,
    CalendarWeekRule.FirstDay, DayOfWeek.Sunday);
```

DateSerial Method

Visual Basic's `DateSerial` method returns an instance of a `Date` value based on distinct year, month, and day components. In C#, create a new instance of the `DateTime` type, passing the component values to one of its constructor overloads.

VISUAL BASIC
```
Dim targetDate As Date = DateSerial(year, month, day)
```

C#
```csharp
DateTime targetDate = new DateTime(year, month, day);
```

DateString Property

Visual Basic's `DateString` property retrieves or sets the current date. To obtain the current date as a string in C#, access members of the `DateTime` type.

VISUAL BASIC
```
Dim result As String = DateString
```

C#
```csharp
// ----- Adjust the format as needed.
string result = DateTime.Today.ToString("MM-dd-yyyy");
```

To set the date in C#, you must use features exposed by the Win32 API.

```csharp
// ----- Define at the top of the file.
using System.Runtime.InteropServices;

// ----- Define outside of a method.
[DllImport("kernel32.dll")]
static extern void GetLocalTime(out SystemTime timeInfo);
[DllImport("kernel32.dll")]
static extern bool SetLocalTime(ref SystemTime timeInfo);

[StructLayout(LayoutKind.Sequential)]
struct SystemTime
{
    public ushort Year;
    public ushort Month;
    public ushort DayOfWeek;
    public ushort Day;
    public ushort Hour;
    public ushort Minute;
    public ushort Second;
    public ushort Milliseconds;
}

// ----- A method similar to setting DateString.
static bool SetDate(string dateText)
{
    // ----- Convert from a string to a true date.
    DateTime newDate;
    if (DateTime.TryParse(dateText, out newDate) == false)
        return false;

    // ----- Retrieve the current date.
    SystemTime timeInfo = new SystemTime();
    GetLocalTime(out timeInfo);

    // ----- Modify the date and set it.
    timeInfo.Year = (ushort)newDate.Year;
    timeInfo.Month = (ushort)newDate.Month;
    timeInfo.Day = (ushort)newDate.Day;
    try
    {
        return SetLocalTime(ref timeInfo);
    }
    catch
    {
        return false;
    }
}
```

You must have the appropriate system permissions to set the date or time from your application.

DateValue Method

Use the `Convert.ToDateTime` method to return a value similar to what Visual Basic's `DateValue` method returns. Once converted, use the `Date` property to remove any time component.

```vb
Dim targetDate As Date = DateValue(dateAsString)
```

```csharp
DateTime targetDate =
    Convert.ToDateTime(dateAsString).Date;
```

Day Method

The `DateTime` type's `Day` property returns the same information as Visual Basic's `Day` method.

```vb
Dim whichDay As Integer = Day(oneOrder.OrderDate)
```

```csharp
int whichDay = oneOrder.OrderDate.Day;
```

DDB Method

See

Financial Methods

Decimal Data Type

C#'s intrinsic `decimal` data type is identical to Visual Basic's `Decimal` data type. Both types are aliases for .NET's `System.Decimal` type. For decimal literals, VB uses a *D*, *d*, or *@* suffix after the value; in C#, use *M* or *m* instead.

```vb
Dim cost As Decimal = 0@   ' or 0D or 0d
```

```csharp
decimal cost = 0m;   // or 0M
```

Declare Statement

Visual Basic's `Declare` statement imports methods from an external source.

```vb
Private Declare Sub InitAVI Lib "avifil32.dll" _
    Alias "AVIFileInit" ()
```

VB also supports an alternative syntax that depends on attributes for many of the declaration particulars.

```
<DllImport("avifil32.dll")>
Private Shared Sub AVIFileInit()
End Sub
```

This second form is identical to the import method used in C#. The *extern* keyword indicates that the declared method is coming from an external source identified in the attached attribute.

C#

```
[DllImport("avifil32.dll")]
private static extern void AVIFileInit();
```

See Also

Methods

Default Modifier

In Visual Basic, the *Default* modifier identifies a type's default property.

VISUAL BASIC

```
' ----- You may indicate the name, "Item" in this case.
Default Public Property Item(
        ByVal index As Integer) As String
    Get
        Return InternalStorage(index)
    End Get
    Set(ByVal value As String)
        ' ----- If the "value" declaration is omitted,
        '       it is still implicitly defined. You can
        '       change the name from "value" if desired.
        InternalStorage(index) = value
    End Set
End Property
```

In C#, default properties are known as "indexers," and use the *this* declaration keyword as the name portion of the property declaration.

C#

```
// ----- C# does not allow you to name the
//       default property.
public string this[int index]
{
    get
    {
        return InternalStorage[index];
    }
    set
    {
        // ----- "value" is implicitly defined.
        InternalStorage[index] = value;
    }
}
```

As indicated in the sample code, Visual Basic allows you to specify a custom name for the index, while C# provides no such naming opportunity. To assign an indexer name that can be used from other .NET languages, apply the *IndexerName* attribute to the declaration.

C#
```
[System.Runtime.CompilerServices.IndexerName("Item")]
public string this[int index]
{
```

Both languages support overloading of the default property via a different argument signature. The name of the property must be the same across all overloads in VB, and *Default* must appear as a modifier in each overload. Both languages allow indexers to appear in classes, structures, or interfaces.

VISUAL BASIC
```
' ----- Interface-based indexer.
Interface IIndexed
    Default Property Item(ByVal index As Integer) As String
End Interface
```

C#
```
// ----- Interface-based indexer.
interface IIndexed
{
    string this[int index] {get; set;}
}
```

In addition to Visual Basic's *Default* modifier, default properties and indexers support the following modifiers in each language.

Visual Basic Modifier	C# Modifier
Friend	internal
MustOverride	abstract
NotOverridable	sealed
Overridable	virtual
Overrides	override
Private	private
Protected	protected
Protected Friend	protected internal
Public	public
ReadOnly	Not supported
Shadows	new
WriteOnly	Not supported
Not supported	extern

See Also

( ) Member Access Operator, Property Statement

Delegate Statement

C#'s *delegate* statement is equivalent to Visual Basic's *Delegate* statement.

VISUAL BASIC

```
Public Delegate Function PerformCalculation( _
    ByVal x As Integer, ByVal y As Integer) As Integer
```

C#

```
public delegate int PerformCalculation(int x, int y);
```

As with standard C# methods, delegates destined to return a value indicate the return type as part of the declaration; those that do not use *void* as the return type. These two styles are comparable to *Function* and *Sub* modifiers in VB.

Delegates support the following modifiers in each language.

Visual Basic Modifier	C# Modifier
Friend	internal
Private	private
Protected	protected
Protected Internal	protected internal
Public	public
Shadows	new
Shared	static

See Also

Anonymous Methods

DeleteSetting Method

Visual Basic's *DeleteSetting* method removes a single key or a set of related keys from a standardized Visual Basic section of the Windows registry.

VISUAL BASIC

```
' ----- Delete single key.
DeleteSetting(appName, sectionName, keyName)

' ----- Delete all keys in the same section.
DeleteSetting(appName, sectionName)
```

C#

```
// ----- Assumes: using Microsoft.Win32;
const string settingRoot =
    "Software\\VB and VBA Program Settings";
string settingLocation = string.Format("{0}\\{1}\\{2}",
    settingRoot, appName, sectionName);

// ----- Delete a single key.
RegistryKey keyAccess =
    Registry.CurrentUser.OpenSubKey(settingLocation, true);
keyAccess.DeleteValue(keyName);
keyAccess.Close();

// ----- Delete all keys in the same section.
Registry.CurrentUser.DeleteSubKeyTree(settingLocation);
```

```
// ----- Delete an entire application.
settingLocation = string.Format("{0}\\{1}",
    settingRoot, appName);
Registry.CurrentUser.DeleteSubKeyTree(settingLocation);
```

Destructors

In Visual Basic, you can add destructors to a type by overriding the base *Finalize* method.

VISUAL BASIC
```
Class Customer
    Protected Overrides Sub Finalize()
        Try
            ' ----- Cleanup logic appears here.
        Finally
            MyBase.Finalize()
        End Try
    End Sub
End Class
```

C# supports this implementation as well, although the call to the base *Finalize* method is provided automatically.

C#
```
class Customer
{
    protected override void Finalize()
    {
        try
        {
            // ----- Cleanup logic appears here.
        }
        finally
        {
            // ----- This is called automatically.
            // base.Finalize();
        }
    }
}
```

However, it is more common to implement C# destructors by creating a method with the same name as the class, prefixed with a tilde character (~).

C#
```
class Customer
{
    ~Customer()
    {
        // ----- Cleanup logic appears here.
    }
}
```

In both languages, the garbage collector determines when to call the destructor.

Dim Statement

In Visual Basic, the *Dim* statement declares local variables.

VISUAL BASIC

```
Dim basicValue As Integer      ' No initializer
Dim greeting As String = "hi"  ' With initializer
Dim storage() As Byte          ' Array
```

In C#, local variable declaration occurs without any special keyword.

C#

```
int basicValue;                // No initializer
string greeting = "hi";        // With initializer
byte[] storage;                // Array
```

Just like in VB, C# allows multiple variables to be declared in a single statement, using a comma to separate the identifiers.

VISUAL BASIC

```
' ----- Both variables typed as Date.
Dim startDate, endDate As Date

' ----- Three Integer, two Short.
Dim i1, i2, i3 As Integer, s4, s5 As Short
```

C#

```
// ----- Both variables typed as DateTime.
DateTime startDate, endDate;

// ----- Different types require different statements.
int i1, i2, i3;
short s4, s5;
```

In Visual Basic, all variables are initialized automatically to their default values: *Nothing* for reference types; some variation of zero for intrinsic value types and enumerations; and an instance with initialized members for structures. In C#, all variables must be assigned an initial value before they can be used elsewhere in code.

In Visual Basic, the *Dim* statement can declare local variables with inferred types by leaving off the *As* clause. *Option Infer On* must be used at the file or project level for this to work.

VISUAL BASIC

```
' ----- Inferred as string.
Dim message = "Hello, world."
```

Inferred variables in C# use the *var* instance type.

C#

```
// ----- Inferred as string.
var message = "Hello, world.";
```

Locally defined variables in VB can be used as the iteration variable in a *For Each* loop. In C#, the iteration variable must be defined as part of the *foreach* loop declaration itself.

See Also

( ) Array Declaration, Fields, Identifiers, Initializers, Lifetime and Scope, Query Expressions, Static Modifier

Dir Method

Visual Basic's *Dir* method returns the first matching file or directory name based on a name pattern and attribute mask, or the subsequent match when called without arguments. C# does not include a direct equivalent for the *Dir* method. Instead, you can use members of the *System.IO* namespace to access file and directory results. For instance, the following code retrieves all files in a directory as a collection of strings.

C#

```
// ----- Return text files with a .txt extension in
//       the target directory, ignore subdirectories.
string[] result =
    System.IO.Directory.GetFiles("C:\\WorkArea", "*.txt",
    System.IO.SearchOption.TopDirectoryOnly);
```

A related *GetDirectories* method returns matching directories instead of files. To return results limited by file attribute, obtain a *DirectoryInfo* object for the target directory, use its *GetFiles* method to return all files, and then examine each file for an attribute match.

C#

```
// ----- Assumes: using System.IO;
DirectoryInfo targetFolder =
    new DirectoryInfo("C:\\WorkArea");
FileInfo[] targetFiles = targetFolder.GetFiles();
foreach (FileInfo scanFile in targetFiles)
{
    if ((scanFile.Attributes & FileAttributes.Hidden) ==
        FileAttributes.Hidden)
    {
        // ----- Found a hidden file.
    }
}
```

DirectCast Casting Operator

C# includes a casting operator that provides the same results as Visual Basic's *DirectCast* operator. To perform this type of cast, prefix the object to be cast with the name of the new type, enclosing that type name in parentheses.

VISUAL BASIC

```
Dim someElephant As Elephant = DirectCast(
    someAnimal, Elephant)
```

C#

```
Elephant someElephant = (Elephant)someAnimal;
```

As in Visual Basic, either the source or target type used in the C# casting operation needs to be derived from the other type.

Directives

See

Preprocessing Directives

Distinct Query Expression Operator (LINQ)

C# does not include a direct equivalent for Visual Basic's `Distinct` query expression operator. However, you can use LINQ's `Distinct` extension method to accomplish the same thing.

VISUAL BASIC

```
Dim lateCusts = From cust In customers, ord In orders
                Where cust.ID = ord.CustomerID _
                And ord.PaymentOverdue = True
                Select cust.FullName
                Distinct
```

C#

```
var lateCusts = (from cust in customers
                from ord in orders
                where cust.ID == ord.CustomerID
                & ord.PaymentOverdue == true
                select new {cust.FullName}).Distinct();
```

See Also

Query Expressions

Do Statement

Visual Basic's *Do* statement loops while (or until) a condition is true. The exit condition appears as a *While* or *Until* clause, either at the top of the loop (after the *Do* keyword) or the bottom (after the *Loop* keyword).

VISUAL BASIC

```
' ----- Example using While at bottom of loop.
Do
    content = ProcessChunkOfContent(content)
Loop While content.Length > 0
```

```
' ----- Example using Until at top of loop.
Do Until content.Length = 0
    content = ProcessChunkOfContent(content)
Loop
```

C# includes two related statements, one with the condition at the top (the `while` statement), and one with the condition at the bottom (the `do` statement). The condition is always associated with the `while` clause; to emulate a VB `Until` clause, negate the Boolean value of the condition.

C#
```
// ----- Example using condition at bottom of loop.
do
{
    content = ProcessChunkOfContent(content);
} while (content.Length > 0);

// ----- Example using condition at top of loop.
while (content.Length > 0)
{
    content = ProcessChunkOfContent(content);
}
```

C# requires parentheses around the condition, something that is optional in Visual Basic.

Double Data Type

C#'s intrinsic `double` data type is identical to Visual Basic's `Double` data type. Both types are aliases for .NET's `System.Double` type. For double literals, Visual Basic uses an *R*, *r*, or *#* suffix after the value; C# uses *D* or *d* instead.

VISUAL BASIC
```
Dim factor As Double = 0#    ' or 0R or 0r
```

C#
```
double factor = 0d;   // or 0D
```

Else Clause

See

If Statement

ElseIf Clause

See

If Statement

End Block Clause

Visual Basic includes several block statements that terminate using an *End* block clause. One example is in class definitions, where an *End Class* clause ends the statement.

```
Class Example
End Class
```

Visual Basic includes the following *End* clauses.

- *End AddHandler*
- *End Class*
- *End Enum*
- *End Event*
- *End Function*
- *End Get*
- *End If*
- *End Interface*
- *End Module*
- *End Namespace*
- *End Operator*
- *End Property*
- *End RaiseEvent*
- *End RemoveHandler*
- *End Select*
- *End Set*
- *End Structure*
- *End Sub*
- *End SyncLock*
- *End Try*
- *End While*
- *End With*

In C#, a closing curly brace ends similar block statements. When certain block statements include only a single subordinate statement, that statement by itself is often sufficient to end the block, and curly braces are not required.

```
// ----- Block statement requiring ending curly brace.
class Example
{
}

// ----- Block statement with single-line
//       subordinate statement.
if (errorCount == 0)
    CompleteProcessing();
```

For information about each *End* clause and its equivalent within C#, see the associated entry in this chapter. For example, to learn about the *End Enum* statement, see the "Enum Statement" entry in this chapter.

End Statement

C# does not include a language equivalent for Visual Basic's *End* statement. Instead, to abort an application in C#, you can use one of two .NET Framework methods.

In Windows Forms applications, the *Application.Exit* method asks each form to close, causing control to return to the *Main* method. This typically causes the application to end, although logic within the *Main* method can delay a standard termination.

C#
```
System.Windows.Forms.Application.Exit();
```

A more generic way of terminating an application is via the *Environment.Exit* method. This method is more abrupt, aborting the application immediately and returning an exit code to the shell that originally invoked the application. Visual Basic's *End* statement calls this method behind the scenes.

C#
```
System.Environment.Exit(0);
```

Entry Point

See

   Main Method

Enum Statement

C#'s *enum* statement is equivalent to Visual Basic's *Enum* statement.

VISUAL BASIC
```
Enum DoorState
    Closed = 1
    Ajar
    Open
End Enum
```

C#
```
enum DoorState
{
    Closed = 1,
    Ajar,
    Open
}
```

Both languages default each enumeration member to zero (for the first item) or one more than the item that precedes it, unless overridden with a specific value, as was done with `DoorState.Closed` in the prior sample. VB separates members with line breaks, while C# uses commas.

Both C# and Visual Basic support enumerations based on the eight core integer types (`Byte`, `SByte`, `Short`, `UShort`, `Integer`, `UInteger`, `Long`, `ULong`, and their C# counterparts), with `Integer` (VB) and `int` (C#) used by default.

VISUAL BASIC
```
Enum DoorState As Long
```

C#
```
enum DoorState : long
```

Visual Basic enumerations can appear within namespaces, classes, structures, or interfaces. C# does not allow enumerations to appear within interfaces, but supports inclusion within the other three types.

Enumerations support the following modifiers in each language.

Visual Basic Modifier	C# Modifier
Friend	internal
Private	private
Protected	protected
Protected Friend	protected internal
Public	public
Shadows	new

New with Visual Studio 2015

Both languages use a dotted notation when using enumeration members in code. When combined with an `Imports` statement that specifies the enumeration, Visual Basic expressions can use enumeration members without specifying the name of the enumeration. C# added this functionality in 2015 with its new `using static` directive.

VISUAL BASIC
```
' ----- At the top of the file.
Imports DoorNamespace
Imports DoorNamespace.DoorState

' ----- Later, within a method.
Dim frontDoor As DoorState = DoorState.IsClosed

' ----- This will also work thanks to the Imports.
Dim backDoor As DoorState = IsClosed
```

C#
```
// ----- Before 2015.
DoorState frontDoor = DoorState.IsClosed;

// ----- Starting in 2015, at the top of the file.
using static DoorNamespace;
using static DoorNamespace.DoorState;
```

```
// ----- Later, within a method.
DoorState backDoor = IsClosed;
```

Environin Method

The *Environment* class' *GetEnvironmentVariable* method is an exact replacement for Visual Basic's *Environ* method when called with an environment variable name.

VISUAL BASIC
```
Dim result As String = Environ("PATH")
```

C#
```
string result = Environment.GetEnvironmentVariable("PATH");
```

The *Environ* method also accepts a 1-based numeric value, returning the variable at that position. In C#, you must retrieve all elements and locate the correct item.

VISUAL BASIC
```
result = Environ(oneBasedPosition)
```

C#
```
System.Collections.SortedList allVars =
    new System.Collections.SortedList(
    Environment.GetEnvironmentVariables());
if (oneBasedPosition <= allVars.Count)
    result = allVars[oneBasedPosition - 1].ToString();
```

EOF Method

Visual Basic's *EOF* method indicates whether the current reading or writing position for an open file is at the end of that file.

VISUAL BASIC
```
Dim atEndOfFile As Boolean = EOF(fileNumber)
```

C# does not include the same file-management features included with VB. Instead, it is common to work with the *System.IO.FileStream* class to read and write files. This class does not include a direct equivalent for the *EOF* method. Instead, you can compare the length of the file with its current 0-based position, or you can attempt to read data from the file.

C#
```
// ----- Comparing position to length.
bool atEndOfFile = (openedStream.Position >=
    openedStream.Length);

// ----- Attempting to read more data.
int nextByte = openedStream.ReadByte();
atEndOfFile = (nextByte == -1);
```

If you opened a file using the *System.IO.StreamReader* class, the returned *TextReader* instance includes a *Peek* method that can be used to check for the end of the file.

C#
```
atEndOfFile = (openedReader.Peek() == -1);
```

See Also

FileOpen Method

Erase Statement

Although C# does not have a dedicated statement similar to Visual Basic's *Erase* statement, you can release an array by assigning it the value *null*.

VISUAL BASIC
```
Erase arrayOfData
```

C#
```
arrayOfData = null;
```

Erl Property

C# methods do not allow numeric line labels, and therefore the language has no counterpart for Visual Basic's *Erl* property.

Err Object

Visual Basic's *Err* object is used to identify error details as part of the language's unstructured error handling system. Because C# only includes structured error handling, it does not include an equivalent for *Err*. However, because *Err* uses internally a reference to the active structured *Exception*, converting your unstructured error handling code to the structured equivalent will provide you with comparable error access.

VISUAL BASIC
```
On Error GoTo ErrorHandler
' ----- Later...
ErrorHandler:
    LogError(Err.Description)
    Resume Next
```

C#
```
try
{
    // ----- Error-prone code here.
}
catch (System.Exception ex)
{
    LogError(ex.Message);
}
```

Err Property

Visual Basic's `Err` property presents the most recent error as part of the language's unstructured error handling system. C# only includes support for structured error handling. The closest equivalent for the `Err` property is the exception included with the `catch` clause of a `try` statement.

VISUAL BASIC
```
On Error GoTo ErrorHandler
' ----- Later in the same method...
ErrorHandler:
    LogError(Err)
    Resume Next
```

C#
```
try
{
    // ----- Error-prone statements here.
}
catch (System.Exception ex)
{
    LogError(ex);
}
```

Error Handling

See

Err Object, Error Statement, On Error Statement, Resume Statement, Throw Statement, Try Statement

Error Statement

Visual Basic's `Error` statement exists for backward compatibility only. The Visual Studio documentation recommends that it be replaced with the `Err.Raise` method instead. Neither `Error` nor `Err.Raise` exists in C#. Instead, use C#'s `throw` statement to raise an error condition within your code.

VISUAL BASIC
```
' ----- Obsolete.
Error vbErrors.FileNotFound    ' Or 53

' ----- Newer equivalent.
Err.Raise(vbErrors.FileNotFound)
```

C#
```
throw new System.IO.FileNotFoundException();
```

ErrorToString Method

Visual Basic's `ErrorToString` method returns an error message based on a numeric code. C# does not support this core list of numeric codes, and therefore contains no equivalent for the `ErrorToString` method. The closest equivalent would be the `Message` property of the `System.Exception` class or its derivatives.

Event Statement

As in Visual Basic, C# includes support for delegate-based event declaration. Its `event` statement, when used in this way, closely parallels the functionality of VB's `Event` statement.

VISUAL BASIC
```
Public Delegate Sub SampleEventHandler(
    ByVal sender As Object, ByVal e As SampleEventArgs)
Public Event SampleEvent As SampleEventHandler
```

C#
```
public delegate void SampleEventHandler(
    object sender, SampleEventArgs e);
public event SampleEventHandler SampleEvent;
```

Visual Basic also supports a combined syntax, where the signature of the delegate is included in the event declaration.

VISUAL BASIC
```
Public Event SampleEvent(ByVal sender As Object,
    ByVal e As SampleEventArgs)
```

This standalone syntax is not available in C#. Instead, you must declare a delegate before using it in an `event` statement.

Events support the following modifiers in each language.

Visual Basic Modifier	C# Modifier
Friend	internal
Private	private
Protected	protected
Protected Friend	protected internal
Public	public
Shadows	new
Shared	static
Not supported	abstract
Not supported	extern
Not supported	override
Not supported	sealed
Not supported	virtual

Exceptions

See

Err Object, Error Statement, On Error Statement, Resume Statement, Throw Statement, Try Statement

Exit Statement

Visual Basic's various *Exit* statements allow your code to exit a block construct, such as a loop or a method. The following table shows the equivalent C# statements for each *Exit* variation.

Visual Basic Statement	C# Statement
Exit Do	*break*
Exit For	*break*
Exit Function	*return*
Exit Property	*return*
Exit Select	*break*
Exit Sub	*return*
Exit Try	Not supported
Exit While	*break*

In general, C#'s *return* statement exits out of methods and properties, while its *break* statement leaves other subordinate block constructs. To exit a *try* block in C#, you need to jump out to an external label using a *goto* statement; C# has no direct equivalent for the *Exit Try* statement.

In Visual Basic *Select Case* statements, jumping out of a *Case* block using *Exit Select* is optional. You use the statement only when you need to explicitly exit a block early. In C#, you must always employ a *break* statement (or some other block-exiting statement, such as a *return* statement) to leave each *case* block.

VISUAL BASIC
```
' ----- No need for Exit Select in any of these blocks.
Select Case customerType
    Case CustType.New
        message = "Welcome!"
    Case CustType.Existing
        Message = "Welcome back!"
End Select
```

C#
```
// ----- break is required in both case blocks.
switch (customerType)
{
    case CustType.New:
        message = "Welcome!";
        break;
```

```
        case CustType.Existing:
            message = "Welcome back!";
            break;
}
```

Because Visual Basic lets you identify a specific exit type, it is possible to exit some types of nested constructs simultaneously.

VISUAL BASIC

```
For counter As Integer = 0 To 9
    Do While (content.Length > 0)
        ' ----- This will exit both loops.
        Exit For
    Loop
Next counter
```

C#'s combined *break* statement doesn't support this level of jumping. Instead, for constructs that use *break* to exit a block, you must use other methods, such as a *goto* statement, to exit multiple constructs immediately.

C#

```
for (int counter = 0; counter < 10; counter++)
{
    while (content.Length > 0)
    {
        // ----- A "break" statement would only exit
        //       the while loop. Use a "goto" instead.
        goto AfterAllLoops;
    }
}
AfterAllLoops:
```

Extension Methods

In Visual Basic, extension methods always appear within a *Module* statement. The method must be decorated with the *Extension* attribute (from *System.Runtime.CompilerServices*). Although not marked with any special modifier, the first argument to the method is the target of the extension.

VISUAL BASIC

```
' ----- Assumes: Imports System.Runtime.CompilerServices
Friend Module LocalExtensions
    <Extension> Public Function DigitsOnly(
            ByVal originalText As String) As String
        ' ----- Returns a string result.
    End Function
End Module
```

In C#, extension methods appear in static classes (akin to VB modules), and use the *this* modifier to indicate the target type being extended.

C#

```csharp
internal static class LocalExtensions
{
    public static string DigitsOnly(
        this string originalText)
    {
        // ----- Returns a string result.
    }
}
```

False Boolean Literal

C#'s *false* literal is identical to Visual Basic's *False* literal.

Fields

Fields are variables declared within a class or structure (plus modules in Visual Basic), but outside of any method. The syntax closely parallels that of local variable declaration. (See the "Variables" entry in this chapter for more declaration details.)

VISUAL BASIC

```vbnet
' ----- Field declared with initializer.
Private MonitoredValue As Integer = 0

' ----- The "Dim" keyword is optional, but required
'       when no access modifier is used.
Dim AnotherValue As Integer
```

C#

```csharp
// ----- Field declared with initializer.
private int MonitoredValue = 0;
```

Access modifiers are optional in field declarations. When missing, the access level defaults to *Private* in Visual Basic classes and modules, and *Public* by default in structures. Within C# classes and structures, fields are *private* by default.

Fields support the following modifiers in each language.

Visual Basic Modifier	C# Modifier
Friend	internal
Private	private
Protected	protected
Protected Friend	protected internal
Public	public
ReadOnly	readonly
Shadows	new
Shared	static
WithEvents	Not supported
Not supported	volatile

See Also

() Array Declaration, Access Modifiers, Identifiers, Initializers, New Operator, Shared Modifier, Variables

FileAttr Method

Visual Basic's *FileAttr* method indicates the *OpenMode* enumeration value originally used to open a file with the *FileOpen* method. The possible values are *Append*, *Binary*, *Input*, *Output*, or *Random*.

VISUAL BASIC
```
Dim whichMode As OpenMode = FileAttr(fileNumber)
```

C# does not include the same file-management features included with VB. Instead, it is common to work with the *System.IO.FileStream* class to read and write files. This class does not include a direct equivalent for the *FileAttr* method. It does include *CanRead*, *CanSeek*, and *CanWrite* properties that may provide some limited information similar to what is offered through the *FileAttr* method.

See Also

FileOpen Method

FileClose Method

Visual Basic's *FileClose* method closes one, some, or all files previously opened with the *FileOpen* method. The closing method accepts zero or more file numbers, indicating which files to close.

VISUAL BASIC
```
FileClose()       ' All files
FileClose(1)      ' Just file #1
FileClose(2, 3) ' Files #2 and #3
```

C# does not include the same file-management features included with VB. Instead, it is common to work with the *System.IO.FileStream* class to read and write files. To close an opened file stream, call its *Close* method.

C#
```
openedStream.Close();
```

See Also

FileOpen Method

FileCopy Method

The *System.IO.File.Copy* method provides file-copying services similar to those provided by Visual Basic's *FileCopy* method.

VISUAL BASIC
```
FileCopy(sourcePath, destinationPath)
```

C#

```
// ----- Third argument is the "overwrite" argument.
//       Visual Basic's FileCopy method always overwrites.
System.IO.File.Copy(sourcePath, destinationPath, true);
```

When using *File.Copy*, the attributes of the original file are retained on the new file. Visual Basic's *FileCopy* method clears the target file's attributes, setting only the archive flag. The following C# statement, when used after the copy, emulates VB's behavior.

C#

```
System.IO.File.SetAttributes(destinationPath,
    FileAttributes.Archive);
```

FileDateTime Method

In C#, use the *System.IO.FileInfo* class' *LastWriteTime* property to return the same information as Visual Basic's *FileDateTime* method.

VISUAL BASIC
```
Dim updateDate As Date = FileDateTime(pathToFile)
```

C#
```
DateTime updateDate =
    (new System.IO.FileInfo(pathToFile)).LastWriteTime;
```

FileGet Method

Visual Basic's *FileGet* method reads a piece of data from a file that was previously written using the *FilePut* method. C# does not have a direct equivalent for the *FileGet* method. Instead, data can be serialized to a file or any other stream, and then later read back in, using a stream formatter.

The .NET Framework includes a binary formatter and an XML formatter, among others. Any object decorated with the *System.SerializableAttribute* attribute can be serialized to a stream for later retrieval, and all of the core data types included in C# automatically support this attribute.

Note

Files written through .NET serialization methods are not identical to those written using the *FilePut* method. The output format of *FilePut* is proprietary to Visual Basic. You can learn about the specific content written with *FilePut* by accessing the Microsoft Reference Sources at http://referencesource.microsoft.com, and searching for "FilePut." A full discussion of its output is beyond the scope of this book.

The following code shows how to retrieve some basic data values from a file stream in a binary format. The "FilePut Method" entry in this chapter includes the C# code used to write the content that is being read by the sample code shown here.

C#
```
// ----- At the top of the file.
using System.IO;
using System.Runtime.Serialization;
using System.Runtime.Serialization.Formatters.Binary;

// ----- In a method.
bool booleanData;
int numericData;
string textData;

// ----- Open the input stream.
IFormatter formatter = new BinaryFormatter();
Stream inputFile = new FileStream(
    "C:\\temp\\output.dat", FileMode.Open,
    FileAccess.Read, FileShare.Read);

// ----- Read the data values.
booleanData = (bool)formatter.Deserialize(inputFile);
numericData = (int)formatter.Deserialize(inputFile);
textData = (string)formatter.Deserialize(inputFile);
inputFile.Close();
```

FileGetObject Method

Visual Basic's *FileGetObject* method reads an instance of a type from a file that was previously written using the *FilePutObject* method. C# does not have a direct equivalent for the *FileGetObject* method. Instead, data can be serialized to a file or any other stream, and then later read back in, using a stream formatter. The "FileGet Method" entry in this chapter includes an example of how to read data from a file using binary formatting.

See Also

FileGet Method

FileLen Method

The *FileInfo* class' *Length* property returns the length of a file in bytes, just like Visual Basic's *FileLen* method.

VISUAL BASIC
```
Dim result As Long = FileLen(pathToFile)
```
C#
```
long result = (new System.IO.FileInfo(pathToFile)).Length;
```

FileOpen Method

C# has no direct equivalent for Visual Basic's *FileOpen* method, or for its numeric file identifiers. However, internally this method uses standard

System.IO.FileStream instances to manage files. You can use this same class in C# to open a file.

VISUAL BASIC

```
Dim fileID As Integer = FreeFile()
FileOpen(fileID, "C:\temp\work.txt", OpenMode.Input)
```

C#

```
System.IO.FileStream sourceFile =
    new System.IO.FileStream("C:\\temp\\work.txt",
    System.IO.FileMode.Open);
```

Both the *FileOpen* method and the *FileStream* constructor include overloads and optional arguments that let you specify mode (input, output, and so on), access (read, write, or both), and sharing options. The required mode setting is indicated by the *OpenMode* enumeration in VB, and the *System.IO.FileMode* enumeration when using streams. The following table shows the equivalent values.

OpenMode Member	FileMode Member
Append	Append
Binary	OpenOrCreate
Input	Open
Output	OpenOrCreate
Random	OpenOrCreate

By default, files are opened for read and write access in VB. The optional *OpenAccess* enumeration modifies this access if desired. When using streams, the *System.IO.FileAccess* enumeration provides the same options. The following table shows the equivalent access values.

OpenAccess Member	FileAccess Member
Default	ReadWrite
Read	Read
ReadWrite	ReadWrite
Write	Write

In VB, opened files are locked to prevent access by other users. To override this default, the *OpenShare* enumeration includes relevant options. The following table compares these values to those in the *System.IO.FileShare* enumeration, which is used when working with file streams.

OpenShare Member	FileShare Member
Default	None
LockRead	Write
LockReadWrite	None
LockWrite	Read
Shared	ReadWrite

One additional feature of the *FileOpen* method lets you specify a record length. Streams do not include an equivalent for reading and writing data in record blocks. Instead, you must position reads and writes within a file using the stream's *Seek* method or other similar features. When determining file locations, the first position in a file opened with Visual Basic's *FileOpen* method is *1* (one). When working with streams, the first position is identified as *0* (zero).

Another alternative is to open a file for dedicated reading or writing using the *StreamReader* or *StreamWriter* classes, also found in the *System.IO* namespace. These classes provide more text-friendly access to the files, allowing you to simulate fixed-size records by reading or writing data in blocks of a specified size.

C#
```
// ----- Open a file for reading.
System.IO.TextReader inputFile =
    new System.IO.StreamReader("C:\\temp\\work.txt");

// ----- Open a file for writing.
System.IO.TextWriter outputFile =
    new System.IO.StreamWriter("C:\\temp\\output.txt");
```

FilePut Method

Visual Basic's *FilePut* method writes a piece of data to a file opened for binary or random access output. At the file level, *FilePut* first writes out a code to indicate the type or length of the content being written, followed by the content itself.

C# does not have a direct equivalent for the *FilePut* method. Instead, data can be serialized to a file or any other stream using a stream formatter. The .NET Framework includes a binary formatter and an XML formatter, among others. Any object decorated with the *System.SerializableAttribute* attribute can be serialized to a stream, and all of the core data types included in C# automatically support this attribute.

Note

Files written through .NET serialization methods are not identical to those written using the *FilePut* method. The output format of *FilePut* is proprietary to Visual Basic. You can learn about the specific content written with *FilePut* by accessing the Microsoft Reference Sources at http://referencesource.microsoft.com, and searching for "FilePut." A full discussion of its output is beyond the scope of this book.

The following code shows out to serialize some basic data values to a file stream in a binary format.

C#
```
// ----- At the top of the file.
using System.IO;
using System.Runtime.Serialization;
using System.Runtime.Serialization.Formatters.Binary;

// ----- In a method.
bool booleanData = true;
int numericData = 123;
string textData = "Hello, World";
```

```
// ----- Open the output stream.
IFormatter formatter = new BinaryFormatter();
Stream outputFile = new FileStream(
    "C:\\temp\\output.dat", FileMode.Create,
    FileAccess.Write, FileShare.None);

// ----- Write the data values.
formatter.Serialize(outputFile, booleanData);
formatter.Serialize(outputFile, numericData);
formatter.Serialize(outputFile, textData);
outputFile.Close();
```

More complex types can also be serialized as long as the type is marked with the *Serializable* attribute.

FilePutObject Method

Visual Basic's *FilePutObject* method writes an instance of a type to a file opened for binary or random access output. At the file level, *FilePutObject* writes both a description of the content being written plus the content itself.

C# does not have a direct equivalent for the *FilePutObject* method. Instead, data can be serialized to a file or any other stream using a stream formatter. The "FilePut Method" entry in this chapter includes an example of how to write data to a file using binary formatting.

See Also

FilePut Method

FileWidth Method

Visual Basic's *FileWidth* method indicates the width of any text lines written to a file opened with the *FileOpen* method.

VISUAL BASIC
```
' ----- Set the line width to 35 characters.
FileWidth(fileNumber, 35)
```

C# does not include the same file-management features included with VB. Instead, it is common to work with the *System.IO.StreamWriter* class to output text data. When writing text using this class, you must manually insert line breaks at the appropriate positions as you emit your text data.

See Also

FileOpen Method, Print Method, Write Method

Filter Method

Visual Basic's *Filter* method returns a subset of string array elements that match a substring pattern.

```
' ----- Just cities in Montana.
Dim montanaOnly() As String = Filter(allCities, ", MT")
```

C# does not have a direct equivalent for the *Filter* method. Instead, you can manually extract the matching elements within a loop, or use LINQ to retrieve the matches in one statement.

C#
```
// ----- Loop-based filtering.
List<string> montanaOnly = new List<string>();
foreach (string oneCity in allCities)
{
    if (oneCity.Contains(", MT"))
        montanaOnly.Add(onecity);
}
// ----- If an array is really needed.
string[] montanaAsArray = montanaOnly.ToArray();

// ----- LINQ-based filtering.
string[] montanaOnly =
    (from oneCity in allCities
    where oneCity.Contains(", MT")
    select oneCity).ToArray();
```

Finalize Method

See

Destructors

Finally Clause

See

Try Statement

Financial Methods

The *Microsoft.VisualBasic.Financial* class contains several methods that perform common financial and statistical calculations. The following table lists those methods.

Method	Description
DDB	Double-declining balance depreciation of an asset
FV	Future value of an annuity
IPmt	Interest payment for an annuity
IRR	Internal rate of return
MIRR	Modified internal rate of return
NPer	Number of periods for an annuity

Method	Description
NPV	Net present value of an investment
Pmt	Payment for an annuity
PPmt	Principal payment for an annuity
PV	Present value of an investment
Rate	Interest rate for an annuity
SLN	Straight-line depreciation of an asset
SYD	Sum-of-years depreciation of an asset

No equivalents exist in C# for these methods. A conversion of the logic for each method into C# is beyond the scope of this book. You can find the complete Visual Basic source code for these methods at Microsoft's Reference Source web site. The code for the financial methods can be found at the following location: http://referencesource.microsoft.com/#Microsoft.VisualBasic/Financial.vb

Fix Method

In C#, use the `System.Math.Floor` method to produce results identical to those returned by Visual Basic's `Fix` method. Integer values always return the original value. For decimal inputs, the method returns the integer portion of the number, with rounding toward zero.

VISUAL BASIC
```
result = Fix(originalDecimal)
```

C#
```
if (originalDecimal >= 0)
    result = System.Math.Floor(originalDecimal);
else
    result = -System.Math.Floor(-originalDecimal);
```

For Each Statement

C#'s `foreach` statement is equivalent to Visual Basic's `For Each` statement.

VISUAL BASIC
```
For Each scanRow As DataRow In customerTable.Rows
    ' ----- Logic using scanRow variable.
Next scanRow
```

C#
```
foreach (DataRow scanRow in customerTable.Rows)
{
    // ----- Logic using scanRow variable.
}
```

Visual Basic allows the iteration variable to be declared outside of the loop.

VISUAL BASIC
```
Dim scanRow As DataRow
For Each scanRow In customerTable.Rows
```

This is not permitted in C#; you must indicate the loop variable type as part of the statement declaration. (The type can be *var* for implicitly typed iterators.)

For Statement

Visual Basic's *For* loop iterates from a starting value to an ending value, incrementing by *1* or an optional custom stepping amount.

VISUAL BASIC
```
' ----- Standard loop.
For counter As Integer = 0 To 9
    ' ----- Loops 10 times, from 0 to 9, inclusive.
Next counter

' ----- Loop with custom step.
For counter As Integer = 9 To 0 Step -1
    ' ----- Loops 10 times, from 9 to 0, inclusive.
Next counter

' ----- Outside-of-loop declaration of counter
'       is also valid.
Dim counter As Integer
For counter = 0 To 9
Next counter
```

The syntax of C#'s *for* loops is a little more complex—or a little more flexible, depending on your perspective. Instead of starting, ending, and step values, the declaration includes *initialization, condition,* and *iteration* expressions, which all work together to determine the starting, ending, and increment rules for the loop. The three expressions appear within a set of parentheses, each separated by a semicolon.

C#
```
for (initialization; condition; iteration)
{
    // ----- Loop body appears here.
}
```

In basic *for* loops, the initialization expression defines the loop variable. As in VB, the loop variable can be declared outside of the loop, and initialized with a starting value in the loop declaration.

C#
```
// ----- For example, to declare an integer counter
//       starting at zero.
int counter = 0
```

The condition expression is a Boolean test expression that should return *true* as long as the loop should continue. For example, if your loop's counter will start at *0* (zero), and continue up to and including a value of *9*, a condition that returns *true* while the counter is less than *10* gives the loop the correct ending condition.

C#
```
counter < 10

// ----- This would also work.
counter <= 9

// ----- Or even this.
(counter * 2) < 19
```

The third part, the iteration expression, provides instructions on how the loop should alter the loop counter before starting a new iteration, and before checking the condition expression. A simple increment adds *1* to the loop counter.

C#
```
counter++

// ----- This will also work.
++counter

// ----- As will this.
counter += 1
```

Putting it all together, the three expressions declare the bounds and phases of the loop's lifetime.

C#
```
for (int counter = 0; counter < 10; counter++)
{
    // ----- Loops 10 times, from 0 to 9.
}

// ----- Outside-of-loop declaration of counter
//       is also valid.
int counter;
for (counter = 9; counter >= 0; counter -= 1)
{
    // ----- Loops 10 times, from 9 to 0.
}
```

Visual Basic loops support integer, floating-point, or enumeration values. Because of its flexible syntax, C# supports all of these options and more. For example, you can design a loop that uses a string for its loop monitoring.

C#
```
for (string content = GetContent(); content.Length > 0;
    content = (content.Length > 0 ?
    content.Substring(1) : ""))
{
    // ----- Loop while content has characters in it.
}
```

C#'s *for* statement permits even more complex looping scenarios, with support for multiple comma-delimited initializers (of the same data type) and iterators. In Visual Basic, such loops would normally be created using a *Do* statement, or a *For* loop that also took other variables into account within the body of the loop. C#'s *for* statement can also be used to create an infinite loop by leaving the condition portion (or all portions) blank, a format not permitted in VB.

C#
```
for (;;) { }
```

In both languages, you can alter the counter variable within the body of the loop.

Format Method

In general, the `string` type's `Format` method is a good replacement for Visual Basic's `Format` method. Both methods accept a formatting template string, and they share some of their custom formatting codes in common. The biggest difference between the two methods is that VB's `Format` method accepts an object or expression to be formatted, followed by the template. In the `string.Format` method, the template appears first in the argument list, followed by one or more objects or expressions to be formatted according to the template.

VISUAL BASIC
```
Dim holidayName As String = "Christmas"
Dim targetDate As Date = New Date(2000, 12, 25)
Dim result As String = holidayName &
    " in " & targetDate.Year & " occurs on " &
    Format(targetDate, "M/d/yyyy") & "."
```

C#
```
// ----- Build the string via concatenation, as in VB.
string holidayName = "Christmas";
DateTime targetDate = new DateTime(2000, 12, 25);
string result = holidayName + " in " + targetDate.Year +
    " occurs on " + string.Format("{0:M/d/yyyy}",
    targetDate) + ".";

// ----- Build the string using a composite template.
result = string.Format(
    "{0} in {1:yyyy} occurs on {1:M/d/yyyy}.",
    holidayName, targetDate);
```

Placeholders in the `string.Format` template appear in curly braces, each containing the position number of the argument to use, and an optional colon and formatting code. The list of available formatting codes varies somewhat between those used in the `Format` method and those used by `string.Format`. For a full description of the custom and predefined codes used by the latter, see the Visual Studio documentation for the `System.String.Format` method.

FormatCurrency Method

Visual Basic's `FormatCurrency` method converts a numeric value (or a string representation of a number) to the monetary format of the current culture. All numbers are coerced to the `System.Double` type before formatting.

The *ToString* method of the *double* type in C# accepts a formatting string. The *"C"* format code outputs a value using the default currency format for the current culture.

VISUAL BASIC
```
Dim result As String = FormatCurrency(moneyValue)
```

C#
```
string result = moneyValue.ToString("C");
```

Additional formatting codes provide greater flexibility in the output of the monetary content. The *ToString* method also has overloads that let you specify culture-specific options, some of which match the optional arguments of the *FormatCurrency* method. See the .NET documentation for the *System.Globalization.NumberFormatInfo* class for additional information.

FormatDateTime Method

Visual Basic's *FormatDateTime* method uses the *System.DateTime* class' *ToString* method to output formatted date and time strings. *FormatDateTime* accepts a formatting enumeration value that indicates the output format.

VISUAL BASIC
```
Dim result As String =
    FormatDateTime(workDate, DateFormat.LongDate)
```

C#
```
string result = workDate.ToString("D");
```

The following table shows the matching *ToString* argument needed for each *DateFormat* enumeration value.

DateFormat Value	ToString Argument
LongDate	*"D"*
ShortDate	*"d"*
LongTime	*"T"*
ShortTime	*"HH:mm"*
GeneralDate	*"T"* for times with no dates, *"d"* for dates with midnight times, otherwise *"G"*

FormatNumber Method

Visual Basic's *FormatNumber* method returns a numeric value formatted as a string according to the optional arguments passed to the method. In C#, use the *ToString* method attached to the source variable or expression to generate this string, passing a formatting template.

C#
```
decimal sourceValue = 65.4321;
result = sourceValue.ToString("0.00");   // 65.43
```

The following table shows some sample formatting templates that relate to the optional arguments that can be passed to the *FormatNumber* method.

Feature to Emulate	Formatting Template
Default formatting style	*0*
Four digits after decimal	*0.0000*
Exclude leading digit	*#.00*
Parentheses around negatives	*0;(0)*
Include grouping before decimal	*#,##0.0*

FormatPercent Method

Visual Basic's *FormatPercent* method returns a numeric value formatted as a string, with a trailing % symbol included. In C#, use the *ToString* method attached to the source variable or expression to generate this string, passing a formatting template.

C#
```
decimal sourceValue = 0.853m;
result = sourceValue.ToString("0.00%");   // 85.30%
```

The following table shows some sample formatting templates that relate to the optional arguments that can be passed to the *FormatPercent* method.

Feature to Emulate	Formatting Template
Default formatting style	*0.00%*
Four digits after decimal	*0.0000%*
Exclude leading digit	*#.00%*
Parentheses around negatives	*0.00%;(0.00%)*
Include grouping before decimal	*#,##0.00%*

FreeFile Method

Visual Basic's *FreeFile* method returns a numeric file identifier compatible with pre-.NET Visual Basic file management features. C# does not include support for this older system, and therefore has no equivalent to the *FreeFile* method. Instead, C# file management typically uses stream features, including those classes that derive from *System.IO.Stream*.

Friend Access Modifier

C#'s *internal* access modifier is equivalent to Visual Basic's *Friend* access modifier.

See Also

Access Modifiers

From Clause

See

Initializers

From Query Expression Operator (LINQ)

C#'s *from* query expression operator is identical to Visual Basic's *From* operator. For queries with multiple sources, Visual Basic supports multiple *From* clauses, or a single *From* clause with multiple comma-delimited sources. In C#, multiple *from* clauses may appear, but each clause can reference only one source.

VISUAL BASIC
```
' ----- Single source.
Dim result = From item In Employees
             Select item.FullName, item.HireDate

' ----- Multiple comma-delimited sources.
Dim result = From item In Employees, site In Divisions
             Where item.Division = site.ID
             Select Division = site.Name, item.FullName

' ----- Multiple distinct sources.
Dim result = From item In Employees
             From site In Divisions
             Where item.Division = site.ID
             Select Division = site.Name, item.FullName
```

C#
```
// ----- Single source.
var result = from item in Employees
             select new {item.FullName, item.HireDate};

// ----- Multiple sources.
var result = from item in Employees
             from site in Divisions
             where item.Division == site.ID
             select new {Division = site.Name,
                         item.FullName};
```

Visual Basic supports multiple *From* clauses when processing nested results. In C#, a *let* clause generates similar results.

VISUAL BASIC
```
Dim result = From customer In GetActiveCustomers()
             From order In customer.Orders
             Select order
```

C#
```
var result = from customer in GetActiveCustomers()
             let order = customer.Orders
             select order;
```

Normally, the range variable is inferred from the collection type. To explicitly identify the range variable type, include an *As* clause. In C# prefix the range variable with the target data type.

VISUAL BASIC
```
Dim result = From item As Employee In AllEmployees
```

C#
```
var result = from Employee item in AllEmployees
             select item;
```

When building VB queries using the *Aggregate* operator, the *From* clause is not required. The *from* clause is required in all C# query expressions.

See Also

Query Expressions

Function Lambda Statement

See

Lambda Expressions

Function Statement

See

Methods

FV Method

See

Financial Methods

Garbage Collection

See

Destructors

Generics

Both Visual Basic and C# support generics, also known as "constructed types." One key difference is the syntax used to specify the type placeholders. In Visual Basic, these appear in parentheses as part of an *Of* clause, while in C#, they appear within angle brackets after the generic type name.

VISUAL BASIC
```
' ----- As part of a generic declaration.
Class SpecialList(Of T)
    Private InternalList As T
End Class

' ----- As part of a generic instantiation.
Dim trackNumbers As New SpecialList(Of Integer)
```
C#
```
// ----- As part of a generic declaration.
class SpecialList<T>
{
    private T InternalList;
}

// ----- As part of a generic instantiation.
SpecialList<int> trackNumbers = new SpecialList<int>();
```
Generic constructs can be applied to classes, structures, interfaces, methods, and delegates in both languages. Generic methods can appear within generic or non-generic types.

VISUAL BASIC
```
Shared Sub ReverseItems(Of T)(ByRef firstItem As T,
        ByRef secondItem As T)
    Dim holdingArea As T = firstItem
    firstItem = secondItem
    secondItem = holdingArea
End Sub
```
C#
```
static void ReverseItems<T>(ref T firstItem,
    ref T secondItem)
{
    T holdingArea = firstItem;
    firstItem = secondItem;
    secondItem = holdingArea;
}
```
In both Visual Basic and C#, the generic type parameter list can include type-specific modifiers that provide limits for each parameter. VB's *As* clause, like C#'s *where* clause, lets you limit the specific types that can be used for a type parameter during instantiation. See the "As Clause" entry in this chapter for more information.

When defining interfaces, optional modifiers specify the variance associated with each type parameter. By default, type parameters are invariant. The "out" modifier in each language specifies covariance, while "in" specifies contravariance.

VISUAL BASIC
```
Interface IVariant(Of TInvariant, Out TCovariant,
    In TContravariant)
End Interface
```

```
interface IVariant<TInvariant, out TCovariant,
    in TContravariant>
{
}
```

See Also

As Clause

Get Declaration

See

Properties

GetAllSettings Method

Visual Basic's *GetAllSettings* method returns a two-dimensional array of key-value pairs from a standardized Visual Basic section of the Windows registry.

VISUAL BASIC

```
Dim allSettings(,) As String =
    GetAllSettings(appName, sectionName)
```

C#

```
// ----- Assumes: using Microsoft.Win32;
string[,] results;
string[] keyNames;
const string settingRoot =
    "Software\\VB and VBA Program Settings";
string settingLocation = string.Format("{0}\\{1}\\{2}",
    settingRoot, appName, sectionName);
RegistryKey keyAccess =
    Registry.CurrentUser.OpenSubKey(settingLocation);
if (keyAccess.ValueCount == 0)
    results = null;
else
{
    keyNames = keyAccess.GetValueNames();
    results = new string[keyNames.Length, 2];
    for (int counter = 0; counter < keyNames.Length;
        counter++)
    {
        results[counter, 0] = keyNames[counter];
        results[counter, 1] = (string)keyAccess.GetValue(
            keyNames[counter], "");
    }
}
keyAccess.Close();
```

GetAttr Method

In Visual Basic, the *GetAttr* method retrieves the attributes for a file path. In C#, this operation is done via .NET's *File.GetAttributes* method.

VISUAL BASIC
```
Dim result As FileAttribute = GetAttr(targetFile)
```

C#
```
System.IO.FileAttributes result =
    System.IO.File.GetAttributes(targetFile);
```

The two language variations use a different set of attribute flags. VB uses a language-specific *FileAttribute* enumeration, while the .NET method uses members from the *System.IO.FileAttributes* enumeration. The two enumerations are similar in purpose, though incompatible in their member values.

GetChar Method

Visual Basic's *GetChar* method returns a single character form a string, throwing an exception for invalid 1-based position references.

VISUAL BASIC
```
' ----- Returns the fifth character.
Dim result As Char = GetChar(largeString, 5)
```

In C#, you can access individual characters of a string as if they were 0-based array elements.

C#
```
// ----- Returns the fifth character.
char result = largeString[4];
```

GetObject Method

Visual Basic's *GetObject* method returns a COM component based on its path, class, or both. In C#, use members of the *System.Marshal* class to retrieve COM component instances.

VISUAL BASIC
```
' ----- Assumes: Option Strict Off
Dim comComponent As Object

' ----- Create component from path, default class.
comComponent = GetObject(pathName)

' ----- Retrieve running instance of the indicated class.
comComponent = GetObject(, className)

' ----- Create new instance for the indicated class.
comComponent = GetObject("", className)
```

```
' ----- Create component from path, specific class.
comComponent = GetObject(pathName, className)
```

C#
```
// ----- At top of file.
using System.Runtime.InteropServices;
using System.Runtime.InteropServices.ComTypes;

// ----- In a method.
dynamic comComponent;

// ----- Create component from path, default class.
comComponent = Marshal.BindToMoniker(pathName);

// ----- Retrieve running instance of the indicated class.
comComponent = Marshal.GetActiveObject(className);

// ----- Create new instance for the indicated class.
Type whichType = Type.GetTypeFromProgID(className);
comComponent = System.Activator.CreateInstance(whichType);

// ----- Create component from path, specific class.
IPersistFile interimObject =
    (IPersistFile)Marshal.GetActiveObject(className);
interimObject.Load(pathName, 0);
comComponent = interimObject;
```

GetSetting Method

Visual Basic's *GetSetting* method returns the key value from a standardized Visual Basic section of the Windows registry.

VISUAL BASIC
```
Dim savedSetting As String =
    GetSetting(appName, sectionName, keyName)
```

C#
```
// ----- Assumes: using Microsoft.Win32;
const string settingRoot =
    "Software\\VB and VBA Program Settings";
string settingLocation = string.Format("{0}\\{1}\\{2}",
    settingRoot, appName, sectionName);
RegistryKey keyAccess =
    Registry.CurrentUser.OpenSubKey(settingLocation);
string savedSetting = (string)keyAccess.GetValue(
    keyName, "");
keyAccess.Close();
```

GetType Operator

C#'s *typeof* operator is identical to Visual Basic's *GetType* operator.

```
Dim numberType As System.Type = GetType(Integer)
```
C#
```
System.Type numberType = typeof(int);
```

GetXmlNamespace Operator

Visual Basic's `GetXmlNamespace` operator exists to support the language's XML Literals feature. C# does not include this feature, and therefore it has no equivalent for the intrinsic VB operator.

`GetXmlNamespace` returns an instance of type `XNamespace`, a class designed for .NET's LINQ to XML implementation. This class and the other classes from the `System.Xml.Linq` namespace can be used directly in C# as needed for XML content manipulation.

Global Namespace Alias

When used to indicate the root of the namespace hierarchy, C#'s `global` namespace alias is equivalent to Visual Basic's `Global` alias.

VISUAL BASIC
```
Dim theProblem As Global.System.Exception
```
C#
```
// ----- Perhaps you defined a MyApp.System.Exception
//       class in your application's code. This makes
//       it clear that you want .NET's Exception class.
global::System.Exception theProblem;
```

GoTo Statement

For ordinary jumps to line labels, C#'s `goto` statement is identical to Visual Basic's `GoTo` statement.

C#
```
goto SkipProcessing;
```
See Also

Labels, On Error Statement

Group Join Query Expression Operator (LINQ)

C#'s `join` query expression operator, when used with its `into` clause, provides functionality that parallels Visual Basic `Group Join` operator.

VISUAL BASIC

```
Dim result = From dept In Departments
             Group Join emp In Employees
             On dept.ID Equals emp.Department Into Group
             Select dept.DeptName, RecentHires = Group
```

C#

```
var result = from dept in Departments
             join emp in Employees
             on dept.ID equals emp.Department into empSets
             select new {dept.DeptName,
             RecentHires = empSets};
```

See Also

Join Query Expression Operator, Query Expressions

Group Query Expression Operator (LINQ)

C#'s *group* query expression operator parallels Visual Basic's *Group* operator. In Visual Basic, the target to be grouped can be an expression, a range variable, a comma-delimited list of expressions, or missing altogether, which implies that the target should include all range variables or fields. In C#, the target to be grouped must be a single expression or range variable.

VISUAL BASIC

```
' ----- Grouping of range variable.
Dim result = From item In Employees
             Group By item.Department Into Group

' ----- Grouping of specific field.
Dim result = From item In Employees
             Group item.FullName
             By item.Department Into Group

' ----- Grouping of multiple fields.
Dim result = From item In Employees
             Group item.FullName, item.HireDate
             By item.Department Into Group
```

C#

```
// ----- Grouping of range variable.
var result = from item in Employees
             group item by item.Department;

// ----- Grouping of specific field.
var result = from item in Employees
             group item.FullName by item.Department;

// ----- Grouping of multiple fields.
var result = from item in Employees
             group new {item.FullName, item.HireDate}
             by item.Department;
```

In Visual Basic, the *Into Group* clause is required, although a variation of this clause lets you specify a temporary identifier for subsequent processing. In C#, the *into* clause is needed only when performing additional processing on the grouped results.

VISUAL BASIC
```
Dim result = From item In Employees
             Group By item.Department Into deptSets = Group
             Order By Department
             Select deptSets
```

C#
```
var result = from item in Employees
             group item by item.Department into deptSets
             orderby deptSets.Key
             select deptSets;
```

Visual Basic's *Into* clause supports additional aggregate functions. This syntax is not supported directly in C#, but requires an additional *select* clause.

VISUAL BASIC
```
' ----- In this variation, the results will also include
'       subordinate "item" records, although C# version
'       will only include department name and count.
Dim result = From item In Employees
             Group By item.Department
             Into Group, Count()
```

C#
```
var result = from item in Employees
             group item by item.Department into deptSets
             select new { DeptName = deptSets.Key,
                          DeptMembers = deptSets.Count() };
```

See Also

Query Expressions

Handles Clause

C# does not have an equivalent statement for Visual Basic's *Handles* clause. Instead, event handlers must be attached to instance events manually using the *+=* event subscription operator. See the "AddHandler Statement" in this chapter for information on attaching events in C#.

See Also

AddHandler Statement

Hex Method

Visual Basic's *Hex* method returns a string showing the hexadecimal representation of a numeric value. Passing *"X"* as an argument to the *ToString* method of any integer value type in C# will generate the same results.

```
Dim result As String = Hex(someInteger)
```

```
string result = someInteger.ToString("X");
```

Hour Method

The *DateTime* type's *Hour* property returns the same information as Visual Basic's *Hour* method.

```
Dim whichHour As Integer = Hour(oneOrder.OrderDate)
```

```
int whichHour = oneOrder.OrderDate.Hour;
```

Identifiers

Both Visual Basic and C# use a common set of identifier naming rules, allowing for a mixture of letters, digits, and underscores, with some limitations, such as not starting an identifier with a digit.

In Visual Basic, identifiers are case-insensitive. Two VB identifiers are identical if they are the same when converted to all lower-case letters. Identifiers in C# are case-sensitive. Two variables named *customerName* and *CustomerName* in the same method would not conflict since the first letter is a different case. It is possible to create an assembly in C# with two exposed type or member names that differ only by case. Such naming would cause problems when consumed by a Visual Basic project, although VB does have rules that attempt to access the most accessible element when there is a conflict.

Visual Basic allows you to give the same (case-insensitive) name to a type and one of its members.

```
' ----- This is valid in Visual Basic.
Public Class ItemData
    Public ItemText As String
    Public ItemData As Long
End Class
```

C# does not allow this combination. You must not name a type member the same as its enclosing type in C#. If you create a Visual Basic assembly that has this shared naming of type and member, a C# project will not be able to access the member directly.

Both languages allow you to create identifiers that conflict with reserved language keywords. To use such identifiers, surround them with square brackets in Visual Basic, or prefix them with the @ symbol in C#.

```
Dim [For] As Long = 0&
```

C#

```
long @for = 0L;
```

Microsoft recommends that identifier names be either Pascal-cased or camel-cased. In Pascal casing, every distinct word within the name has an initial capital, including the start of the identifier. Camel casing is similar, but the initial letter is lowercase.

C#

```
int PascalCaseExample;
int camelCaseExample;
```

As indicated in Visual Studio's documentation, camel casing is recommended for parameter names, local variable names, and protected instance fields within types. All other identifiers, including line labels, should use Pascal casing.

If Statement

C#'s *if* statement closely parallels the *If* statement in Visual Basic.

VISUAL BASIC

```
If (testDate < Now) Then
    era = "Past"
ElseIf (testDate = Now) Then
    era = "Present"
Else
    era = "Future"
End If
```

C#

```
if (testDate < DateTime.Now)
    era = "Past";
else if (testDate == DateTime.Now)
    era = "Present";
else
    era = "Future";
```

Each condition in C# begins with *if* or *else if* (two words), and appears within a set of parentheses. While Visual Basic needs a terminating *End If* clause, C# has no such ending marker.

Visual Basic's condensed *If* statement, where the *Then* and *Else* parts appear in a single logical line, can be replicated in C#. However, this is the case only because of C#'s flexibility with whitespace, and not due to any special syntax construction.

VISUAL BASIC

```
' ----- Simple If with no Else component.
If problemOccurred Then ErrorField.Visible = True

' ----- Simple If with Else component.
If (IsValidZip(zipCode) = True) Then _
    city = GetZipCity(zipCode) Else city = "Unknown"
```

C#
```
// ----- Simple if with no else component.
if (problemOccurred) ErrorField.Visible = true;

// ----- Simple if with else component.
if (IsValidZip(zipCode) == true) city =
    GetZipCity(zipCode); else city = "Unknown";
```

As in Visual Basic, C#'s conditional statements can include any mix of expressions or logical operators, just as long as the result of each expression is a Boolean value. You must surround the condition in C# with a set of parentheses; these parentheses are optional in VB. C# supports any number of `else if` clauses, and you can nest `if` statements, just like in Visual Basic.

If Operator

When used with three arguments, Visual Basic's `If` operator finds its equal in C#'s `?:` conditional operator, traditionally called the ternary operator.

VISUAL BASIC
```
Dim result As String = If(amount > 100, "Overflow",
    amount.ToString())
```

C#
```
string result = amount > 100 ? "Overflow" :
    amount.ToString();
```

As with the `If` operator, the `?:` operator includes three expressions, separated by the distinct `?` and `:` symbols: (1) a Boolean test condition, (2) the value to return if the condition is true, and (3) the value to return if the condition is false. As in Visual Basic, the `?:` operator short-circuits; either the true or false part is evaluated, but not both.

C#'s conditional operator is right-associative. Consider the following expressions, which are all equivalent.

VISUAL BASIC
```
result1 = If(a, b, If(c, d, e))
```

C#
```
result1 = a ? b : c ? d : e;
result2 = a ? b : (c ? d : e);
```

Visual Basic also includes a two-argument version of the `If` operator, which returns the second argument if the first one evaluates to *Nothing*. In C#, the `??` coalescence operator performs this same task.

VISUAL BASIC
```
' ----- Assumes: Dim suppliedName As String
Dim customerName As String = If(suppliedName, "Customer")
```

C#
```
// ----- Assumes: string suppliedName;
string customerName = suppliedName ?? "Customer";
```

IIf Method

Both the *IIf* method and the *If* operator return one of two expressions based on a Boolean test condition. Visual Basic's *IIf* method, retained for historical reasons from the pre-.NET version of the language, lacks the short-circuiting behavior found in the *If* operator. Also, *If* does a better job at implicitly identifying the return type of the expression; *IIf* always returns a value of type *Object*.

C# does not have an exact equivalent for the *IIf* method. However, its *?:* conditional operator is equivalent to VB's *If* operator. See the "If Operator" entry in this chapter for information on using its C# counterpart.

Implements Clause

In Visual Basic, all interface member implementations are explicit, and require the *Implements* clause as part of the method declaration.

VISUAL BASIC
```
Interface IDomesticate
    Sub Train(ByVal daysRequired As Integer)
End Interface

Class Dog
    Implements IDomesticate

    Public Sub Train(ByVal daysRequired As Integer) _
            Implements IDomesticate.Train
        ' ----- Implementation code here.
    End Sub
End Class
```

When a C# class or structure implements an interface member, it does so implicitly via the name and argument signature, or explicitly by including the interface name in the method definition.

C#
```
interface IDomesticate
{
    void Train(int daysRequired);
}

class Dog : IDomesticate
{
    // ----- Implicit implementation.
    public void Train(int daysRequired) { }

    // ----- Explicit implementation
    public void IDomesticate.Train(int daysRequired) { }
}
```

One advantage (or disadvantage, depending on your perspective) of Visual Basic's syntax is that the name of the implementing member need not be the same as the interface member being implemented.

```
Public Sub TeachTheDog(ByVal daysRequired As Integer) _
        Implements IDomesticate.Train
```
This ability to change the implementation name is not supported in C#.

See Also

Implements Statement

Implements Statement

Visual Basic types that implement interfaces include the *Implements* statement immediately after the type declaration. Multiple interfaces appear as a comma-delimited list of interface names.

VISUAL BASIC
```
Public Class Dog
    Implements IDomesticate
```
In C#, the comma-delimited list of interface names appears immediately after the declared type name, separated from the name by a colon. This list may also include a single class name if the new type derives from a base class.

C#
```
public class Dog : IDomesticate
{
```
See Also

Implements Clause

Imports Statement

Visual Basic's *Imports* statement identifies namespaces that will be used within the current source file without the need to provide the full, absolute namespace path to its members.

VISUAL BASIC
```
' ----- At the top of a source code file.
Imports System.Text

' ----- Later, in a method in the same file, you don't
'       need the full System.Text.StringBuilder path.
Dim content As New StringBuilder()
```
C#'s *using* directive performs this same identification of namespaces.

C#
```
// ----- At the top of a source code file.
using System.Text;

// ----- Later, in a method in the same file, you don't
//       need the full System.Text.StringBuilder path.
StringBuilder content = new StringBuilder();
```

Both languages support the assignment of alias names to imported namespaces.

```
Imports TextStuff = System.Text
```

```
using TextStuff = System.Text;
```

The alias can be prefixed to member names within that same file.

```
Dim content As New TextStuff.StringBuilder()
```

```
TextStuff.StringBuilder content =
    new TextStuff.StringBuilder();
```

Visual Basic also provides project-wide importing of namespaces, allowing programmers to reference such namespaces without the need to include an *Imports* statement in every file. C# does not support this project-level feature. Instead, you must include the appropriate *using* directive in every file that references imported namespaces.

New with Visual Studio 2015

In addition to namespaces, VB's *Imports* statement lets you specify the full name hierarchy of a container type (class, structure, module, interface, or enumeration), and have the accessible members of that type available for use in the current file without qualification, at least when the use of a member name by itself is unambiguous. C#'s *using static* directive duplicates this feature, but only in the 2015 edition of the language and beyond.

```
Imports System.Drawing.SystemColors

' ----- Later, in method code in the same file, members
'        of SystemColors can be used directly.
displayColor = ControlText
```

```
using static System.Drawing.SystemColors;

// ----- Later, in method code in the same file, members
//        of SystemColors can be used directly.
displayColor = ControlText;
```

Visual Basic allows alias assignments when importing a type, but this is not permitted in C# *using static* statements.

In Modifier

See

Generics

Indexers

See

> Default Modifier

Inheritance

See

> Inherits Statement

Inherits Statement

In Visual Basic, a derived class specifies its base class using the *Inherits* statement. This statement appears on the first line within the class definition.

VISUAL BASIC
```
' ----- Dog derives from Animal, and
'       implements IDomesticate.
Public Class Dog
    Inherits Animal
    Implements IDomesticate
```

In C#, the base class appears after the declared derived class name, separated from the name by a colon. Implemented interfaces may also appear after this colon, with commas used to separate multiple interfaces and the base class name.

C#
```
// ----- Dog derives from Animal, and
//       implements IDomesticate.
public class Dog : Animal, IDomesticate
```

Initializers

Visual Basic automatically initializes all fields and local variables to their default values (typically *Nothing* or some variation of zero) when no other initialization is used. In C#, while you don't need to provide initialization at the moment of declaration for fields and local variables, you must initialize these variables before they are used in code. Neither language allows you to provide in-line initialization of instance fields in structures. These must be initialized within a constructor.

Basic initialization of variables and constants in both languages is done with an assignment.

VISUAL BASIC
```
Const closeToPi As Decimal = 3.2@
Dim notInitialized As Integer
Dim startingZero As Integer = 0
Dim startingUnused As String = Nothing
Dim startingEmpty As String = ""
```

```
Dim readyToUse As Customer = Nothing
Dim fromExpression As Customer = GetCustomer(123)
```

C#
```
const decimal closeToPi = 3.2m;
int notInitialized;
int startingZero = 0;
string startingUnused = null;
string startingEmpty = "";
Customer readyToUse = null;
Customer fromExpression = GetCustomer(123);
```

In both languages, object initializers let you set member fields and properties as part of instance declaration. The member values appear in a set of curly braces. In Visual Basic, this block appears as part of a *With* clause, and each member is prefixed with a period; C# leaves out both the *With* keyword and the periods.

VISUAL BASIC
```
' ----- Explicit type.
Dim cat1 As New Animal With {.Age = 5, .Name = "Fluffy"}
Dim cat2 As Animal = New Animal With {.Age = 10,
    .Name = "Fang"}

' ----- Implicit type.
Dim kitten = New Animal With {.Age = 0, .Name = "Kitty"}

' ----- With custom constructor.
Dim boss As New Employee("John Smith") With {
    .Title = "President"}
```

C#
```
// ----- Explicit type.
Animal cat = new Animal {Age = 5, Name = "Fluffy"};

// ----- Implicit type.
var kitten = new Animal {Age = 0, Name = "Kitty"};

// ----- With custom constructor.
Employee boss = new Employee("John Smith")
    {Title = "President"};
```

Both Visual Basic and C# can initialize arrays and collections as part of instance declaration. Visual Basic requires a *From* clause when initializing a collection, but no such keyword is required in C#.

VISUAL BASIC
```
' ----- Array. In the explicitSize declaration, "3"
'        refers to the upper bound, not the size.
Dim implicitSize() As Integer = {2, 3, 5, 7, 11}
Dim explicitSize() As Integer =
    New Integer(3) {13, 17, 19, 23}
Dim simpler() As Integer = {29, 31, 37}

Dim multiDimension(,) As Integer = {{1, 2}, {3, 4}}
```

```
Dim jagged()() As Integer = New Integer(1)() _
    {New Integer() {1, 2, 3},
    New Integer() {4, 5, 6, 7, 8}}

' ----- Collection.
Dim basicList As New List(Of Integer) From {1, 2, 3, 4, 5}
Dim dayInfo = New Dictionary(Of Integer, String) _
    From {{0, "Sunday"}, {1, "Monday"}}
```

C#

```
// ----- Array. In the explicitSize declaration, "4"
//       refers to the size, not the upper bound.
int[] implicitSize = new int[] {2, 3, 5, 7, 11};
int[] explicitSize = new int[4] {13, 17, 19, 23};
int[] simpler = {29, 31, 37};

int[,] multiDimension = {{1, 2}, {3, 4}};
int[][] jagged = {new int[] {1, 2, 3},
                    new int[] {4, 5, 6, 7, 8}};

// ----- Collection.
List<int> basicList = new List<int> {1, 2, 3, 4, 5};
var dayInfo = new Dictionary<int, string>
    {{0, "Sunday"}, {1, "Monday"}};
```

Here is a more involved example that combines collection and object initializers.

VISUAL BASIC

```
Dim moreCats As New List(Of Cat) From
{
    New Cat() With {.Name = "Furrytail", .Age = 5},
    New Cat() With {.Name = "Peaches", .Age = 4}
}
```

C#

```
List<Cat> moreCats = new List<Cat>
{
    new Cat() {Name = "Furrytail", Age = 5},
    new Cat() {Name = "Peaches", Age = 4}
};
```

Collection initializers can be used as expressions, wherever a collection or array is expected.

VISUAL BASIC

```
Dim result As Integer = CondenseArray(
    New Integer() {1, 2, 3})
```

C#

```
int result = CondenseArray(new int[] {1, 2, 3});
```

Initialization of anonymous types in both languages follows the syntax of standard initialization.

VISUAL BASIC

```
Dim pet = New With {.Age = 3, .Name = "Rover"}
```

C#

```
var pet = new {Age = 3, Name = "Rover"};
```

When working with generics, Visual Basic's *Nothing* literal lets you assign the default value of a type to a variable. In C#'s, the *default* operator provides the same functionality.

VISUAL BASIC

```
Class Special(Of T)
    Public watchValue As T = Nothing
End Class
```

C#

```
class Special<T>
{
    public T watchValue = default(T);
}
```

New with Visual Studio 2015

Before 2015, Visual Basic already included in-line initialization features for read-write auto-properties, but initialization of read-only automatic properties came about with the 2015 release. In that same year, C# gained the ability to assign a value to an automatic property during declaration for both read-only and read-write properties.

VISUAL BASIC

```
' ----- Read-write property.
Public Property CoreName As String = "Unknown"

' ----- Read-only property.
Public ReadOnly Property CoreName As String = "Unknown"
```

C#

```
// ----- Read-write property.
public string CoreName { get; set; } = "Unknown";

// ----- Read-only property.
public string CoreName { get; } = "Unknown";
```

InStr Method

In C#, use the *string* type's *IndexOf* method to return results similar to that of Visual Basic's *InStr* method. *IndexOf* returns *-1* if the sought-after substring is not found, while *InStr* returns *0* when there is no match. Also, *InStr*'s result is 1-based, where a match at the start of a string returns *1*. The *IndexOf* method, by contrast, is 0-based, returning *0* when a match occurs with the first character of the source string. When indicating a starting position with *InStr*, that value is also 1-based, while the related index in *IndexOf* is 0-based.

VISUAL BASIC

```
' ----- The results will be 1-based.
position = InStr(internetUrl, "://")
```

```
' ----- The index is also 1-based.
afterDomain = InStr(position + 3, internetUrl, "/")
```

C#
```
// ----- The results will be 0-based.
position = internetUrl.IndexOf("://");

// ----- The index is also 0-based.
afterDomain = internetUrl.IndexOf("/", position + 3);
```

Both methods let you specify binary (case-sensitive) or text (case-insensitive) search methods through an optional argument.

VISUAL BASIC
```
' ----- Perform a case-insensitive match.
position = InStr(originalText, pattern, CompareMethod.Text)
```

C#
```
// ----- Perform a case-insensitive match.
position = originalText.IndexOf(pattern,
    StringComparison.CurrentCultureIgnoreCase);
```

InStrRev Method

In C#, use the *string* type's *LastIndexOf* method to return results similar to that of Visual Basic's *InStrRev* method. *LastIndexOf* returns *-1* if the sought-after substring is not found, while *InStrRev* returns *0* when there is no match. Also, *InStrRev*'s result is 1-based, where a match at the start of a string returns *1*. The *LastIndexOf* method, by contrast, is 0-based, returning *0* when a match occurs with the first character of the source string. When indicating a starting position with *InStrRev*, that value is also 1-based, while the related index in *LastIndexOf* is 0-based.

VISUAL BASIC
```
' ----- The results will be 1-based.
filePart = InStrRev(fullPath, "\")

' ----- The index is also 1-based.
directoryPart = InStrRev(fullPath, "\", filePart - 1)
```

C#
```
// ----- The results will be 0-based.
filePart = fullPath.LastIndexOf(@"\");

// ----- The index is also 0-based.
directoryPart = fullPath.LastIndexOf(@"\", filePart - 1);
```

Both methods let you specify binary (case-sensitive) or text (case-insensitive) search methods through an optional argument.

VISUAL BASIC
```
' ----- Perform a case-insensitive match.
position = InStrRev(originalText, pattern,
    CompareMethod.Text)
```

```
// ----- Perform a case-insensitive match.
position = originalText.LastIndexOf(pattern,
    StringComparison.CurrentCultureIgnoreCase);
```

Input Method

Visual Basic's *Input* method reads content from a file opened with the *FileOpen* method. The method typically retrieves data previously written with the *Write* and *WriteLine* methods, data that is structured, comma-delimited, and qualified with quotation marks or similar enveloping characters.

C# does not have a direct equivalent for the *Input* statement, or for the entire *Write* and *Input* file management system. Instead, delimited files must be parsed manually by reading in each character and interpreting fields and lines appropriately. For sample code on how to read in such files, see the "OpenTextFieldParser Method" entry in Chapter 3.

InputBox Method

C# does not include an equivalent for Visual Basic's *InputBox* method. Internally, the *InputBox* method creates a standard *Form*-derived instance with its own *TextBox*, *Label*, and *Button* controls. In C#, you would need to add a custom *Form* to your project with the relevant controls. The code would have an instantiating routine similar to the following.

C#
```
public string InputBox(string prompt, string title = "",
    string defaultResponse = "", int xPos = -1,
    int yPos = -1)
{
    // ----- Set up the presentation. Many of these
    //       statements could be enhanced.
    label1.Text = prompt;
    textBox1.Text = defaultResponse;
    if ((title == null) || (title.Trim().Length == 0))
        this.Text = System.Reflection.Assembly.
            GetCallingAssembly().GetName().FullName;
    else
        this.Text = title;
    if ((xPos == -1) | (yPos == -1))
        this.StartPosition =
            FormStartPosition.CenterScreen;
    else
    {
        this.StartPosition = FormStartPosition.Manual;
        this.DesktopLocation = new Point(xPos, yPos);
    }
```

```
//  ----- Prompt the user. Return "" on Cancel.
if (this.ShowDialog() == DialogResult.OK)
    return textBox1.Text;
else
    return "";
}
```

Calling the code would be not too different from an *InputBox* call.

C#
```
string result = (new MyInputBoxForm()).InputBox(
    "Type in your name.", "Name Request");
```

InputString Method

Visual Basic's *InputString* method returns a text string, up to a maximum length, from a file opened using the *FileOpen* method.

VISUAL BASIC
```
Dim zipCode As String = InputString(fileNumber, 5)
```

C# does not include the same file-management features found in VB. Instead, it is common to work with the *System.IO.StreamReader* class to read text files. This class does not include a direct equivalent for the *InputString* method. Instead, you can read in bytes one at a time, and join them to build the target string.

C#
```
string zipCode = "";
for (int counter = 0; counter < 5; counter++)
{
    if (openedStream.Peek() == -1)
        break;
    zipCode += (char)openedStream.Read();
}
```

See Also

FileOpen Method

Int Method

In C#, use the *System.Math.Floor* method to produce results identical to those returned by Visual Basic's *Int* method. Integer values always return the original value. For decimal inputs, the method returns the integer portion of the number, with rounding toward negative infinity.

VISUAL BASIC
```
result = Int(originalDecimal)
```

C#
```
result = System.Math.Floor(originalDecimal);
```

Integer Data Type

C#'s intrinsic *int* data type is identical to Visual Basic's *Integer* data type. Both types are aliases for .NET's *System.Int32* type. For integer literals, Visual Basic uses an *I*, *i*, or *%* suffix after the value; C# does not include such a suffix. Instead, all integer literals that will fit into the range of the *int* data type are automatically typed as *int*.

VISUAL BASIC
```
Dim counter As Integer = 0%   ' or 0I or 0i
```

C#
```
int counter = 0;
```

Interface Statement

C#'s *interface* statement is equivalent to Visual Basic's *Interface* statement. When declaring an interface that derives from one or more interfaces, VB's *Inherits* clause lists those interfaces, appearing as the first line within the *Interface* statement. In C#, the base interfaces appear as a comma-delimited list after the defined interface name, separated from that name by a colon.

VISUAL BASIC
```
Interface ISomethingNew
    Inherits ISomethingOld
    ' ----- Members appear here.
End Interface
```

C#
```
interface ISomethingNew : ISomethingOld
{
    // ----- Members appear here.
}
```

Interfaces in both Visual Basic and C# can include methods, properties, events, and indexers (default properties). Visual Basic interfaces also support subordinate interfaces, classes, and structures, none of which can be included in C# interfaces.

VISUAL BASIC
```
Interface IOptions
    ' ----- Methods with and without return
    Function MethodWithData(ByVal incoming As String) _
        As Integer
    Sub WorkOnlyMethod()

    ' ----- Property and Indexer
    Property Name() As String
    Default ReadOnly Property Item(
        ByVal index As Integer) As String

    ' ----- Event (with and without defined delegate)
    Event EventFromDelegate As DelegateSignature
    Event EventDefinedInline(ByVal source As Object)
```

```
' ----- Class
Class SubordinateClass
    ' ----- Members here
End Class

' ----- Structure
Structure SubordinateStructure
    ' ----- Members here
End Structure

' ----- Interface
Interface ISubordinate
    ' ----- Members here
End Interface
End Interface
```

C#
```
interface IOptions
{
    // ----- Methods with and without return
    int MethodWithData(string incoming);
    void WorkOnlyMethod();

    // ----- Property and Indexer
    string Name {get; set;}
    string this[int index] {get;}

    // ----- Event (with delegate defined elsewhere)
    event DelegateSignature EventName;
}
```

Interfaces support the following modifiers in each language.

Visual Basic Modifier	C# Modifier
Friend	internal
Partial (starting in 2015)	partial
Private	private
Protected	protected
Protected Friend	protected internal
Public	public
Shadows	new

Interfaces in Visual Basic are *Friend* by default, just as interfaces in C# are *internal* by default. In both languages, all members are public by definition.

During implementation of an interface, Visual Basic uses the *Implements* modifier, both on the type and explicitly on each implementing member. When performing explicit interface implementations in C#, the name of each member is prefixed with the interface name.

VISUAL BASIC
```
Class Employee
    Implements IPerson
```

```
    Public Property Name As String Implements IPerson.Name
        ' ----- Implementation here.
    End Property
End Class
```

C#
```
class Employee : IPerson
{
    public string IPerson.Name
    {
        // ----- Implementation here.
    }
}
```

Because the *Implements* clause on the member includes the name of the interface member, the name of the class member implementing the item does not have to be the same in Visual Basic. In C#, the implementing member name is always the same as the interface member name being implemented.

IPmt Method

See

Financial Methods

IRR Method

See

Financial Methods

Is Comparison Operator

C#'s == comparison operator provides functionality similar to Visual Basic's *Is* operator when used with reference types. In both languages, the comparison can be between two possibly identical instances, or between one type and *Nothing* (VB) or *null* (C#).

VISUAL BASIC
```
' ----- Standard instance comparison.
If (firstInstance Is secondInstance) Then

' ----- Comparisons with Nothing.
If (anotherInstance Is Nothing) Then
```

C#
```
// ----- Standard instance comparison.
if (firstIntance == secondInstance)

// ----- Comparisons with Nothing (null in C#).
if (anotherInstance == null)
```

IsArray Method

Visual Basic's *IsArray* method returns true for all non-null instances that derive from *System.Array*.

VISUAL BASIC
```
If (IsArray(someVariable)) Then
```

C#
```
if ((someVariable != null) &&
    (someVariable is System.Array))
```

IsDBNull Method

Visual Basic's *IsDBNull* method returns true for all non-null instances that derive from *System.DBNull*.

VISUAL BASIC
```
If (IsDBNull(someVariable)) Then
```

C#
```
if ((someVariable != null) &&
    (someVariable is System.DBNull))
```

IsDate Method

Visual Basic's *IsDate* method returns true for all non-null instances of *System.DateTime*.

VISUAL BASIC
```
If (IsDate(someVariable)) Then
```

C#
```
if ((someVariable != null) &&
    (someVariable is System.DateTime))
```

IsDate also returns true for strings that include valid date or time content. The *DateTime* structure's *TryParse* method can indicate this as well.

C#
```
if (DateTime.TryParse(testString, out resultingDate))
```

IsError Method

Visual Basic's *IsError* method returns true for all non-null instances that derive from *System.Exception*.

VISUAL BASIC
```
If (IsError(someVariable)) Then
```

C#

```
if ((someVariable != null) &&
    (someVariable is System.Exception))
```

IsFalse Operator

See

Operator Statement

IsNot Comparison Operator

C#'s `!=` comparison operator provides functionality similar to Visual Basic's *IsNot* operator when used with reference types. In both languages, the comparison can be between two possibly identical instances, or between one type and *Nothing* (VB) or *null* (C#).

VISUAL BASIC

```
' ----- Standard instance comparison.
If (firstInstance IsNot secondInstance) Then

' ----- Comparisons with Nothing.
If (anotherInstance IsNot Nothing) Then
```

C#

```
// ----- Standard instance comparison.
if (firstIntance != secondInstance)

// ----- Comparisons with Nothing (null in C#).
if (anotherInstance != null)
```

IsNothing Method

Visual Basic's *IsNothing* method indicates whether a reference instance is undefined. In C#, compare the instance to *null* to produce the same result.

VISUAL BASIC

```
If (IsNothing(someVariable)) Then
```

C#

```
if (someVariable == null)
```

See Also

Nothing Literal, Nullable Types

IsNumeric Method

C# lacks an equivalent for Visual Basic's *IsNumeric* method. The closest option is to use a *TryParse* method from one or more of the numeric data types. For example, consider using *double.TryParse* to determine if a string contains a valid *double*.

C#
```
double tempValue;
if (double.TryParse(sourceText, out tempValue) == true)
    // ----- Is numeric.
```

VB's *IsNumeric* method allows much greater flexibility in the format of the incoming test string. For example, currency symbols found in strings like *"$100"* return *True* when using *IsNumeric*, but *False* when using the various *TryParse* methods.

IsReference Method

Visual Basic's *IsReference* method returns true for all instances other than those that derive from *System.ValueType*.

VISUAL BASIC
```
If (IsReference(someVariable)) Then
```

C#
```
if (!(someVariable is System.Value))
```

IsTrue Operator

See

Operator Statement

Iterator Modifier

In Visual Basic, iterators are functions or properties declared with the *Iterator* modifier, and that make use of the *Yield* statement. In C#, iterators are also built from functions or properties, and include the *yield return* statement.

VISUAL BASIC
```
Public Iterator Function FirstFivePrimes() As _
        IEnumerable(Of Integer)
    Yield 2
    Yield 3
    Yield 5
    Yield 7
    Yield 11
End Function
```

C#
```
public IEnumerable<int> FirstFivePrimes()
{
    yield return 2;
    yield return 3;
    yield return 5;
    yield return 7;
    yield return 11;
}
```

When implemented as a read-only property, Visual Basic uses both the *Iterator* and *ReadOnly* modifiers on the property declaration. As with all read-only properties in C#, there is no special read-only modifier applied to the declaration. Instead, the omission of the *set* accessor makes the property read-only.

VISUAL BASIC
```
Public ReadOnly Iterator Property EvensOnly(
        ByVal maximum As Integer) _
        As IEnumerable(Of Integer)
    Get
        For counter As Integer = 2 To maximum
            Yield counter
        Next counter
    End Get
End Property
```

C#
```
public IEnumerable<int> EvensOnly(int maximum)
{
    get
    {
        for (int counter = 2; counter <= maximum;
             counter++)
            yield return counter;
    }
}
```

Visual Basic allows the *Iterator* modifier to be used with an anonymous method. This variation is not supported in C#.

See Also

Yield Statement

Iterators

See

Iterator Modifier

Join Method

The *string* type's *Join* method produces the same delimited merger of a source array as Visual Basic's *Join* method. In VB, the source array argument comes before the delimiter in the argument list. In C#, the arguments are reversed.

VISUAL BASIC
```
result = Join(sourceArray, ":")
```

C#
```
result = string.Join(":", sourceArray);
```

Join Query Expression Operator (LINQ)

C#'s *join* query expression operator is the same as the *Join* operator in Visual Basic.

VISUAL BASIC
```
Dim result = From item In Employees
             Join dept In Departments
             On item.Department Equals dept.ID
             Select item.FullName, dept.DeptName
```

C#
```
var result = from item in Employees
             join dept in Departments
             on item.Department equals dept.ID
             select new {item.FullName, dept.DeptName};
```

In both languages, you can use multiple "from" and "where" clauses to perform joins between different range sources. See the "From Query Expression Operator" entry in this chapter for an example that uses this syntax.

See Also

Query Expressions

Key Modifier

See

Anonymous Types

Kill Method

Visual Basic's *Kill* method deletes a file or directory, including any subordinate items within the directory. In C#, deleting files and deleting directories are two distinct operations, each using a method within the *System.IO* namespace. File removals use the *File.Delete* method, while directories use the *Directory.Delete* method. An optional Boolean argument on this second method indicates whether the contents of a directory should be deleted recursively.

VISUAL BASIC
```
Kill(pathToFileOrDirectory)
```

C#
```
// ----- Deleting a file.
System.IO.File.Delete(pathToFile);

// ----- Deleting an empty directory.
System.IO.Directory.Delete(pathToDirectory);

// ----- Deleting a non-empty directory.
System.IO.Directory.Delete(pathToDirectory, True);
```

Labels

Both Visual Basic and C# support line labels within methods. A colon (:) follows the label in both languages.

```
StartOver:
    ' ----- Later...
    GoTo StartOver
```

```
StartOver:
    // ----- Later...
    goto StartOver;
```

Line labels are case-sensitive in C#; you can include two identically named labels in the same method as long as they vary by case. This differs from Visual Basic's case-insensitive labels; VB does not allow two identically spelled labels in the same method, even if they differ by case.

Visual Basic allows labels to be wholly numeric. This is not supported in C#.

```
100:
    ' ----- Some code here.
```

See Also

GoTo Statement

Lambda Expressions

C# includes lambda expressions and anonymous functions that parallel the same features in Visual Basic. Single-line lambda expressions in both languages are quite similar, although the C# version includes a special => lambda operator not required in VB implementations.

```
' ----- NOTE: These expressions are not meant to be
'             used alone, but are shown here out of context
'             for demonstration purposes only.

' ----- With typed arguments.
Function(ByVal limit As Integer, ByVal code As String) _
    code.Length > limit

' ----- With inferred arguments.
Function(first, second) first <> second

' ----- With no arguments.
Sub() LogAction()
```

```
// ----- With typed arguments.
(int limit, string code) => code.Length > limit

// ----- With inferred arguments.
(first, second) => first != second

// ----- With no arguments.
() => LogAction()
```

Multiline anonymous functions in Visual Basic appear by starting the logic on the line following the argument list, and ending the block with an *End Sub* or *End Function* statement. C# uses a set of curly braces after the => operator to enable such logic blocks.

VISUAL BASIC

```
Sub(ByVal someArgument As Integer)
    ' ----- This could also be Function...End Function.
End Sub
```

C#

```
(int someArgument) =>
{
    // ----- Code appears here.
};
```

Anonymous functions in both languages can be asynchronous by preceding the entire expression with *Async* (Visual Basic) or *async* (C#).

Late Binding

In Visual Basic, late-bound instances are created as *Object*, and must be defined in a source file or project that uses *Option Strict Off*.

VISUAL BASIC

```
' ----- At the top of the file.
Option Strict Off

' ----- Later, in method code.
Dim basicValue As Object = 20
Dim complexValue As Object = New ExampleType()

' ----- This method call is not checked at compile-time.
complexValue.ProcessData()
```

In C#, late binding (often called "dynamic binding" in that language) occurs through the *dynamic* type declaration expression.

C#

```
dynamic basicValue = 20;
dynamic complexValue = new ExampleType();

// ----- This method call is not checked at compile-time.
complexValue.ProcessData();
```

In both languages, when assigning a value type to a dynamic variable, boxing and unboxing will occur as the value is used throughout your code.

LBound Method

The `System.Array` class' `GetLowerBound` method returns the same information as Visual Basic's `LBound` method. For multidimensional arrays, `LBound` assumes the first rank, unless another 1-based rank is specified. The `GetLowerBound` method requires a 0-based rank.

VISUAL BASIC
```
' ----- Default, first rank assumed.
result = LBound(someArray)

' ----- 1-based rank specified (third rank).
result = LBound(someArray, 3)
```

C#
```
// ----- 0-based rank specified (third rank).
result = someArray.GetLowerBound(2);
```

For standard .NET arrays, the lower bound of any array rank is always zero.

LCase Method

The `char` and `string` data types in C# each include a `ToLower` method that is an exact replacement for Visual Basic's intrinsic `LCase` method.

VISUAL BASIC
```
result = LCase(someStringOrChar)
```

C#
```
result = someStringOrChar.ToLower();
```

Left Method

Visual Basic's `Left` method returns the leftmost characters of a source string. Use the `Substring` method of C#'s `string` class to return similar content.

VISUAL BASIC
```
' ----- Return first three characters.
Dim areaCode As String = Left(phoneNumber, 3)
```

C#
```
// ----- Return first three characters.
string areaCode = phoneNumber.Substring(0, 3);
```

The `Left` method will silently return the entire string if the length requested exceeds the full length of the string. In C#, the `Substring` method will throw an exception if the length requested is too long. Always verify the length of the string before using the `Substring` method.

Len Method

Visual Basic's `Len` method returns the length of a string, or the number of bytes occupied by a value type. The following table shows the return value for expressions of specific Visual Basic data types.

Expression Type	C# Data Type	Return Value
`Boolean`	`bool`	2
`Byte`	`byte`	1
`Char`	`char`	2
`Char` array	`char` array	`expression.Length`
`Date`	Not available	8
`Decimal`	`decimal`	8
`Double`	`double`	8
`Integer`	`int`	4
`Long`	`long`	8
`SByte`	`sbyte`	1
`Short`	`short`	2
`Single`	`float`	4
`String`	`string`	`expression.Length`
`UInteger`	`uint`	4
`ULong`	`ulong`	8
`UShort`	`ushort`	2
`structure`	`structure`	Length of structure members, with adjustments

The `sizeof` operator in C# returns results that are similar to VB's `Len` method when used with basic value types. For the intrinsic value types listed in the above table, `sizeof` returns the same values as `Len` with two exceptions: (1) `sizeof(bool)` returns *1* instead of the `Len(Boolean)` value of *2*; and (2) `sizeof(decimal)` returns *16* instead of the `Len(Decimal)` value of *8*.

Let Query Expression Operator (LINQ)

C#'s `let` query expression operator is identical to Visual Basic's `Let` operator.

VISUAL BASIC
```
Dim result = From oneEmployee in Employees
             Let annualSalary =
             oneEmployee.WeeklySalary * 52
             Where annualSalary >= 50000
             Select oneEmployee.FullName, annualSalary
```

C#
```
var result = from oneEmployee in Employees
             let annualSalary =
             oneEmployee.WeeklySalary * 52
             where annualSalary >= 50000
             select new {oneEmployee.FullName,
             annualSalary};
```

See Also

Query Expressions

Lifetime and Scope

With one significant difference within method code, C# and Visual Basic generally follow the same lifetime and scoping rules for variables.

Lifetime

Lifetime indicates how long the value stored within a variable remains available. Both languages mostly follow the same rules for managing variable lifetime. *Shared* (VB) and *static* (C#) fields declared outside of methods have application lifetime, as do fields that appear within Visual Basic *Module* statements. Non-static and non-shared type-level fields have lifetimes that last as long as the instance does. Local *Static* variables in Visual Basic methods have application or instance lifetime, depending on whether the containing method is *Shared* or not, respectively. C# does not support local static variables.

The key difference between the languages appears when using non-static local variables. In Visual Basic, all local non-static variables, whether declared inside or outside of a given block, have procedure-lifetime. If you declare a variable within an *If* statement, its value will remain throughout the entire procedure, although scoping rules limit access to that variable to just that block. This means that if you reenter the block, the variable may retain the value it had the last time you passed through that block. Because of this, you should always initialize variables defined within a block.

In C#, variables have block-level lifetimes. If you declare a variable within an *if* statement block, its lifetime ends once your code leaves that block.

Scope

Scope refers to which parts of your source code have access to a specific identifier. Visual Basic and C# follow the same scoping rules for type-level, procedure-level, and block-level variables.

Like Comparison Operator

C# does not have an equivalent for Visual Basic's *Like* operator. Instead, you can use features from .NET's *System.Text.RegularExpressions* namespace to match text patterns.

VISUAL BASIC
```
If (seriesName Like "A*") Then
    ' ----- Code for items that begin with "A".
```

C#
```
//' ----- At the top of a file.
using System.Text.RegularExpressions;
```

```
// ----- Later, in a method.
if ((new Regex("A.*")).IsMatch(seriesName))
{
    // ----- Code for items that begin with "A".
```

The pattern language used in regular expressions is very different and much more extensive than the expressions used with the *Like* operator. Read the Visual Studio documentation to learn about the full set of regular expression patterns.

Line Continuation Character

See

> _ Line Continuation Character

Line Numbers

See

> Labels

LineInput Method

Visual Basic's *LineInput* method returns a text string containing the next line of text from a file opened using the *FileOpen* method. The trailing newline is not appended to the returned string.

VISUAL BASIC
```
Dim content As String = LineInput(fileNumber)
```

C# does not include the same file-management features included with VB. Instead, it is common to work with the *System.IO.StreamReader* class to read text files. This class includes a *ReadLine* method that is comparable to VB's *InputString* method.

C#
```
string zipCode = openedStream.ReadLine();
```

See Also

> FileOpen Method

LINQ

See

> Query Expressions

Literals

Visual Basic and C# both support a wide range of value type literals, although there are some significant feature differences between the languages.

Unicode Sequences

Although they are not included in Visual Basic, you may encounter string and character literals in C# with Unicode escape sequences, each prefixed with the \U or \u escape code. Comparable VB strings embed the target character directly in the text, or use the *ChrW* function to obtain the character representation of a Unicode value.

VISUAL BASIC
```
' ----- Embed the symbol directly.
Dim currencySymbol As Char = "£"c

' ----- Use the ChrW function.
Dim currencySymbol As Char = ChrW(&H00A3)
```

C#
```
// ----- \u00a3 is the British Pound symbol.
char currencySymbol = '\u00a3';
```

C# also supports a \x escape code that is similar the \u, but that can be followed by a variable-length hex value that indicates the character to embed. This is another text-specific feature not supported in Visual Basic.

Character and String Literals

In Visual Basic, string literals are enclosed in a set of double quotes, and any embedded double-quotes are doubled within the text. C# supports this format via verbatim strings. Such strings are prefixed with the @ symbol.

VISUAL BASIC
```
Dim notice As String = "This is ""verbatim"" text."
```

C#
```
string notice = @"This is ""verbatim"" text.";
```

> **New with Visual Studio 2015**
> C# verbatim strings can break across physical line boundaries, resulting in an embedded line break in the literal string. This matches the behavior in Visual Basic beginning with VB's 2015 release. Before that release, such line breaks in VB would normally be included in strings using one of the intrinsic literals, such as *vbCrLf*.

VISUAL BASIC
```
' ----- 2015 and later only.
Dim multiLine As String = "First Line
Second Line"

' ----- Before 2015 release.
Dim multiLine As String = "First Line" & vbCrLf & _
    "Second Line"
```

C#
```
string multiLine = @"First Line
Second Line";
```

C# supports a second string format that it uses as its standard method of defining string literals. While still surrounded by double quotes, the content can include any number of escape sequences, each beginning with a backslash (\) character. The @ symbol is not used to start these strings.

C#
```
string notice = "This is \"regular\" text.";
```

The following table lists the escape sequences that you can use in these strings, along with the most compatible VB intrinsic literal (found in `Microsoft.VisualBasic.Constants`) for each sequence.

Character	Hex	C#	Visual Basic
Alert	0x07	\a	Chr(7)
Backslash	0x5c	\\	\ within text
Backspace	0x08	\b	vbBack
Carriage Return	0x0d	\r	vbCr
Double Quote	0x22	\"	"" within text
Form Feed	0x0c	\f	vbFormFeed
Horizontal Tab	0x09	\t	vbTab
Line Feed	0x0a	\n	vbLf
MS-DOS Line Ending	0x0d,0x0a	\r\n	vbCrLf
Null Character	0x00	\0	vbNullChar
Single Quote	0x27	\'	' within text
Vertical Tab	0x0b	\v	vbVerticalTab

Unicode (\u) and hex (\x) escape sequences, described in the previous section, can also appear in strings.

Character literals in Visual Basic appear in double quotes, followed by the c character. In C#, they appear in single quotes with no special suffix.

VISUAL BASIC
```
Dim oneDigit As Char = "0"c
```

C#
```
char oneDigit = '0';
```

New with Visual Studio 2015
In 2015, both Visual Basic and C# added string interpolation, a method of generating formatted strings using string literals. Both languages share an identical syntax for such strings, prefixing them with a $ symbol, and using curly braces to contain the interpolated sections.

Integer Literals

In Visual Basic, integer literals are `Integer` by default, or if too large for that type, then `Long`. In C#, a plain integer literal will be typed as `int` if it fits in that type. If not, it is coerced into the smallest of `uint`, `long`, or `ulong`.

Each language supports a set of suffixes that force an integer literal to become a specific type. The following sample includes a long integer value in each language.

VISUAL BASIC
```
PassALongValue(123&)
```

C#
```
PassALongValue(123L);
```

The following table lists the suffixes for each integer type. Each suffix can be uppercase, lowercase, or for suffixes with more than one character, a mix of casing.

Data Type	Visual Basic Suffix	C# Suffix
Short	*S*	No suffix
Unsigned Short	*US*	No suffix
Integer	% or *I*	No suffix
Unsigned Integer	*UI*	*U*
Long	& or *L*	*L*
Unsigned Long	*UL*	*UL* or *LU*

Floating-Point Literals

In both languages, floating-point literals are *Double/double* by default. You can also alter this default by appending a type suffix to the literal value. The following table lists the suffixes for each floating-point type. Each suffix can be uppercase or lowercase.

Data Type	Visual Basic Suffix	C# Suffix
Single	! or *F*	*F*
Double	# or *R*	*D*
Decimal	@ or *D*	*M*

Both C# and Visual Basic also accept numbers in exponential format (scientific notation). Either the base or the exponent can include a unary + or − sign, and an optional type character can appear as well.

VISUAL BASIC
```
bigValue = 9.24E+22#    ' Double
```

C#
```
bigValue = 9.24E22D;   // double
```

Boolean Literals

C#'s *true* and *false* Boolean literals are exact replacements for Visual Basic's *True* and *False* literals. See the "Boolean Data Type" entry in this chapter for information on differences between the languages when converting a true value to an integer.

Hexadecimal and Octal Literals

Visual Basic offers both hexadecimal and octal literals via the *&H* and *&O* prefixes. C# supports hexadecimal literals using the *0x* prefix, but does not support octal literals.

VISUAL BASIC
```
decimal25 = &H19
decimal25 = &O31
```

C#
```
decimal25 = 0x19;
```

The various type suffixes, listed earlier in this entry, can follow the hexadecimal and octal literals to force the expression to a specific type.

Date Literals

Visual Basic includes intrinsic support for date and time literals, with the literal text appearing between a set of # symbols. C# does not include support for date or time literals. Instead, you must create instances of the *System.DateTime* type manually.

The Nothing Literal

For reference types, C#'s *null* literal is identical to Visual Basic's *Nothing* literal, indicating an undefined reference. For value types, *Nothing* acts like C#'s *default* operator, returning the default value of a value type.

Loc Method

Visual Basic's *Loc* method returns the current 0-based byte, sequential block, or record position within a file opened with the *FileOpen* method.

VISUAL BASIC
```
Dim position As Long = Loc(fileNumber)
```

C# does not include the same file-management features included with VB. Instead, it is common to work with the *System.IO.FileStream* class to read and write files. This class does not include a direct equivalent for the *Loc* method, with its adjustments made for user-defined record sizes or 128-byte sequential blocks. Instead, you can use the *FileStream* class' *Position* property to determine the current 0-based byte position within the file. You must calculate the record or block-based position yourself based on this byte position.

C#
```
long position = openedStream.Position;
```

See Also

FileOpen Method

Local Variables

See

Variables

Lock Method

Visual Basic's *Lock* method locks a portion of a file or an entire file opened with the *FileOpen* method. Optional arguments indicate the starting and ending bytes or records to lock. All positions are 1-based.

VISUAL BASIC
```
' ----- Lock the whole file.
Lock(fileNumber)

' ----- Lock one byte or record.
Lock(fileNumber, targetPosition)
```

```
' ----- Lock a range of bytes or records.
Lock(fileNumber, startPosition, stopPosition)
```

C# does not include the same file-management features included with VB. Instead, it is common to work with the *System.IO.FileStream* class to read and write files. This class includes a *Lock* method that is similar to VB's *Lock* method. The key differences are that the *FileStream*'s *Lock* method only indicates byte positions and not record positions, and that its positions are 0-based. Also, when specifying a range of data to lock, the final argument to the stream's method indicates the length of the lock, not the final position of the lock.

C#
```csharp
// ----- Lock the whole file.
openedStream.Lock(0, openedStream.Length);

// ----- Lock one byte.
openedStream.Lock(targetPosition - 1, 1);

// ----- Lock a range of bytes.
openedStream.Lock(startPosition - 1,
    stopPosition - startPosition + 1);
```

See Also

FileOpen Method

LOF Method

Visual Basic's *LOF* method returns the length of a file opened with the language's *FileOpen* method. C# has no direct equivalent for these methods, or for their numeric file identifiers. However, internally these methods use standard *System.IO.FileStream* instances to manage files. You can use this same class in C# to obtain the length of an open file.

VISUAL BASIC
```vbnet
Dim fileID As Integer = FreeFile()
FileOpen(fileID, "C:\temp\work.txt", OpenMode.Input)
Dim fileLength As Long = LOF(fileID)
```

C#
```csharp
System.IO.FileStream sourceFile =
    new System.IO.FileStream("C:\\temp\\work.txt",
    System.IO.FileMode.Open);
long fileLength = sourceFile.Length;
```

Logical Operators

See

Operators

Long Data Type

C#'s intrinsic `long` data type is identical to Visual Basic's `Long` data type. Both types are aliases for .NET's `System.Int64` type. For long literals, Visual Basic uses an `L`, `l`, or `&` suffix after the value; in C#, use `L` or `l` instead.

VISUAL BASIC
```
Dim distance As Long = 0&   ' or 0L or 0l
```

C#
```
long distance = 0L;   // or 0l
```

LSet Method

Visual Basic's `LSet` method returns a string with the original string trimmed or padded with spaces to a specific length. You can accomplish this in C#, although there is no single language feature that is equivalent to `LSet`.

VISUAL BASIC
```
result = LSet(originalString, 10)
```

C#
```
if (originalString.Length < 10)
    result = originalString.PadRight(10);
else
    result = originalString.Substring(0, 10);
```

LTrim Method

The `TrimStart` method of C#'s `string` data type does the same thing as Visual Basic's `LTrim` method.

VISUAL BASIC
```
result = LTrim(someString)
```

C#
```
result = someString.TrimStart();
```

Main Method

In both Visual Basic and C#, an application uses a `Main` method as the program's entry point. These routines are always `Shared` (VB, although the `Shared` modifier is assumed if the method appears in a `Module`) or `static` (C#), return either no result (`Sub` or `void`) or an integer, and can be defined with one argument, an array of command line argument strings. C# allows these methods to be `private`, although this is not allowed in Visual Basic.

VISUAL BASIC
```
' ----- Plain version with no return or arguments.
Shared Friend Sub Main()
End Sub
```

```
' ----- Version with both a return code and arguments.
Shared Friend Function Main(
    ByVal cmdArgs() As String) As Integer
End Function
```

C#
```csharp
// ----- Plain version with no return or arguments.
static void Main()
{
}

// ----- Version with both a return code and arguments.
static int Main(string[] args)
{
}
```

In Visual Basic Windows Forms applications, a form can be defined as the startup object, and in the absence of a *Main* method, the compiler will provide one. In C#, you must supply the *Main* method yourself, and identify it through the Project Properties. In C# Windows Forms applications, the *Main* method must be decorated with the *STAThread* attribute, something that the Visual Basic compiler provides behind the scenes.

C#
```csharp
[STAThread] static void Main()
```

In a Windows Forms application in C#, you must display the main form manually through the code in the *Main* method.

C#
```csharp
static void Main()
{
    Application.Run(new Form1());
}
```

An application normally exits when it reaches the end of the *Main* method. A program can be made to exit early by using one of the following features, sorted from most polite to most abrupt. Note that C# does not include a direct equivalent for VB's *End* statement.

- Calling *System.Windows.Forms.Application.Exit()*
- Calling *System.Environment.Exit(exitCode)*
- Using Visual Basic's *End* statement

Visual Basic includes its Visual Basic Application Model, activated using the Enable Application Framework checkbox in the Project Properties. When activated, the model enables features that provide for a more structured startup process, plus support for application-wide unhandled error monitoring. C# does not include project-level support for these features, although you can emulate them in standard code. For more information on these features and how to employ equivalents in C#, access the following entries in Chapter 3 of this book:

- MinimumSplashScreenDisplayTime Property
- NetworkAvailabilityChanged Event (My.Application)
- SplashScreen Property
- Startup Event
- StartupNextInstance Event
- UnhandledException Event

Me Instance Expression

C#'s *this* expression provides access to members of the local type, just like Visual Basic's *Me* expression.

VISUAL BASIC

```
Class SimpleAdder
    Public Value As Integer = 0

    Public Sub Increment()
        Me.Value += 1
    End Sub
End Class
```

C#

```
class SimpleAdder
{
    public int Value = 0;

    public void Increment()
    {
        this.Value++;
    }
}
```

See Also

MyClass Instance Expression

Methods

Visual Basic differentiates between *Function* and *Sub* statements, that is, between methods that return a value, and those that don't. In C#, these two method types share a common syntax, differing primarily in the format of the *return* statement used to exit the method.

The syntax of functions in C# isn't too different from what appears in Visual Basic. Each includes an identifier name followed by a parameter list in parentheses. Both languages support a similar complement of declaration modifiers. In C#, the return data type declaration moves from the trailing *As* clause to just before the method identifier.

VISUAL BASIC

```
Public Function ParseTimeText(ByVal timeText As String, _
        ByRef hours As Integer, ByRef minutes As Integer) _
        As Boolean
```

```
' ----- Core logic, then...
    Return success
End Function
```

C#

```
public bool ParseTimeText(string timeText,
    ref int hours, ref int minutes)
{
    // ----- Core logic, then...
    return success;
}
```

Methods that don't return a value—*Sub* statements in Visual Basic—look almost identical to those that do have a return value. The key change is the replacement of the return data type with the *void* keyword.

VISUAL BASIC

```
Public Sub LogError(ByVal errorText As String)
    ' ----- May optionally include this statement:
    Return
End Sub
```

C#

```
public void LogError(string errorText)
{
    // ----- May optionally include this statement:
    return;
}
```

As shown in these examples, the body of a C# method appears in a set of curly braces.

When implementing a member of a specific interface in Visual Basic, the *Implements* clause identifies the interface member being implemented explicitly by the method.

VISUAL BASIC

```
Public Sub Speak(ByVal textToSpeak As String) _
    Implements IVocal.Speak
```

In C#, the name of the method is prefixed with the name of the interface.

C#

```
public void IVocal.Speak(string textToSpeak)
{
```

Visual Basic's *Handles* clause, when attached to a method declaration, connects an event to an event hander. C# does not include an equivalent keyword. Instead, you must attach event handlers as part of standard method logic. See the "AddHandler Statement" in this chapter for details on equivalent C# syntax.

Methods support the following modifiers in each language.

Visual Basic Modifier	C# Modifier
Async	async
Friend	internal
Iterator	Not supported

Visual Basic Modifier	C# Modifier
MustOverride	abstract
NotOverridable	sealed
Overloads	Not supported
Overridable	virtual
Overrides	override
Partial	partial
Private	private
Protected	protected
Protected Friend	protected internal
Public	public
Shadows	new
Shared	static
Not supported	extern

In Visual Basic, all methods are *Public* by default. When defined without an access modifier, methods are *private* by default in C# classes and structures.

See Also

, Punctuator, Arguments and Parameters, Access Modifiers, Event Handlers, Identifiers, Named Arguments

Mid Assignment Statement

C# does not have an equivalent for Visual Basic's *Mid* assignment statement. To replace a portion of an existing string in C#, use the *string* data type's *Substring* method to extract the surrounding portions, and concatenate them back together with the new content.

VISUAL BASIC
```
Dim content As String = "Update this text."
Mid(content, 8, 4) = "that"
' ----- content now contains "Update that text."
```

C#
```
string content = "Update this text.";
content = content.Substring(0, 7) + "that" +
    content.Substring(11);
// ----- content now contains "Update that text."
```

Visual Basic's *Mid* statement is very forgiving about string lengths, and it silently trims off extra content, and doesn't complain when there isn't enough text in the original string to replace. The *Substring* method is more strict, and will throw an exception if you attempt to access portions of a string that do not exist. Before using *Substring*, verify that all portions exist by checking string lengths.

Mid Method

The `Substring` method of C#'s `string` data type provides functionality somewhat similar to Visual Basic's `Mid` method. `Mid` uses 1-based positions; `Substring` uses 0-based positions.

VISUAL BASIC
```
' ----- Get YYY part of XXXYYYZZZZ phone number.
phoneExchange = Mid(phoneNumber, 4, 3)

' ----- Get last four digits.
phoneSuffix = Mid(phoneNumber, 7)
```

C#
```
// ----- Get YYY part of XXXYYYZZZZ phone number.
phoneExchange = phoneNumber.Substring(3, 3);

// ----- Get last four digits.
phoneSuffix = phoneNumber.Substring(6);
```

VB's `Mid` method will silently return valid strings even when the position or length would extend past the end of the original string. In C#, such requests will throw an exception. You must ensure that you retrieve only valid portions of the source string.

Minute Method

The `DateTime` type's `Minute` property returns the same information as Visual Basic's `Minute` method.

VISUAL BASIC
```
Dim whichMinute As Integer = Minute(oneOrder.OrderDate)
```

C#
```
int whichMinute = oneOrder.OrderDate.Minute;
```

MIRR Method

See

Financial Methods

MkDir Method

Visual Basic's `MkDir` method creates a directory. To do the same thing in C#, use the `System.IO.Directory.CreateDirectory` method.

VISUAL BASIC
```
MkDir(pathToDirectory)
```

C#
```
System.IO.Directory.CreateDirectory(pathToDirectory);
```

Mod Modulo Operator

C#'s % operator is identical to Visual Basic's *Mod* operator.

```
Dim penniesNeeded As Integer = totalInCents Mod 5
```

```
int penniesNeeded = totalInCents % 5;
```

Module Modifier

See

Attributes

Module Statement

C# does not include a direct equivalent for Visual Basic's *Module* statement. The closest equivalent is to use a *class* statement with the *static* modifier applied. The *static* modifier is like VB's *Shared* modifier, tying each member to the class itself instead of to each specific instance.

```
Module UsefulFunctions
    Public Function Reverse(ByVal originalText As String) _
            As String
        Dim buffer() As Char
        If (originalText Is Nothing) Then
            Return ""
        Else
            buffer = originalText.ToCharArray()
            Array.Reverse(buffer)
            Return New String(buffer)
        End If
    End Function
End Module
```

```
static class UsefulFunctions
{
    public static string Reverse(string originalText)
    {
        char[] buffer;
        if (originalText == null)
            return "";
        else
        {
            buffer = originalText.ToCharArray();
            Array.Reverse(buffer);
```

```
                return new string(buffer);
          }
        }
      }
```

As shown in this example, the `static` modifier must be applied to each member.

New with Visual Studio 2015

When using module members in a Visual Basic application, "type promotion" allows access to those members without including the module name as a qualifier. Before its 2015 release, C# did not support such unqualified usage; you needed to specify the class name when accessing static class members. Beginning in 2015, C# allows unqualified access when paired with its new `using static` statement.

VISUAL BASIC
```
' ----- Assumes previous code sample.
Dim funText As String = Reverse(originalText)
```

C#
```
// ----- Assumes previous code sample. Before 2015.
string funText = UsefulFunctions.Reverse(originalText);

// ----- Beginning in 2015, at the top of the file.
using static UsefulFunctions;

// ----- Later, in a method.
string funText = Reverse(originalText);
```

See the "Class Statement" entry in this chapter for additional information on creating static classes in C#.

See Also

Class Statement

Month Method

The `DateTime` type's `Month` property returns the same information as Visual Basic's `Month` method.

VISUAL BASIC
```
Dim whichMonth As Integer = Month(oneOrder.OrderDate)
```

C#
```
int whichMonth = oneOrder.OrderDate.Month;
```

MonthName Method

Visual Basic's `MonthName` method returns a full or abbreviated month name when given a numeric month value. In C#, use the `DateTimeFormat` member of the current culture for the running assembly.

VISUAL BASIC

```
' ----- Full month name, "January" in en-US culture.
result = MonthName(1)

' ----- Abbreviation, "Jan" in en-US culture.
result = MonthName(1, True)
```

C#

```
// ----- Full month name, "January" in en-US culture.
result = System.Threading.Thread.CurrentThread.
    CurrentCulture.DateTimeFormat.GetMonthName(1);

// ----- Abbreviation, "Jan" in en-US culture.
result = System.Threading.Thread.CurrentThread.

CurrentCulture.DateTimeFormat.GetAbbreviatedMonthName(1);
```

When working with an instance of the *DateTime* type, you can use its *ToString* method with a formatting code to return the full or abbreviated month name.

C#

```
// ----- Full month name, "January" in en-US culture.
result = orderDate.ToString("MMMM");

// ----- Abbreviation, "Jan" in en-US culture.
result = orderDate.ToString("MMM");
```

MsgBox Method

Visual Basic's *MsgBox* method is a wrapper around the Windows Form's *MessageBox.Show* method. In general, you can call that method in C#, keeping in mind that the parameter list for *MsgBox* appears in a different order from that of *MessageBox*'s *Show* method. Also, the enumerations used by each method, though similar, are not identical.

VISUAL BASIC

```
MsgBox("Sample message text.",
    MsgBoxStyle.OKOnly Or MsgBoxStyle.Exclamation,
    "Message Title")
```

C#

```
System.Windows.Forms.MessageBox.Show(
    "Sample message text.", "Message Title",
    System.Windows.Forms.MessageBoxButtons.OK,
    System.Windows.Forms.MessageBoxIcon.Exclamation);
```

The *MessageBox.Show* method offers many more options that what is offered with the *MsgBox* method. The .NET Framework documentation includes details on all of the available overloads for the *Show* method.

MustInherit Modifier

When applied to a class, C#'s *abstract* modifier is equivalent to Visual Basic's *MustInherit* modifier.

```
MustInherit Class Creature
    ' ----- Include members marked as MustOverride
    '       as needed.
End Class
```

```
abstract class Creature
{
    // ----- Include members marked as abstract as needed.
}
```

C# also uses the *abstract* keyword as a class-member modifier. In that case, it is equivalent to VB's *MustOverride* modifier.

See Also

MustOverride Modifier

MustOverride Modifier

When applied to class members, C#'s *abstract* modifier is the same as Visual Basic's *MustOverride* modifier. The decorated member will not include an implementation.

```
' ----- Abstract method.
Public MustOverride Sub ProcessResults()

' ----- Abstract property.
Public MustOverride Property MaxLevel() As Integer

' ----- Abstract read-only indexer.
Public MustOverride Default ReadOnly Property Item(
    ByVal index As Integer) As String
```

```
// ----- Abstract method.
public abstract void ProcessResults();

// ----- Abstract property.
public abstract int MaxLevel { get; set; }

// ----- Abstract read-only indexer.
public abstract string this[int index] { get; }
```

In Visual Basic, the *MustOverride* modifier can be applied to methods and properties, but not events. C#'s *abstract* member modifier can be applied to methods, and properties, indexers, and events.

C# also uses the *abstract* keyword as a class modifier. In that case, it is equivalent to VB's *MustInherit* modifier. Just as Visual Basic *MustOverride* members can only appear in a class marked with *MustInherit*, C# *abstract* members can only appear in an *abstract* class.

See Also

MustInherit Modifier

My Namespace

C# does not have a direct equivalent for Visual Basic's *My* namespace. However, C# and .NET Framework features can be used to implement its members, some with a single statement or method call, others with more involved code.

See Chapter 3, "My Namespace," for details on how to replicate *My* namespace member functionality in C#.

MyBase Instance Expression

C#'s *base* expression provides the same type of access to base type members as does Visual Basic's *MyBase* expression.

VISUAL BASIC
```
MyBase.RefreshStatus()
```

C#
```
base.RefreshStatus();
```

Within constructors, Visual Basic code sometimes includes a call to the base constructor as its first statement. This same logic can be performed in C#. But C# also provides a special syntax that automatically calls a base constructor before entering the body of the derived constructor. To use this implementation, the keyword *base* appears at the end of the constructor's signature declaration, separated from the signature by a colon.

C#
```
// ----- Assumes BaseClass with a default constructor,
//       plus a constructor that accepts an int.
class DerivedClass : BaseClass
{
    public DerivedClass() : base()
    {
        // ----- Default constructor logic here.
    }
    public DerivedClass(int value) : base(value)
    {
        // ----- Constructor logic here.
    }
}
```

MyClass Instance Expression

Visual Basic's *MyClass* expression is similar to the *Me* expression, but provides access to a member of a base class even when an overriding member exists in the derived class.

C# does not include an equivalent for *MyClass*. To simulate it, you must add a *public* or *protected* member in the base class, and access it directly from derived code.

See Also

MyBase Instance Expression

NameOf Operator

New with Visual Studio 2015
C#'s *nameof* operator is identical to Visual Basic's *NameOf* operator.

VISUAL BASIC
```
Dim variableName As String = NameOf(customerName)
```

C#
```
string variableName = nameof(customerName);
```

Namespace Statement

C# includes a *namespace* statement that is functionally equivalent to Visual Basic's *Namespace* statement. Both languages support nesting of namespaces, either with individual namespaces at each level, or through a dotted-name syntax.

VISUAL BASIC
```
Namespace Level1
    Namespace Level2.Level3
    End Namespace
End Namespace
```

C#
```
namespace Level1
{
    namespace Level2.Level3
    {
    }
}
```

Within the Project Properties, Visual Basic includes support for a project's Root Namespace, which is the enclosing namespace for all code in the project (unless the *Global* namespace alias is used in a file). C# includes a Default Namespace option in its Project Properties, but that option is used by Visual Studio to create the initial *namespace* statement when each new source code file is added to a project. It has no other impact on the hierarchy of types within a project.

See Also

Global Namespace Alias

Narrowing Modifier

Visual Basic's *Narrowing* modifier indicates that an overloaded conversion from one type to another must be performed explicitly, as the destination type may be too narrow for all the source type's possible values.

VISUAL BASIC

```
Class BigType
    Public Shared Narrowing Operator CType(
            ByVal source As BigType) As SmallType
        Return New SmallType(source.GetCondensed())
    End Operator
End Class
```

The equivalent C# overload uses the *explicit* modifier to express this same limiting conversion.

C#

```
class BigType
{
    public static explicit operator SmallType(
        BigType source)
    {
        return new SmallType(source.GetCondensed());
    }
}
```

See Also

Operator Statement, Widening Modifier

New Constructor Declaration

In Visual Basic, constructors are always named *New*. In C#, constructors are named for the type in which they appear; a class named *Employee* has constructors that are named *Employee* as well. Constructors in both languages provide functionality that is generally equivalent.

VISUAL BASIC

```
Class Employee
    Public Sub New()
        ' ----- Default constructor.
    End Sub
    Public Sub New(ByVal empName As String)
        ' ----- Custom constructor.
    End Sub
End Class
```

C#

```
class Employee
{
    public Employee()
    {
        // ----- Default constructor.
    }
    public Employee(string empName)
    {
        // ----- Custom constructor.
    }
}
```

By default, the constructor in a derived class calls the default constructor in the base class, if it exists. In Visual Basic, you can alter this default and call the base constructor or another local constructor in the first line of the new constructor.

VISUAL BASIC

```
Class Employee
    Inherits Person

    Public Sub New(ByVal empName As String)
        ' ----- Base class handles person's name.
        MyBase.New(empName)
    End Sub
    Public Sub New(ByVal empName As String,
            ByVal salary As Decimal)
        ' ----- Another constructor handles the name.
        Me.New(empName)
        ' ----- Salary-specific code here.
    End Sub
End Class
```

To call a custom base constructor in C#, or to use another custom constructor as the starting point for a constructor, use the *base* and *this* constructor declarations, respectively. These appear immediately after the constructor signature, separated from that signature by a colon.

C#

```
class Employee : Person
{
    public Employee(string empName) : base(empName)
    {
        // ----- Base class handles person's name.
    }
    public Employee(string empName,
        decimal salary) : this(empName)
    {
        // ----- Salary-specific code here.
    }
}
```

Constructors support the following modifiers in each language.

Visual Basic Modifier	C# Modifier
Friend	internal
Private	private
Protected	protected
Protected Friend	protected internal
Public	public
Shared	static
Not supported	extern

New Operator

C#'s *new* operator is functionally equivalent to Visual Basic's *New* operator when used to create new type instances. In both languages, the name of the type being instantiated and any parentheses-enclosed constructor arguments follow the operator.

VISUAL BASIC

```
' ----- Examples with default and custom constructor.
Dim oneManager As Employee = New Employee
Dim namedManager As Employee = New Employee("Jones")
```

C#

```
// ----- Examples with default and custom constructor.
Employee oneManager = new Employee();
Employee namedManager = new Employee("Jones");
```

As shown in the previous example, parentheses are always required after the type name being instantiated C#, but they are optional in VB when the default constructor is used. VB supports a compressed format that combines the type identification and assignment of a new instance.

VISUAL BASIC

```
Dim oneManager As New Employee
```

This syntax is not available in C#.

As in Visual Basic, instance creation using the *new* operator can appear within expressions.

VISUAL BASIC

```
authenticated = (New PasswordDialog).PromptUser()
```

C#

```
authenticated = (new PasswordDialog()).PromptUser();
```

Anonymous types in Visual Basic use the *New* operator followed by *With* and a list of properties in curly braces.

VISUAL BASIC

```
Dim namedAndNumbered = New With { .ID = 5, .Name = "test" }
```

C# employs a similar syntax, but omits both the *With* keyword and the period before each member name.

C#
```
var namedAndNumbered = new { ID = 5, Name = "test" };
```

VB also allows you to specify which anonymous type properties are "key" properties, those that can be used for equivalence testing between two instances.

VISUAL BASIC
```
Dim numberedByID = New With { Key .ID = 5, .Name = "test" }
```

C# does not include support for these key fields. Instead, you must create a standard named type, and provide your own custom overrides for the *Equals* and *GetHashCode* base methods.

See Also

Initializers

Not Negation/Complement Operator

When used with Boolean operands, C#'s *!* negation operator is equivalent to Visual Basic's *Not* operator.

VISUAL BASIC
```
Dim opposite As Boolean = Not originalValue
```

C#
```
bool opposite = !originalValue;
```

When used with integer operands, C#'s *~* bitwise complement operator is equivalent to Visual Basic's *Not* operator.

VISUAL BASIC
```
Dim complement As Integer = Not originalValue
```

C#
```
int complement = ~originalValue;
```

Nothing Literal

Visual Basic's *Nothing* literal is a null reference for reference types and nullable value types.

VISUAL BASIC
```
Dim oneManager As Employee = Nothing        ' No instance
Dim optionalNumber As Integer? = Nothing    ' No value
```

Note

When working with "null" values in database interactions, use *System.DbNull* instead of *Nothing.*

In C#, the *null* literal serves a similar purpose.

C#
```
Employee oneManager = null;  // No instance
int? optionalNumber = null;  // No value
```

However, *Nothing* can also be assigned to a standard (non-nullable) value type to set that instance to its default value. C#'s *default* operator carries out this function.

VISUAL BASIC
```
Dim requiredNumber As Integer = Nothing    ' Set to zero
```

C#
```
int requiredNumber = default(int);    // Set to zero
```

When comparing variables or expressions to *Nothing* in Visual Basic, the *Is* and *IsNot* comparison operators indicate equivalence or non-equivalence, respectively.

VISUAL BASIC
```
' ----- To check for the absence of an instance.
If (customerRecord Is Nothing) Then

' ----- To check for the presence of an instance.
If (customerRecord IsNot Nothing) Then
```

In C#, such comparisons occur using the standard == and != comparison operators.

C#
```
// ----- To check for the absence of an instance.
if (customerRecord == null)

// ----- To check for the presence of an instance.
if (customerRecord != null)
```

Visual Basic propagates or discards *Nothing* in ways that are somewhat different from how C# uses *null*. This is both for reasons of backward compatibility in VB, and also because of *Nothing*'s dual nature as a null reference and a default value type. Compare the following examples to see just one difference.

VISUAL BASIC
```
' ----- result will be set to "5".
Dim result As String = (5 + Nothing).ToString()
```

C#
```
// ----- result will be set to "".
string result = (5 + null).ToString();
```

Visual Basic treats empty strings and *Nothing* as equivalent; C# distinguishes between *null* and empty strings.

VISUAL BASIC
```
' ----- result will be set to "Empty".
Dim testValue As String = Nothing
If (testValue = "") Then
    result = "Empty"
Else
    result = "Not Empty"
End If
```

C#
```
// ----- result will be set to "Not Empty".
string testValue = null;
```

```
if (testValue == "")
    result = "Empty";
else
    result = "Not Empty";
```

To check for true null equivalence, use *Is Nothing* in Visual Basic, and compare the expression to *null* in C#.

VISUAL BASIC
```
If (testValue Is Nothing) Then
```

C#
```
if (testValue == null)
```

NotInheritable Modifier

When applied to a class, C#'s *sealed* modifier is the same as Visual Basic's *NotInheritable* modifier.

VISUAL BASIC
```
NotInheritable Class CoreSettings
```

C#
```
sealed class CoreSettings
```

See Also

NotOverridable Modifier

NotOverridable Modifier

When applied to members of a derived class overriding the matching *Overridable* member in the base class, C#'s *sealed* modifier is the same as Visual Basic's *NotOverridable* modifier. In both languages, the *Overrides* (VB) or *override* (C#) modifier must also be present.

VISUAL BASIC
```
Protected NotOverridable Overrides Sub Refresh()
```

C#
```
sealed protected override void Refresh()
```

For such members, Visual Basic's *NotOverridable* modifier can apply to methods and properties. C#'s *sealed* modifier supports these, as well as indexers (the same as VB's default properties) and events.

See Also

NotInheritable Modifier

Now Property

In C#, use the *System.DateTime.Now* property as an equivalent for Visual Basic's intrinsic *Now* property.

```
Dim result As Date = Now
```
```
DateTime result = DateTime.Now;
```

NPer Method

See

Financial Methods

NPV Method

See

Financial Methods

Nullable Types

Both Visual Basic and C# use the *?* symbol after a value type name to indicate a nullable value type.

VISUAL BASIC
```
Dim optionalNumber As Integer? = Nothing

' ----- This is also a valid syntax.
Dim optionalNumber? As Integer = Nothing
```

C#
```
int? optionalNumber = null;
```

In Visual Basic, you check the nullable instance for the presence of data using the *Is* and *IsNot* operators, or by calling the variable's *HasValue* method.

VISUAL BASIC
```
If (optionalNumber Is Nothing) Then

' ----- This will also work, in both languages.
If (optionalNumber.HasValue() = False) Then
```

In C#, nullable variables can be compared directly to *null* with the *==* or *!=* comparison operators, or as in VB with the *HasValue* method.

C#
```
if (optionalNumber == null)

// ----- This will also work, in both languages.
if (optionalNumber.HasValue() == false)
```

In both languages, the nullable syntax is an alias for *Nullable(Of T)* (in Visual Basic) or *Nullable<T>* (in C#).

Object Data Type

C#'s intrinsic *object* data type is identical to Visual Basic's *Object* data type. Both types are aliases for .NET's *System.Object* type.

VISUAL BASIC
```
Dim result As Object = Nothing
```

C#
```
object result = null;
```

Object Initializers

See

Initializers

Oct Method

An overload of the *Convert.ToString* method accepts a target numeric base. Passing a base of *8* to this method replicates the output of Visual Basic's *Oct* method.

VISUAL BASIC
```
Dim result As String = Oct(123)   ' --> "173"
```

C#
```
string result = System.Convert.ToString(123, 8);
```

Of Clause

Visual Basic uses an *Of* clause within a set of parentheses to indicate the data types in a generic declaration. In C#, this declaration appears in a set of angle brackets.

VISUAL BASIC
```
Dim lookupSet As Dictionary(Of Long, String)
```

C#
```
Dictionary<long, string> lookupSet;
```

This syntax extends to class definitions, and anywhere else Visual Basic would normally place the *Of* clause in parentheses.

See Also

Generics

On Error Statement

C# does not include support for unstructured error handling, and therefore it has no equivalent for Visual Basic's *On Error* statement. Instead, you must use structured error handling constructs.

Operator Statement

C#'s *operator* statement is equivalent to Visual Basic's *Operator* statement. In both languages, the "operator" keyword is followed by the specific operator symbol being overloaded, and the operands appear as parameters in the method-style definition.

VISUAL BASIC

```
Public Shared Operator +(ByVal op1 As Team,
        ByVal op2 As Player) As Team
    ' ----- Logic to add player to team, then...
    Return updatedTeam
End Operator
```

C#

```
public static Team operator +(Team op1, Player op2)
{
    // ----- Logic to add player to team, then...
    return updatedTeam;
}
```

The overload must be declared as *Public Shared* in Visual Basic, and the equivalent *public static* in C#. VB also allows the *Overloads* modifier to appear between *Public* and *Shared*, but it has no impact on the logic of the overload; this optional keyword is not needed in C# code. In both languages, for unary operators, the parameter list will include only one parameter.

The following table lists the different operators that can be overloaded in each language.

Type	Visual Basic	C#
Addition	+	+
And-also False Test	IsFalse	false
Bitwise Complement	Not	~
Concatenation	&	+
Conjunction	And	&
Conversion	CType	See below
Decrement	Not supported	--
Disjunction	Or		
Division	/	/
Equality	=	==
Exclusive Or	Xor	^
Exponentiation	^	Not supported
Greater Than	>	>
Greater Than Equal	>=	>=
Increment	Not supported	++
Inequality	<>	!=

Type	Visual Basic	C#
Integer Division	\	Not supported
Left Shift	<<	<<
Less Than	<	<
Less Than Equal	<=	<=
Modulo	Mod	%
Multiplication	*	*
Negation	Not	!
Or-else True Test	IsTrue	true
Pattern Match	Like	Not supported
Right Shift	>>	>>
Subtraction	-	-
Unary Minus	-	-
Unary Plus	+	+

In both languages, a few of these operators must be overloaded in pairs.

Type	Visual Basic	C#
Equality Testing	= and <>	== and !=
Less/Greater	> and <	> and <
Less/Greater Equal	>= and <=	>= and <=
And-also/Or-else	IsFalse and IsTrue	false and true

Operator overloads support the following modifiers in each language.

Visual Basic Modifier	C# Modifier
Narrowing	explicit
Overloads	Not supported
Public	public
Shadows	Not supported
Shared	static
Widening	implicit
Not supported	extern

User-defined conversions are implemented as part of the operator overloading syntax in both languages. In Visual Basic, CType is used as the operator name for all such conversions. The source type appears in the parameter list, and the target type appears as the return type for the method. In C#, the source type appears in the parameter list, and the target type is used as the operator name. In both languages, the type containing the conversion declaration must match either the source or the target type.

VISUAL BASIC

```
Class CountMonitor
    Public Shared Narrowing Operator CType(
            ByVal source As CountMonitor) As Integer
        ' ----- Converts CountMonitor to int, then...
        Return newInt
    End Operator
```

```
Public Shared Widening Operator CType(
        ByVal source As Integer) As CountMonitor
    ' ----- Converts int to CountMonitor, then...
        Return newCountMonitor
    End Operator
End Class
```

C#

```
class CountMonitor
{
    public static explicit operator int(
        CountMonitor source)
    {
        // ----- Converts CountMonitor to int, then...
        return newInt;
    }
    public static implicit operator CountMonitor(
        int source)
    {
        // ----- Converts int to CountMonitor, then...
        return newCountMonitor;
    }
}
```

C#'s *implicit* modifier is the same as Visual Basic's *Widening* modifier, while C#'s *explicit* modifier matches VB's *Narrowing* modifier. One of these modifiers must be used in each user-defined conversion declaration.

Operator Overloading

See

Operator Statement

Operator Precedence and Associativity

When an expression includes more than one operator, both Visual Basic and C# use specific precedence and associativity rules to determine, in the absence of grouping parentheses, which operations to apply first. The following table lists the precedence rules for Visual Basic, in order from highest (applied first) to lowest (applied last). Operators at the same precedence level are treated as equal in terms of application order.

Category	Operators
Await	*Await*
Exponentiation	^
Unary	+, −
Multiplicative	*, /
Integer division	\
Modulo	*Mod*

Category	Operators
Additive	+, -
Concatenation	&
Shift	<<, >>
Comparison	=, <>, <, <=, >, >=, Is, IsNot, Like, TypeOf...Is, TypeOf...IsNot
Negation	Not
Conjunction	And, AndAlso
Disjunction	Or, OrElse
Exclusive disjunction	Xor

The following table lists C#'s operators by order of precedence.

Category	Operators
Primary	x.y, f(x), a[x], x++, x--, new, typeof, default, checked, unchecked, delegate, nameof
Unary	+, -, !, ~, ++x, --x, (T)x
Multiplicative	*, /, %
Additive	+, -
Shift	<<, >>
Comparison	<, >, <=, >=, is, as
Equality	==, !=
Conjunction	&
Exclusive disjunction	^
Disjunction	|
Conditional conjunction	&&
Conditional disjunction	||
Coalescence	??
Conditional	?:
Assignment and lambda	=, *=, /=, %=, +=, -=, <<=, >>=, &=, ^=, |=, =>

In both languages, assignment operators are right-associative; the right side of the operator is evaluated first. For most other binary operators at the same precedence level, operations are left-associative; the expression on the left-side of the operator is determined first, from left to right. For example, $x + y + z$ is evaluated as $(x + y) + z$. The two exceptions are C#'s ?: conditional operator and its ?? null coalescence operator, both of which are right-associative. For an example of how this impacts conditional operations, see the "?: Conditional Operator" entry in Chapter 1.

Operators

The following table lists the operators available in both languages. Use the "See Also" column below to locate related entries in this chapter.

Visual Basic Operator	C# Operator	See Also
&	+	& Concatenation Operator
( )	[ ]	( ) Member Access Operator
*	*	* Multiplication Operator
*=	*=	*= Assignment Operator
+	+	+ Addition Operator, + Unary-Plus Operator
+=	+=	+= Assignment Operator
–	–	- Subtraction Operator, - Unary-Minus Operator
-=	-=	-= Assignment Operator
?.	?.	?. Null Conditional Operator
.	.	. Member Access Operator
/	/	/ Division Operator
/=	/=	/= Assignment Operator
<	<	< Comparison Operator
<<	<<	<< Left Shift Operator
<<=	<<=	<<= Assignment Operator
<=	<=	<= Comparison Operator
<>	!=	<> Comparison Operator
=	=	= Assignment Operator
=	==	= Comparison Operator
>	>	> Comparison Operator
>=	>=	>= Comparison Operator
>>	>>	>> Right Shift Operator
>>=	>>=	>>= Assignment Operator
\	/	\ Division Operator
\=	/=	\= Assignment Operator
^	Not supported	^ Exponentiation Operator
And	&	And Conjunction Operator
AndAlso	&&	AndAlso Conjunction Operator
Function()	=>	Lambda Expressions
If(x,y)	?? or :?	If Operator
Is	==	Is Comparison Operator
IsNot	!=	IsNot Comparison Operator
Like	Not supported	Like Comparison Operator
Mod	%	Mod Modulo Operator
Not	! or ~	Not Negation Operator, ~ Bitwise Complement Operator
Or	|	Or Disjunction Operator
OrElse	||	OrElse Disjunction Operator
Sub()	=>	Lambda Expressions
Xor	^	Xor Exclusive-Or Operator

Option Compare Statement

By default, all text comparisons in both Visual Basic and C# use binary sorting rules, resulting in case-sensitive comparisons. Visual Basic allows the *Option Compare Text* statement to be used within a source file, or set at the project level. C# does not include an equivalent for this setting.

Some .NET features, such as the *String* data type's *Compare* method, let you indicate whether case should be taken into account when doing text comparison or sorting. Some of these features also let you specify the culture used to compare and sort data. In C#, you must use such features to enable text comparison rules that are comparable to *Option Compare Text*.

Option Explicit Statement

C# does not include an equivalent for Visual Basic's *Option Explicit* statement, either at the file or project level. Declaration is required for all variables in C#.

Option Infer Statement

C# does not include an equivalent for Visual Basic's *Option Infer* statement, either at the file or project level. Type inference in C# is done using the *var* statement. See the "Dim Statement" entry in this chapter for details on this C# equivalent.

Option Strict Statement

C# does not include an equivalent for Visual Basic's *Option Strict* statement, either at the file or project level. In general, narrowing conversions in C# must be explicitly cast to the appropriate target type.

Although C# lacks an *Option Strict* equivalent, it does support late binding through its *dynamic* type keyword. See the "Late Binding" entry in this chapter for information on using this feature in C#.

See Also

Conversion and Casting, Late Binding

Optional Arguments

See

Optional Modifier

Optional Modifier

In Visual Basic, parameters that accept optional arguments include the *Optional* modifier, and also require the assignment of a constant expression in the parameter definition.

VISUAL BASIC
```
' ----- The times parameter is optional, defaulting to 2.
Public Function CopyText(ByVal original As String,
    Optional ByVal times As Integer = 2) As String
```

C# does not require an *Optional*-like modifier in its method signatures. Instead, any parameter that includes an assignment becomes an optional argument to the calling procedure.

C#
```
// ----- The times parameter is optional, defaulting to 2.
public string CopyText(string original, int times = 2)
```

The rules surrounding the use of optional arguments in both languages are similar: no non-optional arguments may appear after an optional argument; parameter arrays and optional arguments cannot be used together; and so on.

See Also

, Punctuator, Arguments and Parameters, Methods

Or Disjunction Operator

In general, C#'s | disjunction operator is identical to Visual Basic's *Or* operator, both for integer (bitwise) and Boolean (logical) operations.

VISUAL BASIC
```
Dim complain As Boolean = (hot Or humid)
```

C#
```
bool complain = (hot | humid);
```

When applying *Option Strict Off* to a Visual Basic project or source file, using the *Or* operator with one integer operand and one Boolean operand forces the Boolean value to an integer (*0* or *-1*), and then performs a bitwise operation. C# does not allow this mixture of operand types.

Order By Query Expression Operator (LINQ)

C#'s *orderby* query expression operator is identical to Visual Basic's *Order By* operator. Both languages support a comma-delimited list of sorting fields. Each field is sorted in ascending order by default, or explicitly with the *Ascending* (VB) or *ascending* (C#) option. To sort in descending order, use the *Descending* (VB) or *descending* (C#) option.

```
Dim result = From oneEmployee in Employees
             Order By oneEmployee.FullName Descending
             Select oneEmployee
```

C#

```
var result = from oneEmployee in Employees
             orderby oneEmployee.FullName descending
             select oneEmployee;
```

In Visual Basic, the *Select* clause can appear before or after the *Order By* clause. If *Select* appears first, any calculated fields it includes become available within the *Order By* clause. In C#, the *orderby* clause must appear before the *select* clause.

See Also

Query Expressions

OrElse Disjunction Operator

C#'s || operator is generally identical to Visual Basic's *OrElse* short-circuiting disjunction operator.

VISUAL BASIC

```
If ((result Is Nothing) OrElse (result.Length == 0)) Then
```

C#

```
if ((result == null) || (result.Length == 0))
```

Out Modifier

See

Generics

Overloading

See

Operator Statement, Overloads Modifier

Overloads Modifier

Visual Basic's *Overloads* modifier appears on methods within a type that share the same name, but a different argument signature.

VISUAL BASIC

```
Public Overloads Function RetrieveCustomer(
        ByVal customerID As Long) As Customer
    ' ----- Retrieve customer record by numeric ID.
End Function
```

```
Public Overloads Function RetrieveCustomer(
        ByVal email As String) As Customer
    ' ----- Retrieve customer record by email address.
End Function
```

Although the modifier is included for clarity, it is optional. The Visual Basic compiler will detect overloaded methods even when the modifier is excluded from each definition. In the same way, C# provides method overloading without requiring a specific modifier.

C#
```
public Customer RetrieveCustomer(long customerID)
{
    // ----- Retrieve customer record by numeric ID.
}

public Customer RetrieveCustomer(string email)
{
    // ----- Retrieve customer record by email address.
}
```

See Also

Operator Statement

Overridable Modifier

C#'s *virtual* modifier is equivalent to Visual Basic's *Overridable* modifier.

VISUAL BASIC
```
Public Overridable Function DetermineImpact() As Long
```

C#
```
public virtual long DetermineImpact()
```

Visual Basic's *Overridable* modifier can be used with class methods and properties. C#'s *virtual* modifier supports these uses, plus indexers (the same as VB's default properties) and events.

Overrides Modifier

C#'s *override* modifier is equivalent to Visual Basic's *Overrides* modifier.

VISUAL BASIC
```
Public Overrides Function DetermineSize() As Integer
```

C#
```
public override int DetermineSize()
```

Visual Basic's *Overrides* modifier applies to methods and properties. In C#, the *override* includes these uses, as well as indexers (the same as VB's default properties) and events.

ParamArray Modifier

C#'s *params* modifier is functionally identical to Visual Basic's *ParamArray* modifier.

VISUAL BASIC
```
Public Function AverageValue(
    ByVal ParamArray values() As Integer) As Integer
```

C#
```
public int AverageValue(params int[] values)
```

Parameter Arrays

See

> ParamArray Modifier

Parameters

See

> Arguments and Parameters, Methods

Partial Modifier

When applied to classes, structures, and interfaces, Visual Basic's *Partial* modifier allows you to split the type across multiple files. One of the type portions can omit the *Partial* keyword.

VISUAL BASIC
```
' ----- From the first *.vb file.
Partial Class ComplexContent
    ' ----- Some members defined here.
End Class

' ----- From the second *.vb file.
Class ComplexContent
    ' ----- Other members defined here. The
    '       "Partial" modifier was left off this part,
    '       although it could have been retained.
End Class
```

C#'s *partial* modifier does the same thing. The *partial* keyword is required on all portions of the split type.

C#
```
// ----- From the first *.cs file.
partial class ComplexContent
{
    // ----- Some members defined here.
}
```

```
// ----- From the second *.cs file.
partial class ComplexContent
{
    // ----- Other members defined here.
}
```

New with Visual Studio 2015
Visual Basic initially did not allow the `Partial` modifier to be used with interface declarations. This feature has been added to VB starting in 2015, although it has long been allowed in C#. Also starting in 2015, VB's `Partial` modifier can be used with `Module` types, a change that has no counterpart in C#.

Partial methods allow you to define a method in one file, and provide its implementation in another file, with both parts belonging to the same partial class.

VISUAL BASIC
```
' ----- From the first *.vb file.
Partial Class ComplexContent
    ' ----- Declaration includes no method body.
    '       Always begins with "Partial Private Sub."
    Partial Private Sub RecordTraceData(
        ByVal data As String)
    End Sub
End Class

' ----- From the second *.vb file.
Partial Class ComplexContent
    ' ----- Implementation excludes "Partial" modifier.
    '       Signature must still match.
    Private Sub RecordTraceData(ByVal data As String)
        ' ----- Implementation here.
    End Sub
End Class
```

C#
```
// ----- From the first *.cs file.
partial class ComplexContent
{
    // ----- "private" is implied.
    partial void RecordTraceData(string data);
}

// ----- From the second *.cs file.
partial class ComplexContent
{
    // ----- Same "partial void" and signature.
    partial void RecordTraceData(string data)
    {
        // ----- Implementation here.
    }
}
```

In VB, only classes support partial methods. C# permits partial methods in both classes and structures.

Partition Method

C# has no feature that is similar to Visual Basic's `Partition` method. The following code returns results similar to that of `Partition`.

C#

```
public static string Partition(long number, long start,
    long stop, long interval)
{
    // ----- Handle invalid data.
    if ((start < 0L) | (stop < start) | (interval < 1))
        throw new ArgumentException();

    // ----- Handle boundary conditions.
    if (number < start)
        return string.Format(":{0}", start - 1);
    else if (number > stop)
        return string.Format("{0}:", stop + 1);
    else if (interval == 1)
        return string.Format("{0}:{0}", start);

    // ----- Within valid range.
    for (long counter = start; counter <= stop;
        counter += interval)
    {
        if ((number >= counter) & (number =<
                Math.Min(stop, counter + interval - 1)))
            return string.Format("{0}:{1}", counter,
                Math.Min(stop, counter + interval - 1));
    }

    // ----- Should be unreachable.
    throw new ArgumentException();
}
```

VB's `Partition` method pads the resulting value with spaces so that both colon-delimited portions are the same length. The sample code shown here does not perform padding.

Pmt Method

See

Financial Methods

PPmt Method

See

Financial Methods

Preprocessing Directives

See

#Const Directive, #ExternalChecksum Directive, #ExternalSource Directive, #If Directive, #Region Directive

Print Method

Visual Basic's *Print* method (and the related *PrintLine* method) outputs content to a file opened with the *FileOpen* method. The output can include columnar data via the *SPC* and *TAB* methods. *PrintLine* adds a carriage-return and line-feed pair.

VISUAL BASIC
```
' ----- Output a string and a number, like:
'         Seattle          84
PrintLine(fileNumber, cityName, TAB(15), totalMatches)
```

C# does not include the same file-management features included with VB. Instead, it is common to work with the *System.IO.StreamWriter* class to output text data. This class includes *Write* and *WriteLine* methods with overloads for outputting different types of data. Space and tabular output must be handled manually.

C#
```
// ----- Output a string and a number, like:
//         Seattle          84
outFile.Print(cityName);
outFile.Print(new String(' ', 15 - cityName.Length));
outFile.PrintLine(totalMatches);
```

See Also

FileOpen Method

PrintLine Method

See

Print Method

Private Access Modifier

C#'s *private* access modifier is equivalent to Visual Basic's *Private* access modifier.

See Also

Access Modifiers

Project Properties

Visual Basic and C# offer nearly identical settings through the Project Properties window. Visual Studio presents a tabbed presentation of settings, and most of the tabs that exist in VB are found in C#, and in an identical configuration. The set of available tabs and features on each tab will vary based on the type of project.

This entry describes a few of the differences you will encounter when moving from Visual Basic to C#. To see a list of differences from the perspective of moving from C# to Visual Basic, see the "Project Properties" entry in Chapter 1.

Application Tab

In general, C# and Visual Basic offer the same selection of project types. In some projects, VB's Application Type field offers "Windows Service" and "Web Control Library" options. These appear as distinct project types in C#.

In Windows Forms applications, Visual Basic offers a selection of startup forms, plus any compatible *Main* methods once the Enable Application Framework field is cleared. In any C# project that generates an executable, the equivalent Startup Object field only displays *Main* methods, not forms. If you want to use a form as the startup object, you must display the form via code in your *Main* method. See the "Main Method" entry in this chapter for a C# example that does this.

C# has no direct equivalent for the Windows Application Framework or its subordinate features. For information about handling Application Framework events in C#, see the event-specific entries in Chapter 3. Enabling XP Visual Styles in a C# program can be accomplished in code through the following statement.

C#
```
Application.EnableVisualStyles();
```

To enforce a single-instance application in C#, you must manually check for a conflicting instance via a mutex or some other shared-memory functionality. The following code demonstrates one possible way of doing this from your *Main* method.

C#
```
System.Threading.Mutex checkApp =
    new System.Threading.Mutex(true, "AppSpecificString");
if (checkApp.WaitOne(0, false))
    // ----- Allow program to run.
else
    MessageBox.Show("App already running");
```

Likewise, elements like authentication and splash-screen features must be managed through standard code, although specific implementations are beyond the scope of this book.

Visual Basic's View Windows Settings button adds an *app.manifest* file to the project that can be edited manually. C# includes comparable manifest features directly on the Application Tab, plus some other resource options not normally accessible in VB.

Compile Tab

Most of the features on the Compile tab appear in Visual Basic's equivalent Build tab, although many of the names are altered. In most cases, you should be able to determine fairly quickly what the equivalent field is. Both tabs include an Advanced button, and some of the fields considered advanced compile options in VB (including settings for

DEBUG, TRACE, and custom constants) appear on the main Build tab in C#. The fields displayed via VB's Build Events button appear on a distinct Build Events tab in C#'s project properties.

C# does not include direct equivalents for the four *Option* settings (such as *Option Explicit*) on VB's Compile tab. See the specific *Option* entries in this chapter for information on how to manage these features in C#.

Visual Basic's Advanced compile options include a Remove Integer Overflow Checks option. C#'s Advanced build options include a similar Check for Arithmetic Overflow/Underflow option. Because integer operations are checked by default in VB, but unchecked by default in C#, selecting these options results in different behavior between the languages. If you check the option in Visual Basic, you should leave it unchecked in C#, and vice versa.

References Tab
C# does not have a direct equivalent for Visual Basic's References tab. Instead, the list of project references appears in the project's Solution Explorer view. (The list of project references can also be accessed through the Solution Explorer in VB, although some editions require that the Show All Files feature of that panel be activated.) The References branch of the project tree gives you access to included references. Right-click on elements of this branch to make changes.

The Reference Paths button on VB's References tab exists in C# as a distinct Reference Paths tab. VB's Imported Namespace region, however, cannot be found in C#'s project settings. Instead, you must add *using* statements to individual C# source code files.

My Extensions Tab
C# does not support Visual Basic's *My* namespace, and therefore has no equivalent for the My Extensions tab.

Properties

See

> Property Statement

Property Statement

C#'s implementation of properties closely parallels Visual Basic's *Property* statement, although C# includes no specific language keyword to identify property declarations. Instead, the declarations resemble field declarations followed by getter and setter implementations within a set of curly braces.

VISUAL BASIC
```
' ----- Many properties use backing fields.
Private _maxAmount As Integer = 0
```

```vbnet
' ----- Here is the property itself.
Public Property Maximum As Integer
    Get
        Return Me._maxAmount
    End Get
    Set(ByVal value As Integer)
        ' ----- Although "value" is the default,
        '       you can rename this variable.
        If (value > 100) Then
            Me._maxAmount = 100
        ElseIf (value < 0) Then
            Me._maxAmount = 0
        Else
            Me._maxAmount = value
        End If
    End Set
End Property
```

C#

```csharp
// ----- Many properties use backing fields.
private int _maxAmount = 0;

// ----- Here is the property itself.
public int Maximum
{
    get
    {
        return this._maxAmount;
    }
    set
    {
        // ----- A "value" incoming variable is implied.
        if (value > 100)
            this._maxAmount = 100;
        else if (value < 0)
            this._maxAmount = 0;
        else
            this._maxAmount = value;
    }
}
```

In addition to using the *Return* statement, you can indicate the return value in a Visual Basic property getter by assigning the result to the property name and using the *Exit Property* statement.

VISUAL BASIC

```vbnet
' ----- Within Get block.
Maximum = Me._maxAmount
Exit Property
```

C# only supports the return of property values via the *return* statement, equivalent to using VB's *Return* statement in a property getter.

Read-only and write-only properties in Visual Basic include the *ReadOnly* and *WriteOnly* modifiers, respectively, and omit the unneeded getter or setter. In C#, omission of the unneeded setter or getter is sufficient to indicate the property's read-only or write-only status. No special modifier is required.

VISUAL BASIC

```
Public ReadOnly Property Status As Integer
    Get
        ' ----- Return statement appears here.
    End Get
    ' ----- But no setter appears.
End Property
```

C#

```
public int Status
{
    get
    {
        // ----- return statement appears here.
    }
    // ----- But no setter appears.
}
```

When crafting a read-write property, both languages allow you to apply an access modifier to either the getter or setter (but not both) that differs from the modifier applied to the property itself. Properties are *Public* by default in Visual Basic classes and structures, but *private* by default in C# types.

VISUAL BASIC

```
Public Property Status As Integer
    Get
        ' ----- Publicly accessible getter code.
    End Get
    Private Set
        ' ----- Privately accessible setter code.
    End Set
End Property
```

C#

```
public int Status
{
    get
    {
        // ----- Publicly accessible getter code.
    }
    private set
    {
        // ----- Privately accessible setter code.
    }
}
```

In Visual Basic, when a property explicitly implements an interface member, an *Implements* clause appears after the *As* clause. In C#, the name is modified to include the interface name.

VISUAL BASIC

```
Public Property Status As Integer _
    Implements IMonitor.Status
```

C#

```
public int IMonitor.Status
```

Properties support the following modifiers in each language.

Visual Basic Modifier	C# Modifier
Default	Not supported
Friend	internal
Iterator	Not supported
MustOverride	abstract
NotOverridable	sealed
Overloads	Not supported
Overridable	virtual
Overrides	override
Private	private
Protected	protected
Protected Friend	protected internal
Public	public
ReadOnly	Not supported
Shadows	new
Shared	static
WriteOnly	Not supported
Not supported	extern

Properties in Visual Basic can include parameters, as with methods. The parameter list appears after the property name in the initial declaration.

VISUAL BASIC

```
Public Property Status(ByVal day As DayOfWeek) As Integer
    Get
        ' ----- Return day-specific status.
    End Get
    Set(ByVal value As Integer)
        ' ----- Set day-specific status to value.
    End Set
End Property
```

This method for creating parameterized properties is not supported in C#. Also, a Visual Basic property can be passed to a method by reference, that is, to a parameter that includes the *ByRef* modifier. C# does not allow this.

See Also

Automatic Properties

Protected Access Modifier

C#'s *protected* access modifier is equivalent to Visual Basic's *Protected* access modifier.

See Also

Access Modifiers

Protected Friend Access Modifier

C#'s *protected internal* access modifier is equivalent to Visual Basic's *Protected Friend* access modifier.

See Also

Access Modifiers

Public Access Modifier

C#'s *public* access modifier is equivalent to Visual Basic's *Public* access modifier.

See Also

Access Modifiers

PV Method

See

Financial Methods

QBColor Method

Visual Basic's *QBColor* method returns an integer RGB value based on a set of sixteen predefined color IDs. The following table shows the appropriate hexadecimal RGB value for each color ID. The resulting hex values can be used in both Visual Basic and C# code.

QB Color ID	Color Name	Hexadecimal Value
0	Black	0x000000
1	Blue	0x800000
2	Green	0x008000
3	Cyan	0x808000
4	Red	0x000080
5	Magenta	0x800080
6	Yellow	0x008080
7	White	0xC0C0C0
8	Grey	0x808080
9	Light Blue	0xFF0000

QB Color ID	Color Name	Hexadecimal Value
10	Light Green	0x00FF00
11	Light Cyan	0xFFFF00
12	Light Red	0x0000FF
13	Light Magenta	0xFF00FF
14	Light Yellow	0x00FFFF
15	Bright White	0xFFFFFF

For values in the appropriate QB color code range, the following C# code will return the appropriate hexadecimal value.

VISUAL BASIC

```
result = QBColor(colorID)
```

C#

```
int[] QBColorTable = {
    0x0, 0x800000, 0x8000, 0x808000,
    0x80, 0x800080, 0x8080, 0xc0c0c0,
    0x808080, 0xff0000, 0xff00, 0xffff00,
    0xff, 0xff00ff, 0xffff, 0xffffff};
result = QBColorTable[colorID];
```

Query Expressions (LINQ)

Both Visual Basic and C# include native support for many features of LINQ. Each language includes a set of query operators, and many of them have counterparts in the other language. The following table lists the methods supported by LINQ's `Queryable` class, and indicates the equivalent query operator available within each language.

Queryable Member	Visual Basic Operator	C# Operator
Aggregate	Not supported	Not supported
All	Aggregate...Into All	Not supported
Any	Aggregate...Into Any	Not supported
AsEnumerable	Not supported	Not supported
AsQueryable	From...As	from with TypeName
Average	Aggregate...Into Average	Not supported
Cast	Not supported	Not supported
Concat	Not supported	Not supported
Contains	Not supported	Not supported
Count	Aggregate...Into Count	Not supported
DefaultIfEmpty	Not supported	Not supported
Distinct	Distinct	Not supported
ElementAt	Not supported	Not supported
ElementAtOrDefault	Not supported	Not supported
Empty	Not supported	Not supported
Except	Not supported	Not supported

Queryable Member	Visual Basic Operator	C# Operator
First	Not supported	Not supported
FirstOrDefault	Not supported	Not supported
GroupBy	*Group By*	*group*
GroupJoin	*Group Join*	*join...into*
Intersect	Not supported	Not supported
Join	*Join*	*join*
Last	Not supported	Not supported
LastOrDefault	Not supported	Not supported
LongCount	*Aggregate...Into LongCount*	Not supported
Max	*Aggregate...Into Max*	Not supported
Min	*Aggregate...Into Min*	Not supported
OfType	Not supported	Not supported
OrderBy	*Order By*	*orderby*
OrderByDescending	*Order By*	*orderby*
Range	Not supported	Not supported
Repeat	Not supported	Not supported
Reverse	Not supported	Not supported
Select	*From* and *Select*	*from* and *select*
SelectMany	*From* (multiple)	*from* (multiple)
SequenceEqual	Not supported	Not supported
Single	Not supported	Not supported
SingleOrDefault	Not supported	Not supported
Skip	*Skip*	Not supported
SkipWhile	*Skip While*	Not supported
Sum	*Aggregate...Into Sum*	Not supported
Take	*Take*	Not supported
TakeWhile	*Take While*	Not supported
ThenBy	*Order By*	*orderby*
ThenByDescending	*Order By*	*orderby*
ToArray	Not supported	Not supported
ToDictionary	Not supported	Not supported
ToList	Not supported	Not supported
ToLookup	Not supported	Not supported
Union	Not supported	Not supported
Where	*Where*	*where*
Not applicable	*Let*	*let*

To see specific examples of these native operators, use the "See Also" block later in this entry to locate related query expression entries in this chapter.

When a specific LINQ method is not supported natively, each language allows that method to be included directly as part of the query expression syntax.

VISUAL BASIC

```
Dim allNames = (From set1 In oldCustomers
                Select set1.FullName).Union(
                From set2 In newCustomers
                Select set2.FullName)
```

C#

```
var allNames = (from set1 in oldCustomers
                select set1.FullName).Union(
                from set2 in newCustomers
                select set2.FullName);
```

Both languages support the LINQ providers supplied with Visual Studio: LINQ to Objects, LINQ to DataSet, LINQ to Entities, and LINQ to XML. (LINQ to SQL, formerly supported in both languages, has been deprecated in favor of LINQ to DataSet and LINQ to Entities.) Visual Basic's interaction with LINQ to XML includes the ability to generate new XML content natively as part of its XML Literals support. C# does not include this feature.

In Visual Basic, the compiler attempts to detect the end of a LINQ statement syntactically. However, there may be times when the compiler will not be able to correctly determine whether the statement that follows a query expression is part of the query or not. In such cases, a blank line must appear between the query expression and the subsequent statement. Because all statements in C#, including LINQ statements, end with a semicolon, this type of ambiguity is not an issue.

See Also

Aggregate Query Expression Operator, Distinct Query Expression Operator, From Query Expression Operator, Group Join Query Expression Operator, Group Query Expression Operator, Join Query Expression Operator, Let Query Expression Operator, Order By Query Expression Operator, Select Query Expression Operator, Skip Query Expression Operator, Skip While Query Expression Operator, Take Query Expression Operator, Take While Query Expression Operator, Where Query Expression Operator

RaiseEvent Custom Event Declaration

See

Custom Event Statement

RaiseEvent Statement

C# does not include an equivalent to Visual Basic's `RaiseEvent` statement. Instead, you must manually issue a call to the event handler method.

Randomize Method

Random numbers in C# are generated through the `System.Random` class. Creating an instance of this class, with or without a seed value, resets the generator. A distinct statement similar to Visual Basic's `Randomize` method is not needed.

VISUAL BASIC

```
' ----- With default seed.
Randomize()

' ----- With custom seed.
Randomize CInt(Now.Ticks And &H0000FFFF)
```

C#

```
// ----- With default seed.
System.Random generator = new System.Random();

// ----- With custom seed.
System.Random generator = new System.Random(
    (int)(DateTime.Now.Ticks & 0x0000FFFF));
```

Rate Method

See

Financial Methods

ReadOnly Modifier

When used with field definitions, C#'s `readonly` modifier is identical to Visual Basic's `ReadOnly` modifier.

VISUAL BASIC

```
Class TaxInformation
    ' ----- Must be set in a constructor or declaration.
    Private ReadOnly TaxYear As Integer
End Class
```

C#

```
class TaxInformation
{
    // ----- Must be set in a constructor or declaration.
    private readonly int TaxYear;
}
```

Visual Basic's `ReadOnly` modifier is also used to create read-only properties. In such definitions, the `Set` portion of the property is left off. C# also leaves off the `set` portion, but it does not require that any other special modifier be present to indicate the property's read-only format.

VISUAL BASIC

```
Public ReadOnly Property Status As Integer
    Get
        ' ----- Return statement appears here.
    End Get
    ' ----- But no setter appears.
End Property
```

C#

```
public int Status
{
    get
    {
        // ----- return statement appears here.
    }
    // ----- But no setter appears.
}
```

ReDim Statement

C# does not include an equivalent for Visual Basic's *ReDim* statement. To resize an array, you create a new array with the desired dimensions, use the *System.Array* class' *Resize* method (for one-dimensional arrays), or use other features of the *Array* class to build a new array based on the old array.

VISUAL BASIC

```
Dim infoArray(4, 8) As Integer

' ----- Later, resize the array, discarding old content.
ReDim infoArray(2, 10) ' 3x11 array
```

C#

```
int[,] infoArray = new int[5, 9];

// ----- Later, resize the array, discarding old content.
infoArray = new int[3, 11];
```

The *ReDim* statement's *Preserve* modifier retains existing content in the new array. In C#, you must manually copy old elements to the new array. For one-dimensional arrays, you can use the *Array.Resize* method to change the array length while preserving existing elements.

VISUAL BASIC

```
ReDim Preserve storageArea(0 to 9)
```

C#

```
Array.Resize(ref storageArea, 10);
```

REM Statement

When adding a full-line comment to your source, C#'s // comment symbol is an exact replacement for Visual Basic's *REM* statement.

VISUAL BASIC

```
REM ----- This is a full-line comment.
```

C#

```
// ----- This is a full-line comment.
```

See Also

' Comment Symbol

RemoveHandler Custom Event Declaration

See

Custom Event Statement

RemoveHandler Statement

Visual Basic uses the *RemoveHandler* statement, in conjunction with the *AddressOf* operator, to detach event handlers from object instances.

VISUAL BASIC
```
RemoveHandler Form1.Click, AddressOf ClickEventHandler
```

In C#, the -= event unsubscription operator does the same thing. An *AddressOf*-style operator is not required.

C#
```
Form1.Click -= ClickEventHandler;
```

Rename Method

When renaming a file, the *System.IO.File.Move* method provides functionality similar Visual Basic's *Rename* method, with the same limitations and restrictions.

VISUAL BASIC
```
Rename(oldFileName, newFileName)
```

C#
```
System.IO.File.Move(oldFileName, newFileName);
```

When renaming directories, *Directory.Move* is the equivalent method to call in C#.

VISUAL BASIC
```
Rename(oldDirectory, newDirectory)
```

C#
```
System.IO.Directory.Move(oldDirectory, newDirectory);
```

Replace Method

For basic replacements of all occurrences of one substring with another, the *string* type's *Replace* method produces the same results as Visual Basic's *Replace* method.

VISUAL BASIC
```
sourceString = "I vote yes."
result = Replace(sourceString, "yes", "no")
```

C#

```
sourceString = "I vote yes.";
result = sourceString.Replace("yes", "no");
```

The *Replace* method accepts additional arguments that indicate the starting 1-based position and the number of occurrences to replace. The *string* type's *Replace* method lacks these features. Instead, you can use regular expressions to perform this replacement. The start position in the C# version is 0-based.

VISUAL BASIC

```
result = Replace(sourceString, "A", "Z", startAt, count)
```

C#

```
// ----- Assumes: using System.Text.RegularExpressions;

// ----- For a case-sensitive replacement.
Regex replaceEngine = new Regex("A");

// ----- For a case-insensitive replacement.
Regex replaceEngine = new Regex("A",
    RegexOptions.IgnoreCase);

// ----- Finally, perform the replacement.
result = replaceEngine.Replace(
    sourceString, "Z", count, startAt - 1);
```

The pattern to match and the replacement pattern may both need to be adjusted using regular expression rules if they contain special characters. See Visual Studio's documentation on regular expressions for more information.

Reset Method

C# does not include an equivalent for Visual Basic's *Reset* method. To close all open files in C#, you must close each stream or other file-management class individually.

Resume Statement

C# does not include support for unstructured error handling, and therefore it has no equivalent for Visual Basic's *Resume* statement. Instead, you must use structured error handling constructs.

See Also

Try Statement

Return Statement

C#'s *return* statement is identical in use and syntax to Visual Basic's *Return* statement, both for *Function* and *Sub* methods.

VISUAL BASIC
```
' ----- For methods without a return type (Subs).
Return

' ----- For methods with a return type (Functions).
Return someValue
```
C#
```
// ----- For methods with void return type.
return;

// ----- For methods with non-void return type.
return someValue;
```

For *Sub* methods that do not return a value, Visual Basic also supports the *Exit Sub* statement, which is functionally equivalent to *Return*, and the same as C#'s *return* statement.

In Visual Basic *Function* methods that return a value, you can assign the return value to the name of the function instead of using the *Return* statement. This variation is not supported in C#. Instead, use the *return* statement to indicate the return value.

RGB Method

Visual Basic's *RGB* method produces an integer RGB value from individual red, green, and blue values. In C#, you must combine the color components manually.

VISUAL BASIC
```
' ----- Negative values will throw an exception.
Dim result As Integer =
    RGB(redValue, greenValue, blueValue)
```
C#
```
// ----- Assumes all values are in 0-to-255 range.
int result = (blueValue * 0x10000) +
    (greenValue * 0x100) + redValue;
```

Right Method

Visual Basic's *Right* method returns the rightmost characters of a source string. Use the *Substring* method of C#'s *string* class to return similar content.

VISUAL BASIC
```
' ----- Return last two characters.
Dim cents As String = Right(dollarsAndCents, 2)
```
C#
```
// ----- Return last two characters.
string cents = dollarsAndCents.Substring(
    dollarsAndCents.Length - 2, 2);
```

The *Right* method will silently return the entire string if the length requested exceeds the full length of the string. In C#, the *Substring* method will throw an exception if the starting position or length requested is too long. Always verify the length of the string before using the *Substring* method.

RmDir Method

Visual Basic's *RmDir* method deletes a directory. To do the same thing in C#, use the *System.IO.Directory.Delete* method.

VISUAL BASIC
```
RmDir(pathToDirectory)
```

C#
```
System.IO.Directory.Delete(pathToDirectory);
```

Rnd Method

Random numbers in C# are generated through the *System.Random* class. The class' *NextDouble* method returns a value between *0* and *1*, similar to that returned by Visual Basic's *Rnd* method.

VISUAL BASIC
```
Randomize()
Dim nextSample As Double = Rnd()
```

C#
```
System.Random generator = new System.Random();
double nextSample = generator.NextDouble();
```

The *Random* class also includes methods that return random integers within specific ranges.

RSet Method

Visual Basic's *RSet* method returns a string with the original string trimmed or padded with spaces to a specific length. You can accomplish this in C#, although there is no single language feature that is equivalent to *RSet*.

VISUAL BASIC
```
result = RSet(originalString, 10)
```

C#
```
if (originalString.Length < 10)
    result = originalString.PadLeft(10);
else
    result = originalString.Substring(0, 10);
```

RTrim Method

The *TrimEnd* method of C#'s *string* data type does the same thing as Visual Basic's *RTrim* method.

```
result = RTrim(someString)
```

C#
```
result = someString.TrimEnd();
```

SaveSetting Method

Visual Basic's *SaveSetting* method adds a single key to a standardized Visual Basic section of the Windows registry.

VISUAL BASIC
```
SaveSetting(appName, sectionName, keyName, newValue)
```

C#
```
// ----- Assumes: using Microsoft.Win32;
const string settingRoot =
    "Software\\VB and VBA Program Settings";
string settingLocation = string.Format("{0}\\{1}\\{2}",
    settingRoot, appName, sectionName);

RegistryKey keyAccess =
    Registry.CurrentUser.CreateSubKey(settingLocation);
keyAccess.SetValue(keyName, newValue);
keyAccess.Close();
```

SByte Data Type

C#'s intrinsic *sbyte* data type is identical to Visual Basic's *sbyte* data type. Both types are aliases for .NET's *System.SByte* type.

VISUAL BASIC
```
Dim offset As SByte = 0
```

C#
```
sbyte offset = 0;
```

Scope

See

Lifetime and Scope

ScriptEngine Property

Visual Basic's *ScriptEngine* property always returns the short text *"VB"* to indicate the Visual Basic language. It has no equivalent in C#.

ScriptEngineBuildVersion Property

Visual Basic's *ScriptEngineBuildVersion* property has no equivalent in C#.

ScriptEngineMajorVersion Property

Visual Basic's *ScriptEngineMajorVersion* property has no equivalent in C#.

ScriptEngineMinorVersion Property

Visual Basic's *ScriptEngineMinorVersion* property has no equivalent in C#.

Second Method

The *DateTime* type's *Second* property returns the same information as Visual Basic's *Second* method.

VISUAL BASIC
```
Dim whichSecond As Integer = Second(oneOrder.OrderDate)
```

C#
```
int whichSecond = oneOrder.OrderDate.Second;
```

Seek Method

Visual Basic's *Seek* method gets or sets the current read or write position in a file opened with the *FileOpen* method. All positions are 1-based, and can indicate a byte, record, or sequential block position based on the open mode of the file.

VISUAL BASIC
```
' ----- Return the current 1-based position.
Dim currentPos As Long = Seek(fileNumber)

' ----- Set a new 1-based position.
Seek(fileNumber, targetPosition)
```

C# does not include the same file-management features included with VB. Instead, it is common to work with the *System.IO.FileStream* class to read and write files. This class includes a *Position* property and a *Seek* method that together provide functionality similar to VB's *Seek* method. The key differences are that the *FileStream*'s features only indicate byte positions and not record or block positions, and that its positions are 0-based.

C#
```
// ----- Return the current 0-based position.
Dim currentPos As Long = openedStream.Position;

// ----- Set a new 0-based position.
openedStream.Seek(targetPosition,
    System.IO.SeekOrigin.Begin);
```

See Also

FileOpen Method

Select Case Statement

C#'s *switch* statement is generally equivalent to Visual Basic's *Select Case* statement. Both statements include "case" blocks, plus an optional else/default block.

VISUAL BASIC
```
Select Case position
    Case 1
        positionName = "ones"
    Case 10
        positionName = "tens"
    Case 100
        positionName = "hundreds"
    Case Else
        positionName = "too large!"
End Select
```

C#
```
switch (position)
{
    case 1:
        positionName = "ones";
        break;
    case 10:
        positionName = "tens";
        break;
    case 100:
        positionName = "hundreds";
        break;
    default:
        positionName = "too large!";
        break;
}
```

As with other C# block statements, the condition that appears after the *switch* keyword must be enclosed in parentheses, something Visual Basic does not require. VB's *Case* clause becomes *case* with a trailing colon in C#; *Case Else* becomes *default*. In both languages, the first block that matches is used; those that follow, even if they match the test value, will be skipped.

In Visual Basic, a matched block is automatically exited after its last statement. Each *case* block in C# must be explicitly exited using a *break* statement or similar block-exiting statement.

C#
```
case "A":
    // ----- Case-specific processing, then...
    break;
```

C# allows you to jump from one *case* block to another via the *goto case* and *goto default* statements, something that would require distinct line labels and *GoTo* statements in Visual Basic.

C#

```
case DayOfWeek.Monday:
    // ----- Monday-specific processing, such as...
    if (HolidayMonday())
        goto case DayOfWeek.Tuesday;
    else
        goto default;
case DayOfWeek.Tuesday:
    // ----- Tuesday-specific processing, then...
    break;
default:
    // ----- General processing.
```

In Visual Basic, the test value supported by a *Case* clause can be an integer number, a character or string, a Boolean literal, an enumeration value, a floating-point number, a date, a general *Object* instance, or *Nothing*. In C#, the list includes literals from a more restricted set of value types: integers, strings, characters, Boolean literals, enumeration values, and *null*. VB *Case* clauses support value ranges, expressions, and relative comparisons.

VISUAL BASIC

```
Case 1, 2
    ' ----- Matches one of comma-delimited values.
    tableSize = "small"
Case 3 To 6
    ' ----- Matches inclusive range.
    tableSize = "medium"
Case TableForSeven()
    ' ----- Matches result of expression or method call.
    tableSize = "oddball"
Case Is > 7
    ' ----- Matches using comparison operator.
    tableSize = "large"
```

C# supports none of these complex test expressions. Instead, each *case* clause presents precisely one value to be compared to the statement's incoming test value. The only flexibility beyond this single-value format is that two or more adjacent *case* clauses can all share the same logic block.

C#

```
case DayOfWeek.Monday:
case DayOfWeek.Wednesday:
    // ----- Code for both Monday and Wednesday.
```

Select Query Expression Operator (LINQ)

C#'s *select* query expression operator is identical to Visual Basic's *Select* operator. When crafting query expressions in VB, the *Select* clause is optional, with the resulting fields indicated by the *From*, *Aggregate*, or *Group* clause. In C#, the *select* clause is required in all query types. Additionally, Visual Basic allows some flexibility concerning the placement of the *Select* clause within the query expression. For standard queries, C# requires that *select* be the terminating clause.

VISUAL BASIC

```
' ----- The Select clause can also appear before Where.
Dim result = From oneEmployee In Employees
             Where oneEmployee.IsManager = True
             Select oneEmployee
```

C#

```
var result = from oneEmployee in Employees
             where oneEmployee.IsManager == true
             select oneEmployee;
```

As in Visual Basic, C# supports the return of anonymous types, either implicitly with a restricted selection list, or explicitly via the *new* operator. You can also create new instances of named types using this same syntax.

VISUAL BASIC

```
' ----- Anonymous type.
Dim result = From oneEmployee In Employees
             Where oneEmployee.IsManager = True
             Select New With {.Name = oneEmployee.FullName,
             oneEmployee.Salary, oneEmployee.HireDate}

' ----- Named type.
Dim result = From oneEmployee In Employees
             Where oneEmployee.IsManager = True
             Select New Person With {
             .Name = oneEmployee.FullName}
```

C#

```
// ----- Anonymous type.
var result = from oneEmployee in Employees
             where oneEmployee.IsManager == true
             select new {Name = oneEmployee.FullName,
             oneEmployee.Salary, oneEmployee.HireDate};

// ----- Named type.
var result = from oneEmployee in Employees
             where oneEmployee.IsManager == true
             select new Person {
             Name = oneEmployee.FullName};
```

See Also

Query Expressions

Set Declaration

See

Properties

SetAttr Method

In Visual Basic, the `SetAttr` method sets the attributes for a file path. In C#, this operation is done via .NET's `File.SetAttributes` method.

VISUAL BASIC
```
SetAttr(targetFile, attributeFlags)
```

C#
```
System.IO.File.SetAttributes(targetFile, attributeFlags);
```

The two variations use a different set of attribute flags. VB uses a language-specific `FileAttribute` enumeration, while the .NET method uses members from the `System.IO.FileAttributes` enumeration. The two enumerations are similar in purpose, though incompatible in their member values.

Shadows Modifier

C#'s *new* modifier hides a base member of the same name from being expressed in the derived class, just like Visual Basic's *Shadows* modifier. The *new* modifier is optional in such cases, but should be included to make the hiding explicit.

VISUAL BASIC
```
Class DerivedClass
    Inherits BaseClass

    ' ----- Hides whatever BaseClass.BaseElement was.
    Public Shadows Sub BaseElement()
    End Sub
End Class
```

C#
```
class DerivedClass : BaseClass
{
    // ----- Hides whatever BaseClass.BaseElement was.
    new public void BaseElement()
    {
    }
}
```

Shared Modifier

In Visual Basic, the *Shared* modifier identifies members of a class or structure that are accessible outside of any specific instance of that type.

VISUAL BASIC
```
Class CoreFeatures
    Public Shared Sub LogError(ByVal errorText As String)
        ' ----- Callable as CoreFeatures.LogError()
    End Sub
End Class
```

In C#, the `static` modifier—unrelated to VB's own `Static` modifier—performs the same function.

C#
```csharp
class CoreFeatures
{
    public static void LogError(string errorText)
    {
        // ----- Callable as CoreFeatures.LogError()
    }
}
```

While this syntax works for individual members, C# also allows the `static` modifier to be applied to an entire class or structure. All members of such types become static (shared) as well, and must be decorated with the `static` modifier.

C#
```csharp
static class CoreFeatures
{
    // ----- All members will be static, including...
    public static void LogError(string errorText)
    {
        // ----- Callable as CoreFeatures.LogError()
    }
}
```

In Visual Basic, the `Module` statement provides this type-level sharing of all members.

See Also

Module Statement

Shell Method

Visual Basic's `Shell` method starts an external application. In C#, you can do the same thing using the `Process.Start` method, found in the `System.Diagnostics` namespace.

VISUAL BASIC
```vb
' ----- Basic startup of an application. Program will be
'       minimized, but will have the focus by default.
Shell("Notepad.exe")

' ----- Startup with different position/focus setting.
'       The process ID is also retained.
Dim processID As Integer =
    Shell("IExplore.exe", AppWinStyle.MaximizedFocus)

' ----- Start and wait for the program to finish.
Shell("ComponentSetup.exe",
    AppWinStyle.NormalFocus, True, -1)
```

C#
```
// ----- Basic startup of an application. Program will be
//       displayed in its default presentation with focus.
//       Assumes: using System.Diagnostics;
Process.Start("Notepad.exe");

// ----- Startup with different position/focus setting.
Process browserProcess = new Process();
browserProcess.StartInfo.UseShellExecute = true;
browserProcess.StartInfo.FileName = "IExplore.exe";
browserProcess.StartInfo.WindowStyle =
    ProcessWindowStyle.Maximized; // Will have focus also.
browserProcess.Start();
int processID = browserProcess.Id;

// ----- Start and wait for the program to finish.
Process setupProcess = Process.Start("ComponentSetup.exe");
setupProcess.WaitForExit();
```

Short Circuiting

See

AndAlso Conjunction Operator, OrElse Disjunction Operator, If Operator

Short Data Type

C#'s intrinsic *short* data type is identical to Visual Basic's *Short* data type. Both types are aliases for .NET's *System.Int16* type. For short literals, Visual Basic uses an *S* or *s* suffix after the value; C# does not include such a suffix.

VISUAL BASIC
```
Dim baseYear As Short = 0s   ' or 0S
```

C#
```
short baseYear = 0;
```

Single Data Type

C#'s intrinsic *float* data type is identical to Visual Basic's *Single* data type. Both types are aliases for .NET's *System.Single* type. For single literals, Visual Basic uses an *F*, *f*, or *!* suffix after the value; in C#, use *F* or *f* instead.

VISUAL BASIC
```
Dim factor As Single = 0!   ' or 0F or 0f
```

C#
```
float factor = 0f;   // or 0F
```

Skip Query Expression Operator (LINQ)

C# does not include a direct equivalent for Visual Basic's *Skip* query expression operator. However, you can use LINQ's *Skip* extension method to accomplish the same thing.

VISUAL BASIC
```
' ----- Identify less-active customers for follow-up.
Dim followUp = From cust In customers
               Order By cust.TotalSales Descending
               Select cust.FullName
               Skip 20
```

C#
```
// ----- Identify less-active customers for follow-up.
var followUp = (from cust in customers
                orderby cust.TotalSales descending
                select new {cust.FullName}).Skip(20);
```

See Also

Query Expressions

Skip While Query Expression Operator (LINQ)

C# does not include a direct equivalent for Visual Basic's *Skip While* query expression operator. However, you can use LINQ's *SkipWhile* extension method to accomplish the same thing.

VISUAL BASIC
```
' ----- Identify less-active customers for follow-up.
Dim followUp = From cust In customers
               Order By cust.TotalSales Descending
               Select cust.FullName, cust.TotalSales
               Skip While TotalSales >= 10000
```

C#
```
// ----- Identify less-active customers for follow-up.
var followUp = (from cust in customers
                orderby cust.TotalSales descending
                select new {cust.FullName,
                cust.TotalSales})
                .SkipWhile(test => test.TotalSales
                >= 10000);
```

See Also

Query Expressions

SLN Method

See

Financial Methods

Space Method

Visual Basic's *Space* method returns a string with a specified number of space characters. In C#, create a new instance of a *string*, passing the count of space characters to the constructor.

VISUAL BASIC

```
' ----- Creates a string of five spaces.
Dim result As String = Space(5)
```

C#

```
// ----- Creates a string of five spaces.
string result = new string(' ', 5);
```

SPC Method

C# does not include an equivalent for Visual Basic's *SPC* method. When outputting columnar text data, you must manually manage the spacing in the result by counting the length of each output value yourself.

Split Method

In C#, the *string* type's *Split* method returns results similar to that of Visual Basic's *Split* method. VB's *Split* method accepts a single string delimiter; The *string.Split* method accepts an array of *string* or *char* values, all of which are treated as delimiters.

VISUAL BASIC

```
' ----- Return all delimited components.
Dim source As String = "Hello,World"
Dim delim As String = ","
Dim result() As String = Split(source, delim)

' ----- Split off only the first delimited component.
result = Split(source, delim, 1)
```

C#

```
// ----- Return all delimited components.
string source = "Hello,World";
char[] delim = new char[] {','};
string[] result = source.Split(delim);

// ----- Split off only the first delimited component.
result = source.Split(delim, 1);
```

The *Split* method includes an option that specifies whether to use text (case-insensitive) or binary (case-sensitive) sorting rules when searching for the delimiter. The *string* type's *Split* method lacks this option. Instead, it has one additional option that indicates whether to omit zero-length strings in the returned array.

```
result = source.Split(delim,
    StringSplitOptions.RemoveEmptyEntries);
```

Statements

In Visual Basic, the end of a physical line indicates where a statement ends. For block statements (such as *For* loops), opening, closing, and subordinate portions each terminate at the end of a physical line.

VISUAL BASIC

```
' ----- A simple single-line statement.
quotient = numerator / denominator

' ----- An If condition, with its subordinate statement.
If (totalPercent > 100) Then
    totalPercent = 100
End If

' ----- An If condition with a subordinate block.
If (totalPercent > 100) Then
    ReportOverage(totalPercent)
    totalPercent = 100
End If
```

In C#, a semicolon indicates the end of a statement. For the purposes of statement structure, a block of statements surrounded with a set of curly braces is treated as a single semicolon-terminated statement.

C#

```
// ----- A simple single-line statement.
quotient = numerator / denominator;

// ----- An if condition, with its subordinate statement.
if (totalPercent > 100)
    totalPercent = 100;

// ----- An if condition with a subordinate block.
if (totalPercent > 100)
{
    ReportOverage(totalPercent);
    totalPercent = 100;
}
```

Visual Basic allows one logical line to span multiple physical lines by adding a line continuation character—a trailing underscore—to all but the last line. Newer versions of VB attempt to identify spanned lines by context, without requiring the underscore.

VISUAL BASIC

```
' ----- Explicit: Using the line continuation character.
expirationDate = String.Format("{0:00}/{1:0000}", _
    monthPortion, yearPortion)
```

```
'  ----- Implicit: A comma indicates continuation.
expirationDate = String.Format("{0:00}/{1:0000}",
    monthPortion, yearPortion)
```

C# allows a single logical line to span physical lines by employing as much or as little whitespace as needed, as long as the entire statement ends with a semicolon.

C#
```
expirationDate = string.Format("{0:00}/{1:0000}",
    monthPortion, yearPortion);
```

Visual Basic allows multiple statements to sit on a physical line, separated by the colon character.

VISUAL BASIC
```
'  ----- Two simple statements on one line.
firstName = "John" : lastName = "Doe"

'  ----- A block statement can be single-line as well.
Do While (status > 0) : status = DoMoreWork() : Loop
```

In C#, placing multiple statements on a single line is another whitespace decision. The placement of semicolons is the determining factor in separating statements. As long as the semicolons appear in the correct positions, it seldom matters where you break a logical line.

C#
```
// ----- Two simple statements on one line.
firstName = "John"; lastName = "Doe";

// ----- A block statement can be single-line as well.
while (status > 0) status = DoMoreWork();
```

A special case of statement joining in VB occurs in the single-line form of the *If* statement, where linked statements are processed in response to the condition.

VISUAL BASIC
```
'  ----- Both assignments will occur if true.
If (counter > 100) Then overflow = True : counter = 0
```

In C#, these subordinate statements must be enclosed in a set of curly braces. Using a syntax that more closely parallels that of VB will produce the wrong results.

C#
```
// ----- This is equivalent to the earlier VB code.
if (counter > 100) { overflow = true; counter = 0; }

// ----- This code is wrong; counter will be reset
//       whether the condition is true or false.
if (counter > 100) overflow = true; counter = 0;
```

C# permits you to start a distinctly scoped block by using a set of curly braces without an associated block construct, something not available in Visual Basic.

C#

```
{
    // ----- Code here is locally scoped.
}
```

Static Modifier

C# does not include support for local static variables, and therefore does not include an equivalent for Visual Basic's *Static* modifier. One workaround is to define an instance field within the same type that contains the method needing a local static variable.

VISUAL BASIC

```
Class Example
    Public Sub WorkWithPersistentData()
        Static tracking As Integer = 0
        ' ----- Manipulate tracking variable as needed.
    End Sub
End Class
```

C#

```
class Example
{
    private int tracking = 0;
    public void WorkWithPersistentData()
    {
        // ----- Manipulate tracking variable as needed.
    }
}
```

Stop Statement

C# does not include a language substitute for Visual Basic's *Stop* statement. Instead, you must call the equivalent .NET Framework method, *Debugger.Break*.

VISUAL BASIC

```
Stop
```

C#

```
System.Diagnostics.Debugger.Break();
```

Str Method

Visual Basic's *Str* method returns the string representation of a number. In general, a numeric expression's *ToString* method provides similar results, although the output of *Str* for floating-point values may differ in format from what *ToString* produces. When a string-formatted number is provided to *Str*, it attempts to convert the source value to *Double* before reissuing it as a string.

VISUAL BASIC

```
Dim result As String = Str(sourceValue)
```

C#

```
// ----- For signed or unsigned integer expressions.
string result = sourceValue.ToString();

// ----- For floating-point expressions.
result = ((double)sourceValue).ToString();

// ----- For strings that contain numeric values.
double convertedValue;
if (double.TryParse(sourceValue, out convertedValue))
    result = convertedValue.ToString();
```

The *Str* method also includes a few non-standard outputs for specific expressions.

- If the source value is of type *System.DBNull*, the output is "Null."
- If the source is a Boolean true value, the output is "True."
- If the source is a Boolean false value, the output is "False."

StrComp Method

Visual Basic's *StrComp* returns an integer that indicates the relative order of two source strings. In C#, use the *string* type's *Compare* method to provide similar results.

VISUAL BASIC

```
' ----- Case-sensitive comparison
Dim result As Integer = StrComp(firstString,
    secondString, CompareMethod.Binary)

' ----- Case-insensitive comparison
Dim result As Integer = StrComp(firstString,
    secondString, CompareMethod.Text)
```

C#

```
// ----- Case-sensitive comparison
int result = Math.Sign(string.Compare(firstString,
    secondString, String.Comparison.Ordinal));

// ----- Case-insensitive comparison
int result = Math.Sign(string.Compare(firstString,
    secondString, String.Comparison.OrdinalIgnoreCase));
```

The *StrComp* method always returns 0, -1, or 1 depending on the order of the items. The *Compare* method returns positive or negative values, or zero, and the *Math.Sign* method (or a similar calculation) must be used to coalesce the values into those presented by Visual Basic.

StrConv Method

Visual Basic's *StrConv* method transforms text into a variant format based on flags provided to the method. The method is useful for transforming text between various Asian-language formats, but it can also produce "proper case" text and other conversions, all in a locale-specific manner.

C# does not include a direct equivalent for the *StrConv* method. Instead, you can call the same underlying Win32 method used by *StrConv*. The following code provides a simplified wrapper around that call to Win32's *LCMapStringEx* method.

C#

```
// ----- Define at the top of the file.
using System.Runtime.InteropServices;
using System.Globalization;

// ----- Define the following in a class.
[DllImport("kernel32.dll", CharSet = CharSet.Unicode,
    SetLastError = true)]
private static extern int LCMapStringEx(
    string localeName, uint mappingFlags,
    string source, int sourceLen,
    [Out] IntPtr dest, int destLen,
    IntPtr versionInfo, IntPtr reserved,
    IntPtr sortHandle);

public enum StrConvFlags : uint
{
    Hiragana           = 0x00100000,
    Katakana           = 0x00200000,
    LinguisticCasing   = 0x01000000,
    Lowercase          = 0x00000100,
    Narrow             = 0x00400000,
    ProperCase         = 0x00000300,
    SimplifiedChinese  = 0x02000000,
    TraditionalChinese = 0x04000000,
    Uppercase          = 0x00000200,
    Wide               = 0x00800000
}

// ----- Then use the following method to
//       simulate StrConv.
public static string StrConv(string originalText,
    StrConvFlags convFlags, int localeID = 0)
{
    CultureInfo whichLocale;
    string result = originalText;
    IntPtr destBuffer;
    int destLen;

    // ----- Ignore if no text supplied.
    if ((originalText == null) ||
            (originalText.Length == 0))
        return originalText;
```

```
// ----- Get the default or specified locale.
if ((localeID == 0) || (localeID == 1))
    whichLocale = System.Threading.Thread.
        CurrentThread.CurrentCulture;
else
    whichLocale = new CultureInfo(localeID);

// ----- Make room for the converted version.
destLen = LCMapStringEx(whichLocale.Name,
    (uint)convFlags, originalText, originalText.Length,
    IntPtr.Zero, 0, IntPtr.Zero,
    IntPtr.Zero, IntPtr.Zero);
destLen = destLen * sizeof(char);
destBuffer = Marshal.AllocHGlobal(destLen);
try
{
    // ----- Perform the conversion. destLen=0
    //       on failure.
    destLen = LCMapStringEx(whichLocale.Name,
        (uint)convFlags,
        originalText, originalText.Length,
        destBuffer, destLen, IntPtr.Zero,
        IntPtr.Zero, IntPtr.Zero);
    if (destLen > 0)
        result = Marshal.PtrToStringUni(
            destBuffer, destLen);
    else
        result = originalText;
}
catch
{
    result = originalText;
}
finally
{
    Marshal.FreeHGlobal(destBuffer);
}
return result;
}
```

StrDup Method

Visual Basic's *StrDup* method creates a new string with a certain number of repetitions of a specified character. In C#, create a new instance of the *string* class, and use one of its constructors to specify the base character and the number of repetitions.

VISUAL BASIC

```
' ----- Creates the string "*****"
Dim result As String = StrDup(5, "*"c)
```

```
C#
// ----- Creates the string "*****"
string result = new string('*', 5);
```

String Data Type

C#'s intrinsic *string* data type is identical to Visual Basic's *String* data type. Both types are aliases for .NET's *System.String* type.

VISUAL BASIC
```
Dim name As String = ""
```

C#
```
string name = "";
```

Historically, Visual Basic has provided a *$* suffix that could be attached to string identifiers or certain intrinsic functions. Although the .NET versions of Visual Basic still support this for backward compatibility, no equivalent syntax exists in C#.

StrReverse Method

Visual Basic's *StrReverse* method returns a new string with its characters in the reverse order from a source string. To do this in C#, convert the string to an array of characters, reverse the array, then reassemble the string.

VISUAL BASIC
```
Dim result As String = StrReverse(originalString)
```

C#
```
char[] tempArea = originalString.ToCharArray();
System.Array.Reverse(tempArea);
string result = new string(tempArea);
```

The *StrReverse* method performs special processing when the source string includes certain Unicode characters, such as surrogates that reference extended characters. If you will work with certain international character sets, the source code for the *StrReverse* can provide guidance on how to perform such reversals. See the source code at: http://referencesource.microsoft.com/#Microsoft.VisualBasic/Strings.vb

Structure Statement

C#'s *struct* statement is equivalent to Visual Basic's *Structure* statement. When declaring a structure that implements one or more interfaces in C#, a comma-delimited list of those interfaces appears after the structure name, separated from the name by a colon.

VISUAL BASIC
```
Structure Variable
    Implements IDataPart
    ' ----- Members appear here.
End Structure
```

C#

```
struct Variable : IDataPart
{
    // ----- Members appear here.
}
```

Structures in both languages contain the same types of members: constructors, fields, constants, properties, methods, operator overloads and user-defined conversions, indexers, events, and nested types (including delegates and enumerations). Instance fields in structures cannot include an initialization value with the declaration, but static (shared) fields can.

Structures support the following modifiers in each language.

Visual Basic Modifier	C# Modifier
Friend	internal
Partial	partial
Private	private
Protected	protected
Protected Friend	protected internal
Public	public
Shadows	new

Structures in Visual Basic are *Friend* by default, just as structures in C# are *internal* by default. In VB, structure members are *Public* by default; they are *private* by default in C#. Structure members cannot use the *Protected* (VB) or *protected* (C#) modifier.

See Also

Access Modifiers, Constructors

Sub Statement

See

Methods

Sub Lambda Statement

See

Lambda Expressions

Switch Method

Visual Basic's *Switch* method accepts a parameter array of conditions and matching objects, returning the first object whose condition is *True*, or *Nothing* when no conditions match.

```
Dim playerMessage As String = Switch(
    players < 9, "Too few players!",
    players > 9, "Too many players!",
    players = 9, "Play ball!")
```

C# lacks a language equivalent for the *Switch* method. Instead, you can use a conditional statement, such as the *select case* or *if* statement, to achieve the same results.

C#

```
string playerMessage = null;
if (players < 9)
    playerMessage = "Too few players!";
else if (players > 9)
    playerMessage = "Too many players!";
else
    playerMessage = "Play ball!";
```

SYD Method

See

Financial Methods

SyncLock Statement

C#'s *lock* statement is equivalent to Visual Basic's *SyncLock* statement.

VISUAL BASIC

```
Class VitalMethods
    Private HoldLock As New Object
    Public Sub PerformVitalAction()
        SyncLock HoldLock
            ' ----- Protected code here.
        End SyncLock
    End Sub
End Class
```

C#

```
class VitalMethods
{
    private object HoldLock = new object();
    public void PerformVitalAction()
    {
        lock (HoldLock)
        {
            // ----- Protected code here.
        }
    }
}
```

SystemTypeName Method

Visual Basic's *SystemTypeName* method accepts input from a set of pre-.NET VB type names, and returns the system (.NET in this case) type name equivalent. No direct replacement for this method exists in C#. However, the following table shows the full set of results produced by this *SystemTypeName*. The case of the input term is ignored.

Input Value	Output Value
Boolean	*System.Boolean*
Byte	*System.Byte*
Char	*System.Int64*
Date	*System.DateTime*
Decimal	*System.Decimal*
Double	*System.Double*
Integer	*System.Int32*
Long	*System.Char*
Object	*System.Object*
Short	*System.Int16*
Single	*System.Single*
String	*System.String*

All other inputs return *Nothing*, the equivalent of *null* in C#.

TAB Method

C# does not include an equivalent for Visual Basic's *TAB* method. When outputting columnar text data, you must manually manage the spacing in the result by counting the length of each output value yourself.

Take Query Expression Operator (LINQ)

C# does not include a direct equivalent for Visual Basic's *Take* query expression operator. However, you can use LINQ's *Take* extension method to accomplish the same thing.

VISUAL BASIC
```
' ----- Get top 10 customers.
Dim topCusts = From cust In customers
               Order By cust.TotalSales Descending
               Select cust.FullName
               Take 10
```

C#
```
// ----- Get top 10 customers.
var topCusts = (from cust in customers
                orderby cust.TotalSales descending
                select new {cust.FullName}).Take(10);
```

See Also

Query Expressions

Take While Query Expression Operator (LINQ)

C# does not include a direct equivalent for Visual Basic's `Take While` query expression operator. However, you can use LINQ's `TakeWhile` extension method to accomplish the same thing.

VISUAL BASIC
```
' ----- Get top customers.
Dim topCusts = From cust In customers
               Order By cust.TotalSales Descending
               Select cust.FullName, cust.TotalSales
               Take While TotalSales >= 10000
```

C#
```
// ----- Get top 10 customers.
var topCusts = (from cust in customers
               orderby cust.TotalSales descending
               select new {cust.FullName,
               cust.TotalSales})
               .TakeWhile(test => test.TotalSales
               >= 10000);
```

See Also

Query Expressions

Ternary Operator

See

If Operator

Throw Statement

C#'s `throw` statement is identical to Visual Basic's `Throw` statement.

VISUAL BASIC
```
Throw New System.Exception("Something bad happened.")
```

C#
```
throw new System.Exception("Something bad happened.");
```

Within the `Catch` block of a `Try` statement, the `Throw` statement can be used by itself (without any operand) to re-throw the `Catch` block's exception.

VISUAL BASIC
```
Catch ex As System.Exception
    ' ----- Local logic, then...
    Throw
```

C# supports this same syntax.

C#
```
catch (System.Exception ex)
{
    // ----- Local logic, then...
    throw;
}
```

TimeOfDay Property

Visual Basic's *TimeOfDay* property retrieves or sets the current time. To obtain the current time as a *DateTime* instance in C#, access members of the *DateTime* type.

VISUAL BASIC
```
Dim result As Date = TimeOfDay
```

C#
```
// ----- Truncate milliseconds, just like TimeOfDay
long timeAsTicks = DateTime.Now.TimeOfDay.Ticks;
DateTime result = new DateTime(timeAsTicks -
    (timeAsTicks % TimeSpan.TicksPerSecond));
```

To set the time in C#, you must use features exposed by the Win32 API. The "TimeString Property" entry in this chapter includes sample C# code that sets the system time.

See Also

TimeString Property

Timer Property

Visual Basic's *Timer* property returns the number of seconds and milliseconds since midnight. In C#, use the members of the *System.DateTime* type to calculate this same value.

VISUAL BASIC
```
Dim result As Double =
    Microsoft.VisualBasic.DateAndTime.Timer
```

C#
```
double result =
    (System.DateTime.Now.Ticks %
    System.TimeSpan.TicksPerDay) /
    (TimeSpan.TicksPerMillisecond * 1000d);
```

TimeSerial Method

Visual Basic's *TimeSerial* method returns an instance of a *Date* value based on distinct hour, minute, and second components. In C#, create a new instance of the *DateTime* type, using the total calculated ticks to indicate the target time.

VISUAL BASIC
```
Dim targetTime As Date = TimeSerial(hour, minute, second)
```

C#

```
int totalSeconds = (hour * 60 * 60) +
    (minute * 60) + second;
DateTime targetTime = new DateTime(totalSeconds *
    System.TimeSpan.TicksPerSecond);
```

The .NET Framework also includes a *TimeSpan* structure that provides additional features for working with non-date time values.

C#

```
TimeSpan targetTime = new TimeSpan(hour, minute, second);
```

TimeString Property

Visual Basic's *TimeString* property retrieves or sets the current time. To obtain the current time as a string in C#, access members of the *DateTime* type.

VISUAL BASIC
```
Dim result As String = TimeString
```

C#
```
// ----- Locale-neutral, just like TimeString
string result = new DateTime(DateTime.Now.TimeOfDay.Ticks))
    .ToString("HH:mm:ss", System.Globalization
    .CultureInfo.InvariantCulture)

// ----- Locale-specific
string result = DateTime.Now.ToString("HH:mm:ss");
```

To set the time in C#, you must use features exposed by the Win32 API.

C#
```
// ----- Define at the top of the file.
using System.Runtime.InteropServices;

// ----- Define outside of a method.
[DllImport("kernel32.dll")]
static extern void GetLocalTime(out SystemTime timeInfo);
[DllImport("kernel32.dll")]
static extern bool SetLocalTime(ref SystemTime timeInfo);

[StructLayout(LayoutKind.Sequential)]
struct SystemTime
{
    public ushort Year;
    public ushort Month;
    public ushort DayOfWeek;
    public ushort Day;
    public ushort Hour;
    public ushort Minute;
    public ushort Second;
    public ushort Milliseconds;
}
```

```
// ----- A method similar to setting TimeString.
static bool SetTime(string timeText)
{
    // ----- Convert from a string to a true time.
    DateTime newTime;
    if (DateTime.TryParse(timeText, out newTime) == false)
        return false;

    // ----- Retrieve the current time.
    SystemTime timeInfo = new SystemTime();
    GetLocalTime(out timeInfo);

    // ----- Modify the time and set it.
    timeInfo.Hour = (ushort)newTime.Hour;
    timeInfo.Minute = (ushort)newTime.Minute;
    timeInfo.Second = (ushort)newTime.Second;
    timeInfo.Milliseconds = (ushort)newTime.Millisecond;
    try
    {
        return SetLocalTime(ref timeInfo);
    }
    catch
    {
        return false;
    }
}
```

You must have the appropriate system permissions to set the date or time from your application.

TimeValue Method

To emulate Visual Basic's *TimeValue* method in C#, convert the time string to a *DateTime* instance, and then extract just the time portion.

VISUAL BASIC
```
Dim result As Date = TimeValue(timeAsString)
```

C#
```
DateTime result = new DateTime(Convert.ToDateTime(
    timeAsString).Ticks % System.TimeSpan.TicksPerDay);
```

The .NET Framework also includes a *TimeSpan* structure that provides additional features for working with non-date time values.

C#
```
TimeSpan result =
    Convert.ToDateTime(timeAsString).TimeOfDay;
```

Today Property

Visual Basic's *Today* property retrieves or sets the current date. To obtain the current time as a *DateTime* instance in C#, access that type's *Today* property.

```
Dim result As Date = Today
```

```
DateTime result = DateTime.Today;
```

To set the date in C#, you must use features exposed by the Win32 API. The "DateString Property" entry in this chapter includes sample C# code that sets the system date.

See Also

DateString Property

Trim Method

The `Trim` method of C#'s `string` data type does the same thing as Visual Basic's `Trim` method.

```
result = Trim(someString)
```

```
result = someString.Trim();
```

True Boolean Literal

When limited to Boolean operations, C#'s `true` literal is identical to Visual Basic's `True` literal. When a Boolean value is converted or cast to an integer, VB's `True` value will become 1 or -1 depending on the type of cast or conversion. C#'s `true` value will always become 1 (one). See the "Boolean Data Type" entry in this chapter for details.

See Also

Boolean Data Type

Try Statement

C#'s `try` statement is generally equivalent to Visual Basic's `Try` statement.

```
Try
    customerRecord = RetrieveCustomer(customerID)
Catch ex As System.Expression
    LogError("Problem with customer record.", ex)
    Return
Finally
    InProcessField.Visible = False
End Try
```

C#

```
try
{
    customerRecord = RetrieveCustomer(customerID);
}
catch (System.Expression ex)
{
    LogError("Problem with customer record.", ex);
    return;
}
finally
{
    InProcessField.Visible = false;
}
```

Both languages share a common set of rules surrounding the use of try/catch statements: at least one catch or finally block must appear; nesting is supported; jumps into any of the blocks from outside is restricted; multiple catch blocks may appear, and are processed in order; and so on.

> **New with Visual Studio 2015**
> Visual Basic's *Catch* clauses can include conditions that limit access to a given exception handler via an additional *When* clause. C# added this feature in 2015 with the introduction of *if* clauses. In C# applications written before 2015, you must use standard conditional code within a *catch* block to differentiate between various situations that trigger the same exception.

VISUAL BASIC

```
Try
    customerRecord = RetrieveCustomer(customerID)
Catch ex As System.Exception When (errorCount < 5)
    errorCount += 1
    LogWarning("Problem with customer record.", ex)
Catch ex As System.Exception When (errorCount >=5)
    LogFatalError("Problem with customer record.", ex)
    Return
End Try
```

C#

```
try
{
    customerRecord = RetrieveCustomer(customerID);
}
catch (System.Exception ex) if (errorCount < 5)
{
    errorCount += 1;
    LogWarning("Problem with customer record.", ex);
}
catch (System.Exception ex) if (errorCount >=5)
{
    LogFatalError("Problem with customer record.", ex);
    return;
}
```

Visual Basic includes an *Exit Try* statement that can be used in a *Try* or *Catch* block (but not a *Finally* block) to exit the innermost *Try* structure. Execution continues with the statement after the entire *Try* statement; the *Finally* block, when present, will be processed. In C#, such a jump out of the *try* statement requires a line label after the statement, and the use of *goto* to perform the jump out of the *try* or *catch* block.

VISUAL BASIC
```
Try
     ' ----- Some code, then...
     Exit Try
     ' ----- More code.
Finally
     ' ----- Or a catch block.
End Try
' ----- Exit Try jumps to here.
```

C#
```
try
{
    // ----- Some code, then...
    goto EscapeTryBlock;
    // ----- More code.
}
finally
{
    // ----- Or a catch block.
}
EscapeTryBlock:
// ----- goto jumps to here.
```

TryCast Operator

In Visual Basic, when working with reference types, the *TryCast* operator performs a cast operation, returning *Nothing* if the conversion fails instead of throwing an exception.

VISUAL BASIC
```
Dim boss As Manager = TryCast(employeeRecord, Manager)
```

C#'s *as* conversion operator performs a similar action, returning *null* when the cast or conversion fails.

C#
```
Manager boss = employeeRecord as Manager;
```

TypeName Method

Visual Basic's *TypeName* method returns the type name for a variable or expression passed to the method. In both languages, accessing the *GetType().Name* property for any expression returns similar information, although the *TypeName* method uses VB-centric names when relevant.

```vbnet
Dim integerValue As Integer = 123
Dim decimalValue As Double = 456#
Dim someList As New List(Of String)
Dim notMuch As Object = Nothing

result = TypeName(integerValue) ' --> Integer
result = TypeName(decimalValue) ' --> Double
result = TypeName(someList)     ' --> List(Of String)
result = TypeName(notMuch)      ' --> Nothing
```

C#
```csharp
int integerValue = 123;
double decimalValue = 456.0;
List<string> someList = new List<string>();
object notMuch = null;

result = integerValue.GetType().Name; // --> Int32
result = decimalValue.GetType().Name; // --> Double
result = someList.GetType().Name;     // --> List`1
result = notMuch.GetType().Name;      // Throws Exception
```

The value returned in C# for the *someList* variable in the sample code can vary due to the way that .NET builds names for generic types.

TypeOf...Is Operator

Both Visual Basic's *TypeOf...Is* operator and C#'s *is* operator return true if the object being tested is of a specified type, or can be implicitly converted to that type.

VISUAL BASIC
```vbnet
If (TypeOf personVariable Is Customer) Then
```

C#
```csharp
if (personVariable is Customer)
```

TypeOf...IsNot Operator

New with Visual Studio 2015
The *TypeOf...IsNot* operator is new in the 2015 release of Visual Basic. It's equivalent in C# would be the *is* operator used in conjunction with the *!* negation operator.

VISUAL BASIC
```vbnet
If (TypeOf personVariable IsNot Customer) Then
```

C#
```csharp
if (!(personVariable is Customer))
```

UBound Method

The `System.Array` class' `GetUpperBound` method returns the same information as Visual Basic's `UBound` method. For multidimensional arrays, `UBound` assumes the first rank, unless another 1-based rank is specified. The `GetUpperBound` method requires a 0-based rank.

VISUAL BASIC
```
' ----- Default, first rank assumed.
result = UBound(someArray)

' ----- 1-based rank specified (third rank).
result = UBound(someArray, 3)
```

C#
```
// ----- 0-based rank specified (third rank).
result = someArray.GetUpperBound(2);
```

UCase Method

The `char` and `string` data types in C# each include a `ToUpper` method that is an exact replacement for Visual Basic's intrinsic `UCase` method.

VISUAL BASIC
```
result = UCase(someStringOrChar)
```

C#
```
result = someStringOrChar.ToUpper();
```

UInteger Data Type

C#'s intrinsic `uint` data type is identical to Visual Basic's `UInteger` data type. Both types are aliases for .NET's `System.UInt32` type. For unsigned integer literals, Visual Basic uses a `UI` or `ui` suffix after the value; in C#, use `U` or `u` instead.

VISUAL BASIC
```
Dim counter As UInteger = 0UI   ' or 0ui
```

C#
```
uint counter = 0u;
```

ULong Data Type

C#'s intrinsic `ulong` data type is identical to Visual Basic's `ULong` data type. Both types are aliases for .NET's `System.UInt64` type. For unsigned long literals, both Visual Basic and C# use a `UL` suffix after the value, or some uppercase/lowercase variation of `UL`.

VISUAL BASIC
```
Dim counter As ULong = 0UL
```

```csharp
ulong counter = 0ul;
```

Unlock Method

Visual Basic's *Unlock* method unlocks a previously locked portion of a file opened with the *FileOpen* method. Optional arguments indicate the starting and ending bytes or records to unlock. All positions are 1-based.

VISUAL BASIC
```vb
' ----- Unlock the whole file.
Unlock(fileNumber)

' ----- Unlock one byte or record.
Unlock(fileNumber, targetPosition)

' ----- Unlock a range of bytes or records.
Unlock(fileNumber, startPosition, stopPosition)
```

C# does not include the same file-management features included with VB. Instead, it is common to work with the *System.IO.FileStream* class to read and write files. This class includes an *Unlock* method that is similar to VB's *Unlock* method. The key differences are that the *FileStream*'s *Unlock* method only indicates byte positions and not record positions, and that its positions are 0-based. Also, when specifying a range of data to unlock, the final argument to the stream's method indicates the length of the lock, not the final position of the lock.

C#
```csharp
// ----- Unlock the whole file.
openedStream.Unlock(0, openedStream.Length);

// ----- Unlock one byte.
openedStream.Unlock(targetPosition - 1, 1);

// ----- Unlock a range of bytes.
openedStream.Unlock(startPosition - 1,
    stopPosition - startPosition + 1);
```

See Also

FileOpen Method

Until Clause

See

Do Statement

UShort Data Type

C#'s intrinsic *ushort* data type is identical to Visual Basic's *UShort* data type. Both types are aliases for .NET's *System.UInt16* type. For unsigned short literals, Visual

Basic uses a *US* suffix after the value, or some uppercase/lowercase variation of *US*; C# does not include such a suffix.

VISUAL BASIC
```
Dim counter As UShort = 0US
```

C#
```
ushort counter = 0;
```

Using Statement

C#'s *using* statement is generally equivalent to Visual Basic's *Using* statement. Parentheses are optional around the block variable declaration in VB, but they are required in C#.

VISUAL BASIC
```
Using myDB As SqlConnection = New SqlConnection(dbPath)
    ' ----- myDB is disposed on exit of Using block.
End Using

' ----- This compressed format is also supported.
Using myDB As New SqlConnection(dbPath)
End Using
```

C#
```
using (SqlConnection myDB = new SqlConnection(dbPath))
{
    // ----- myDB is disposed on exit of using block.
}
```

Both languages allow multiple resources to be created at once in the same *Using* or *using* statement. The compiler converts these to nested blocks, which are also permitted in each language. In VB, each variable declared within the same *Using* statement can be of a different data type; in C#, all such variables share a single data type.

VISUAL BASIC
```
' ----- Variables of the same type.
Using firstVal As New Type1, secondVal As New Type1

' ----- Variables of different types.
Using firstVal As New Type1, secondVal As New Type2
```

C#
```
using (Type1 firstVal = new Type1(),
    secondVal = new Type1())
```

Val Method

C# lacks an equivalent for Visual Basic's *Val* method. The closest option is to use a *TryParse* method from one or more of the numeric data types. For example, consider using *double.TryParse* to determine if a string contains a valid *double*.

C#

```
double result;
if (double.TryParse(sourceText, out result) == false)
    // ----- sourceText contained an invalid number.
```

VB's *Val* method allows much greater flexibility in the format of the incoming string. For example, currency symbols found in strings like *"$100"* convert appropriately to their non-currency equivalents when using *Val*, but fail to convert when using the various *TryParse* methods.

Variables

See

( ) Array Declaration, Const Statement, Dim Statement, Fields, Identifiers, Initializers, Lifetime and Scope, Static Modifier

VarType Method

Visual Basic's *VarType* method returns an enumeration value that indicates the variant type of an instance. Variant types are a feature from pre-.NET versions of Visual Basic. Though these types are no longer supported, *VarType* was retained for backward-compatibility reasons.

VarType has no direct equivalent in C#. However, the *GetType* method intrinsic in every .NET type provides general functionality that is comparable to what *VarType* provides, albeit returning true .NET types instead of an enumerated value.

VBFixedArrayAttribute Class

The *VBFixedArrayAttribute* class is used to indicate that an array field should be treated as if it has a fixed length when used with certain file operations. For example, VB's *FileGet* and *FilePut* methods use this attribute when reading and writing structured data. The attribute itself does not alter its associated array, but provides information to code within methods like *FileGet* via reflection. Outside of these specific Visual Basic methods, the attribute has no impact on application logic, and is therefore not useful in a C# context.

VBFixedStringAttribute Class

The *VBFixedStringAttribute* class is used to indicate that a string field should be treated as if it has a fixed length when used with certain file operations. For example, VB's *FileGet* and *FilePut* methods use this attribute when reading and writing structured data. The attribute itself does not alter its associated string, but provides information to code within methods like *FileGet* via reflection. Outside of these specific Visual Basic methods, the attribute has no impact on application logic, and is therefore not useful in a C# context.

VbTypeName Method

Visual Basic's *VbTypeName* method accepts input from a set of .NET type names, and returns a similar pre-.NET VB type name. No direct equivalent for this method exists in C#. However, the following table shows the full set of results produced by *VbTypeName*. The case of the input term is ignored.

Input Value	Output Value
Boolean or *System.Boolean*	*Boolean*
Byte or *System.Byte*	*Byte*
Char or *System.Char*	*Char*
DateTime or *System.DateTime*	*Date*
Decimal or *System.Decimal*	*Decimal*
Double or *System.Double*	*Double*
Short or *System.Int16*	*Short*
Integer or *System.Int32*	*Integer*
Long or *System.Int64*	*Long*
Object or *System.Object*	*Object*
Single or *System.Single*	*Single*
String or *System.String*	*String*

All other inputs return *Nothing*, the equivalent of *null* in C#.

Weekday Method

The *DateTime* type's *DayOfWeek* property returns the same type of information as Visual Basic's *Weekday* method.

VISUAL BASIC
```
' ----- Returns 1 for the first day of the week, using
'       the system default for the first-day-of-week.
Dim whichDay As Integer = Weekday(oneOrder.OrderDate)

' ----- Using a specified first-day-of-week.
whichDay = Weekday(oneOrder.OrderDate,
    FirstDayOfWeek.Sunday)
```

C#
```
System.DayOfWeek whichDay = oneOrder.OrderDate.DayOfWeek;
```

The *Weekday* method returns a 1-based integer value that indicates the weekday from the current system setting for the cultural first-day-of-week, or based on a specified first-day-of-week argument. The *DateTime.DayOfWeek* property always returns a *System.DayOfWeek* enumeration value. In that enumeration, zero is the equivalent of Sunday.

WeekdayName Method

Visual Basic's `WeekdayName` method returns a full or abbreviated weekday name when given a numeric value, where *1* is the first day of the week. In C#, use the `DateTimeFormat` member of the current culture for the running assembly.

VISUAL BASIC
```
' ----- Full weekday name, returning the Sunday value when
'       the system default first-day-of-week is Sunday.
result = WeekdayName(1)

' ----- Abbreviation, with specified first-day-of-week.
result = WeekdayName(1, True, FirstDayOfWeek.Sunday)
```

C#
```
// ----- Full month name.
result = System.Threading.Thread.CurrentThread.
    CurrentCulture.DateTimeFormat.GetDayName(
    DayOfWeek.Sunday);

// ----- Abbreviation.
result = System.Threading.Thread.CurrentThread.
    CurrentCulture.DateTimeFormat.GetAbbreviatedDayName(
    DayOfWeek.Sunday);
```

The `WeekdayName` function allows for some flexibility in the numeric values used to indicate the days of the week. In the C# sample shown here, the `DayOfWeek` enumeration is used to specify the target day. In this enumeration, the equivalent of zero is *Sunday*.

When working with an instance of the `DateTime` type, you can use its `ToString` method with a formatting code to return the full or abbreviated weekday name.

C#
```
// ----- Full weekday name.
result = orderDate.ToString("dddd");

// ----- Abbreviation.
result = orderDate.ToString("ddd");
```

Where Query Expression Operator (LINQ)

C#'s `where` query expression operator is identical to Visual Basic's `Where` operator. As in VB, C#'s `where` clause supports the full set of language-specific logical operators.

VISUAL BASIC
```
' ----- The Select clause can also appear before Where.
Dim result = From oneEmployee in Employees
            Where oneEmployee.IsManager = True
            Select oneEmployee
```

C#

```
var result = from oneEmployee in Employees
             where oneEmployee.IsManager == true
             select oneEmployee;
```

Visual Basic offers some flexibility as to the placement of the *where* clause relative to the *select* clause within the query expression. In C#, the *where* clause must appear before the *select* clause.

See Also

Query Expressions

While Clause

See

Do Statement

While Statement

Visual Basic's *While* statement is a variation of its *Do* statement, with the *While* clause at the top of the loop. For information on using this construct in C#, see the "Do Statement" entry in this chapter.

See

Do Statement

Widening Modifier

Visual Basic's *Widening* modifier indicates that an overloaded conversion from one type to another may be performed implicitly, as the destination type is wide enough for all the source type's possible values.

VISUAL BASIC

```
Class SmallType
    Public Shared Widening Operator CType(
            ByVal source As SmallType) As BigType
        Return New BigType(source.GetValue())
    End Operator
End Class
```

The equivalent C# overload uses the *implicit* modifier to express this same conversion.

C#

```
class SmallType
{
    public static implicit operator BigType(
        SmallType source)
    {
```

```
        return new BigType(source.GetValue());
    }
}
```

See Also

Narrowing Modifier, Operator Statement

With Clause

See

Initializers

With Statement

C# does not include an equivalent for Visual Basic's *With* block statement.

WithEvents Modifier

C# does not include an equivalent for Visual Basic's *WithEvents* modifier. You do not need to indicate to the compiler that a variable will use event handlers. Instead, you must manually attach events within method logic as you do in VB through the *AddHandler* statement. See the "AddHandler Statement" entry in this chapter for information on attaching events in C#.

See Also

AddHandler Statement

Write Method

Visual Basic's *Write* method (and the related *WriteLine* method) outputs content to a file opened with the *FileOpen* method. Designed for structured data, *Write* inserts commas and quotation marks as needed to delimit each piece of data. *WriteLine* adds a carriage-return and line-feed pair.

VISUAL BASIC
```
'  ----- Output a string and a number, like:
'        "Seattle",84
WriteLine(fileNumber, cityName, totalMatches)
```

C# does not include the same file-management features included with VB. Instead, it is common to work with the *System.IO.StreamWriter* class to output text data. This class includes *Write* and *WriteLine* methods with overloads for outputting different types of data. You must emit the commas and quotation marks manually.

C#
```
// ----- Output a string and a number, like:
//        "Seattle",84
outFile.Write("\"" + cityName + "\"");
outFile.Write(",");
outFile.WriteLine(totalMatches);
```

See Also

FileOpen Method

WriteLine Method

See

Write Method

WriteOnly Modifier

Visual Basic's `WriteOnly` modifier is used to create write-only properties. In such definitions, the `Get` portion of the property is left off. C# also leaves off the `get` portion, but it does not require that any other special modifier be present to indicate the property's write-only format.

VISUAL BASIC
```
Public WriteOnly Property Status As Integer
    Set(ByVal value As Integer)
        ' ----- Assignment statement appears here.
    End Set
    ' ----- But no getter appears.
End Property
```

C#
```
public int Status
{
    set
    {
        // ----- Assignment statement appears here.
    }
    // ----- But no getter appears.
}
```

XML Documentation Comments

Both Visual Basic and C# support XML comments as a means of documenting code and prompting Visual Studio's IntelliSense to display extended information about types and type members. In VB, these comments begin with the ' ' ' symbol.

VISUAL BASIC
```
''' <summary>
'''     Tracks details about living creatures.
''' </summary>
Class Animal
End Class
```

In C#, use the `///` symbol instead.

C#
```
/// <summary>
///     Tracks details about living creatures.
/// </summary>
class Animal
{
}
```

Although there is no multi-line comment syntax in Visual Basic, C# does allow XML comments within such blocks. Start the block with the /** symbol.

C#
```
/** <summary>
    ...
  */
```

Both languages use the same set of recommended XML tags for documenting code. See Microsoft's MSDN documentation for information on using these tags in your projects.

XML Literals

There is no direct equivalent for Visual Basic's XML Literals in C#. Instead, you must use the various .NET Framework XML-specific classes to manipulate XML content, or process such content yourself using string and file-access features.

Xor Exclusive-Or Operator

C#'s ^ exclusive-or operator is an exact replacement for Visual Basic's *Xor* operator, both for integer and Boolean operands.

VISUAL BASIC
```
currentState = currentState Xor newInput
```

C#
```
currentState = currentState ^ newInput;
```

Year Method

The *DateTime* type's *Year* property returns the same information as Visual Basic's *Year* method.

VISUAL BASIC
```
Dim whichYear As Integer = Year(oneOrder.OrderDate)
```

C#
```
int whichYear = oneOrder.OrderDate.Year;
```

Yield Statement

When defining a method iterator or get-accessor iterator with the *Iterator* modifier, Visual Basic's *Yield* statement identifies the next value to emit. The standard *Return* statement (or the older *Exit Function* and *Exit Property* statements) aborts an iterator early, before any other logic in the iterator code can run.

VISUAL BASIC

```
' ----- Assumes a LimitedEdition value defined elsewhere.
Public Iterator Function SmallNumbers() As _
          IEnumerable(Of Integer)
     Yield 1
     Yield 2
     Yield 3
     If (LimitedEdition) Then Return
     Yield 4
     Yield 5
End Function
```

In C#, the *yield return* statement returns the next iterator value, and appears in a method or property that returns *IEnumerable*, *IEnumerator*, or their generic variations. C#'s *yield break* statement takes the place of VB's *Return* statement within the context of an iterator.

C#

```
// ----- Assumes a LimitedEdition value defined elsewhere.
public IEnumerable<int> SmallNumbers()
{
     yield return 1;
     yield return 2;
     yield return 3;
     if (LimitedEdition)
          yield break;
     yield return 4;
     yield return 5;
}
```

Visual Basic allows *Try* statements that contain *Yield* statements to use both *Catch* and *Finally* clauses. If a *yield* statement appears in a C# *try* statement, that statement cannot have *catch* clauses, only a *finally* clause.

See Also

Iterators

Chapter 3

My Namespace to C#

The Visual Basic *My* namespace entries in this chapter appear alphabetically according to each member name within the hierarchy. For example, to discover the C# equivalent to the `My.Computer.Network.IsAvailable` property, locate the "IsAvailable Property" entry.

Some of the C# code samples in this chapter provide reasonable, but not exact, equivalents for *My* namespace members. For example, some members return a read-only collection of results, but the provided C# code might return an array or a generic collection instead.

Some *My* namespace members perform validation on data supplied to those members. In many cases, the provided C# code simplifies or eliminates such validation, providing just a basic translation for the *My* namespace member.

The full source code for the *My* namespace, written in Visual Basic, is available online. Visit http://referencesource.microsoft.com to access the code.

AllUsersApplicationData Property

♦ My.Computer.FileSystem.SpecialDirectories.AllUsersApplicationData

Returns the path to the "application data" folder shared by all local users.

VISUAL BASIC
```
Dim result As String = My.Computer.FileSystem.
    SpecialDirectories.AllUsersApplicationData
```

C#
```
string result = System.Environment.GetFolderPath(
    System.Environment.SpecialFolder.
    CommonApplicationData);
```

AltKeyDown Property

♦ My.Computer.Keyboard.AltKeyDown

Indicates whether an Alt key is currently pressed.

```
Dim result As Boolean = My.Computer.Keyboard.AltKeyDown
```

C#
```
// ----- For Windows Forms code:
bool result = ((System.Windows.Forms.Control.ModifierKeys &
    System.Windows.Forms.Keys.Alt) != 0);

// ----- For XAML-centric code:
bool result = ((System.Windows.Input.Keyboard.Modifiers &
    System.Windows.Input.ModifierKeys.Alt) != 0);
```

ApplicationContext Property

♦ My.Application.ApplicationContext

Returns the application context for the current application or thread.

VISUAL BASIC
```
Dim result As System.Windows.Forms.ApplicationContext =
    My.Application.ApplicationContext
```

If you start a Windows Forms application by passing in a custom context, this instance is normally not accessible within the application. You must preserve a reference to it in your code if you want to access later.

C#
```
static class Program
{
    // ----- Assumes that a LocalContext class derived
    //       from System.Windows.Forms.ApplicationContext
    //       has been defined elsewhere.
    private static LocalContext TheContext = null;

    [STAThread]
    static void Main()
    {
        Program.TheContext = new LocalContext();
        Program.TheContext.MainForm = new Form1();
        Application.Run(Program.TheContext);
    }

    public static LocalContext GetContext
    {
        get
        {
            return Program.TheContext;
        }
    }
}
```

AssemblyName Property

♦ My.Application.Info.AssemblyName

Retrieves the simple name of the assembly, with the file extension removed.

VISUAL BASIC
```
Dim result As String = My.Application.Info.AssemblyName
```

C#
```
System.Reflection.Assembly currentAssembly =
    System.Reflection.Assembly.GetEntryAssembly();
if (currentAssembly == null) currentAssembly =
    System.Reflection.Assembly.GetCallingAssembly();
string result = currentAssembly.GetName().Name;
```

Audio Object

♦ My.Computer.Audio

See

Play Method, PlaySystemSound Method, Stop Method

AvailablePhysicalMemory Property

♦ My.Computer.Info.AvailablePhysicalMemory

Returns the total number of free bytes of physical memory on the local computer.

VISUAL BASIC
```
Dim result As ULong =
    My.Computer.Info.AvailablePhysicalMemory
```

C#
```
// ----- GetMemoryInfo code discussed below.
ulong result = MemoryQuery.GetMemoryInfo().AvailPhysical;
```

Visual Basic retrieves memory information through the *GlobalMemoryStatusEx* Windows API call. The following code wraps the API call in C# code, and returns a Win32-compatible structure containing the memory information.

C#
```
// ----- This code works only with Windows 2000 and beyond.
public class MemoryQuery
{
    [System.Runtime.InteropServices.StructLayoutAttribute(
        System.Runtime.InteropServices.LayoutKind.
        Sequential)]
    public struct MemoryInfo
    {
        public uint DataLength;
        public uint MemoryLoad;
        public ulong TotalPhysical;
```

```
        public ulong AvailPhysical;
        public ulong TotalPageFile;
        public ulong AvailPageFile;
        public ulong TotalVirtual;
        public ulong AvailVirtual;
        public ulong AvailExtendedVirtual;

        public void Initialize()
        {
            // ----- The API must know the return size.
            this.DataLength = (uint)System.Runtime.
                InteropServices.Marshal.SizeOf(
                typeof(MemoryInfo));
        }
    }

    [System.Runtime.InteropServices.DllImportAttribute(
        "kernel32.dll", EntryPoint="GlobalMemoryStatusEx")]
    [return: System.Runtime.InteropServices.
        MarshalAsAttribute(System.Runtime.
        InteropServices.UnmanagedType.Bool)]
    public static extern bool GlobalMemoryStatusEx(
        [System.Runtime.InteropServices.OutAttribute()]
        out MemoryInfo memoryDetails);

    public static MemoryInfo GetMemoryInfo()
    {
        MemoryQuery.MemoryInfo memoryDetails =
            new MemoryQuery.MemoryInfo();
        memoryDetails.Initialize();
        if (MemoryQuery.GlobalMemoryStatusEx(
                out memoryDetails))
            return memoryDetails;
        else
            throw new System.Exception(
                "Failed to retrieve memory information.");
    }
}
```

AvailableVirtualMemory Property

♦ My.Computer.Info.AvailableVirtualMemory

Returns the total number of free bytes of virtual memory on the local computer.

VISUAL BASIC
```
Dim result As ULong =
    My.Computer.Info.AvailableVirtualMemory
```

C#
```
// ----- GetMemoryInfo code discussed below.
ulong result = MemoryQuery.GetMemoryInfo().AvailVirtual;
```

Visual Basic retrieves memory information through the *GlobalMemoryStatusEx* Windows API call. See the "AvailablePhysicalMemory Property" entry in this chapter for a sample *GetMemoryInfo* method that wraps the API call in C# code.

ButtonsSwapped Property

♦ My.Computer.Mouse.ButtonsSwapped

Indicates whether the standard arrangement of the two primary mouse buttons has been reversed.

VISUAL BASIC
```
Dim result As Boolean = My.Computer.Mouse.ButtonsSwapped
```

C#
```
// ----- For Windows Forms code:
bool result = System.Windows.Forms.SystemInformation.
    MouseButtonsSwapped;

// ----- For XAML-centric code:
bool result = System.Windows.SystemParameters.SwapButtons;
```

CapsLock Property

♦ My.Computer.Keyboard.CapsLock

Indicates whether the Caps Lock key is currently activated.

VISUAL BASIC
```
Dim result As Boolean = My.Computer.Keyboard.CapsLock
```

C#
```
// ----- For Windows Forms code:
bool result = System.Windows.Forms.Form.IsKeyLocked(
    System.Windows.Forms.Keys.CapsLock);

// ----- For XAML-centric code:
bool result = System.Windows.Input.Keyboard.IsKeyToggled(
    System.Windows.Input.Key.CapsLock);
```

ChangeCulture Method

♦ My.Application.ChangeCulture

Given a culture code (such as *en-US*), changes the current culture used for formatting certain values, such as numbers and dates.

VISUAL BASIC
```
My.Application.ChangeCulture("en-US")
```

```
C#
System.Threading.Thread.CurrentThread.CurrentCulture =
    new System.Globalization.CultureInfo("en-US");
```

ChangeUICulture Method

♦ My.Application.ChangeUICulture

Given a culture code (such as *en-US*), changes the current culture used for the user interface.

VISUAL BASIC
```
My.Application.ChangeUICulture("en-US")
```

C#
```
System.Threading.Thread.CurrentThread.CurrentUICulture =
    new System.Globalization.CultureInfo("en-US");
```

ClassesRoot Property

♦ My.Computer.Registry.ClassesRoot

Returns a reference to the *HKEY_CLASSES_ROOT* Windows registry location.

VISUAL BASIC
```
Dim result As Microsoft.Win32.RegistryKey =
    My.Computer.Registry.ClassesRoot
```

C#
```
Microsoft.Win32.RegistryKey result =
    Microsoft.Win32.Registry.ClassesRoot;
```

Clear Method

♦ My.Computer.Clipboard.Clear

Removes all data from the system clipboard.

VISUAL BASIC
```
My.Computer.Clipboard.Clear()
```

C#
```
// ----- For Windows Forms code:
System.Windows.Forms.Clipboard.Clear();

// ----- For XAML-centric code:
System.Windows.Clipboard.Clear();
```

Clipboard Object

♦ My.Computer.Clipboard

See

Clear Method, ContainsAudio Method, ContainsData Method, ContainsFileDropList Method, ContainsImage Method, ContainsText Method, GetAudioStream Method, GetData Method, GetDataObject Method, GetFileDropList Method, GetImage Method, GetText Method, SetAudio Method, SetData Method, SetDataObject Method,SetFileDropList Method, SetImage Method, SetText Method

Clock Object

♦ My.Computer.Clock

See

GmtTime Property, LocalTime Property, TickCount Property

CombinePath Method

♦ My.Computer.FileSystem.CombinePath

Combines an absolute path, such as a directory, with an additional relative path, such as a file name, adding the appropriate punctuation.

VISUAL BASIC
```
Dim result As String = My.Computer.FileSystem.CombinePath(
    "C:\temp", "OutputFile.txt")
```

C#
```
string result = System.IO.Path.Combine(
    "C:\\temp", "OutputFile.txt");
```

CommandLineArgs Property

♦ My.Application.CommandLineArgs

Returns a collection of the command-line arguments used to initiate the application. The application path is not included as the first element; only the arguments themselves are included, if any.

VISUAL BASIC
```
' ----- This code returns a read-only collection of
'       the command-line arguments, excluding the
'       program itself.
Dim result As System.Collections.ObjectModel.
    ReadOnlyCollection(Of String) =
    My.Application.CommandLineArgs
```

C#
```
// ----- This code returns an ordinary string array of
//       the command-line arguments, *including* the
//       program itself as the zeroth array element.
string[] result = System.Environment.GetCommandLineArgs();
```

CompanyName Property

♦ My.Application.Info.CompanyName

Returns the company name as stored in the assembly.

VISUAL BASIC
```
Dim result As String = My.Application.Info.CompanyName
```

C#
```
string result;
System.Reflection.Assembly currentAssembly =
    System.Reflection.Assembly.GetEntryAssembly();
if (currentAssembly == null) currentAssembly =
    System.Reflection.Assembly.GetCallingAssembly();
object[] attrSet = currentAssembly.GetCustomAttributes(
    typeof(System.Reflection.AssemblyCompanyAttribute),
    inherit:true);
if (attrSet.Length == 0)
    result = "";
else
    result = ((System.Reflection.AssemblyCompanyAttribute)
        attrSet[0]).Company;
```

Computer Object

♦ My.Computer

See

Audio Object, Clipboard Object, Clock Object, FileSystem Object, Info Object (My.Computer), Keyboard Object, Mouse Object, Name Property (My.Computer), Network Object, Ports Object, Registry Object, Screen Property

ContainsAudio Method

♦ My.Computer.Clipboard.ContainsAudio

Indicates whether the system clipboard contains audio data.

VISUAL BASIC
```
Dim result As Boolean =
    My.Computer.Clipboard.ContainsAudio()
```

C#
```
// ----- For Windows Forms code:
bool result =
    System.Windows.Forms.Clipboard.ContainsAudio();

// ----- For XAML-centric code:
bool result = System.Windows.Clipboard.ContainsAudio();
```

ContainsData Method

♦ My.Computer.Clipboard.ContainsData

Indicates whether the system clipboard contains content with a specific data format.

VISUAL BASIC
```
Dim result As Boolean = My.Computer.Clipboard.ContainsData(
    "CustomerRecord")
```

C#
```
// ----- For Windows Forms code:
bool result = System.Windows.Forms.Clipboard.ContainsData(
    "CustomerRecord");

// ----- For XAML-centric code:
bool result = System.Windows.Clipboard.ContainsData(
    "CustomerRecord");
```

ContainsFileDropList Method

♦ My.Computer.Clipboard.ContainsFileDropList

Indicates whether the system clipboard contains a list of target file paths.

VISUAL BASIC
```
Dim result As Boolean = My.Computer.Clipboard.
    ContainsFileDropList()
```

C#
```
// ----- For Windows Forms code:
bool result = System.Windows.Forms.Clipboard.
    ContainsFileDropList();

// ----- For XAML-centric code:
bool result =
    System.Windows.Clipboard.ContainsFileDropList();
```

ContainsImage Method

♦ My.Computer.Clipboard.ContainsImage

Indicates whether the system clipboard contains image data.

VISUAL BASIC
```
Dim result As Boolean =
    My.Computer.Clipboard.ContainsImage()
```

C#
```
// ----- For Windows Forms code:
bool result =
    System.Windows.Forms.Clipboard.ContainsImage();
```

```
// ----- For XAML-centric code:
bool result = System.Windows.Clipboard.ContainsImage();
```

ContainsText Method

♦ My.Computer.Clipboard.ContainsText

Indicates whether the system clipboard contains text, optionally in a specified format.

VISUAL BASIC
```
Dim result As Boolean =
    My.Computer.Clipboard.ContainsText()
```

C#
```
// ----- For Windows Forms code:
bool result =
    System.Windows.Forms.Clipboard.ContainsText();

// ----- For XAML-centric code:
bool result = System.Windows.Clipboard.ContainsText();
```

The *ContainsText* method accepts one optional argument that indicates the type of text to check, such as HTML or Unicode. In the *My* and Windows Forms versions of the code, this argument is of type *System.Windows.Forms.TextDataFormat*; for XAML code, use the *System.Windows.TextDataFormat* enumeration instead.

CopyDirectory Method

♦ My.Computer.FileSystem.CopyDirectory

Copies a directory and all files within it to a new destination directory.

VISUAL BASIC
```
' ----- Basic syntax. Third (optional) argument is
'       the overwrite flag.
My.Computer.FileSystem.CopyDirectory(
    source, destination, True)

' ----- UI-invoking syntax.
My.Computer.FileSystem.CopyDirectory(source, destination,
    UIOption.OnlyErrorDialogs)
```

C# does not include a feature that will copy a complete directory. For basic directory copy operations, your code must manually create the target directory and copy each file and subdirectory within the source directory to the target using features in the *System.IO* namespace.

C#
```
private void CopyDirectory(string source,
    string destination)
{
    string destItem;
```

```
// ----- Create the target directory.
System.IO.Directory.CreateDirectory(destination);

// ----- Scan each source file.
foreach (string oneFile in System.IO.
    Directory.GetFiles(source))
{
    // ----- Copy a file to the target.
    destItem = System.IO.Path.Combine(destination,
        System.IO.Path.GetFileName(oneFile));
    System.IO.File.Copy(oneFile, destItem);
}

// ----- Scan each source subdirectory.
foreach (string oneDirectory in System.IO.
    Directory.GetDirectories(source))
{
    // ----- Recurse to copy the subdirectory.
    destItem = System.IO.Path.Combine(destination,
        System.IO.Path.GetFileName(oneDirectory));
    CopyDirectory(oneDirectory, destItem);
}
}
```

C# does not include features that invoke the Windows directory copy dialog. Instead, you must access the Win32 API directly and call the appropriate function. In the case of directory copying and similar file-based actions, you call the *SHFileOperation* API. See the "CopyFile Method" entry in this chapter for sample code that calls this API.

CopyFile Method

♦ My.Computer.FileSystem.CopyFile

Copies a file to a new location.

VISUAL BASIC
```
' ----- Basic syntax. Third (optional) argument is
'       the overwrite flag.
My.Computer.FileSystem.CopyFile(source, destination, True)

' ----- UI-invoking syntax.
My.Computer.FileSystem.CopyFile(source, destination,
    UIOption.OnlyErrorDialogs)
```

For basic file copy operations, the *File.Copy* method in the *System.IO* namespace provides functionality similar to the basic VB syntax.

C#
```
// ----- Third argument is the "overwrite" flag.
System.IO.File.Copy(source, destination, true);
```

C# does not include features that invoke the Windows file copy dialog. Instead, you must access the Win32 API directly and call the appropriate function. In the case of file copying and similar file-based actions, you call the *SHFileOperation* API. The following code shows how to call this method to perform a basic file copy.

```
using System;
using System.Runtime.InteropServices;

public class FileCopy
{
    // ----- Type of shell operation.
    private enum FileFuncFlags : uint
    {
        FO_MOVE   = 0x1,
        FO_COPY   = 0x2,
        FO_DELETE = 0x3,
        FO_RENAME = 0x4
    }

    // ----- Additional flags for some operations.
    [Flags] public enum FileOpFlags : ushort
    {
        FOF_MULTIDESTFILES        = 0x1,
        FOF_CONFIRMMOUSE          = 0x2,
        FOF_SILENT                = 0x4,
        FOF_RENAMEONCOLLISION     = 0x8,
        FOF_NOCONFIRMATION        = 0x10,
        FOF_WANTMAPPINGHANDLE     = 0x20,
        FOF_ALLOWUNDO             = 0x40,
        FOF_FILESONLY             = 0x80,
        FOF_SIMPLEPROGRESS        = 0x100,
        FOF_NOCONFIRMMKDIR        = 0x200,
        FOF_NOERRORUI             = 0x400,
        FOF_NOCOPYSECURITYATTRIBS = 0x800,
        FOF_NORECURSION           = 0x1000,
        FOF_NO_CONNECTED_ELEMENTS = 0x2000,
        FOF_WANTNUKEWARNING       = 0x4000,
        FOF_NORECURSEREPARSE      = 0x8000
    }

    // ----- Structure for operation details.
    [StructLayout(LayoutKind.Sequential,
        CharSet=CharSet.Unicode)]
    private struct SHFILEOPSTRUCT
    {
        public IntPtr hwnd;
        public FileFuncFlags wFunc;
        [MarshalAs(UnmanagedType.LPWStr)]
            public string pFrom;
        [MarshalAs(UnmanagedType.LPWStr)]
            public string pTo;
        public FileOpFlags fFlags;
        [MarshalAs(UnmanagedType.Bool)]
            public bool fAnyOperationsAborted;
```

```
        public IntPtr hNameMappings;
        [MarshalAs(UnmanagedType.LPWStr)]
            public string lpszProgressTitle;
    }

    // ----- Main shell file operation method.
    [DllImport("shell32.dll",CharSet = CharSet.Unicode)]
    static extern int SHFileOperation(
        [In] ref SHFILEOPSTRUCT lpFileOp);

    public static void CopyFiles(
        string sourceFile, string destination)
    {
        // ----- Copy a file using the Windows copy.
        SHFILEOPSTRUCT fileDetail;
        int result;

        fileDetail.wFunc = FileFuncFlags.FO_COPY;
        fileDetail.fFlags = FileOpFlags.FOF_ALLOWUNDO;
        fileDetail.pFrom = sourceFile + "\0\0";
        fileDetail.pTo = destination + "\0\0";
        fileDetail.hwnd = IntPtr.Zero;
        fileDetail.fAnyOperationsAborted = false;
        fileDetail.hNameMappings = IntPtr.Zero;
        fileDetail.lpszProgressTitle = "";

        try
        {
            result = SHFileOperation(ref fileDetail);
            if (result != 0)
                System.Windows.Forms.MessageBox.Show(
                    "Error occurred during copy.");
        }
        catch (Exception ex)
        {
            System.Windows.Forms.MessageBox.Show(
                ex.Message);
        }
    }
}
```

Microsoft's MSDN web site (msdn.microsoft.com) includes full documentation on this
and other "shell" features.

Copyright Property

♦ My.Application.Info.Copyright

Returns the copyright owner notice as stored in the assembly.

VISUAL BASIC
```
Dim result As String = My.Application.Info.Copyright
```

C#
```
string result;
System.Reflection.Assembly currentAssembly =
    System.Reflection.Assembly.GetEntryAssembly();
if (currentAssembly == null) currentAssembly =
    System.Reflection.Assembly.GetCallingAssembly();
object[] attrSet = currentAssembly.GetCustomAttributes(
    typeof(System.Reflection.AssemblyCopyrightAttribute),
    inherit:true);
if (attrSet.Length == 0)
    result = "";
else
    result = ((System.Reflection.
        AssemblyCopyrightAttribute)attrSet[0]).Copyright;
```

CreateDirectory Method

♦ My.Computer.FileSystem.CreateDirectory

Creates the directory and subdirectories in a path.

VISUAL BASIC
```
My.Computer.FileSystem.CreateDirectory("C:\temp")
```

C#
```
System.IO.Directory.CreateDirectory("C:\\temp");
```

CtrlKeyDown Property

♦ My.Computer.Keyboard.CtrlKeyDown

Indicates whether a Control key is currently pressed.

VISUAL BASIC
```
Dim result As Boolean = My.Computer.Keyboard.CtrlKeyDown
```

C#
```
// ----- For Windows Forms code:
bool result = ((System.Windows.Forms.Control.ModifierKeys &
    System.Windows.Forms.Keys.Control) != 0);

// ----- For XAML-centric code:
bool result = ((System.Windows.Input.Keyboard.Modifiers &
    System.Windows.Input.ModifierKeys.Control) != 0);
```

Culture Property

♦ My.Application.Culture

Returns an object that describes the active data-formatting culture for numbers, dates, and other values.

```
Dim result As System.Globalization.CultureInfo =
    My.Application.Culture
```

C#
```
System.Globalization.CultureInfo result =
    System.Threading.Thread.CurrentThread.CurrentCulture;
```

CurrentConfig Property

♦ My.Computer.Registry.CurrentConfig

Returns a reference to the *HKEY_CURRENT_CONFIG* Windows registry location.

VISUAL BASIC
```
Dim result As Microsoft.Win32.RegistryKey =
    My.Computer.Registry.CurrentConfig
```

C#
```
Microsoft.Win32.RegistryKey result =
    Microsoft.Win32.Registry.CurrentConfig;
```

CurrentDirectory Property

♦ My.Computer.FileSystem.CurrentDirectory

Returns the full path to the directory used for relative directory references.

VISUAL BASIC
```
Dim result As String =
    My.Computer.FileSystem.CurrentDirectory
```

C#
```
string result = System.IO.Directory.GetCurrentDirectory();
```

CurrentPrincipal Property

♦ My.User.CurrentPrincipal

Returns the in-effect security context.

VISUAL BASIC
```
Dim result As System.Security.Principal.IPrincipal =
    My.User.CurrentPrincipal
```

C#
```
System.Security.Principal.IPrincipal result =
    System.Threading.Thread.CurrentPrincipal;
```

CurrentUser Property

♦ My.Computer.Registry.CurrentUser

Returns a reference to the *HKEY_CURRENT_USER* Windows registry location.

```
Dim result As Microsoft.Win32.RegistryKey =
    My.Computer.Registry.CurrentUser
```

C#
```
Microsoft.Win32.RegistryKey result =
    Microsoft.Win32.Registry.CurrentUser;
```

CurrentUserApplicationData Property

♦ My.Computer.FileSystem.SpecialDirectories.CurrentUserApplicationData

Returns the path to the "application data" folder for the current user.

VISUAL BASIC
```
Dim result As String = My.Computer.FileSystem.
    SpecialDirectories.CurrentUserApplicationData
```

C#
```
string result = System.Environment.GetFolderPath(
    System.Environment.SpecialFolder.ApplicationData);
```

DefaultFileLogWriter Property

♦ My.Application.Log.DefaultFileLogWriter (for Desktop applications)

♦ My.Log.DefaultFileLogWriter (for ASP.NET applications)

C# applications do not configure logging features by default. Therefore, there is no default listener for logging purposes.

See Also

TraceSource Property

DeleteDirectory Method

♦ My.Computer.FileSystem.DeleteDirectory

Deletes a directory or moves it to the Recycle Bin.

VISUAL BASIC
```
' ----- Basic syntax. Directory is deleted permanently.
My.Computer.FileSystem.DeleteDirectory(targetDirectory,
    DeleteDirectoryOption.DeleteAllContents)

' ----- UI-invoking syntax.
My.Computer.FileSystem.DeleteDirectory(targetDirectory,
    UIOption.OnlyErrorDialogs,
    RecycleOption.SendToRecycleBin)
```

For basic directory delete operations, the `Directory.Delete` method in the `System.IO` namespace provides functionality comparable to the basic VB syntax.

C#
```
// ----- Directory is deleted permanently. The
//       second argument deletes even when the
//       target is not empty.
System.IO.Directory.Delete(targetFile, true);
```

C# does not include features that invoke the Windows directory delete dialog. Instead, you must access the Win32 API directly and call the appropriate function. In the case of directory removal and similar file-based actions, you call the `SHFileOperation` API. See the "CopyFile Method" entry in this chapter for sample code that calls this API.

DeleteFile Method

♦ My.Computer.FileSystem.DeleteFile

Deletes a file or moves it to the Recycle Bin.

VISUAL BASIC
```
' ----- Basic syntax. File is deleted permanently.
My.Computer.FileSystem.DeleteFile(targetFile)

' ----- UI-invoking syntax.
My.Computer.FileSystem.DeleteFile(targetFile,
    UIOption.OnlyErrorDialogs,
    RecycleOption.SendToRecycleBin)
```

For basic file delete operations, the `File.Delete` method in the `System.IO` namespace provides functionality comparable to the basic VB syntax.

C#
```
// ----- File is deleted permanently.
System.IO.File.Delete(targetFile);
```

C# does not include features that invoke the Windows file delete dialog. Instead, you must access the Win32 API directly and call the appropriate function. In the case of file removal and similar file-based actions, you call the `SHFileOperation` API. See the "CopyFile Method" entry in this chapter for sample code that calls this API.

Deployment Property

♦ My.Application.Deployment

Returns the current application's ClickOnce (installation) deployment object.

VISUAL BASIC
```
Dim result As System.Deployment.Application.
    ApplicationDeployment = My.Application.Deployment
```

C#

```
System.Deployment.Application.ApplicationDeployment
    result = System.Deployment.Application.
    ApplicationDeployment.CurrentDeployment;
```

Description Property

♦ My.Application.Info.Description

Returns the application description as stored in the assembly.

VISUAL BASIC

```
Dim result As String = My.Application.Info.Description
```

C#

```
string result;
System.Reflection.Assembly currentAssembly =
    System.Reflection.Assembly.GetEntryAssembly();
if (currentAssembly == null) currentAssembly =
    System.Reflection.Assembly.GetCallingAssembly();
object[] attrSet = currentAssembly.GetCustomAttributes(
    typeof(System.Reflection.AssemblyDescriptionAttribute),
    inherit:true);
if (attrSet.Length == 0)
    result = "";
else
    result = ((System.Reflection.
        AssemblyDescriptionAttribute)
        attrSet[0]).Description;
```

Desktop Property

♦ My.Computer.FileSystem.SpecialDirectories.Desktop

Returns the path to the "desktop" folder for the current user.

VISUAL BASIC

```
Dim result As String = My.Computer.FileSystem.
    SpecialDirectories.Desktop
```

C#

```
string result = System.Environment.GetFolderPath(
    System.Environment.SpecialFolder.DesktopDirectory);
```

DirectoryExists Method

♦ My.Computer.FileSystem.DirectoryExists

Indicates whether a directory path exists.

VISUAL BASIC

```
Dim result As Boolean = My.Computer.FileSystem.
    DirectoryExists("C:\temp")
```

```csharp
C#
bool result = System.IO.Directory.Exists("C:\\temp");
```

DirectoryPath Property

♦ My.Application.Info.DirectoryPath

Returns the path for the directory containing the current application.

VISUAL BASIC
```vbnet
Dim result As String = My.Application.Info.DirectoryPath
```

```csharp
C#
System.Reflection.Assembly currentAssembly =
    System.Reflection.Assembly.GetEntryAssembly();
if (currentAssembly == null) currentAssembly =
    System.Reflection.Assembly.GetCallingAssembly();
string result = System.IO.Path.GetDirectoryName(
    currentAssembly.Location);
```

DoEvents Method

♦ My.Application.DoEvents

In Windows Forms applications, temporarily suspends the current code to allow processing of messages in other threads and processes.

VISUAL BASIC
```vbnet
My.Application.DoEvents()
```

```csharp
C#
// ----- For Windows Forms code only:
System.Windows.Forms.Application.DoEvents();
```

XAML-based applications use a "dispatcher" or a "background worker thread" to achieve this same purpose.

DownloadFile Method

♦ My.Computer.Network.DownloadFile

Downloads a file from a network address to the local computer.

VISUAL BASIC
```vbnet
My.Computer.Network.DownloadFile(sourceAddress,
    destinationFile, userName, password);
```

```csharp
C#
System.Net.WebClient client = new System.Net.WebClient();
System.Uri sourceUri = new System.Uri(sourceAddress);

// ----- Default credentials.
client.UseDefaultCredentials = true;
```

```
// ----- Or, supply specific credentials.
client.UseDefaultCredentials = false;
client.Credentials = new System.Net.NetworkCredential(
    userName, password);

// ----- Synchronous copy.
client.DownloadFile(sourceUri, destinationFile);

// ----- Or, asynchronous copy, providing your own
//       custom complete/cancel event handler.
client.DownloadFileCompleted += new
    AsyncCompletedEventHandler(CompletedCallback);
client.DownloadFileAsync(sourceUri, destinationFile);
```

The *WebClient* class' download methods will overwrite the target file if it exists. You must manually check for the file if you do not want it overwritten. Also, it provides no visual cues as to the state of the transfer. You must provide your own progress dialog if desired.

To override the default timeout value, derive a new class from the *WebClient* class, and manually configure the *WebRequest*'s *TimeOut* property. Then use this class instead of the standard *WebClient* class to perform the download.

C#
```
class WebClientTimeout : System.Net.WebClient
{
    public int Timeout { get; set; }
    public WebClientTimeout(int timeoutOverride)
    {
        // ----- Save the user-specified timeout.
        this.Timeout = timeoutOverride;
    }

    protected override System.Net.WebRequest
        GetWebRequest(System.Uri sourceAddress)
    {
        // ----- Modify the request with the timeout.
        System.Net.WebRequest coreRequest =
            base.GetWebRequest(sourceAddress);
        if (coreRequest != null)
            coreRequest.Timeout = this.Timeout;
        return coreRequest;
    }
}
```

Drives Property

♦ My.Computer.FileSystem.Drives

Returns a collection of objects describing the workstation's logical disk drives.

```
' ----- This code returns a read-only collection of drives.
Dim result As System.Collections.ObjectModel.
    ReadOnlyCollection(Of System.IO.DriveInfo) =
    My.Computer.FileSystem.Drives
```

C#
```
// ----- This code returns an ordinary array of drives.
System.IO.DriveInfo[] result =
    System.IO.DriveInfo.GetDrives();
```

DynData Property

♦ My.Computer.Registry.DynData

Returns a reference to the *HKEY_DYN_DATA* Windows registry location.

VISUAL BASIC
```
' ----- This code is obsolete.
Dim result As Microsoft.Win32.RegistryKey =
    My.Computer.Registry.DynData
```

C#
```
// ----- This code is obsolete.
Microsoft.Win32.RegistryKey result =
    Microsoft.Win32.Registry.DynData;
```

This code is useful only on Windows 98 and Windows ME platforms. It is not valid on Windows NT-based systems or later.

FileExists Method

♦ My.Computer.FileSystem.FileExists

Indicates whether a file path exists.

VISUAL BASIC
```
Dim result As Boolean = My.Computer.FileSystem.FileExists(
    "C:\temp\WorkFile.txt")
```

C#
```
bool result = System.IO.File.Exists(
    "C:\\temp\\WorkFile.txt");
```

FileSystem Object

♦ My.Computer.FileSystem

See

CombinePath Method, CopyDirectory Method, CopyFile Method, CreateDirectory Method, CurrentDirectory Property, DeleteDirectory Method, DeleteFile Method, DirectoryExists Method, Drives Property, FileExists Method, FindInFiles Method,

GetDirectories Method, GetDirectoryInfo Method, GetDriveInfo Method, GetFileInfo Method, GetFiles Method, GetName Method, GetParentPath Method, GetTempFileName Method, MoveDirectory Method, MoveFile Method, OpenTextFieldParser Method, OpenTextFileReader Method, OpenTextFileWriter Method, ReadAllBytes Method, ReadAllText Method, RenameDirectory Method, RenameFile Method, SpecialDirectories Object, WriteAllBytes Method, WriteAllText Method

FindInFiles Method

♦ My.Computer.FileSystem.FindInFiles

Returns a collection of file paths from a target directory that contains a specified search string.

VISUAL BASIC
```
Dim result As System.Collections.ObjectModel.
    ReadOnlyCollection(Of String) =
    My.Computer.FileSystem.FindInFiles(targetDirectory,
    searchText, ignoreCase,
    SearchOption.SearchAllSubDirectories, "*.txt")
```

C# does not include an equivalent for VB's *FindInFiles* method. Instead, you must examine each file in a target directory to see if it contains the search string. The following code provides one example of how you can search for matches.

C#
```
private static List<string> FindInFiles(
    string targetDirectory, string searchText,
    bool ignoreCase, System.IO.SearchOption depthType,
    string fileMask = "*.*")
{
    List<string> results = new List<string>();
    bool foundMatch;
    string content;

    foreach (string oneFile
        in System.IO.Directory.GetFiles(
        targetDirectory, fileMask, depthType))
    {
        // ----- WARNING: Large files could fill memory.
        content = System.IO.File.ReadAllText(oneFile);
        if (ignoreCase)
            foundMatch = content.ToUpper().Contains(
                searchText.ToUpper());
        else
            foundMatch = content.Contains(searchText);
        if (foundMatch)
            results.Add(oneFile);
    }
    return results;
}
```

Forms Object

♦ My.Forms

Provides access to any form within the current Windows Forms project.

VISUAL BASIC
```
' ----- Full syntax
My.Forms.Form1.Show()

' ----- Shortened syntax
Form1.Show()
```

Windows Forms applications written in C# do not maintain a list of the current active or available forms within the project. Each form must be manually instantiated, and any monitoring of all active forms must be done through custom code.

GetAudioStream Method

♦ My.Computer.Clipboard.GetAudioStream

Returns a stream object of audio data from the system clipboard.

VISUAL BASIC
```
Dim result As System.IO.Stream =
    My.Computer.Clipboard.GetAudioStream()
```

C#
```
// ----- For Windows Forms code:
System.IO.Stream result = System.Windows.Forms.
    Clipboard.GetAudioStream();

// ----- For XAML-centric code:
System.IO.Stream result = System.Windows.
    Clipboard.GetAudioStream();
```

GetData Method

♦ My.Computer.Clipboard.GetData

Returns an object from the system clipboard in the specified format.

VISUAL BASIC
```
Dim result As Object = My.Computer.Clipboard.
    GetData("MyAppFormat")
```

C#
```
// ----- For Windows Forms code:
object result = System.Windows.Forms.Clipboard.
    GetData("MyAppFormat");
```

```
// ----- For XAML-centric code:
object result = System.Windows.Clipboard.
    GetData("MyAppFormat");
```

GetDataObject Method

♦ My.Computer.Clipboard.GetDataObject

Returns an object from the system clipboard that supports the *IDataObject* interface. When the clipboard contains data in multiple formats at once, this interface provides access to each of those formats.

VISUAL BASIC
```
Dim result As System.Windows.Forms.IDataObject =
    My.Computer.Clipboard.GetDataObject()
```

C#
```
// ----- For Windows Forms code:
System.Windows.Forms.IDataObject result =
    System.Windows.Forms.Clipboard.GetDataObject();

// ----- For XAML-centric code:
System.Windows.IDataObject result =
    System.Windows.Clipboard.GetDataObject();
```

GetDirectories Method

♦ My.Computer.FileSystem.GetDirectories

Returns a collection of directory names in a specified directory, optionally checking in subdirectories, and optionally matching a pattern.

VISUAL BASIC
```
' ----- Return directories starting with "A" in
'        the target directory, ignore subdirectories.
Dim result As ReadOnlyCollection(Of String) =
    My.Computer.FileSystem.GetDirectories(
    "C:\WorkArea", SearchOption.SearchTopLevelOnly, "A*")
```

C#
```
// ----- Return directories starting with "A" in
//        the target directory, ignore subdirectories.
string[] result = System.IO.Directory.GetDirectories(
    "C:\\WorkArea", "A*",
    System.IO.SearchOption.TopDirectoryOnly);
```

As shown in this sample code, the C# equivalent returns an array of strings instead of a collection.

GetDirectoryInfo Method

♦ My.Computer.FileSystem.GetDirectoryInfo

Returns an informational object for the indicated directory.

VISUAL BASIC
```
Dim result As System.IO.DirectoryInfo =
    My.Computer.FileSystem.GetDirectoryInfo("C:\temp")
```

C#
```
System.IO.DirectoryInfo result =
    new System.IO.DirectoryInfo("C:\\temp");
```

GetDriveInfo Method

♦ My.Computer.FileSystem.GetDriveInfo

Returns an informational object for the indicated drive letter.

VISUAL BASIC
```
Dim result As System.IO.DriveInfo =
    My.Computer.FileSystem.GetDriveInfo("C:")
```

C#
```
System.IO.DriveInfo result = new System.IO.DriveInfo("C:");
```

GetEnvironmentVariable Method

♦ My.Application.GetEnvironmentVariable

Retrieves the value of the specified Windows environment variable.

VISUAL BASIC
```
' ----- Throws an exception if the variable is not found.
Dim result As String =
    My.Application.GetEnvironmentVariable("PATH")
```

C#
```
// ----- Returns null if the variable is not found.
string result = System.Environment.
    GetEnvironmentVariable("PATH");
```

GetFileDropList Method

♦ My.Computer.Clipboard.GetFileDropList

Returns a collection of file-path strings from the system clipboard.

VISUAL BASIC
```
Dim result As System.Collections.
    Specialized.StringCollection =
    My.Computer.Clipboard.GetFileDropList()
```

C#

```
// ----- For Windows Forms code:
System.Collections.Specialized.StringCollection result =
    System.Windows.Forms.Clipboard.GetFileDropList();

// ----- For XAML-centric code:
System.Collections.Specialized.StringCollection result =
    System.Windows.Clipboard.GetFileDropList();
```

GetFileInfo Method

♦ My.Computer.FileSystem.GetFileInfo

Returns an informational object for the indicated file.

VISUAL BASIC

```
Dim result As System.IO.FileInfo =
    My.Computer.FileSystem.GetFileInfo(
    "C:\temp\WorkFile.txt")
```

C#

```
System.IO.FileInfo result =
    new System.IO.FileInfo("C:\\temp\\WorkFile.txt");
```

GetFiles Method

♦ My.Computer.FileSystem.GetFiles

Returns a collection of file names in a specified directory, optionally checking in subdirectories, and optionally matching a pattern.

VISUAL BASIC

```
' ----- Return text files with a .txt extension in
'        the target directory, ignore subdirectories.
Dim result As ReadOnlyCollection(Of String) =
    My.Computer.FileSystem.GetFiles("C:\WorkArea",
    SearchOption.SearchTopLevelOnly, "*.txt")
```

C#

```
// ----- Return text files with a .txt extension in
//        the target directory, ignore subdirectories.
string[] result =
    System.IO.Directory.GetFiles("C:\\WorkArea", "*.txt",
    System.IO.SearchOption.TopDirectoryOnly);
```

As shown in this sample code, the C# equivalent returns an array of strings instead of a collection.

GetImage Method

♦ My.Computer.Clipboard.GetImage

Returns an image from the system clipboard.

```
Dim result As System.Drawing.Image =
    My.Computer.Clipboard.GetImage()
```

C#

```
// ----- For Windows Forms code:
System.Drawing.Image result =
    System.Windows.Forms.Clipboard.GetImage();

// ----- For XAML-centric code:
System.Drawing.Image result =
    System.Windows.Clipboard.GetImage();
```

GetName Method

♦ My.Computer.FileSystem.GetName

Returns the file name portion of a file path.

VISUAL BASIC

```
' ----- Returns "WorkFile.txt"
Dim result As String = My.Computer.FileSystem.GetName(
    "C:\temp\WorkFile.txt")
```

C#

```
// ----- Returns "WorkFile.txt"
string result = System.IO.Path.GetFileName(
    "C:\\temp\\WorkFile.txt");
```

GetParentPath Method

♦ My.Computer.FileSystem.GetParentPath

Returns the parent directory for a specified file or directory path.

VISUAL BASIC

```
' ----- Returns "C:\temp"
Dim result As String =
    My.Computer.FileSystem.GetParentPath(
    "C:\temp\WorkFile.txt")
```

C#

```
// ----- Returns "C:\temp"
string result = System.IO.Path.GetDirectoryName(
    "C:\\temp\\WorkFile.txt");
```

GetParentPath accepts absolute or relative paths. The C# equivalent requires an absolute path.

GetTempFileName Method

♦ My.Computer.FileSystem.GetTempFileName

Creates a temporary file, and returns the path to that file.

VISUAL BASIC

```
Dim result As String =
    My.Computer.FileSystem.GetTempFileName()
```

C#

```
string result = System.IO.Path.GetTempFileName();
```

GetText Method

♦ My.Computer.Clipboard.GetText

Returns text from the system clipboard.

VISUAL BASIC

```
Dim result As String = My.Computer.Clipboard.GetText()
```

C#

```
// ----- For Windows Forms code:
string result = System.Windows.Forms.Clipboard.GetText();

// ----- For XAML-centric code:
string result = System.Windows.Clipboard.GetText();
```

The *GetText* method accepts one optional argument that indicates the type of text to check, such as HTML or Unicode. In the *My* and Windows Forms versions of the code, this argument is of type *System.Windows.Forms.TextDataFormat*; for XAML code, use the *System.Windows.TextDataFormat* enumeration instead. By default, the text is retrieved in Unicode format.

GetValue Method

♦ My.Computer.Registry.GetValue

Returns data from a specified Windows registry value.

VISUAL BASIC

```
Dim result As Long = CLng(My.Computer.Registry.GetValue(
    "HKEY_CURRENT_USER\Software\Example\MyApp",
    "ErrorCount", 0&))
```

C#

```
long result = (long)Microsoft.Win32.Registry.GetValue(
    "HKEY_CURRENT_USER\\Software\\Example\\MyApp",
    "ErrorCount", 0L);
```

GmtTime Property

♦ My.Computer.Clock.GmtTime

Returns the current date and time in the UTC (Universal Coordinated Time) time zone.

```
Dim result As Date = My.Computer.Clock.GmtTime
```
```
DateTime result = DateTime.UtcNow;
```

Info Object (My.Application)

♦ My.Application.Info

See

AssemblyName Property, CompanyName Property, Copyright Property, Description Property, DirectoryPath Property, LoadedAssemblies Property, ProductName Property, StackTrace Property, Title Property, Trademark Property, Version Property, WorkingSet Property

Info Object (My.Computer)

♦ My.Computer.Info

See

AvailablePhysicalMemory PropertyAvailableVirtualMemory Property, InstalledUICulture Property, OSFullName Property, OSPlatform Property, OSVersion Property, TotalPhysicalMemory Property, TotalVirtualMemory Property

InitializeWithWindowsUser Method

♦ My.User.InitializeWithWindowsUser

Resets *My.User* to refer to the user that started the application.

```
My.User.InitializeWithWindowsUser()
```
```
System.Threading.Thread.CurrentPrincipal =
    new System.Security.Principal.WindowsPrincipal(
    System.Security.Principal.WindowsIdentity.GetCurrent);
```

InstalledUICulture Property

♦ My.Computer.Info.InstalledUICulture

Returns an object that describes the user interface culture of the operating system.

```
Dim result As System.Globalization.CultureInfo =
    My.Computer.Info.InstalledUICulture
```

C#
```
System.Globalization.CultureInfo result =
    System.Globalization.CultureInfo.InstalledUICulture;
```

IsAuthenticated Property

♦ My.User.IsAuthenticated

Returns a value indicating the authentication status of the current user.

VISUAL BASIC
```
Dim result As Boolean = My.User.IsAuthenticated
```

C#
```
bool result = System.Threading.Thread.
    CurrentPrincipal.Identity.IsAuthenticated;
```

IsAvailable Property

♦ My.Computer.Network.IsAvailable

Indicates whether a network connected to the local computer is available for use.

VISUAL BASIC
```
Dim result As Boolean = My.Computer.Network.IsAvailable
```

C#
```
bool result = System.Net.NetworkInformation.
    NetworkInterface.GetIsNetworkAvailable();
```

IsInRole Method

♦ My.User.IsInRole

Returns a value indicating whether the current user belongs to the specified role.

VISUAL BASIC
```
' Option 1: Dim role As String = "Administrator"
' Option 2: Dim role As BuiltInRole =
'               BuiltInRole.Administrator
Dim result As Boolean = My.User.IsInRole(role)
```

C#
```
// ----- Option 1: String-based lookup.
string role = "Administrator";
bool result = System.Threading.Thread.
    CurrentPrincipal.IsInRole(role);

// ----- Option 2: Windows role-based lookup.
//       Assumes: using System.Security.Principal;
bool result;
WindowsBuiltInRole role = WindowsBuiltInRole.Administrator;
```

```
IPrincipal activePrincipal =
    System.Threading.Thread.CurrentPrincipal;
if (activePrincipal is WindowsPrincipal)
    result = ((WindowsPrincipal)activePrincipal).
        IsInRole(role);
else
{
    TypeConverter converter = TypeDescriptor.GetConverter(
        typeof(WindowsBuiltInRole));
    result = activePrincipal.IsInRole(
        converter.ConvertToString(role));
}
```

The *My* namespace includes a *BuiltInRole* enumeration that is closely related to the *WindowsBuiltInRole* enumeration indicated in the sample code. The members are identical, so it is valid to use the Windows-specific version in C# code. To check role membership for Windows users, you can use either the string-based or enumeration-based versions. For non-Windows role verifications, use the string version only.

IsNetworkDeployed Property

♦ My.Application.IsNetworkDeployed

Returns a value that indicates whether the application was deployed from a network using ClickOnce.

VISUAL BASIC
```
Dim result As Boolean = My.Application.IsNetworkDeployed
```

C#
```
bool result = System.Deployment.Application.
    ApplicationDeployment.IsNetworkDeployed;
```

Keyboard Object

♦ My.Computer.Keyboard

See

AltKeyDown PropertyCapsLock Property, CtrlKeyDown Property, NumLock Property, ScrollLock Property, SendKeys Method, ShiftKeyDown Property

LoadedAssemblies Property

♦ My.Application.Info.LoadedAssemblies

Returns a collection of the current application's loaded assemblies.

VISUAL BASIC
```
' ----- Returns a read-only collection of the results.
Dim result As System.Collections.ObjectModel.
    ReadOnlyCollection(Of System.Reflection.Assembly) =
    My.Application.Info.LoadedAssemblies
```

```
// ----- Returns a standard array of the results.
System.Reflection.Assembly[] result =
    AppDomain.CurrentDomain.GetAssemblies();
```

LocalMachine Property

♦ My.Computer.Registry.LocalMachine

Returns a reference to the *HKEY_LOCAL_MACHINE* Windows registry location.

VISUAL BASIC
```
Dim result As Microsoft.Win32.RegistryKey =
    My.Computer.Registry.LocalMachine
```

C#
```
Microsoft.Win32.RegistryKey result =
    Microsoft.Win32.Registry.LocalMachine;
```

LocalTime Property

♦ My.Computer.Clock.LocalTime

Returns the current date and time within the current time zone.

VISUAL BASIC
```
Dim result As Date = My.Computer.Clock.LocalTime
```

C#
```
DateTime result = DateTime.Now;
```

Log Object

♦ My.Application.Log (for Desktop applications)

♦ My.Log (for ASP.NET applications)

See

DefaultFileLogWriter Property, TraceSource Property, WriteEntry Method, WriteException Method

MinimumSplashScreenDisplayTime Property

♦ My.Application.MinimumSplashScreenDisplayTime

Specifies the minimum time, in milliseconds, that the splash screen should appear.

VISUAL BASIC
```
' ----- Show for at least two seconds.
My.Application.MinimumSplashScreenDisplayTime = 2000
```

This property is part of Visual Basic's Windows Forms Application Framework, a set of classes not included in C# projects. There is no direct C# equivalent for the *MinimumSplashScreenDisplayTime* property. Instead, you must manage the display of any splash screen in your application by hand. See the "SplashScreen Property" entry in this chapter for additional information.

See Also

SplashScreen Property

Mouse Object

♦ My.Computer.Mouse

See

ButtonsSwapped Property, WheelExists Property, WheelScrollLines Property

MoveDirectory Method

♦ My.Computer.FileSystem.MoveDirectory

Moves a directory to a new location.

VISUAL BASIC
```
' ----- Basic syntax. Third (optional) argument is
'       the overwrite flag.
My.Computer.FileSystem.MoveDirectory(
    source, destination, True)

' ----- UI-invoking syntax.
My.Computer.FileSystem.MoveDirectory(source, destination,
    UIOption.OnlyErrorDialogs)
```

For basic directory move operations, the *Directory.Move* method in the *System.IO* namespace provides functionality comparable to the basic VB syntax.

C#
```
// ----- Directory.Move lacks the overwrite option.
System.IO.Directory.Move(source, destination);
```

C# does not include features that invoke the Windows directory move dialog. Instead, you must access the Win32 API directly and call the appropriate function. In the case of directory moving and similar file-based actions, you call the *SHFileOperation* API. See the "CopyFile Method" entry in this chapter for sample code that calls this API.

MoveFile Method

♦ My.Computer.FileSystem.MoveFile

Moves a file to a new directory.

VISUAL BASIC

```
' ----- Basic syntax. Third (optional) argument is
'          the overwrite flag.
My.Computer.FileSystem.MoveFile(source, destination, True)

' ----- UI-invoking syntax.
My.Computer.FileSystem.MoveFile(source, destination,
    UIOption.OnlyErrorDialogs)
```

For basic file move operations, the *File.Move* method in the *System.IO* namespace provides functionality comparable to the basic VB syntax.

C#

```
// ----- File.Move lacks the overwrite option.
System.IO.File.Move(source, destination);
```

C# does not include features that invoke the Windows file move dialog. Instead, you must access the Win32 API directly and call the appropriate function. In the case of file moving and similar file-based actions, you call the *SHFileOperation* API. See the "CopyFile Method" entry in this chapter for sample code that calls this API.

My Namespace

♦ My

See

Application Object, Computer Object, Forms Object, Log Object (My), Request Object, Resources Object, Response Object, Settings Object, User Object, WebServices Object

MyDocuments Property

♦ My.Computer.FileSystem.SpecialDirectories.MyDocuments

Returns the path to the "documents" folder for the current user.

VISUAL BASIC

```
Dim result As String = My.Computer.FileSystem.
    SpecialDirectories.MyDocuments
```

C#

```
string result = System.Environment.GetFolderPath(
    System.Environment.SpecialFolder.MyDocuments);
```

MyMusic Property

♦ My.Computer.FileSystem.SpecialDirectories.MyMusic

Returns the path to the "music" folder for the current user.

```
Dim result As String = My.Computer.FileSystem.
    SpecialDirectories.MyMusic
```

C#
```
string result = System.Environment.GetFolderPath(
    System.Environment.SpecialFolder.MyMusic);
```

MyPictures Property

♦ My.Computer.FileSystem.SpecialDirectories.MyPictures

Returns the path to the "pictures" folder for the current user.

VISUAL BASIC
```
Dim result As String = My.Computer.FileSystem.
    SpecialDirectories.MyPictures
```

C#
```
string result = System.Environment.GetFolderPath(
    System.Environment.SpecialFolder.MyPictures);
```

Name Property (My.Computer)

♦ My.Computer.Name

Returns the name of the local computer.

VISUAL BASIC
```
Dim result As String = My.Computer.Name
```

C#
```
string result = System.Environment.MachineName;
```

Name Property (My.User)

♦ My.User.Name

Returns the current Windows user name.

VISUAL BASIC
```
Dim result As String = My.User.Name
```

C#
```
string result = System.Threading.Thread.
    CurrentPrincipal.Identity.Name;
```

Network Object

♦ My.Computer.Network

See

DownloadFile Method, IsAvailable Property, NetworkAvailabilityChanged Event (My.Computer.Network), Ping Method, UploadFile Method

NetworkAvailabilityChanged Event (My.Application)

♦ My.Application.NetworkAvailabilityChanged

This event is limited to Windows Forms applications. The same event as exposed through the `My.Computer.Network` class is identical in purpose, and is available to all application types. See that event's entry for the C# equivalent for both VB events.

See Also

NetworkAvailabilityChanged Event (My.Computer.Network)

NetworkAvailabilityChanged Event (My.Computer.Network)

♦ My.Computer.Network.NetworkAvailabilityChanged

Calls an event handler when network availability changes.

VISUAL BASIC

```
' ----- Event handler logic.
Public Sub NetworkPresenceHandler(ByVal sender As Object,
    ByVal e As NetworkAvailableEventArgs)
End Sub

' ----- Elsewhere, associating handler with event.
AddHandler My.Computer.Network.NetworkAvailabilityChanged,
    AddressOf NetworkPresenceHandler
```

C#

```
// ----- Event handler logic.
public static void NetworkPresenceHandler(object sender,
    System.Net.NetworkInformation.
    NetworkAvailabilityEventArgs e)
{
}

// ----- Elsewhere, associating handler with event.
System.Net.NetworkInformation.NetworkChange
    .NetworkAvailabilityChanged += NetworkPresenceHandler;
```

NumLock Property

♦ My.Computer.Keyboard.NumLock

Indicates whether the Num Lock key is currently activated.

```
Dim result As Boolean = My.Computer.Keyboard.NumLock
```

C#
```
// ----- For Windows Forms code:
bool result = System.Windows.Forms.Form.IsKeyLocked(
    System.Windows.Forms.Keys.NumLock);

// ----- For XAML-centric code:
bool result = System.Windows.Input.Keyboard.IsKeyToggled(
    System.Windows.Input.Key.NumLock);
```

OpenForms Property

♦ My.Application.OpenForms

Returns a collection of the forms currently open within a Windows Forms application.

VISUAL BASIC
```
Dim result As System.Windows.Forms.FormCollection =
    My.Application.OpenForms
```

C#
```
System.Windows.Forms.FormCollection result =
    System.Windows.Forms.Application.OpenForms;
```

OpenSerialPort Method

♦ My.Computer.Ports.OpenSerialPort

Opens a connection to a serial port on the local workstation.

VISUAL BASIC
```
Dim portAccess As System.IO.Ports.SerialPort =
    My.Computer.Ports.OpenSerialPort(
    portName, baudRate, parity, dataBits, stopBits)
```

C#
```
System.IO.Ports.SerialPort portAccess =
    new System.IO.Ports.SerialPort(
    portName, baudRate, parity, dataBits, stopBits);
```

OpenTextFieldParser Method

♦ My.Computer.FileSystem.OpenTextFieldParser

C# does not include a direct equivalent for the *OpenTextFieldParser* method, or the underlying *TextFieldParser* class that it employs. It is possible to add a reference to the *Microsoft.VisualBasic* assembly to a C# application and use these VB-targeted features. For applications that need to forgo access to all Visual Basic components, the equivalent functionality will need to be obtained from another source, or developed from scratch.

To open a file for reading in C#, open it as a stream using the appropriate encoding. Once opened, each line can be read in using the *StreamReader* class' *ReadLine* method.

C#
```
string filePath = "C:\\temp\\FileWithFields.txt";
System.Text.Encoding useEncoding =
    System.Text.Encoding.UTF8;
bool autoDetectEncoding = true;
System.IO.StreamReader inStream =
    new System.IO.StreamReader(
    filePath, useEncoding, autoDetectEncoding);

// ----- Later, in a loop.
string lineContent = inStream.ReadLine();
```

For fixed-width fields, extract specific portions of the line text.

C#
```
// ----- Line begins with a 2-character state followed
//       by a 30-character city name.
string stateShort = lineContent.Substring(0, 2);
string cityName = lineContent.Substring(2, 30).Trim();
```

For delimited files that do not use text qualifiers around individual columns, use the *string* object's *Split* method to get the individual fields.

C#
```
// ----- A tab-delimited file.
string[] allFields = lineContent.Split(new char[] {'\t'});
string stateShort = allFields[0];
string cityName = allFields[1];
```

For delimited files that include text qualifiers, with the optional inclusion of the delimiter within the quoted fields, you will need to process the characters of the line individually, or use some complex regular expressions that may vary based on the format of the input. The following code represents one way to parse the data, looking for quote-qualified comma-delimited strings.

C#
```
List<string> results = new List<string>();
int fieldPos = 0;
bool inQuote = false;
string tempField = "";

for (int counter = 0; counter < lineContent.Length;
    counter++)
{
    if (lineContent[counter] == ',')
    {
        // ----- Might be a new field or within quotes.
        if (!inQuote)
        {
```

```
              // ----- Finished a field.
              tempField = lineContent.Substring(
                  fieldPos, counter - fieldPos);
              if ((tempField.Length >= 2) &&
                      (tempField.Substring(0, 1) == "\"") &&
                      (tempField.Substring(
                          tempField.Length - 1, 1) == "\""))
                  tempField = tempField.Substring(
                      1, tempField.Length - 2);
              results.Add(tempField);
              fieldPos = counter + 1;
          }
      }
      else if (lineContent[counter] == '"')
      {
          // ----- Start or end a quoted field.
          inQuote = !inQuote;
      }
  }

  // ----- Finish the last field.
  tempField = "";
  if (lineContent.Length > fieldPos)
      tempField = lineContent.Substring(fieldPos,
          lineContent.Length - fieldPos);
  if ((tempField.Length >= 2) &&
          (tempField.Substring(0, 1) == "\"") &&
          (tempField.Substring(
              tempField.Length - 1, 1) == "\""))
      tempField = tempField.Substring(1,
          tempField.Length - 2);
  results.Add(tempField);
  string[] lineFields = results.ToArray();
```

This code does not handle all complex cases. For example, if a quoted field is surrounded by whitespace, the quotation marks will not be removed.

OpenTextFileReader Method

♦ My.Computer.FileSystem.OpenTextFileReader

Opens an existing file for text input.

VISUAL BASIC

```
Dim filePath As String = "C:\temp\WorkFile.txt"
Dim useEncoding As System.Text.Encoding =
    System.Text.Encoding.UTF8
Dim result As System.IO.StreamReader =
    My.Computer.FileSystem.OpenTextFileReader(
    filePath, useEncoding)
```

C#
```
string filePath = "C:\\temp\\WorkFile.txt";
System.TextEncoding useEncoding =
    System.Text.Encoding.UTF8;
bool autoDetectEncoding = true;
System.IO.StreamReader result = new System.IO.StreamReader(
    filePath, useEncoding, autoDetectEncoding);
```

In Visual Basic, the encoding parameter is optional; when absent, output defaults to UTF8 encoding. The equivalent *StreamReader* class accepts a wider variety of parameter options in its constructor. See the Visual Studio documentation for these options.

OpenTextFileWriter Method

♦ My.Computer.FileSystem.OpenTextFileWriter

Opens an existing file, or creates a new one, for text output.

VISUAL BASIC
```
Dim filePath As String = "C:\temp\WorkFile.txt"
Dim appendIfFound As Boolean = True
Dim useEncoding As System.Text.Encoding =
    System.Text.Encoding.UTF8
Dim result As System.IO.StreamWriter =
    My.Computer.FileSystem.OpenTextFileWriter(
    filePath, appendIfFound, useEncoding)
```

C#
```
string filePath = "C:\\temp\\WorkFile.txt";
bool appendIfFound = true;
System.TextEncoding useEncoding =
    System.Text.Encoding.UTF8;
System.IO.StreamWriter result = new System.IO.StreamWriter(
    filePath, appendIfFound, useEncoding);
```

In Visual Basic, the encoding parameter is optional; when absent, output defaults to UTF8 encoding. The equivalent *StreamWriter* class accepts a wider variety of parameter options in its constructor. See the Visual Studio documentation for these options.

OSFullName Property

♦ My.Computer.Info.OSFullName

Returns the full name of the operating system.

VISUAL BASIC
```
Dim result As String = My.Computer.Info.OSFullName
```

C#
```
// Assumes: using System.Management;
```

```
// ----- Default to My.Computer.Info.OSPlatform equivalent.
string result =
    System.Environment.OSVersion.Platform.ToString();
try
{
    SelectQuery querySet =
        new SelectQuery("Win32_OperatingSystem");
    ManagementObjectSearcher queryScan =
        new ManagementObjectSearcher(querySet);
    ManagementObjectCollection results = queryScan.Get();
    if (results.Count > 0)
    {
        ManagementObjectCollection.
            ManagementObjectEnumerator
            resultsEnumerator = results.GetEnumerator();
        resultsEnumerator.MoveNext();
        result = (string)resultsEnumerator.Current.
            Properties["Name"].Value;
        if (result.Contains('|') == true)
            result = result.Substring(0,
                result.IndexOf('|'));
    }
} catch { }
```

OSPlatform Property

♦ My.Computer.Info.OSPlatform

Returns the platform name of the operating system.

VISUAL BASIC
```
Dim result As String = My.Computer.Info.OSPlatform
```

C#
```
string result = System.Environment.
    OSVersion.Platform.ToString();
```

OSVersion Property

♦ My.Computer.Info.OSVersion

Returns the version number of the operating system.

VISUAL BASIC
```
Dim result As String = My.Computer.Info.OSVersion
```

C#
```
string result = System.Environment.
    OSVersion.Version.ToString();
```

PerformanceData Property

♦ My.Computer.Registry.PerformanceData

Returns a reference to the *HKEY_PERFORMANCE_DATA* Windows registry location.

VISUAL BASIC
```
Dim result As Microsoft.Win32.RegistryKey =
    My.Computer.Registry.PerformanceData
```

C#
```
Microsoft.Win32.RegistryKey result =
    Microsoft.Win32.Registry.PerformanceData;
```

Ping Method

♦ My.Computer.Network.Ping

Tests for the presence of another computer or device on a network by issuing an ICMP protocol echo request.

VISUAL BASIC
```
' ----- Using string host or IP address, default timeout.
Dim result As Boolean = My.Computer.Network.Ping(
    "www.example.com")

' ----- Using Uri host, specific timeout.
Dim target As New System.Uri("http://www.example.com")
Dim result As Boolean = My.Computer.Network.Ping(
    target, 3000)
```

C#
```
// ----- Using string host or IP address, default timeout.
bool result = ((new System.Net.NetworkInformation.Ping())
    .Send("www.example.com").Status ==
    System.Net.NetworkInformation.IPStatus.Success);

// ----- Using Uri host, specific timeout.
System.Uri target = new
System.Uri("http://www.example.com");
bool result = ((new System.Net.NetworkInformation.Ping())
    .Send(target.Host, 3000).Status ==
    System.Net.NetworkInformation.IPStatus.Success);
```

Play Method

♦ My.Computer.Audio.Play

Plays a sound contained in a file, byte array, or data stream.

VISUAL BASIC
```
' ----- Play sound file in background mode.
My.Computer.Audio.Play(soundFile, AudioPlayMode.Background)
```

C#

```
// ----- Play sound file in background mode.
System.Media.SoundPlayer audioSource =
    new System.Media.SoundPlayer(soundFile);
audioSource.Play();
```

In addition to specifying a file containing sound content, the *Play* method accepts a byte array or stream. The *SoundPlayer* class will work with a data string, or a byte array wrapped in a stream.

C#

```
// ----- Sound contained in a stream.
System.Media.SoundPlayer audioSource =
    new System.Media.SoundPlayer(existingStream);

// ----- Sound contained in a byte array.
System.IO.MemoryStream bytesAsStream =
    new System.IO.MemoryStream(existingByteArray);
System.Media.SoundPlayer audioSource =
    new System.Media.SoundPlayer(bytesAsStream);
// ----- Later...
bytesAsStream.Close();
```

The *Play* method accepts an argument that indicates how to play the sound, whether in the foreground, the background, or looping in the background. When using the *SoundPlayer* class in C#, call different methods to emulate the related *AudioPlayMode* enumeration value.

AudioPlayMode Value	SoundPlayer Method
Background	Play
BackgroundLoop	PlayLooping
WaitToComplete	PlaySync

PlaySystemSound Method

♦ My.Computer.Audio.PlaySystemSound

Plays a system-defined sound one time.

VISUAL BASIC

```
Dim whichSound As System.Media.SystemSound =
    System.Media.SystemSounds.Beep
My.Computer.Audio.PlaySystemSound(whichSound)
```

C#

```
System.Media.SystemSound whichSound =
    System.Media.SystemSounds.Beep;
whichSound.Play();
```

Ports Object

♦ My.Computer.Ports

See

OpenSerialPort Method, SerialPortNames Property

ProductName Property

♦ My.Application.Info.ProductName

Returns the product name as stored in the assembly.

VISUAL BASIC
```
Dim result As String = My.Application.Info.ProductName
```

C#
```
string result;
System.Reflection.Assembly currentAssembly =
    System.Reflection.Assembly.GetEntryAssembly();
if (currentAssembly == null) currentAssembly =
    System.Reflection.Assembly.GetCallingAssembly();
object[] attrSet = currentAssembly.GetCustomAttributes(
    typeof(System.Reflection.AssemblyProductAttribute),
    inherit:true);
if (attrSet.Length == 0)
    result = "";
else
    result = ((System.Reflection.AssemblyProductAttribute)
        attrSet[0]).Product;
```

ProgramFiles Property

♦ My.Computer.FileSystem.SpecialDirectories.ProgramFiles

Returns the path to the native "program files" folder on the local system.

VISUAL BASIC
```
Dim result As String = My.Computer.FileSystem.
    SpecialDirectories.ProgramFiles
```

C#
```
string result = System.Environment.GetFolderPath(
    System.Environment.SpecialFolder.ProgramFiles);
```

Programs Property

♦ My.Computer.FileSystem.SpecialDirectories.Programs

Returns the path to the "program groups" folder for the current user.

VISUAL BASIC
```
Dim result As String = My.Computer.FileSystem.
    SpecialDirectories.Programs
```

C#

```
string result = System.Environment.GetFolderPath(
    System.Environment.SpecialFolder.Programs);
```

ReadAllBytes Method

♦ My.Computer.FileSystem.ReadAllBytes

Returns a byte array containing a file's content.

VISUAL BASIC

```
Dim result As Byte() = My.Computer.FileSystem.ReadAllBytes(
    "C:\temp\RawData.dat")
```

C#

```
byte[] result = System.IO.File.ReadAllBytes(
    "C:\\temp\\RawData.dat");
```

ReadAllText Method

♦ My.Computer.FileSystem.ReadAllText

Returns a string containing a file's content.

VISUAL BASIC

```
Dim optionalEncoding As System.Text.Encoding =
    System.Text.UnicodeEncoding
Dim result As String = My.Computer.FileSystem.ReadAllText(
    "C:\temp\WorkFile.txt", optionalEncoding)
```

C#

```
System.Text.Encoding optionalEncoding =
    System.Text.UnicodeEncoding;
string result = System.IO.File.ReadAllText(
    "C:\\temp\\WorkFile.txt", optionalEncoding);
```

The second argument to this method specifies an optional text encoding system. If absent, the text is read using the encoding specified by the file itself, if available.

Registry Object

♦ My.Computer.Registry

See

ClassesRoot Property, CurrentConfig Property, CurrentUser Property, DynData Property, GetValue Method, LocalMachine Property, PerformanceData Property, SetValue Method, Users Property

RenameDirectory Method

♦ My.Computer.FileSystem.RenameDirectory

Renames an existing directory, keeping it in the same original directory.

```
My.Computer.FileSystem.RenameDirectory(
    "C:\temp\WorkArea", "BackupArea")
```

C#
```
System.IO.Directory.Move(
    "C:\\temp\\WorkArea", "C:\\temp\\BackupArea");
```

The *RenameDirectory* method requires that the new name be just a directory name, with no path or drive information. The C# alternative allows either the source or destination path to be relative or absolute.

RenameFile Method

♦ My.Computer.FileSystem.RenameFile

Renames a file to a new name, keeping it in the same directory.

VISUAL BASIC
```
My.Computer.FileSystem.RenameFile(
    "C:\temp\WorkFile.txt", "BackupWorkFile.old")
```

C#
```
System.IO.File.Move("C:\\temp\\WorkFile.txt",
    "C:\\temp\\BackupWorkFile.old");
```

The *RenameFile* method requires that the new name be just a file name, with no path or drive information. The C# alternative allows either the source or destination path to be relative or absolute.

Request Object

♦ My.Request

Exposes request details for the current ASP.NET HTTP request.

VISUAL BASIC
```
Dim currentRequest As System.Web.HttpRequest = My.Request
```

C#
```
System.Web.HttpRequest currentRequest =
    System.Web.HttpContext.Current.Request;
```

Resources Object

♦ My.Resources

Accesses resources defined through the Project Properties.

VISUAL BASIC
```
Dim template As String = My.Resources.DisplayTemplate
```

C#

```
string template = Properties.Resources.DisplayTemplate;
```

Response Object

♦ My.Response

Exposes response details for the current ASP.NET HTTP response.

VISUAL BASIC

```
Dim currentResponse As System.Web.HttpResponse =
    My.Response
```

C#

```
System.Web.HttpResponse currentResponse =
    System.Web.HttpContext.Current.Response;
```

Run Method

♦ My.Application.Run

Starts a Windows application using the Windows Forms Application Framework.

VISUAL BASIC

```
My.Application.Run(commandLineArgs)
```

The *Run* method is only available in VB programs that employ the Windows Forms Application Framework. The *Application* class in the *System.Windows.Forms* namespace also exposes a *Run* method. It provides similar functionality, but accepts a *Form* instance or an *ApplicationContext* instance instead of an array of command-line arguments. In C#, you can call the *Environment.GetCommandLineArgs* method to retrieve this information.

C#

```
// ----- Run the application focused on the
//       main form instance.
Application.Run(new MainForm());
```

SaveMySettingsOnExit Property

♦ My.Application.SaveMySettingsOnExit

Indicates whether the settings should be saved when exiting the application.

VISUAL BASIC

```
Dim result As Boolean = My.Application.SaveMySettingsOnExit
```

C# does not include an equivalent for Visual Basic's *SaveMySettingsOnExit* property. Instead, settings must be saved manually on exit. The following code saves any updated settings.

C#

```
Properties.Settings.Default.Save();
```

See Also

Settings Object

Screen Property

♦ My.Computer.Screen

Returns an object containing information and settings about the primary display.

VISUAL BASIC
```
Dim result As System.Windows.Forms.Screen =
    My.Computer.Screen
```

C#
```
// ----- For Windows Forms code:
System.Windows.Forms.Screen result =
    System.Windows.Forms.Screen.PrimaryScreen;
```

In XAML-centric code, the *System.Windows.SystemParameters* class exposes several static properties that provide screen-related information.

ScrollLock Property

♦ My.Computer.Keyboard.ScrollLock

Indicates whether the Scroll Lock key is currently activated.

VISUAL BASIC
```
Dim result As Boolean = My.Computer.Keyboard.ScrollLock
```

C#
```
// ----- For Windows Forms code:
bool result = System.Windows.Forms.Form.IsKeyLocked(
    System.Windows.Forms.Keys.Scroll);

// ----- For XAML-centric code:
bool result = System.Windows.Input.Keyboard.IsKeyToggled(
    System.Windows.Input.Key.Scroll);
```

SendKeys Method

♦ My.Computer.Keyboard.SendKeys

Sends keystrokes to the active window as if typed from the keyboard.

VISUAL BASIC
```
' ----- Send Control-C "copy" sequence to the
'       active window.
Dim waitForProcessing As Boolean = True
My.Computer.Keyboard.SendKeys("^c", waitForProcessing)
```

C#
```
// ----- Send Control-C "copy" sequence to the
//       active window.
System.Windows.Forms.SendKeys.SendWait("^c");

// ----- To return without waiting.
System.Windows.Forms.SendKeys.Send("^c");
```

XAML-based applications typically do not have access to the *SendKeys* class. Instead, such programs must call the *SendInput* Win32 API. Use of this API is beyond the scope of this chapter. Access the "SendInput Function" entry on Microsoft's MSDN web site for information on calling this API.

The SendKeys command uses a set of specially formatted codes, such as *{BACKSPACE}*, to send non-standard characters and sequences to the target window. See the Visual Studio documentation for the full set of codes.

SerialPortNames Property

♦ My.Computer.Ports.SerialPortNames

Returns a collection of serial port names found on the local computer.

VISUAL BASIC
```
' ----- This code returns a read-only collection of
'       the serial port names.
Dim result As System.Collections.Generic.
    ReadOnlyCollection(Of String) =
    My.Computer.Ports.SerialPortNames
```

C#
```
// ----- This code returns an ordinary string array of
//       the serial port names.
string[] result =
    System.IO.Ports.SerialPort.GetPortNames();
```

SetAudio Method

♦ My.Computer.Clipboard.SetAudio

Writes audio data to the system clipboard. The audio content supplied can be in the form of a byte array or a stream (*System.IO.Stream*).

VISUAL BASIC
```
' Option 1: Dim audioContent() As Byte
' Option 2: Dim audioContent As System.IO.Stream
My.Computer.Clipboard.SetAudio(audioContent)
```

C#
```
// Option 1: byte[] audioContent;
// Option 2: System.IO.Stream audioContent;
```

```
// ----- For Windows Forms code:
System.Windows.Forms.Clipboard.SetAudio(audioContent);

// ----- For XAML-centric code:
System.Windows.Clipboard.SetAudio(audioContent);
```

SetData Method

♦ My.Computer.Clipboard.SetData

Writes data in a custom named format to the system clipboard.

VISUAL BASIC
```
Dim formatName As String = "MyCustomFormat"
Dim customData As Object  ' Assign any data you choose
My.Computer.Clipboard.SetData(formatName, customData)
```

C#
```
string formatName = "MyCustomFormat";
object customData;  // Assign any data you choose

// ----- For Windows Forms code:
System.Windows.Forms.Clipboard.SetData(
    formatName, customData);

// ----- For XAML-centric code:
System.Windows.Clipboard.SetData(
    formatName, customData);
```

SetDataObject Method

♦ My.Computer.Clipboard.SetDataObject

Writes data to the system clipboard in multiple formats at once.

VISUAL BASIC
```
Dim toClipboard As New System.Windows.Forms.DataObject
toClipboard.SetText("Some basic text.")
toClipboard.SetData("Backwards", ".txet cisab emoS")
My.Computer.Clipboard.SetDataObject(toClipboard)
```

C#
```
// ----- For Windows Forms code:
System.Windows.Forms.DataObject toClipboard =
    new System.Windows.Forms.DataObject();
toClipboard.SetText("Some basic text.");
toClipboard.SetData("Backwards", ".txet cisab emoS");
System.Windows.Forms.Clipboard.SetDataObject(toClipboard);
```

```
// ----- For XAML-centric code:
System.Windows.DataObject toClipboard =
    new System.Windows.DataObject();
toClipboard.SetText("Some basic text.");
toClipboard.SetData("Backwards", ".txet cisab emoS");
System.Windows.Clipboard.SetDataObject(toClipboard);
```

SetFileDropList Method

♦ My.Computer.Clipboard.SetFileDropList

Writes a collection of file-path strings to the system clipboard.

VISUAL BASIC
```
Dim files As New _
    System.Collections.Specialized.StringCollection
files.Add("C:\temp\FileToShare.txt")
My.Computer.Clipboard.SetFileDropList(files)
```

C#
```
System.Collections.Specialized.StringCollection files =
    new System.Collections.Specialized.StringCollection();
files.Add("C:\\temp\\FileToShare.txt");

// ----- For Windows Forms code:
System.Windows.Forms.Clipboard.SetFileDropList(files);

// ----- For XAML-centric code:
System.Windows.Clipboard.SetFileDropList(files);
```

SetImage Method

♦ My.Computer.Clipboard.SetImage

Writes an image to the system clipboard.

VISUAL BASIC
```
Dim someImage As System.Drawing.Image

' ----- After loading the image.
My.Computer.Clipboard.SetImage(someImage)
```

C#
```
// ----- For Windows Forms code:
System.Drawing.Image someImage;
System.Windows.Forms.Clipboard.SetImage(someImage);

// ----- For XAML-centric code:
System.Windows.Media.Imaging.BitmapSource someImage;
System.Windows.Clipboard.SetImage(someImage);
```

SetText Method

♦ My.Computer.Clipboard.SetText

Writes a text string to the system clipboard.

VISUAL BASIC
```
My.Computer.Clipboard.SetText("Hello, world!")
```

C#
```
// ----- For Windows Forms code:
System.Windows.Forms.Clipboard.SetText("Hello, world!");

// ----- For XAML-centric code:
System.Windows.Clipboard.SetText("Hello, world!");
```

The *SetText* method accepts a second optional argument that indicates the type of text to store, such as HTML or Unicode. In the *My* and Windows Forms versions of the code, this argument is of type *System.Windows.Forms.TextDataFormat*; for XAML code, use the *System.Windows.TextDataFormat* enumeration instead. By default, the text is stored in Unicode format.

Settings Object

♦ My.Settings

Accesses user and application settings defined through the Project Properties.

VISUAL BASIC
```
' ----- Accessing a setting.
Dim result As Point = My.Settings.DisplayLocation

' ----- Modifying a setting (user-scope only).
My.Settings.DisplayLocation = targetForm.Location

' ----- Saving all settings.
My.Settings.Save()
```

C#
```
// ----- Accessing a setting.
Point result = Properties.Settings.Default.DisplayLocation;

// ----- Modifying a setting (user-scope only).
Properties.Settings.Default.DisplayLocation =
    targetForm.Location;

// ----- Saving all settings.
Properties.Settings.Default.Save();
```

SetValue Method

♦ My.Computer.Registry.SetValue

Saves data into a specified Windows registry value.

```
My.Computer.Registry.SetValue(
    "HKEY_CURRENT_USER\Software\Example\MyApp",
    "ErrorCount", 0&, RegistryValueKind.QWord))
```

C#
```
Microsoft.Win32.Registry.SetValue(
    "HKEY_CURRENT_USER\\Software\\Example\\MyApp",
    "ErrorCount", 0L, RegistryValueKind.QWord);
```

ShiftKeyDown Property

♦ My.Computer.Keyboard.ShiftKeyDown

Indicates whether a Shift key is currently pressed.

VISUAL BASIC
```
Dim result As Boolean = My.Computer.Keyboard.ShiftKeyDown
```

C#
```
// ----- For Windows Forms code:
bool result = ((System.Windows.Forms.Control.ModifierKeys &
    System.Windows.Forms.Keys.Shift) != 0);

// ----- For XAML-centric code:
bool result = ((System.Windows.Input.Keyboard.Modifiers &
    System.Windows.Input.ModifierKeys.Shift) != 0);
```

Shutdown Event

♦ My.Application.Shutdown

Occurs when the application shuts down.

VISUAL BASIC
```
Public Sub Me_Shutdown(ByVal sender As Object,
        ByVal e As EventArgs) Handles Me.Shutdown
    ' ----- Relevant shutdown code here.
End Sub
```

The *Shutdown* event is only available in VB programs that employ the Windows Forms Application Framework. However, you can perform shutdown-related processing in any application by adding a handler to the *ProcessExit* event for the current application domain.

C#
```
static void ShutdownLogic(object sender, EventArgs e)
{
    // ----- Relevant shutdown code here.
}
```

```
// ----- In your Main routine, before running the core
//        program logic.
AppDomain.CurrentDomain.ProcessExit += ShutdownLogic;
```

The application context object for an application exposes a similar event that you can use instead of *ProcessExit* to monitor the application's main thread.

C#

```
// ----- In your Main routine.
ApplicationContext appContext = new ApplicationContext();
appContext.ThreadExit += ShutdownLogic;
appContext.MainForm = new Form1();
Application.Run(appContext);
```

SpecialDirectories Object

♦ My.Computer.FileSystem.SpecialDirectories

See

AllUsersApplicationData Property, CurrentUserApplicationData Property, Desktop Property, MyDocuments Property, MyMusic Property, MyPictures Property, Programs Property, Temp Property

SplashScreen Property

♦ My.Application.SplashScreen

Identifies the form used as the splash screen in a Windows Forms application.

VISUAL BASIC

```
My.Application.SplashScreen = New SplashForm
```

Visual Basic includes features that let you display a splash screen with some basic logic. In C#, any splash screen must be displayed manually through custom code. The following method can be called from the *Main* method to display a splash screen.

C#

```
// ----- Call this routine from Main.
private static void ShowSplashScreen()
{
    // ----- Show the splash screen on its own thread.
    System.Threading.Thread splashThread =
        new System.Threading.Thread(DisplaySplash);
    splashThread.Start();
}

private static void DisplaySplash()
{
    // ----- Assume a form with an exposed timer that
    //        will close the form after some time.
    Application.Run(new SplashForm());
}
```

StackTrace Property

♦ My.Application.Info.StackTrace

Returns a string version of the current stack trace.

VISUAL BASIC
```
Dim result As String = My.Application.Info.StackTrace
```

C#
```
string result = System.Environment.StackTrace;
```

Startup Event

♦ My.Application.Startup

Triggered when starting a Windows Forms application that uses VB's Windows Forms Application Framework.

VISUAL BASIC
```
Public Sub Me_Startup(ByVal sender As Object,
        ByVal e As StartupEventArgs) Handles Me.Startup
    ' ----- Custom startup code here. To abort...
    e.Cancel = True
End Sub
```

C# does not include an equivalent to VB's Windows Forms Application Framework. However, because all C# programs begin with a *Main* method, you can place relevant custom code directly in that method.

C#
```
public static void Main()
{
    // ----- Custom code here. To abort...
    Application.Exit();
}
```

StartupNextInstance Event

♦ My.Application.StartupNextInstance

Called when a subsequent instance of a single-instance Windows Forms application starts up. The event occurs in the primary instance.

VISUAL BASIC
```
Public Sub Me_StartupNextInstance(ByVal sender As Object,
        ByVal e As StartupNextInstanceEventArgs) _
        Handles Me.StartupNextInstance
    ' ----- Instance-handling code here.
End Sub
```

The *StartupNextInstance* event is only available in VB programs that employ the Windows Forms Application Framework. In C#, you must monitor the startup of subsequent instances manually. The following *Main* method provides an example of how you can watch for subsequent instances using a shared mutex object.

C#

```csharp
// ----- Assumes: using System.Threading;

public static void Main()
{
    System.Version versionInfo;
    string mutexName;
    Mutex appMutex = null;
    bool firstInstance = false;

    // ----- Provide a reasonably unique mutex name.
    //       GUIDs will also work.
    versionInfo = System.Reflection.Assembly.
        GetExecutingAssembly().GetName().Version;
    mutexName = string.Format(
        "VendorName/AppName({0}.{1})",
        versionInfo.Major, versionInfo.Minor);

    try
    {
        // ----- See if another instance exists.
        appMutex = Mutex.OpenExisting(mutexName);
    }
    catch
    {
        // ----- Not found or other failure.
        //       Try to create one.
        try
        {
            appMutex = new Mutex(true, mutexName,
                out firstInstance);
        }
        catch
        {
            firstInstance = false;
        }
    }

    if (firstInstance)
    {
        // ----- Continue with application logic.
    }
    else
    {
        // ----- This is a subsequent instance.
    }
```

```
// ----- When finished with the app, clean up.
if (appMutex != null)
    appMutex.Close();
}
```

Visual Basic's *StartupNextInstance* shuts down the subsequent instance and passes any of its command-line arguments to the first instance through the event's e argument. It does this through interprocess communications, a demonstration of which is beyond the scope of this entry.

Stop Method

◆ My.Computer.Audio.Stop

Stops a sound that is currently playing.

VISUAL BASIC
```
' ----- Play sound file in background mode.
My.Computer.Audio.Play(soundFile, AudioPlayMode.Background)

' ----- Later, stop the sound.
My.Computer.Audio.Stop()
```

C#
```
// ----- Play sound file in background mode.
System.Media.SoundPlayer audioSource =
    new System.Media.SoundPlayer(soundFile);
audioSource.Play();

// ----- Later, stop the sound.
audioSource.Stop();
```

Temp Property

◆ My.Computer.FileSystem.SpecialDirectories.Temp

Returns the path to the temporary-file folder for the current user.

VISUAL BASIC
```
Dim result As String = My.Computer.FileSystem.
    SpecialDirectories.Temp
```

C#
```
string result = System.IO.Path.GetTempPath();
```

TextFieldParser Object

See

OpenTextFieldParser Method

TickCount Property

♦ My.Computer.Clock.TickCount

Returns the number of milliseconds elapsed since system startup, or since the last time the counter reset, about once every 25 days.

VISUAL BASIC
```
Dim result As Integer = My.Computer.Clock.TickCount
```

C#
```
int result = System.Environment.TickCount;
```

Title Property

♦ My.Application.Info.Title

Returns the application title as stored in the assembly.

VISUAL BASIC
```
Dim result As String = My.Application.Info.Title
```

C#
```
string result;
System.Reflection.Assembly currentAssembly =
    System.Reflection.Assembly.GetEntryAssembly();
if (currentAssembly == null) currentAssembly =
    System.Reflection.Assembly.GetCallingAssembly();
object[] attrSet = currentAssembly.GetCustomAttributes(
    typeof(System.Reflection.AssemblyTitleAttribute),
    inherit:true);
if (attrSet.Length == 0)
    result = "";
else
    result = ((System.Reflection.AssemblyTitleAttribute)
        attrSet[0]).Title;
```

TotalPhysicalMemory Property

♦ My.Computer.Info.TotalPhysicalMemory

Returns the total number of installed bytes of physical memory on the local computer.

VISUAL BASIC
```
Dim result As ULong = My.Computer.Info.TotalPhysicalMemory
```

C#
```
// ----- GetMemoryInfo code discussed below.
ulong result = MemoryQuery.GetMemoryInfo().TotalPhysical;
```

Visual Basic retrieves memory information through the *GlobalMemoryStatusEx* Windows API call. See the "AvailablePhysicalMemory Property" entry in this chapter for a sample *GetMemoryInfo* method that wraps the API call in C# code.

TotalVirtualMemory Property

♦ My.Computer.Info.TotalVirtualMemory

Returns the total number of configured bytes of virtual memory on the local computer.

VISUAL BASIC
```
Dim result As ULong = My.Computer.Info.TotalVirtualMemory
```

C#
```
// ----- GetMemoryInfo code discussed below.
ulong result = MemoryQuery.GetMemoryInfo().TotalVirtual;
```

Visual Basic retrieves memory information through the *GlobalMemoryStatusEx* Windows API call. See the "AvailablePhysicalMemory Property" entry in this chapter for a sample *GetMemoryInfo* method that wraps the API call in C# code.

TraceSource Property

♦ My.Application.Log.TraceSource (for Desktop applications)

♦ My.Log.TraceSource (for ASP.NET applications)

Unlike with Visual Basic, C# does not configure a built-in logging environment by default. Instead, you can add a Logging Application Block from the Microsoft Enterprise Library to your application. The code needed to set up and use trace logging in your application is beyond the scope of this book.

You can find full information on the Logging Application Block, including sample code, on the MSDN web site, msdn.microsoft.com. On that site, search for "Enterprise Library 6." The first result should be a link to the *Developer's Guide* for the Microsoft Enterprise Library. Chapter 5, "As Easy As Falling Off a Log," provides an overview of the logging components.

Visual Basic's logging tools include *WriteEntry* and *WriteException* methods. In the sample code for the Logging Application Block, the *LogWriter.Write* method provides a good substitute for VB's own *WriteEntry* method. However, the Enterprise Library does not include a write method designed for *Exception* instances. Instead, you must format the exception message yourself, and then pass it to the *LogWriter.Write* method.

Trademark Property

♦ My.Application.Info.Trademark

Returns the legal trademark as stored in the assembly.

VISUAL BASIC
```
Dim result As String = My.Application.Info.Trademark
```

C#

```
string result;
System.Reflection.Assembly currentAssembly =
    System.Reflection.Assembly.GetEntryAssembly();
if (currentAssembly == null) currentAssembly =
    System.Reflection.Assembly.GetCallingAssembly();
object[] attrSet = currentAssembly.GetCustomAttributes(
    typeof(System.Reflection.AssemblyTrademarkAttribute),
    inherit:true);
if (attrSet.Length == 0)
    result = "";
else
    result = ((System.Reflection.
        AssemblyTrademarkAttribute)
        attrSet[0]).Trademark;
```

UICulture Property

♦ My.Application.UICulture

Returns an object that describes the user interface culture.

VISUAL BASIC

```
Dim result As System.Globalization.CultureInfo =
    My.Application.UICulture
```

C#

```
System.Globalization.CultureInfo result =
    System.Threading.Thread.CurrentThread.CurrentUICulture;
```

UnhandledException Event

♦ My.Application.UnhandledException

Catches unhandled exceptions within a Windows Forms application that uses VB's Windows Forms Application Framework.

VISUAL BASIC

```
Public Sub Me_UnhandledException(ByVal sender As Object,
        ByVal e As UnhandledExceptionEventArgs) _
        Handles Me.UnhandledException
    ' ----- Relevant error-handling code here.
End Sub
```

The *UnhandledException* event is only available in VB programs that employ the Windows Forms Application Framework. However, you can manage unhandled exceptions in any application by adding a handler to the *UnhandledException* event for the current application domain.

C#

```
static void SurpriseProblem(object sender,
    UnhandledExceptionEventArgs e)
{
    // ----- Relevant error-handling code here.
}

// ----- In your Main routine, before running the core
//       program logic.
AppDomain.CurrentDomain.UnhandledException +=
    SurpriseProblem;
```

You can also add a thread-specific handler that monitors unhandled exceptions in your main (UI) thread.

C#

```
static void ThreadProblem(object sender,
    System.Threading.ThreadExceptionEventArgs e)
{
    // ----- Relevant error-handling code here.
}

// ----- In your Main routine, before running the core
//       program logic.
Application.ThreadException += ThreadProblem;
```

UploadFile Method

♦ My.Computer.Network.UploadFile

Uploads a file from a local computer to a network address.

VISUAL BASIC

```
My.Computer.Network.UploadFile(sourceFile,
    destinationAddress, userName, password)
```

C#

```
System.Net.WebClient client = new System.Net.WebClient();
System.Uri destinationUri =
    new System.Uri(destinationAddress);

// ----- Default credentials.
client.UseDefaultCredentials = true;

// ----- Or, supply specific credentials.
client.UseDefaultCredentials = false;
client.Credentials = new System.Net.NetworkCredential(
    userName, password);

// ----- Synchronous copy.
client.UploadFile(destinationUri, sourceFile);
```

```
// ----- Or, asynchronous copy, providing your own
//       custom complete/cancel event handler.
client.UploadFileCompleted += new
    UploadFileCompletedEventHandler(CompletedCallback);
client.UploadFileAsync(destinationUri, sourceFile);
```

The *WebClient* class' upload methods provide no visual cues as to the state of the transfer. You must provide your own progress dialog if desired.

To override the default timeout value, derive a new class from the *WebClient* class, and manually configure the *WebRequest*'s *TimeOut* property. Then use this class instead of the standard *WebClient* class to perform the upload. For a sample of this override in C#, see the "DownloadFile Method" entry in this chapter.

See Also

DownloadFile Method

User Object

♦ My.User

See

CurrentPrincipal Property, InitializeWithWindowsUser Method, IsAuthenticated Property, IsInRole Method, Name Property (My.User)

Users Property

♦ My.Computer.Registry.Users

Returns a reference to the *HKEY_USERS* Windows registry location.

VISUAL BASIC
```
Dim result As Microsoft.Win32.RegistryKey =
    My.Computer.Registry.Users
```

C#
```
Microsoft.Win32.RegistryKey result =
    Microsoft.Win32.Registry.Users;
```

Version Property

♦ My.Application.Info.Version

Returns the version numbers of the application as stored in the assembly.

VISUAL BASIC
```
Dim result As System.Version = My.Application.Info.Version
```

C#
```
System.Reflection.Assembly currentAssembly =
    System.Reflection.Assembly.GetEntryAssembly();
```

```
if (currentAssembly == null) currentAssembly =
    System.Reflection.Assembly.GetCallingAssembly();
System.Version result = currentAssembly.GetName().Version;
```

WebServices Object

♦ My.WebServices

Accesses web services and their members from a non-ASP.NET application.

VISUAL BASIC
```
' ----- Assumes a MappingService web service with a
'       GetNearestCity member is part of the project.
Dim result As String =
    My.WebServices.MappingService.GetNearestCity(
    targetLatitude, targetLongitude)
```

C#
```
// ----- Assumes a MappingService web service with a
//       GetNearestCity member is part of the project.
MappingNamespace.MappingService theService =
    new MappingNamespace.MappingService();
string result = theService.GetNearestCity(
    targetLatitude, targetLongitude);
```

WheelExists Property

♦ My.Computer.Mouse.WheelExists

Returns a value that indicates whether the installed mouse includes a mouse wheel.

VISUAL BASIC
```
Dim result As Boolean = My.Computer.Mouse.WheelExists
```

C#
```
// ----- For Windows Forms code:
bool result = System.Windows.Forms.SystemInformation.
    MouseWheelPresent;

// ----- For XAML-centric code:
bool result = System.Windows.SystemParameters.
    IsMouseWheelPresent;
```

WheelScrollLines Property

♦ My.Computer.Mouse.WheelScrollLines

Returns the number of lines to scroll during mouse wheel operations.

VISUAL BASIC
```
Dim result As Integer = My.Computer.Mouse.WheelScrollLines
```

```
// ----- For Windows Forms code:
int result = System.Windows.Forms.SystemInformation.
    MouseWheelScrollLines;

// ----- For XAML-centric code:
int result =
    System.Windows.SystemParameters.WheelScrollLines;
```

WorkingSet Property

♦ My.Application.Info.WorkingSet

Returns the size in bytes of physical memory mapped to the current process context.

VISUAL BASIC
```
Dim result As Long = My.Application.Info.WorkingSet
```
C#
```
long result = System.Environment.WorkingSet;
```

WriteAllBytes Method

♦ My.Computer.FileSystem.WriteAllBytes

Writes the content of a byte array to a specified file.

VISUAL BASIC
```
Dim whichFile As String = "C:\temp\SomeData.dat"
Dim theData() As Byte = GetMyByteData()
Dim append As Boolean = False
My.Computer.FileSystem.WriteAllBytes(
    whichFile, theData, append)
```

C#
```
string whichFile = "C:\\temp\\SomeData.dat";
byte[] theData = GetMyByteData();
bool append = false;
System.IO.FileStream outFile;
System.IO.FileMode outMethod;

if (append)
    outMethod = System.IO.FileMode.Append;
else
    outMethod = System.IO.FileMode.Create;

outFile = new System.IO.FileStream(whichFile, outMethod,
    System.IO.FileAccess.Write, System.IO.FileShare.Read);
outFile.Write(theData, 0, theData.Length);
outFile.Close();
```

WriteAllText Method

♦ My.Computer.FileSystem.WriteAllText

Writes text content to a specified file.

VISUAL BASIC

```
Dim filePath As String = "C:\temp\Output.txt"
Dim content As String = "Hello, world!" + vbCrLf
Dim appendFlag As Boolean = False
Dim optionalEncoding As System.Text.Encoding =
    New System.Text.UTF8Encoding
My.Computer.FileSystem.WriteAllText(
    filePath, content, appendFlag, optionalEncoding)
```

C#

```
string filePath = "C:\\temp\\Output.txt";
string content = "Hello, world!\r\n";
System.Text.Encoding optionalEncoding =
    new System.Text.UTF8Encoding();

// ----- To create or overwrite a file:
System.IO.File.WriteAllText(
    filePath, content, optionalEncoding);

// ----- To append to an existing file:
System.IO.File.AppendAllText(
    filePath, content, optionalEncoding);
```

WriteEntry Method

♦ My.Application.Log.WriteEntry (for Desktop applications)

♦ My.Log.WriteEntry (for ASP.NET applications)

Writes a message to the logging system.

See

TraceSource Property

WriteException Method

♦ My.Application.Log.WriteException (for Desktop applications)

♦ My.Log.WriteException (for ASP.NET applications)

Writes an exception to the logging system.

See

TraceSource Property

www.ingramcontent.com/pod-product-compliance
Lightning Source LLC
Chambersburg PA
CBHW071356050326
40689CB00010B/1670